CROSS EXAMINATION
IN A NUTSHELL®

JOSEPH C. BODIFORD, J.D., LL.M.
Florida Bar Board Certified
Criminal Trial Lawyer
National Board of Trial Advocacy
Certified in Criminal Trial Advocacy
Adjunct Professor of Law,
Stetson University College of Law

WEST
ACADEMIC
PUBLISHING

PREFACE

I have been lucky in my time as a trial lawyer, to have some innate cross examination skills. The love of the engagement, the thrill of controlling the course of the trial, and the sheer joy of watching jurors reacting to the drilling of a witness are what drive me. To be totally honest, I enjoy being the center of attention in the courtroom—I certainly don't lack in confidence and showmanship. But I am lucky that way.

Looking back to how my own cross examination skills have developed, I see now that there were things that I always did that were rooted in the skills and techniques discussed herein. It wasn't until I attended the National District Attorney Association prosecutor training school in 1998 that I was shown a method that I could fuse with my natural abilities. Realizing that there was a standardized way that one can always prepare for cross examination was an epiphany. Since then, I have prepared for cross examinations carefully and methodically. And, I have realized that *anyone* can be an effective cross examiner with the right tools and training.

Over the years, I continued to develop that basic method through trial and error. I looked at other methodologies, theories of cross examination, and techniques. I watched countless cross examinations from opposing counsel table and from the gallery. I took things from those live performances—both the good and the bad. While I continually strived to standardize my own cross examination techniques, others seemed to just "wing it" with little or no forethought or practiced techniques. The old quote that "more cross examinations are suicidal than they are homicidal" kept coming to mind. Believing that anyone can cross examine effectively with the right tools and training, I came to understand that practitioners are not being taught the correct way to prepare for and deliver cross examinations.

I realized that while there are many books on cross, very few attorneys have any idea those books exist—much less have read any of them. There are actual tried and true methods available by which to become a great cross examiner. The thought that attorneys—and their clients—were losing trials because of poor cross examinations was depressing. If it is so easy to learn to prepare and deliver, why were practicing attorneys still doing such a lousy job?

Out of my need to spread the word that there is a better way, the Five Fundamentals of Cross Examination were born. I believe that cross examination is a skill that can be taught, no matter the advocate's experience level or natural abilities. Using these techniques, any advocate will have the best fundamental skills by which to be an effective cross examiner in any situation.

I think that understanding cross examination requires an understanding of trial advocacy generally, and so I have attempted to include in this book some discussion of general advocacy skills beyond just cross examination. I have attempted a holistic approach to cross and trial preparation by discussing advocacy and adding commentary on persuasion and storytelling. These concepts should pervade your trial work. My continued mention of them here is to reinforce the concepts and create "advocacy muscle memory."

It is my sincere hope that my contribution to the world of advocacy will help attorneys help their clients and causes. If the reader notes anything that could use clarification or improvement, I welcome the comments and suggestions.

I acknowledge those that have made the dream of practicing law and writing this book come true. My parents, Jane and Jim Bodiford gave me the solid foundation by which to be a good person. My wife, Diane, who has been the best comedy writing partner, intellectual sparring partner, reality checker, and jury consultant I could ever have. Our daughters, Madeleine and Calista, who give me joy, pride, love, and laughter—and great hope that the future will turn out fine because of their leadership. Thank you all—I love you!

Thanks to attorney Gannon Coens (my associate), and attorney Steve Cohen (my former paralegal) for their excellent research contributions.

Thank you to Judge Steve Rushing (who was my Professional Responsibility professor at Stetson Law, and who I appeared before many times in two separate circuits) for sending me his wonderful cartoons for inclusion in the book. And it should be known that the caption under the cartoon at the end of Chapter 2 is his, not mine.

A special thank you to Professor William Eleazer (retired) of the Stetson University College of Law for finding in me something I did not even know I had, and turning me into a trial lawyer. And to the many other law professors I learned from and taught with—you have been an incredible inspiration. To the judges, attorneys, and clients that I have met along the way, I'll simply say this: *I've learned a little something from all of you.*

JOE BODIFORD

Tallahassee, Florida
April 2018

IMPORTANT TERMS

Theory—the overall "why" your case is at trial—the plot in its simplest form

Theme—a large section of facts that support the overall case theory—like a sub-plot

Topic—a specific set of questions that support the particular theme and lead to a target fact—like a scene in a book or movie

Target fact—what you need a witness to say—the whole reason for cross examination-the fundamentals of your story

Tone—adjusting the volume and speaking pattern to the specific questioning

Tempo—the pace in which the questions come, specific to the material being covered

Cross Exposition—a question or a short series of questions placed in the middle of a longer set, in order to lock down an answer or a concept, that leads to the target fact

Transition/Segue—short phrase or question designed to introduce a new theme or topic

Constants—facts that are not disputed or otherwise subject to more than one interpretation

Variables—disputed facts

Pole Position—starting point after a transition, signaling where the line of questions will go toward the ultimate target fact

Safe Harbor Question—a question that is readily at hand and safely delivered, used to get out of a tough spot with a witness, or to avoid sitting down on an objection

OUTLINE

TABLE OF CASES

References are to Pages

CROSS
EXAMINATION
IN A NUTSHELL®

CHAPTER 1

INTRODUCTION

1.1 INTRODUCTION

No doubt, at some point in your life, someone said to you (probably in the middle of an argument), "you know, you argue so well . . . no one can beat you in an argument . . . *you should go to law school.*"

Trial advocacy was the class that person was talking about. Cross examination—the ability to tell your story or make your point through another person—is no doubt one of the skills that you naturally exhibited.

You have thought about being a trial lawyer. Maybe you have decided to take a trial skills class. You may be in an advanced trial skills class, or on the mock trial team, or have already had clinical experience. You may be a practicing attorney, looking to sharpen your knowledge and skill. Wherever you are in your life, you have picked up this book and read this far because you want to learn how to try better a case—*tell a better story.*

You are seeking enlightenment about the most effective of advocacy skills . . . the one hardest to master . . . the one we sit amazed watching a skilled practitioner utilize in the arena of a trial . . . *cross examination.*

Well, this is probably a good time to tell you to forget what you have already learned about cross examination. If you think you are a good at it, surprise . . . *you aren't*. Keep reading. I have seen many trial advocacy students and trial team members who think they are the second coming of Clarence Darrow. Funny, many of them have no idea who Clarence Darrow is (do you?)—or who are F. Lee Bailey, or Johnny Cochran, or Linda Kenney Baden. I heard a story of a trial team student who was not taking constructive criticism from his coach, an assistant United States Attorney who was volunteering his time for the law school. Angrily sneering at the coach, he declared "I've been doing this since high school, and I've done over a dozen mock trials . . . how many actual trials have *you* done?" I laughed at the utter insanity of that statement, and that someone could actually and realistically substitute limited mock trial experience for that of the real world. This stuff takes continual practice and refining, only tempering through the fires of years of trials and hearings.

I, myself, have tried over 100 actual jury trials (way over, as I stopped counting years ago at 100) from both sides of the criminal courtroom. I was on the trial team in law school. I have taught trial advocacy skills at two different law schools and coached many trial teams. I went back to law school and earned an LL.M. in Advocacy. I did all of that because, as my mother always reminds me, *a lawyer never stops learning*. If someone at my place in the game is still looking for the holy grail, then someone at your place in the game should be scared silly at even undertaking such a maniacal endeavor as cross examining someone.

But I assure you, it is well worth it. Think about what a trial lawyer does ... we are the last gunslingers in the world. That's not to say we "shoot from the hip" ... to the contrary, we spend countless hours practicing to becoming experts.

Trial lawyers do someone that no one else does. We stand in an arena and match our wits, intellect, experience, creativity, emotion, and skills against another similarly trained person—winner take all. Nothing compares to that process. Professional sports? That's just a game, and no one has to persuade anyone to award their team points—they just score while the fans watch and hope. Mediation? There's a "neutral" in the middle who you cannot persuade; in fact, he or she is going to persuade you to settle. Arbitration? The arbitrator is as experienced as you are, understands the law, and can readily factor out emotion and focus on the facts.

Trial lawyers are special. What makes lousy trial lawyers is easy to identify: those attorneys who simply go through the motions of a trial, getting from one phase to the next, asking the tired list of questions until done, and then hoping for the best. What makes great trial lawyer is much harder to define.

I have a mug that my wife, Diane, gave me shortly before I graduated from law school in 1995. On it is a simulated want-ad page from a newspaper (for those of you around before eBay and Craigslist, us old folks used to look in the back pages of the newspaper for jobs and used items for sale). Circled in red is "Attorney", and it lists the desired qualities:

ATTORNEY: Looking for a special person. Requirements: Judgement, Intelligence, Sense of History, Diplomacy, Inquisitive, Login, Wisdom, Memory & Caring.

A trial lawyer has to have all of those qualities in order to understand persuasion. We could add to that list several other roles, such as psychologist, sociologist, strategist, actuary, risk assessment manager, etc. A trial lawyer has to have a keen understanding of *life* and *humanity* in order to be able to communicate with others, and to persuade others. So, add to the list storyteller, yarnspinner, raconteur, and "witicist. Think Mark Twain, Walt Disney, or Steven Spielberg.

Trial lawyers are also *emotional* people. They think, they internalize, and they take things personally. How can you persuade someone else if you don't know who you are? Can you do mental combat with an opposing witness, while guiding that very unwilling person before the very people who will decide your fate—whether to believe you or not—if you are unsure of yourself?

In this book, you will learn how to think like a trial lawyer. It requires dedication, and not just going through the motions from week to week. It requires you to concentrate on every word in your case file and every word that comes out of your mouth. Success in trial advocacy demands all of you. It doesn't demand that you be someone else, but it demands all of *you*.

I am known for my post-trial critiques beginning, "well, you already know what you did that was good . . ." and then pointing out problems from there. My philosophy is that I will not be able to teach you anything by not correcting problems, or telling you war stories from my own practice. Neither are helpful to your growth as an advocate—only self-analysis and constructive criticism—coupled with change and adaptation.

A.   THE IMPORTANCE OF
CROSS EXAMINATION

Daniel Cross-Examining the Elders, from The Story of Susanna (Heinrich Aldegrever) (used with permission via Wikimedia Commons)

Cross examination has been a part of human interaction since the time of the Bible:

And when she was led away to death, the Lord raised up the holy spirit of a young boy, whose name was Daniel.

And he cried out with a loud voice, "I am clean of the blood of this one."

And all the people, turning back towards him, said, "What is this word that you are saying?"

But he, while standing in the midst of them, said, "Are you so foolish, sons of Israel, that without judging and without knowing what the truth is, you have condemned a daughter of Israel?

Return to judgment, because they have spoken false witness against her."

Therefore, the people returned with haste, and the old men said to him, "Come and sit down in our midst and show us, since God has given you the honor of old age."

And Daniel said to them, "Separate these at a distance from one another, and I will judge between them."

And so, when they were divided, one from the other, he called one of them, and he said to him, "You deep-rooted ancient evil, now your sins have come out, which you have committed before, judging unjust judgments, oppressing the innocent, and setting free the guilty, though the Lord declares, 'The innocent and the just you must not put to death.'

Now then, if you saw her, declare under which tree you saw them conversing together." He said, "Under an evergreen mastic tree."

But Daniel said, "Truly, you have lied against your own head. For behold, the angel of God, having received the sentence from him, will split you down the middle.

And, having put him aside, he commanded the other to approach, and he said to him, "You offspring of Canaan, and not of Judah, beauty has deceived you, and desire has perverted your heart.

Thus did you do to the daughters of Israel, and they, out of fear, consorted with you, but a daughter of Judah would not tolerate your iniquity.

Now then, declare to me, under which tree you caught them conversing together." He said, "Under an evergreen oak tree."

And Daniel said to him, "Truly, you also have lied against your own head. For the angel of the Lord waits, holding a sword, to cut you down the middle and put you to death."

And then the entire assembly cried out in a loud voice, and they blessed God, who saves those who hope in him.

And they rose up against the two appointed elders, (for Daniel had convicted them, by their own mouth, of bearing false witness,) and they did to them just as they had wickedly done against their neighbor, so as to act according to the law of Moses. And they put them to death, and innocent blood was saved on that day.

Daniel 13:45–62 (http://www.sacredbible.org/catholic/OT-32_Daniel.htm#13) (used with permission).

The importance of cross examination has been discussed and highlighted throughout modern American jurisprudence. Consider these quotes from case law:

The importance of cross-examination—as the majority recognizes—is to reveal a witness' state of mind and, more particularly, the extent of the witness' incentive to testify to the government's satisfaction.

United States v. Larson, 495 F.3d 1094 (9th Cir.) August 2007.

I believe that the importance of cross-examination to a criminal trial is so great that a complete denial of otherwise proper cross-examination concerning the potential bias of a prosecution witness should lead to no less than a reversal of the conviction.

Del. v. Van Arsdall, 475 U.S. 673, 686 (1986).

[T]he right of confrontation and cross-examination is an essential and fundamental

requirement for the kind of fair trial which is this country's constitutional goal.

Pointer v. Texas, 380 U.S. 400, 405 (1965).

"[W]e must also account for the function of cross-examination in the trial process in construing the Sixth Amendment guarantee of counsel. The age-old tool for ferreting out truth in the trial process is the right to cross-examination. 'For two centuries past, the policy of the Anglo-American system of evidence has been to regard the necessity of testing by cross-examination as a vital feature of the law.' 5 Wigmore, Evidence § 1367 (Chadbourn rev. 1974). The importance of cross-examination to the English judicial system, and its continuing importance since the inception of our judicial system in testing the facts offered by the defendant on direct, . . . suggests that the right to assistance of counsel did not include the right to have counsel's advice on cross-examination.

"The Court has consistently acknowledged the vital role of cross-examination in the search for truth. It has recognized that the defendant's decision to take the stand, and to testify on his own behalf, places into question his credibility as a witness and that the prosecution has the right to test his credibility on cross-examination. . . . Once the defendant places himself at the very heart of the trial process, it only comports with basic fairness that the story presented on direct is measured for its accuracy and completeness by uninfluenced testimony on cross-examination."

United States v. DiLapi, 651 F. 2d, at 149–151 (Mishler, J., concurring) (emphasis in original) (2nd Cir. 1981).

There is really one more thing you need to know about cross examination, and to embrace as the ultimate goal of cross examination: *it is your best opportunity for you tell your story to the jury*.

Opening statements are a preview, simply a "movie trailer" that entices your jurors. Closing argument is in fact argument, but delivered at or after the time jurors will likely have drawn their own conclusions after hearing the evidence. If you wait until closing arguments to show the jury your theory of the case, and to start telling your story, *you are too late*.

But cross examination is the time when you can tell the story in real time, using the emotions of the case, and doing it all through the witness that is not expected to help you.

In short, it is your time to shine.

Persuasion is not yelling, it is not being cute . . . it is being genuine and genuinely in control. *Control the witness, control the conversation, and you control the story*. And whoever tells the better story, *wins*.

B.   A GENERAL THEORY
OF TRIAL ADVOCACY

Ask yourself two simple questions about going to trial.

First: ***why am I here?***

Second: *what am I going to do now that I am here?*

The first answer will set the stage for your case— it's the story. It's where you start *storytelling.*

The second answer goes to the heart of your mission as a trial lawyer—*to persuade the jurors to vote for your cause. Persuasion,* plain and simple. All the poise, charisma, and delivery in the world will not work without doing those things to persuade. Going in thinking "I'm a great actor" is dooming your case to form over substance.

Thus, the first thing you should learn is why you are in court and what you have to do while you are there. The technical fundamentals of trial work are important, no doubt. But coming to a true understanding of the power of persuasion will enlighten your approach to the overall case. You will then see that handling evidence, objections, speaking well, etc.—while important—are merely the tools you will use to manipulate your jury.

Let's pause to talk about that phrase— "manipulate your jury." This is not a bad phrase, nor does it in any way suggest that the trial lawyer does anything unethical. Nor does it suggest that jurors are weak-minded and susceptible to "Jedi mind tricks." To the contrary, it is a term imputing skill to the advocate. *Manipulate* means "to handle or control, typically in a skillful manner." It can mean "control or influence cleverly, unfairly, or unscrupulously", which is *not* what a trial lawyer does. Jury manipulation means bringing many into one. When you turn the dial on a combination lock, you are manipulating the dial; when a video gamer plays, he or she manipulates the computer mouse. When addressing a jury, you are using your persuasion knowledge and skills to move many separate opinions, attitudes, backgrounds, and personalities into one verdict for your client.

Back to the two questions—*never stop asking them*. These will guide your through your whole career as a trial lawyer. You must always know why you are in a trial and what you have to do while you are there. I ask them every time I start thinking about a case for trial.

Storytelling. Why are you here? Why is this case here? Who is your client? What does your client need the jury to do for him or her? That's the story.

In any case, you must be able to boil your case down to its *essence*. The essence is the one feeling, the one emotion, the moral or more or ethical value, that connects with your jury.

Advocacy requires you to weave the persuasion into the story. Telling the client's story involves creating an atmosphere where the client's cause is the main concern. You want the story to be present in every aspect of the trial, from jury selection to closing argument.

That requires you to use particular facts, cobbled into topics, woven into themes, which all together make up the whole story. That is the entire theory behind the method of cross examination in this book, as explained beginning in the next chapter.

Persuasion. Persuasion is presenting the story on an emotional level, and by doing so, making the listener come to the conclusion that you want them to—remember, *control the witness, control the conversation, and you control the story*. "Emotional" does not crying, or mad and yelling. Emotional level as used in advocacy means connecting your story to the fundamental and integral human emotions, feelings, and experience that we all share.

Think of just of some of the greatest movies ever— there was a vibe to the story based on a human emotion and the human experience. *Rocky* (adversity and perseverance), *On Golden Pond* (marital love and aging, death of a spouse), *The Shawshank Redemption* (atonement and redemption), *The Godfather* (family), *Shindler's List* (unconditional love of mankind), *Raging Bull* (the pity and sorrow of self-destruction), *The Wizard of Oz* (friendship and finding one's self), *Forrest Gump* (innocence and the loss of innocence), *12 Angry Men* (justice), *Star Wars* (good versus evil). How you persuade a jury is going to depend on the story you tell based on the right word or words that describe your case theory. It depends on the emotion of the case.

Think of the word "mom". What (or who) pops into your head? What about "love", or "justice", or "loss"? What emotions do those words conjure in your mind? How about "boundaries", "trust", "punishment"?

What about "police siren", or "new car smell". All of these word conjure images in your head. They are fairly concrete images—you have heard a police siren blare in traffic and the little pang that sets in your stomach, and we all know and love that "new car" smell and equate it to success and achievement.

Think about the word "spinach." Try "skydiving." Think about "Donald Trump." Those words demonstrate that there are some words that evoke strong reactions (be they emotional, visceral, or otherwise) from some people, but not others. I like spinach; others detest it. I have never been skydiving—I have no basis against which to measure that word, except perhaps in the context of the basic overwhelming fear I have of jumping out of an airplane, and even flying in an airplane. Donald Trump is an enigma beyond explanation.

What you come to realize is that your mind instantly jumps to mental images based on what is already in your head (your own life experiences). These words demonstrate that there are words that invoke *fundamental* and *universal* responses. Everyone can relate to certain words—*everyone*.

What all of this demonstrates to us as trial lawyers is that we can begin to manipulate a jury by carefully choosing words and phrases that will evoke spontaneous mental images and emotions in jurors. If done the correct way, we can get jurors to believe in and vote for our story/side because, quite simply, the jurors cannot help it.

If you present the issue being considered in a way that connects, sticks, and draws only one conclusion, you will persuade your jury to do what you want them to do.

C. THE SEARCH FOR TRUTH THROUGH CROSS EXAMINATION

Courts in America have called cross examination the best tool for reaching the truth. Here are some quotes from courts around the country about the overwhelming importance of cross examination in the search for truth:

Ours is an adversarial system of justice that relies on the ability and resources of adversaries to uncover the truth by testing each other's evidence through a variety of methods, the most important of which is cross-examination. Moreover, in an adversarial system, the defendant has a right to a defense and to cross-examination. Wolford v. JoEllen Smith Psychiatric Hosp., 693 So. 2d 1164, 1168 (La. 1997).

Cross-examination is the principal means by which the believability of a witness and truth of his testimony are tested. Davis v. Alaska, 415 U.S. 308, 316, 94 S.Ct. 1105, 1110, 39 L.Ed.2d 347 (1974).

[Cross examination is] the greatest legal engine ever invented for the discovery of truth." California v. Green, 399 U.S. 149, 158, 90 S.Ct. 1930, 1935, 26 L.Ed.2d 489 (1970) (quoting 5 J. WIGMORE, EVIDENCE § 1367, at 29 (3d ed. 1940)).

Where a witness cannot be cross-examined, the search for truth is severely impaired. Curry v.

United States, 658 A.2d 193, 199 (D.C. App. 1995).

An air of unreality pervaded the trial. Obviously, the [expert] witness had an underlying motivation for testifying. Was there a continuing relationship with either the defendant or some members of the defense team? That factor would remain unexplored if a lawyer could not effectively cross-examine the expert without, at the same time, disclosing the client's initial relationship. One may say that it hinders the search for truth not to permit such a witness to testify. One may say, with equal persuasiveness, that it hinders the search for truth to limit the effective cross-examination of such a witness. It is not a matter of letting lawyers shop for a hired gun. It is simply a matter of placing the lawyer who sought the opinion of such an expert in an impossible situation. Countless claims of malpractice would be leveled against attorneys who put unfavorable expert evidence in as part of their clients' case-in-chief. Certainly there are experts who are wrong, and no unfair advantage should be taken of a lawyer's attempt to evaluate a client's case. Our system is committed to a search for truth within the context of the adversary system. Graham v. Gielchinsky, 599 A.2d 149, 155 (N.J. 1991).

The age-old tool for ferreting out truth in the trial process is the right to cross-examination. For two centuries past, the policy of the Anglo-American system of evidence has been to regard the necessity of testing by cross-examination as a vital feature of the law." Perry v. Leake, 109 S.Ct. 594, 601 n.7, 488 U.S. 272 (1989).

D. CROSS EXAMINER = STORYTELLER

Let's get into the specifics of how cross examination works by looking at direct examination. On direct examination, the witness is the fountain from which facts flow. The direct examiner asks a question, and then the witness responds with a fact-based statement:

Q. Where do you go to school?

A. I am a student at Stetson University College of Law.

The flow of information changes on cross examination. On cross examination, the flow of facts comes from the cross examiner. The cross examination questions constant the facts—not open needed "who, what, when, where, why, and how" questions, but leading questions that hold a fact and demand agreement or disagreement.

Q. You are a student at the Stetson University College of Law, correct?

A. Yes.

This "leading and limiting" (discussed in Chapter 1.5, below). By controlling the flow of the facts, the cross examiner tells the story. The cross examiner choses what facts come out at what time, in what depth the facts are discussed, what the important parts of the story are, and generally where the jury's attention is focused. By leading the witness on cross examination, you control what and how much the witness says.

E. EFFECTIVENESS OF COUNSEL IN IMPEACHING WITNESSES (IMPORTANT CASE LAW)

The Confrontation Clause is a powerful shield and sword. For it to be wielded effectively, advocates must *confront*—test the witnesses and evidence. Effective advocacy requires you to fully put the evidence and witnesses against your client through all the paces, inquires, questioning. By doing so, you can then persuasively tell your story through every part of the trial—but especially on cross examination.

Basic rules of competence exist in most states. Here are some examples, from around the country:

MINNESOTA: Rule of Professional Conduct 1.1 (Competence): *A lawyer shall provide competent representation to a client. Competent representation requires the legal knowledge, skill, thoroughness, and preparation reasonably necessary for the representation.*

NEW YORK: Rule of Professional Conduct 1.1 (Competence): *A lawyer should provide competent representation to a client. Competent representation requires the legal knowledge, skill, thoroughness and preparation reasonably necessary for the representation.*

WYMOING: Rule of Professional Conduct for Attorneys at Law 1.1 (Competence): *A lawyer* *shall provide competent representation to a client. Competent representation requires the legal knowledge, skill, thoroughness and preparation reasonably necessary for the representation.*

HAWAI'I: Rule of Professional Conduct 1.1 (Competence): *A lawyer shall provide competent representation to a client. Competent representation requires the legal knowledge, skill, thoroughness, and preparation reasonably necessary for the representation.*

LOUISIANA: Rule of Professional Conduct 1.1 (Competence): *A lawyer shall provide competent representation to a client. Competent representation requires the legal knowledge, skill, thoroughness and preparation reasonably necessary for the representation.*

See a pattern? Probably because it looks like this one, from the American Bar Association's *Model Rules of Professional Conduct*:

Rule 1.1   Competence

A lawyer shall provide competent representation to a client. Competent representation requires the legal knowledge, skill, thoroughness and preparation reasonably necessary for the representation.[1]

"Skill" appears in every rule. A skill will become rusty if not used, and will not be effective if not practice. I have the skill to dribble a basketball—but certainly not well enough to play in a game. If a team picks me, my basic competence as a player will certainly be in question. I have the skill to play the trumpet—I have played for over thirty years, have a master's degree in trumpet performance, and still seriously practice every day. Although I am a lawyer, I have the skill to play the trumpet professionally in almost any setting.

If you are a trial lawyer, and you have no cross examination skills, or they are not such that are "reasonably necessary for the representation" (i.e. "rusty"), where does that leave you vis-à-vis the rule in your state? Where does it leave your client?

In criminal cases, the Sixth Amendment guarantees effective counsel to defendants. That guarantee includes the duty to properly impeach witnesses and to expose bias, motives, etc. This includes, and probably incurs primarily, on cross examination. Many states and the Federal courts have found attorneys to be ineffective for not properly impeaching a witness in a criminal case, in violation of the Sixth Amendment right to adequate counsel. *See Strickland v. Washington*, 466 U.S. 668 (1984).

1.2 PERSUASION, STORYTELLING, AND BASIC TRIAL PSYCHOLOGY

This is in no way a full treatise on persuasion, storytelling, or trial psychology. But there are some very important fundamentals of those subjects that every advocate, no matter what skill or experience level, must understand.

A. PERSUASION

Persuasion is, as my good friend Professor Charles Rose of Stetson Law says, is presenting a case in a manner that is as easy to understand as "2+2". Think about 2 + 2. What did you think of without hesitation? Of course, 4. Keep that basic exercise in mind throughout your career. It is the most fundamental example of how the mind works. People process information based on (among other things) past experiences, morals, ethics, and personality. They hear information, and filter it through what they already know.

If you present the facts, the jurors get to 4 without the advocate having to say it. Persuasion is setting up the presentation of facts, and the marshaling of those facts into inferences, such that the jurors are left with conclusion you want them to reach as being the *only* conclusion that can be reached. Going back to the old saying, "if it looks like a duck, and it quacks like a duck, then it's a duck." Think about that saying applied to a cross examination:

Q. Mr. Witness, you have seen ducks before, correct?

A. Yes.

Q. And you know what a duck looks like?

A. Yes, I do.

Q. You know what a duck sounds like, correct?

A. Yes.

Q. A duck quacks, doesn't it?

A. Yes.

Q. This thing here, it looks like a duck, doesn't it?

A. Yes.

Q. And it quacks?

A. Yes, it does.

STOP. What were you thinking as you read this? A cute little white bird with an orange bill, making that unmistakable sound that we imitated when we were kids. We all know what a duck looks like and what it sounds like. *You don't need to ask the witness, "So it's a duck, right?"* We all know he knows the thing is a duck. After all, he may say, "I'm not sure, I'm not an ornithologist."

Who cares? *The jury knows it's a duck, and they know that the witness knows that it's a duck.* You gave them 2+2, and their life experiences gave them the 4 = *it's a dadgum duck!*

That's the technical side of persuasion through cross examination, but what about making the point resonate with the jury? That requires use of emotions, feelings, morals, mores, and ethics.

B. EMOTIONS AND FEELINGS, MORALS, MORES, ETHICS

This is not intended as a psychological or theoretical study in the human mind. Rather, this is some basic observations of life that can serve you as a trial lawyer and cross examiner.

One basic thing every advocate must know and implement is that the way to a juror's heart is through his or her ... *heart.* Your story has to connect to common emotions, feelings, morals, mores, and ethics. I often tell my advocacy students, everyone shares emotions feelings, morals, mores, and ethics—*unless he or she is a sociopath.* There are universal truths upon which advocates can build stories and entire cases around.

Emotions and feelings. We all know and feel emotions (and feelings). Think about these basic emotions, and what it conjures inside you:

- Happiness/sadness
- Anger/calm
- Trust/distrust
- Confidence/uncertainty
- Pride/shame
- Attraction/disgust

- Envy/pity

- Offended

These emotions and feelings and the myriad of others that can be infused into litigation, and are very powerful tools for the advocate. For example:

Happiness/sadness	Jury is sad for the plaintiffs in the wrongful death action against the motorist who killed their son
Trust/distrust	Jurors do not believe the witness who has every possible bias against the defendant, and as a result rejects the witness' testimony
Pride/shame	The evidence does not prove the defendant committed the crime, and the jury is proud to find him not guilty as the Constitution requires; vindication of a victim?
Envy/pity	The victim of an aggravated battery lost his eye as a result of the attack on him, and the jury feels pity for him

Anger/calm	The defendant stole millions from the elderly, causing many of them to have to return to work long after retirement, and the jury is angry at the defendant
Confidence/ uncertainty	The expert witness has not done a thorough job in testing the evidence, and the jury has lost confidence in the findings
Attraction/disgust	The defendant is a beautiful and charismatic young woman, the same age as the children of many of the jurors, and they are automatically attracted to her and her story
Offended	The adult female defendant did not have sexual relations with the minor male, but she did cross the line as far as what was appropriate, and the jury is offended by her behavior

Jurors cannot avoid feeling emotions while listening to a story in a courtroom. It is human nature. Constructing a story, and questions sets, that tap into those emotions is powerful. Drawing a juror in by connecting him or her to the story by allowing him or her to feel, and attach emotions to the story, will result in that juror believing your story. And that results in a verdict in your favor.

How do you inject emotions? The emotion of the case will reveal itself in pretrial preparation. Consider these examples. In a theft case, *disgust* at stealing and being a sneaky thief. In a contract breach case, *trust* in the violation caused by the breach of a once-healthy relationship. In a personal injury case, *sadness* at the loss of life, or loss of use of a body part or a standard of living. In a rape case, almost all of the available human emotions run rampant. As jurors listen to facts, they measure them against their own life experiences, and from those experiences the emotions will flow. Use that to your advantage.

Morals. A moral is different than a visceral emotion. A moral is an *internal belief*, a *value*, or even a rule, that guides and governs an individual's actions and behaviors. One of the best examples of a set of guiding morals is found in the Scout Law:

A Scout is Trustworthy, Loyal, Helpful, Friendly, Courteous, Kind, Obedient, Cheerful, Thrifty, Brave, Clean, and Reverent.

I and countless others were taught to recite this mantra as a part of opening Boy Scout troop meetings. These values help guide youths as they begin to learn and take their places in the world. It's a good list, to be sure, and a list by which we all can live.

In litigation, themes and topics can be built around similar morals and values. In a case of theft, "trustworthy" is a value that jurors will understand and relate to . . . and a story that tells of the breach of trust will ring loudly. "Clean" and cleanliness certainly fits into a case involving some sexual deviance. "Obedient" could be used in breach of contract action, or other case involving the breaking of an agreement, oath, or law.

When thinking *"why am I here?"*, think about whether there is any moral theme that summarizes your overall case theory. *See* Chapter 3.2 (Why are we here?).

Mores. Mores are *external* beliefs—those of a society. Mores are adopted by individuals, ostensibly due to the psychology of group dynamics and other socio-environmental pressures.

Examples of mores are:

- *It is not acceptable to be naked in public*
- *You don't burp at the dinner table*
- *Be kind to guinea pigs and bunnies*
- *Marijuana is bad*

In each of those examples, which are totally acceptable to any normal citizen in the United States, are subject to debate and exception in other parts of the world. One is even open to debate in the United States.

In the United States, virtually all (with rare exceptions) beaches are clothed. However, in Europe, topless beaches are no big deal, and are accepted.

In the United States, burping at the dinner table is considered rude. In some parts of Europe and other parts of the world, the host or chef takes it as a compliment that the diner is full and happy.

In the United States, guinea pigs and bunnies are pets (including Sunshine, our guinea pig, and Thumper, our bunny). In other parts of the world, guinea pigs are food. Rabbits are food all over, *including* the United States!

As for marijuana, the debate rages in the United States. Many states have legalized the recreational use of marijuana, while others and the Federal government have not. Its use is polarizing.

In litigation, there are societal norms that can form the basis of a cause of action. Many, many laws are based on mores—one cannot be naked in public lest he or she be charged with indecent exposure or some sort of public disruption of the peace charge. Similarly, sexual cases are based on societal norms of not corrupting children by exposing them to nudity, or improper touches, or worse. Marijuana is still illegal in most states. Using mores as a case theory and thematic material is a powerful tool—even if something is accepted by some, it still may be taboo to others.

Ethics. Ethical behavior, I was taught as a child, is how you act when others are not around to see you. Think of ethics as the personal implementation of morals and mores. It is the personal behavioral adherence to internal (moral) and external (more) beliefs.

When I was a boy, my family went out to eat one Friday evening. Driving home, my father began to wonder aloud if the cashier had given him the right change when he paid. He worried about it all the way home. I remember him taking out his wallet, laying out the bills, and concluding that the cashier had given him too much money back. He told me to get in the car.

We drove back to the restaurant, and talked about why we were going back. He made sure I knew that it was "the right thing" to be honest. Not only that, but he emphasized that if he were to be dishonest and keep the money, someone would suffer. He told me that the shortage would likely be taken out of the cashier's pay, or even cost her a job that she may have desperately needed.

Even though I was there and can recall going back in the restaurant, I can't recall whether he was right or not. But I learned the lesson: that his ethics would not let that mistake stand. It has stayed with me my entire life.

Every juror understands ethics, and has their own personal ethics code. Don't take what is not yours. Don't hurt someone else. Don't make false statements. Don't cheat. Unless one is a sociopath, these are universal ethical standards that we all understand and share.

In litigation, ethical and unethical behavior is easily exposed. It is also easily punishable—maybe not by a fine or imprisonment, but certainly by a contrary verdict.

Overall case theories, themes and topics, and even target facts (see Chapter 2.1, "Structuring the Cross: Theory, Theme, Topic, Target) can and should be based on emotions, morals, mores, and ethics. For example:

Cause of Action	Emotion, Moral, More, or Ethic
Theft	Trust
Elder abuse	Disgust
Breach of contract	One must keep one's word
Assault or battery	Anger
Election fraud	Pride, anger
Identify theft	Fear, distrust
Unjust enrichment	Fairness
Defamation	One must not lie about others
Murder	Retribution, shock, fear, disgust

C.   STORYTELLING

Storytelling is more than just the presentation of the facts. Great trial lawyers are great storytellers. Great advocates persuade juries by telling a better story. So, you have to recognize that and figure out how to do it early in your trial practice career.

There are two aspects of telling a story to a jury. Think in terms of a motion picture. First, there is the movie itself on a broad scale—the *overall story*. Second, there are the individual scenes that require perfect dialogue and acting to unfold the story to the listener.

A jury trial is much the same. There is the overall trial strategy of how the story will be told from jury selection through closing argument. That requires a "story arc" of how the overall case theory will be broken into themes, and in turn, the themes into topics, as they are spread across the various stages of the trial. So you are thinking not only in terms of how to keep the ideas going and in the minds of the jurors, you have to think about how to present those ideas through very different aspects of juror questioning, attorney statements, and witness interrogation.

Within each of the stages of the trial, especially with attorney statements (opening and closing), there is the *art* of being a compelling storyteller. This is where *pathos* of rhetoric comes into play. Being able to "spin a yarn", so to speak . . . creating a verbal painting that draws the listener in and captivates not only the attention but the commitment to believing the story.

Cross examination plays a critical role in telling the story. As discussed above, it is the time when you as the advocate control the flow of the facts. We'll look in depth at how this works in Chapter 2, and work on telling the story on cross examination based on this model:

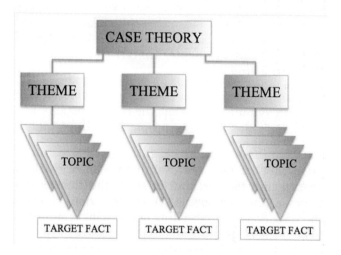

D.   BASIC TRIAL PSYCHOLOGY

Trial psychology is far too complicated to try to condense into a narrow treatise on cross examination. There are some important aspects of it that you need to know in order to have any success at all in trial, and particularly in cross examination. We have already look at some of it in the previous sections.

Personality, attitudes, background, and life experience. It should go without saying that people make decisions based on who they are—and who they are is *complicated*. Then you take six or twelve complicated people and put them together in a room ... That is what makes trial work so incredibly hard—you have to make your case and your story persuasive within a range of commonality. In other words, the specifics of your case have to be packaged and presented in a story that will relate with and resound to just about anyone listening. That is discussed above in Chapter 1.2.B (Emotions, morals, mores, and ethics).

You will learn a great deal about some of your jurors in voir dire. If you ask the right questions, and listen and follow up, some people will tell you quite a bit about themselves.

Personality will generally show itself. Whether someone is a leader or follower, challenges or submits to authority, whether he or she is open- or close-minded . . . those personality traits tend to be at the surface. That will tell you right away if someone might be inclined to listen openly, or whether you will have a problem convincing that person of anything.

People's educational and work backgrounds can shape how they intake, perceive, and process information. Think about how a retired police officer and a retired criminal defense attorney may react to the facts of a criminal case. How might an accountant listen to a financial case? How would a preacher react to the facts in a divorce case? If you are thinking, *these people would never get past jury selection and on to those cases*, you get the point. The problem is what you do with people whose backgrounds are not so polarizing. If your jury is like most juries, you will have a smattering of everyone. So keeping your themes and topics clear, easy to identify with, and approachable is the best practice.

When designing and delivering a cross examination, knowing who is in your audience (i.e. who are the people sitting in the jury box) will help you decide how to present the facts, whether to highlight certain things or not, how intense to make impeachments, and the like.

Using emotions and feelings, morals, mores, ethics, and values and beliefs. As discussed in Chapter 1.2.B, these things will drive your theory, themes, topics, and the importance of your target facts.

Emotions and feelings, morals, mores and ethics tend to be universal thoughts that you can apply to most people—most people know the difference between right and wrong. Similarly, values and beliefs are held be everyone—albeit differently from person to person. Therefore, you can count on themes and topics that generally center around right versus wrong.

Values are one's individual priorities for basic interaction with the world around us. Some people value cleanliness; others are slobs. Some value being prompt or early for appointments; others don't mind being a little late. Some people believe that being courteous and proper is super important (think the South), while others are short and to the point (think the stereotype of hurried urbanites).

Beliefs are deeply rooted convictions about the world around us. Beliefs can be just about anything— some people believe there is life on other planets, others do not. Some believe that law enforcement officers never, ever lie; others do not trust police officers.

Using common values (*e.g.* being honest, being thorough, honoring obligations, obeying the law) and beliefs (cops do not lie, defendants and informants are not to be trusted, felons lie, experts will say anything for money) is a powerful way to sketch out the themes and topics that will support your overall case theory.

Understanding how people intake and process of information. How people learn about a topic or issue varies widely. There are libraries full of research of the intake and processing of information, conducted by psychologists, educators, sociologists, and many other people who are not trial lawyers. But trial lawyers have to understand the basics in order to present a persuasive story.

Think of how the brain works—how you intake information and how you process it. You perceive something (see it, hear it, read it)—it is now trapped in your brain. Once the information is in your brain, your brain will process the information whether you want it to or not. That is because as humans we have to make the information *fit* the world around us. Ever had that moment where you are looking at something and just cannot figure out what it is? That is because your brain is scrambling to try to make sense of it compared to something else the brain has already identified.

A trial situation is no different. Jurors hear testimony and see exhibits, and the intake/process sequence begins. It repeats over and over constantly through the trial. The importance of this sequence is that it is the juror's personal experiences against which the testimony and evidence is measured. Complicated or complex scientific or mathematical testimony is going to have less of a chance of successful comparison to a juror's prior experience than will someone lying to someone else. Not a lot of people have experience in advanced science or math. Everyone has been lied to at some point.

So understand that people's intake and processing will ongoing through the trial, and that it is their individual experiences that will aid in their ability to deal with the information. Knowing that the intake/process sequence permeates the trial must absolutely control how you approach cross examination and trial advocacy in general.

How can you aid your listener in understanding your story? Presenting one fact at a time aids in perception—you don't confuse people, and you keep it simple and direct. A specific and steady tempo will allow jurors to process the information in real time, so they will keep up with your march to the target question. And doing all of that at the same time will allow the jurors to be able to be right with you and understand your case. That is persuasion.

Understanding how information is taken in and processed will guide your preparation and delivery of your cross examination. Remember the organizational chart above—it will guide how you put your story together into the most persuasive order and presentation.

Understanding and using group dynamics. As with the rest of the discussion in this chapter, group dynamics has been the subject of a vast amount of research. Suffice it to say that this book is too limited in scope to delve deeply into the subject, but you should certainly devote study to it.

Remember that the jury you have on any particular day is its own little neighborhood, existing only for a short time and never to exist again. It is populated by six or twelve very different people. Some are leaders, some are followers, and some just want to be left alone and get out of there as quickly as possible. Those people will be keenly aware of the new neighborhood they are in, and trying to figure out how they fit in there.

Group dynamics vary from place to place. The dynamic of a Sunday School class is different than that of a college football game. The dynamic of a family dinner is different than a business luncheon. Why? Because of what is expected and what is permitted by the group in each of those situations. One is going to be much more reserved and careful being in ten or fifteen people on Sunday morning that he or she might be in the middle of fifty thousand screaming fanatics on Saturday afternoon. These situations are governed by mores (don't burp out loud, don't tell off-color jokes, don't talk about politics or religion) and other societal norms.

A jury is no different. There are things you are expected to do and not to do. The judge will even admonish the jury as to certain things. *You don't talk about the case except in deliberation. You stay with the rest of the jurors during breaks.* No one wants to be the person to disobey a judge, so they all comply— if not because the judge told them so, but because of the peer pressure of the group dynamic.

Jurors may not be willing to express who they really are or what they really believe. People do not like to thought of as wrong or different. People want acceptance—or at a minimum do not want to be ostracized or criticized, and will may simply keep quiet to avoid conflict or strife. Understand that people are inherently selfish in this way and very well may stay quiet even if it means the wrong verdict may be rendered.

So when preparing your cross exam (or opening, direct, or closing), know that your themes, topics, and targets have to be made in a way that people can talk about them, and stand by them. Lines of questions about common emotions and feelings, morals, mores, and ethics will hit in the center of whatever group dynamic is in place with your particular jury. No one will feel out of place when expressing agreement with you while in deliberations with the others.

Using primacy, recency, and unforgettable points. Along the lines of how people learn, it is well recognized that people remember the first things and last things in a presentation. Try it sometime, you'll find it to be true. The stuff in the middle can get lost or forgotten.

Ever listen to a comedian, and later try to remember any of the jokes? You laughed consistently for an hour, yet you can only remember one or two jokes. Why is that? Sheer *volume* is probably a contributing factor. You get overloaded, so you have to pick what to recall. Another factor is that not everything was that *memorable*. It was funny at the time, but not memorable.

Contrast that with going to a movie. You can watch it, leave the theater, and tell someone the entire story from start to finish. You can even discuss the meaning behind the movie, what motivated the characters, and how plot twists were interwoven. Not only can you do it right afterward, but if the story is memorable enough, you can tell the story for years to come.

What's the difference between the comedy club and the theater? The jokes are rapid-fire, generally covering a broad spectrum of topics in an almost stream-of-conscious presentation. The move is a *story*. The same effect happens in a trial—you either have a bunch of facts, or you have a *story*. Using the chart in Chapter 2 will help you create a memorable story on cross examination.

Making an unforgettable point is accomplished in two ways. First, by using the persuasion technique of having the juror come to the conclusion (the target fact) on his or her own. Remember "2+2" (Chapter 1.2.A, "Persuasion"). Second, by making that target fact connected to an internal moral or ethical point. That way it resounds—just like the movie you watched and told your friends about.

Not every target fact is a based-on-ethics fact. Some facts are simply "it was", or "it was not". At the time of the accident, the traffic light was red, or it was green. The money went into the account, or it did not. It is ok in those situations to simply present the fact. But do it in a memorable way—get to the target fact *persuasively*. You can ruin the impact of a critical target fact by glossing over it too quickly.

In all of this, during cross examination always keep in mind *why* you are presenting a target fact, and *how* the jury is going to process and use that fact. Everything you do in a trial, you do for a reason. Be sure you know the reason, and that the reason is meaningful and pragmatic to your case.

Be sure to study trial psychology as it relates to cross examination, be sure to read some of the resources listed in Chapter 10.

1.3 CROSS EXAMINATION'S IMPORTANCE TO OTHER PARTS OF THE TRIAL

It has been my experience that jury trials are won in jury selection (picking the right audience) and in cross examination (telling that audience the story myself by controlling the flow of facts). Openings are like the trailer to a movie, and other than hoping to gain conditional acceptance of the story from the jurors, it's not persuasive. But that conditional acceptance is critical—think of it as the jurors opening their minds to you and your story. So, it is a critical part of advocacy storytelling. Closings are summarizing and arguing, but not time to try to start to convince—assume jurors have already made up their minds before you begin your closing. If you wait until closing to start to tell your story or put all the pieces together, you will lose. Direct is when the case *witnesses* tell the story.

But cross examination is when YOU get to tell the story. In a sense you are the puppetmaster, pulling the strings and making the story dance out of the witness. You ask the questions in the form of giving facts—and your story is simply agreed with by your opponent's witness.

So, cross is your time to shine. But you can highlight your story in other parts of the trial in a way that both previews what you are going to do, as well as recaps what you did. Not what the witness said, but your presentation of your side of the story.

A.   CROSS AND JURY SELECTION

Jury selection is a part of the trial susceptible to many different evaluations and conclusions as to its importance. Be brief . . . don't repeat what others have done . . . get everyone talking in a group discussion . . . tell jokes . . . don't pry too deeply . . . every trial lawyer has an opinion as to what to do in jury selections.

Most of them are wrong.

Jury selection is really *juror elimination*. By law, you are weeding out those that cannot be fair and impartial, and/or who are biased or prejudiced. You are also look for those that will give you a fair shot and even early conditional acceptance. You have to eliminate those that are biased—especially those biased to what you know your story will be, or prejudiced against you, your client, or your cause.

However, by necessity and practicality, you are looking for jurors that will listen to you and your story. You are trying to find those that will do their best to carefully listen to and weigh what you are telling them.

Testing your themes and topics. Carefully incorporate your case themes and topics into your jury selection. Prepare open-ended, "how do you feel about . . ." and "what would you think if . . ." types of questions.

If your thematic and topical material (see Chapter 2) includes themes such as lack of trustworthiness, ask jurors how they judge a person's trustworthiness, and what values indicate someone who is trustworthy. If it is self-defense, ask if he or she has had to use self-defense. Ask to what extent people believe it is acceptable to use self-defense. You may find, for example, that a juror is a pacifist who would never find any behavior other than retreat to be acceptable in any situation. That person has to go, because no matter how well put-together your cross examination is, he or she will never accept your premise.

Example. Take this example, in the trial of a battery case, where the defense will be that the defendant hit the accuser first in order to squash the imminent threat of violence by the accuser on the defendant.

Q. Miss Prospective Juror, have you ever had to use self-defense?

A. Me, personally, no, I have not. Thank goodness!

Q. Can you imagine that there are times that someone would have to use self-defense?

A. Oh, certainly.

Q. Well, how about this. What would you think of a situation where someone hit someone in self-defense before he was hit himself? In other words, using self-defense to prevent getting hit. Do you think that could be a thing?

A. I do.

Q. Tell me about your thoughts on that.

In this example, if you were the trial lawyer you would already know that the cross examination of the alleged victim would be that he was hit only because the defendant was scared, and the accuser was actually menacing and creating a serious and substantial threat. What the perspective jurors say about that theory, asked through an open-ended question on the broad topic of self-defense, will tell you everything you need to know.

Consider a business fraud case, which we will get more into below. Certainly you would need to know who has business experience. You also what to know who thinks business is a cut-throat "dog eat dog" world, and who thinks that "honor is honor" no matter the situation.

Q. Mr. Prospective Juror, I see from your questionnaire that you are self-employed, did I ready that correctly?

A. You did and I am.

Q. What do you do?

A. I own a small legal publishing company.

Q. How long have you had it?

A. Started it from scratch twenty years ago. I bought part of another company and incorporated it along the way.

Q. Is it just you, or do you have employees?

A. I have ten employees, the least senior of which has been with us for 5 years. We are like a family.

Q. I would imagine that in addition to dealing with your customers, you have business deals that you do with printers, marketers, et cetera?

A. Yes, we have lots of vendors.

Q. Tell me, what is your philosophy on doing business with the vendors?

A. Well, I don't really expect them to do me any favors, and I try to get the best deal I can. Sometimes they get the better deal, sometimes I do. You do your best to negotiate. But I expect that no matter the deal that is cut, everyone will live up to it. I always honor my end.

Tells you quite a bit about how this juror is going to feel about a crooked business deal, doesn't it?

In other words, don't be afraid to ask about what know will be coming up on cross examination and test people's views on the matters. It certainly helps you adjust your presentation to your audience.

Moreover, it gives the jurors a preview of what is coming up without asking them to pre-try the facts of the case. That, of course, is not permitted. You cannot pre-try your case, which is asking the potential jurors how they would decide the actual facts of your case. Most judges will stop you from that, and they should. The *trial* is for trying your case, not the *voir dire*.

But employing some creative permissible questioning, you can at a minimum find those that are willing to consider your cross examination theories, themes, and topics. Those that are not are, by definition, biased or prejudiced.

B.   CROSS AND OPENING

If the advocate is properly prepared for cross examination, then there is no reason not to talk about the facts in the opening statement to the jury. Why? Because the advocate is sure that the facts *will come out* on cross examination.

Many students avoid referencing any potential points from cross examination in their opening statements. When I point this out, I usually get an excuse to the effect of "well, I don't know what the witness will say on cross." That is the mindset of an amateur, not a master. Using the Five Fundamentals of Cross Examination (see Chapter 1.4) and the techniques in this book, one can master cross examination to the degree that he or she can count on the fact that certain points will be made on cross— either by the witness, or by the advocate.

Lots of thought and planning went into this business deal. Many nights laying awake . . . Many days of agonizing hours of design—getting to a plan and ripping it up, only to start over. Lots and lots of drafting and redrafting, writing and re-writing . . . The countless hours of making sure the deal was "just right" . . . Meeting after meeting with face after face, bad lunches and missing the kids baseball practice to go to a meeting with a stranger over a lousy dinner.

But we're not talking about Ms. Plaintiff's business plan. We're talking about the evil plan Mr. Defendant was developing, the trap he was setting to steal Ms. Plaintiff's business. Mr. Defendant will have to answer today. He will answer to Ms. Plaintiff. He will answer to this jury, as he answers to me on cross examination. You will see first hand his responses to my questions as he sits right over here (indicating witness stand). You will observe his mannerisms, see his demeanor. You get to hear him explain— or try to explain—what all of his "planning" entailed.

You will hear him talk about how he carefully worded the documents, why he used certain words and phrases in certain parts of the contract.

[Getting into the story you are going to tell on cross . . .]

He will admit to you that he had his eyes on this business for a very long time. He will tell you about the trips to visit the shop, the email inquiries, all the online searches about the profitability of this type of business.

He will tell you that he made over thirty drafts of the sale agreement. He will tell you about the changes he made, changes made after visiting lawyers in other towns and seeking advice on how to write unbreakable contracts. He will admit to you going to the law library downtown and educating himself on legal terms, so that he could make the contract sound more enforceable.

Mr. Defendant will admit to you tricking Ms. Plaintiff into entering this deal. He may not agree to the term "trick", but he will tell you that he was very, very careful to spend lots of time with her, asking about every employee, taking notes about the history of the company . . . basically appearing to care deeply about the future of the company. And he will admit to you that he made elderly Ms. Plaintiff come to think of him as the son she never had. He will tell you about spending Christmas with Ms. Plaintiff right before the contract was presented to her. What a fun day they had . . . that is was just like a family would spend together.

Mr. Defendant will take the stand today and during my cross examination he will tell you about how all of this was done, over the course of a year and a half. During cross examination will walk you through his devious plan, and show you just how badly he pulled the wool over Ms. Plaintiff's eyes.

I use the form of a story, of course. No one wants to hear "fact, fact, fact, blah, blah, blah." The jury wants to hear *the story*. And you want to tell it in a way that gets you their conditional acceptance—they believe your story and want to hear more. If your story pans out, they will render a verdict for you.

What I do, and you can do, too, is tell the story as I know it is going to come out on the cross examination of Mr. Defendant. Many attorneys are afraid, because they do not know how to structure (see Chapter 2), prepare (see Chapter 3), and deliver (see Chapter 4) a cross examination. If done correctly, every one of the facts that are in that opening will come out. That is powerful.

C.   CROSS AND CLOSING

I do not advocate writing the closing first. Practically, writing it first helps overall analysis in a general sense. But being married to a canned or scripted closing (or any part of trial) is dangerous. Relying on a pre-planned closing breeds inflexibility and inhibits genuinely persuasive argument. Remember, closing argument is not the time to introduce your case theory; it is the time to tie points up, reinforce the facts with the jury instructions and vice versa. If you wait until closing argument to introduce the case theory, you have probably already lost the trial.

When organizing the cross, the advocate has the points available in which to freely use experience and skill to argue. *Argue*. Not to rehash what the jury heard, but to *argue* why what they heard means they should find for your client.

EXAMPLE OF CROSS EXAMINATION, INCORPORATED INTO CLOSING ARGUMENT

Think back to when Mr. Defendant was on the stand during cross examination. Remember the exchange about the amount of planning that went into this quote-unquote deal:

"Mr. Defendant, you had never written a business purchase agreement before meeting Ms. Plaintiff, correct?

Yes.

You had never written any such proposal prior to deciding that you wanted her business?

That's right.

And your computer logs show you revised just this particular paragraph over 30 times before you presented it, right?

Yes.

You knew she was a widow?

Yes.

You starting spending time with her?

I did

More, and more, and more time?

Yes.

Even spent Christmas Eve and Christmas Day with her?

Yes.

She even starting referring to you as the son she never had, didn't she?

Yes.

And all the while you were working hard on your contract?

Yes.

On December 26, the day she introduced you to her pinochle friends as her son, you presented that contract to her to sign?

I did.

And she did so without even reading it?

Yes."

Folks, it's obvious why he went to such painstaking effort to get the contract just right— it had to be so wonderfully perfect that poor Ms. Plaintiff would think it just another great thing her "son" [makes quotation marks in the air] *had done. And not question . . . just sign. No need for a lawyer when her beloved Mr. Defendant had done it better than anyone could.*

What level of devious thought compels someone to pay lawyers to advise on how to write iron-clad contracts—especially when those lawyers are out of town, and had no chance of running into Ms.

Plaintiff? No chance of finding out she was an elderly widow . . . no chance of getting suspicious.

What level of treacherous scheming does it take to befriend a lonely widow . . . to prey upon her need for companionship . . . to gain her trust . . . and to use the beauty of Christmas as a part of the plot to rip her off?

All of those horrible things are what Mr. Defendant admitted to me, and to you, during his cross examination. From his own mouth, so you know it's true. He could not hide behind the glare of his own actions and statements.

And his own words paint the picture for you—a man who is absolutely guilty of fraud and theft from Ms. Plaintiff.

This is not a case of an arm's length "get the best deal you can" situation. This is a man without honor, and without any intention of keeping the bargain Ms. Plaintiff thought she was entering.

And so on. The jury selection, the cross examination, and the closing are all telling the same story.

D.   CROSS EXAMINATION AND TRIAL MOTIONS/ARGUMENTS

Good advocates engage in meaningful pretrial motion practice. Volumes can be written on that topic alone—more than will be covered here. But good motion practice can narrow issues before the witness takes the stand.

And why is that important? *Control.* The whole issue of controlling the substance of the testimony, the witness, and opposing counsel.

If you think the direct examination could possibly yield damaging irrelevant information that you cannot fix on cross examination, move to have it excluded from the trial. Motions in limine are perfect for that purpose (see Chapter 3.7).

Similarly, if you have issues that you plan on addressing in cross examination, but think the other side may object and impede your delivery, bring them to the court's attention before the trial starts. Most judges will appreciate being made aware of the issues, and having quality time to discuss and consider them outside the presence of the jury. The heat of the moment is not a good time to get a well-informed and well-considered ruling—and it's your fault that happens, not that of the judge!

1.4   FIVE FUNDAMENTALS OF CROSS: THEME, TOPIC, TARGET, TONE, TEMPO

The Five Fundamentals guide the cross examiner in preparation and delivery.

Following the Five Fundamentals permits total control of the story. The case theory *is* the overall arc of the story. The overall case theory is not one of the Five Fundamentals. Rather, the Five Fundamentals are what flashes across the stage to *tell* the story.

The first three fundamentals deal with structuring cross examination into segments that support the case theory (plot), themes (sub-plots), topics (the scenes of the story, play, or movie), and target facts (the "a-ha" moments). The segments work together to persuasively tell your story.

Remember the difference: the themes and topics stem from and organize the overall case theory, while the target fact is a main thing the examiner has to get out of the witness, or get the witness to admit.

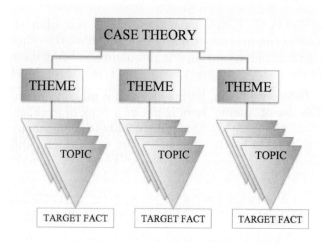

The last two fundamentals, tone and tempo are the governors of the delivery of the cross. How you will deliver a question . . . whether you will be surgical and methodical, or rapid fire machine-gun style.

A. THEME

Your theme is a large section of facts that support the overall case theory—like a sub-plot.

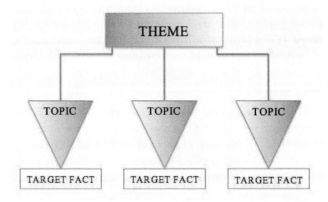

Before we begin, let me clear up a misconception. The use of "theme" here is not as a hook or grabber. Many advocacy teachers tell students to get a snappy one-liner to be the "theme" of the case. Hooks and one-lines are basic theater, at best—you simply cannot persuade a jury in real life by using a one-liner as the overall case theory. Certainly, phrases and hooks can introduce themes and topics within your case story, or summarize parts of the trial. But you cannot substitute a snappy catchphrase for a well thought through and presented story. You didn't read J.R.R. Tolkien or J.K Rowling relying on hooks or grabbers, did you? No.

Think of "theme" as a sub-plot in a move. If the overall case theory is the overall story arc, then the themes are the sub-plots. As your author is a diehard *Star Wars* fan, and has been since age 8 in 1977, this book is full of *Star Wars* references. There are many excellent sub-plots in *Star Wars*—one of the best being that of Han Solo. Solo, the smuggler turned Rebel general and war hero, has his own compelling story. It is a story of self-confidence versus self-doubt, of redemption, and of acceptance. There are three themes right there—all of which support the main story of good triumphing over evil.

Themes support the overall case theory. But remember, it is NOT the overall case theory. Whatever it is, thinking carefully and creatively about your themes will get you organized. It will also get your jury following your story—and believing and buying into it.

B. TOPIC

Topics are the individual scenes. Topics are a specific set of questions that support the particular theme and lead to a target.

TOPIC

BROAD QUESTIONS

NARROWER QUESTIONS

NARROWER QUESTIONS

NARROWER QUESTIONS

NARROWER QUESTIONS

TARGET FACT

Using the Han Solo reference, if the theme is redemption, there are several scenes that demonstrate how he redeemed himself. First, there was the scene in which he gets the gang safely off of the planet Tatooine. There was the scene where he left the rebellion to go and pay his debt. Finally, and most dramatically, there was the scene in which he returned to save Luke and help blow up the Death Star.

Your topics do not have to be long series of questions. In fact, they can be short and to the point. But as with the themes, you have to identify the topics and carefully plot them out, so that the jury clearly understands them. When the jury is following your story, you have them on your side.

C. TARGET FACTS

Target facts are the main points of your topics, and themes. Target facts are the "must gets". They are the piece of gold, the medal, the prize. Above all else, the closing arguments that support the overall case theory will come in the form of statements from the opposing witness. As you work through the topic (scene), from broad questions to narrow questions, you get to the target fact—either directly, or by the jury connecting the dots (2+2): *if it looks like a duck . . . and it quacks like a duck . . .* TARGET FACT: IT'S A DUCK.

As you will see in Chapter 2.5, "Target Facts", there are several ways you can paint a picture. As with music, the silence is just as important as the sound—lack of notes can create as much tension and release as do the notes themselves. With storytelling in trial, a target fact can be an *actual* fact— something that happened, that was said, or that exists (like a report or a photo). These are positive facts, or "positives".

You also can paint a picture with the *absence* of a fact—that something did not happen, or that it was not said, or that there is no tangible items (no report, no photo). Those are negative facts, or "negatives".

For fun, as you will read in Chapter 2.5, there are positive positives, positive negatives, negative positives, and negative negatives. It's not confusing at all!

In Chapter 3.4, you will see that there are many places from which you can get your target facts. Target facts can pertain to the ultimate factual question in dispute at the trial, to the ultimate legal issue to be resolved, or be a critical fact about the witness (going to that person's credibility and believability).

D. TONE

Tone is the approach you take with a witness—a question, or even a word, can be as persuasive as anything else. That is not to say that yelling or being in any way combative or attacking is a good tone. To the contrary, moving away from the bazooka and picking up the scalpel is much more effective.

Think about your normal daily approach to life. Think of how you see others interact. Think about memorable performances on screen or stage. What tone of voice do you associate with certain scenarios or situations?

As you will see in Chapter 4.3, the tone you establish will set the stage for the exchange with the witness. It will define for the jurors who is in control.

Choosing your tone will control the witness, but more importantly, it will control the flow of facts and ultimately the story.

E.   TEMPO

Implementing the right tempo for various sections of the cross make it as interesting and captivating as listening to a symphony.

Cadence is the purposeful selection of the speed of speech.

Ever been fishing? As a boy raised in the South, I can say that I have spent many, may hours fishing, and learned quite a bit about it along the way. For instance, sometimes you run the boat pretty fast, and drag bait behind it. You can get a really big hit that way. Other times, the boat is stationary and you cast your line here and there, searching the waters. In those instances, you vary the speed in which you reel in (retrieve) your line, trying to mimic a live fish and attract your prey. In some cases, you simply stay still and drop your line to the bottom—and something big will gulp it up.

How is fishing like litigation? Because there are times you run full, and other times you "stop and drop". Speed dictates the result.

In this book, you will learn that the tempo YOU select will highlight important parts of the cross examination. The right tempo will also control how the witness act and reacts. Setting and controlling the tempo allows you to control the flow of facts, and where the fish . . . rather, the witness, goes.

1.5 LEADING AND LIMITING

Almost every teacher of advocacy will agree that there is only one way to deliver questions on cross examination: *lead* and *limit*.

Lead. Lead the witness. Control the witness by asking only leading questions. Do not let the witness run away with an open-ended question. You supply the fact, and do so in such a way that the only answer can be "yes" or "no".

Limit. Advocacy teachers will also insist that each cross examination question have a *limit* of one and only one particular fact. No more. When you get your "yes" or "no", there will be no doubt about what fact the witness is affirming or denying.

As you will see, these canons are the most important things to remember about cross examination—and are the most often violated. Strict adherence to leading and limiting will allow you to control the flow of facts and the witness being cross examined.

A. USING LEADING QUESTIONS

The most basic and fundamental part of cross examination is to lead. Leading questions are the only method of questioning during cross examination.

What is a leading question? Certainly not the one posed in the previous sentence! That question is an *open-ended question*. An open-ended question asks the person being questioned to provide the facts that will answer the question. Examples:

Who was your homeroom teacher in twelfth grade?

What is your name?

When did you first vote in a presidential election?

Where do you get your hair cut?

Why do you want to be a lawyer?

How do you make a peanut butter and jelly sandwich?

Who, what, when, where, why, and how. These are *direct* examination questions. They do not suggest an answer, and allows the questionee (the witness) to then give the details.

The best way to think of a leading question is to keep in mind that *the fact is in the question itself*. The question supplies the fact, and the answer will either agree with the fact (yes) or disagree with the fact (no). A well-constructed leading question can only be answered "yes" or "no". Examples:

Your name is Joe Bodiford?

You are a law professor?

You are writing a book on cross examination?

You do not like French toast?

You did not swim the English Channel?

Or, in a sequence:

Q.   You were standing at the corner of Tennessee Street and Monroe Street?

A.   Yes.

Q.   Two particular cars drew your attention.

A.   Yes.

Q.   The first car you noticed was green?

A.   Yes.

Q.   The second car you noticed was red?

A.   Yes.

Q.   The green car was driving west?

A.   Yes.

Q.   The red car was driving south?

A.   Yes.

Q.   The green car had the green light?

A.   Yes.

Q.   The red car did not have a green light?

A.   No, it did not.

Q.   The red car had a red light?

A.   Yes, it did.

Q.   The red car did not stop at the red light?

A.   No, it did not stop.

Q.   The green car was passing through the intersection?

A.   Yes.

Q.   The red car hit the green car? **[TARGET FACT]**

A.   Yes.

In each of the examples above, the questions contain the facts that the cross examiner wants the jury to hear. Each question is designed for an agreement or an acceptable disagreement with the fact. As will be discussed in Chapter 2, the questions are all connected and driving toward a target fact.

Further, leading the witness will place you as the provider of facts in the driver seat to control the flow of facts.

B. LIMITING QUESTIONS TO ONE FACT AT A TIME

In order to maintain control of the questioning and establish the right tempo, you should always be careful to only address one fact per question. It's tough to do, but critical.

Q. Mrs. Witness, you were on the corner of Meridian and Thomasville Roads when the accident occurred?

A. Yes.

Q. The blue truck was moving?

A. Yes.

Q. The red car was stopped at the light?

A. Yes.

Q. Both were in the northbound lane of Thomasville Road?

A. Yes.

Q. And the truck ran into the back of the car?
[TARGET FACT]

Q. Yes.

Simple. One fact at a time. The order is important, and is easy to order and reorder when you are only asking about one fact at a time.

Avoiding compound questions is critical. Consider this mess:

Q. You were at the intersection on Meridian Road when the blue truck that was going north ran into the stopped red car?

A. Yes.

What is the witness saying "yes" to? That she was there, the ordinal, the colors of the vehicles, the models, or what?

Limiting *controls.* You control the material being discussed, you control the witness' by narrowing the subject of the inquiry, and you control the jury's focus. Always limit your question to one fact at a time.

1.6 3D CROSS EXAMINATION

Too many law students, and even attorneys, have a myopic view of cross examination. They only think in terms of the most basic, most general, most readily observable facts. A myopic cross is easily derailed by the recalcitrant witness, an unexpected answer, or any answer that is not within the crosser's limited realm of expectation.

"3D cross examination" is just that—the ability to think on all levels, of all angles, of all routes of escape, and to have the snappy, off-the-cuff response readily available to deliver with confidence and discipline. 3D cross explores all dimensions—time, place, manner.

In other words, you have to be able to think on your feet. This is "cat and mouse" . . . "tit for tat". One-upsmanship. However you identify with it, this is the art of outthinking and outmaneuver your opponent. Have you ever been in an argument with someone, and hours (or days) later thought, "you know, what I should have said was . . ."? That is you recognizing your failure to see a moment of vulnerability in your opponent, and to have the right response (or challenge, or "gotcha" question) on the tip of your tongue.

This skill is part natural talent, part practice. The ability to handily go off on a different line of questions is borne of (1) the ability to recognize the fundamental core parts or facets of any issue, idea, or action, (2) the ability to recognize the need to take the witness by the nose to this place (a Cross Exposition), so that the jury knows you are in control and why, and (3) the advocacy skills to be able to immediately plot the course, lay the questions, and land safely back at the place you left off. The concept of Cross Exposition is discussed futher below.

I teach my students that this is much akin to rubbing a puppy's nose in the mess it made. You have to do it right then, so that the dog associates its mistake with the punishment. If you do it later, then the dog is just confused and distrustful of you. You do not want your jury to be a confused dog.

A.   ONE DIMENSIONAL CHECKERS

Everyone knows checkers. Two players take turns making moves, one square at a time, in one direction (unless of course, you are "kinged"). It's pretty easy to get in a place where there is no move to make, nowhere to go. When you have a "king" checker, it is easier, but if the other player has a king checker, too . . . we all just chase each other around the board *ad nauseum.*

The same applies to cross examination when Player 1—the advocate—is not skilled and/or prepared. Imagine this scenario:

Cross examiner has the case detective on the stand, and wants to make the point that the investigation was shoddy (theme), evidence at the scene of the shooting was not collected and preserved (topic), and because there was no gun shot residue (GSR) evidence from the defendant's hands (target fact), the defendant was not the shooter/murderer (case theory).

Q. Detective, you did not conduct a gunshot residue test on the defendant's hand, did you?

A. I did not see the need to.

Q. Just answer my question with a yes or no.

A. OK.

Q. My question was, you did not conduct a gunshot residue test on the defendant?

A. Like I've already told you, I did not see the need to do such a test.

Q. That did not answer my question, did it?

A. I'm pretty sure it did.

Q. Your Honor, would you instruct the witness to answer my question?

J. Seems like she already did—twice, counselor.

This line of questioning is ineffective. It's shallow, and misses the opportunity to develop serious and important target facts. Of course the jury hears that the GSR was not collected, but why, how, who was responsible, are all lost. And the jury gets tired of your amateur cross examination. In turn, your credibility suffers.

What is glaring about this exchange? Someone who is a detective, and investigating a shooting, is *experienced*. That detective will have had a long career of continual training and tons of experience in policies, writing reports, handling evidence, investigative techniques. That goes to the investigation, and the *credibility* of the detective. Moreover, *not* having the test to rule in or rule out the defendant—leaves a big question looming over the case. All of that is fuel for the cross, to show there were lots of things that were not done and to highlight just how glaring is their omission.

As explained in the next section, "Three Dimensional Chess", the concept of Cross Exposition ("exposition" being a term borrowed from literature) is the skill of being able to weave in and out of an exchange, to shift the story for a moment to add critical relevant facts in the form of a background or back story. Learning this skill is critical to staying in control and telling the jury your story.

B.   THREE DIMENSIONAL CHESS—
CROSS EXPOSITION

Three dimensional chess is a real game, not just something from a science fiction movie. It is chess with multiple boards, wherein the players—who, unlike checkers—already have pieces that can move in a variety of ways. With multiple boards, the players are able to move in three physical dimensions—horizontally, upward, and downward.

Real life cross examination is much like 3D chess. As Mike Tyson once said before a boxing fight against Evander Holyfield, "everyone has a plan until they get punched in the mouth." What seems like a great list of questions turns into a horrible cross. We have all seen it happen—the advocate gets punched in the mouth.

To avoid getting punched in the mouth, one must be able to bob and weave like a boxer. We previewed Cross Exposition in the last section, and will explore it more here.

In cross examination, there are times when you have to break from your normal and planned presentation to get in some important background or otherwise relevant information. Most of the time that occurs when the witness does not want to admit certain facts or avoids admitting a fact by trying to steer the questioning in a different direction. When that happens, you take a short Cross Exposition to provide an iron-clad setting in which to re-ask the question and get the answer you want.

Thinking in 3D and using cross exposition, you break free of the confines of a stodgy list of questions. You are free to stop and explore a theme or topic, or to corral a witness back on track.

The following line of questioning breaks the flat affect of a one-dimensional questioning (and the meltdown you read above). This method uses a short *exposition* to explore more about the issue, and to highlight the ultimate target fact:

TARGET FACT

Q. Detective, you did not conduct a gunshot residue test on the defendant's hand, did you?

A. I did not see the need to.

CROSS EXPOSITION 1 [Detective's duties]:

Q. Well, let's discuss the "needs" [makes quotation marks in the air] *of a crime scene investigation. You were the lead detective on this case, right?*

A. Yes.

Q. That means you are in charge?

A. Yes, I would say so.

Q. And you know what it takes to manage and process a crime scene?

A. I am not a crime scene technician, I am an investigator.

CROSS EXPOSITION 2 [Detective's training and experience]

Q. No. But you were training in crime scene techniques, right?

A. Well, I had a class at the academy.

Q. That was a class taught by experienced crime scene technicians and detectives, right?

A. Yes.

Q. And it was required for you to graduate and get credentialed as a law enforcement officer?

A. Yes.

Q. Now, once you were credentialed, but before you were released to work alone, you went through field training?

A. Yes.

Q. And you were trained on-the-job, in the field, on real cases, how to manage and process a crime scene?

A. Yes.

Q. By your field training officer?

A. Yes.

Q. Who was an experienced officer?

A. Yes.

Q. And then for all the years you have been a police officer, you have managed and processed crime scenes?

A. I have.

Q. And in fact, you have served as a field training officer to others?

A. I have.

BACK TO EXPOSITION 1:

Q. So, detective, while you may not be a crime scene tech, tell this jury, you know very well how to manage and process a crime scene?

A. Yes.

Q. In fact, you had more experience and training on managing and processing a crime scene than anyone at the scene, didn't you?

A. Come to think of it, I did.

BACK TO TARGET FACT [Missing a huge piece of evidence]

Q. As the case detective with the most crime scene experience, the final decision not to collect GSR was ultimately yours, wasn't it?

A. Yes.

Q. Because of your decision not to collect the GSR, these jurors are missing that evidence, aren't they?

A. Unfortunately, yes, they don't have it and I probably should have gotten it.

By use of Cross Exposition, the witness has been contained, using very basic facts in an impromptu manner. Each exposition gives important background, supports the track to the target fact, and helps the jury with the "2+2": the investigation was bad and cannot be trusted. It also prevents any verbal dancing around by the witness.

1.7   A WORD ABOUT DIRECT EXAMINATION

Direct examination is important to cross. I use the term "important" and not "critical" for a reason. In most instances, direct examination is to the cross examiner like a microwave is to a chef . . . it's nice to have, but you can cook without it.

Of course, it is impossible to prepare your opponent's direct examination. If you know your facts, and have carefully structured your own theory, themes, topics, and targets, you certainly know what to expect from your opponent and his or her witness. You can always check your predictions by writing your own direct of your opponent's witness (which is a great exercise in helping structure your cross examination).

However, there are moments of gold that can be mined from a direct examination. By knowing your own strategy for cross, having a method by which to listen and record during direct, and simply paying attention, you can control your opponent's direct more that you think.

A.   RELATION TO CROSS

There are two ways to look at the relationship of direct to cross: (1) the relationship of the direct of the witness you are to cross examine, and (2) the relationship of your crosses to the directs of your own witnesses.

Relationship of the direct of the witness you will cross examine. No more obvious a procedural relationship exists in a trial of that of a direct and cross of a witness. The role of the advocate in cross examination is discussed in Section 1.7.2. Suffice it to say, there is usually gold to be mined in direct. You have to know the witness' testimony in one hundred percent detail, so you can immediately hear contradictions, sudden new additions, and omissions. You note those in the appropriate place on your cross sheets (Section 3.5) for use in cross examination. Listen carefully.

Relationship of the crosses to the directs of your own witness. Remember the overall goal of litigation: *to tell your story*. When you cross examine witnesses, you can use facts that you know your own witnesses will, or have already, supplied.

Clearly you do not want to ask questions on cross that will contradict your own witnesses on direct, or vice versa. You want to harmonize the two; surely the jury will think your own witnesses are there to testify in your favor. The real magic happens when the jurors realize that the opposing witnesses are testifying in your favor as well. Be sure the facts coming from cross witnesses (through you getting them to "yes" and "no" your factual assertions) and those coming from your direct witnesses are the same.

B.   THE CROSS EXAMINER'S JOB DURING DIRECT

Review Chapter 3.6, "Cross exam sheets", for a foolproof method of organizing your cross AND listening to and memorializing comments and testimony from direct.

There are two approaches to the crosser's job during direct—one is a silently aggressive and one is active aggressive. One is played strategically in your mind, and the other is played on your feet.

The mental game—silently aggressive. The mental game is listening and absorbing, hearing what the witness is saying and plugging it into your Cross Sheets (see section 3.6), and plotting. While the outer façade reflects calm coolness, the inside is a perfectly calibrated engine running at full speed. You have to be on top of everything.

The "on your feet" game—actively aggressive. The "on your feet" game is one of controlling the substance of the testimony, the witness and the opposing attorney (see Chapter 5, "Evidentiary Objections"). You must react in real time, or risk (1) overly prejudicial or inadmissible evidence or testimony being blurted out in front of the jury, or (2) not preserving the issue for appeal (see Chapter 5.7, "Contemporaneous objections"). I have seen many instances of an attorney hearing something come out (or about to come out) and they do not object, yet when I glare at them to get up they make a face as if to convey "that's OK, it didn't hurt us". I always wonder if that reaction is because the advocate did not hear what just happened because he or she was busy prepping cross. I also marvel at the fact that a supposedly trained advocate would sit there and let that happen to a client. When in doubt, get up and say "objection!". Take a few seconds then to quickly compose the proper legal objection and argument if needed.

The active game is one of control. There are schools of thought that say "don't object during direct unless you have to, and try not to at all." I do not understand sitting idly by while the rules are being broken. In other words, I do not mind potential damaging information coming out—some say *all* testimony and evidence is prejudicial in some form or fashion. Certainly, if there were not some issues that your client were not contesting, you can ignore it as long as it is not otherwise harmful. Beyond that, controlling the substance, the witness, and your opponent are a part of cross examination.

The Cross Sheet method in Chapter 3.5 gets you organized in a way such that anything that could come out is easily recorded. For example, in an employment discrimination case, you may have laid out themes and topics surrounding diversity training (from discovery exchanges and deposition) on Cross Sheets. Once the direct turns the corner into an exchange about what training the company offered, you quickly access those Cross Sheets and make notes in the appropriate spots. Simple.

I suggest having with you at trial a red and any other color than what you wrote your cross notes in on your Cross Sheets. I create mine with a pencil, so at trial I use a blue pen for notes. I use a red pen for "holy cow" golden nuggets that come out on direct. Those are the direct statements that you want to address in cross ("now, on direct examination you told this jury . . . ."). The blue (or whatever color) is for making notes for you to use on cross, such as "ask this first" within a topic, or even to cross out something you thought was a good idea when you first wrote it.

Whatever you do, *don't sit there idly*. Your job as a crosser starts with your opposing counsel asks the witness to introduce him—or herself to the jury. (Note, asking a witness "what's you name" technically calls for hearsay, but I'll leave that discussion for the evidence book I'll write one day).

1.8 TAKEAWAYS

- Cross examination is the most powerful tool for presenting the *truth*.

- Cross examination is the most powerful tool for presenting your *story*.

- You as the cross examiner control the flow of the facts and therefore tell the story.

- Cross examination is intricately tied to the other parts of the trial.

- Never be afraid to use facts you anticipate you will get out on cross while you are selecting the jury, presenting motions in limine, or giving opening statement (your organization and control will get those facts out for you).

- The themes you chose will form the story arc, and are the main tenets of your cross examination.

- Topics are smaller, narrower areas of questioning within themes.

- Target facts are the points you have to make to weave together into a story.

- Your tone sets the emotion of the exchange with the witness and helps tell the story.

- The tempos you use when questioning will further establish the environment of the exchange with the witness, and is a powerful control tool.

- Leading and limiting are more control techniques.

- Always use leading questions on cross examination. Always.

- Be sure to limit the questions to only one fact. No more.

- Be sure to think outside the box: be able to get away from a list of questions, and look at the witness and the facts from all angles, from all vantages, from all perspectives.

1.9 EXERCISES

Exercise 1:

Think about a common issue that you debate or discuss regularly with a friend. Think about why you cannot convince that person of your point of view. Why persuasion techniques have you used? Next time you engage that person, try asking leading and limiting questions to prove your point.

The Seminoles have a great recruiting class, right?

And they won a national championship just a few seasons ago, right?

The head coach has over two decades of experience, you realize that?

The Seminoles have what it takes to win the conference championship, isn't that correct?

Whatever the topic is, try persuading your opponent calmly and rationally, by presenting one fact at a time, and getting concessions as you go.

Please, do not use politics or religion!

Exercise 2:

Remember the game, "Twenty Questions?" If not, it's a simple game. One person—the answerer—thinks of a person, place, or thing (not too abstract, but something that could ultimately be identified), but does not tell the other player what it is. The other player—the questioner—asks one-part questions that can only be answered "yes" or "no" in order to try to identify what the first player has in mind.

Play Twenty Questions, solely to get in the habit of asking leading, limiting questions, and to think outside the box. It's not technically cross examination, but it trains the brain to lead and limit.

Exercise 3:

Cross examine an inanimate object (have a friend play the object). For instance, cross examine a school bus.

You are large?

You have seats for many students?

More than 5, right?

More than 10, right?

As many as 20 can fit on you?

And you transport those students?

You pick them up in their neighborhoods, right?

They take a seat?

And they ride on you?

Then you drop them off at school, correct?

Later, you pick them up at the school later?

They again take a seat?

And they again ride on you?

You drop them off back in their neighborhood?

You do this every day of the week, correct?

Monday?

Tuesday?

Wednesday?

Thursday?

Friday?

And you care about these students?

You care that they arrive safely to school?

And you care that they return home safely, too?

And so forth. Soda cans, books, just about anything can be used. The idea is to try to think of every aspect and characteristic of the item—its size, its use, anything. Be detailed, and drill down to the minutia. Start broadly, and work down to the narrow. Be creative, and think in "three dimensions."

COUNSEL, PLEASE RE-FRAME YOUR QUESTION.

CHAPTER 2

STRUCTURING THE CROSS
(THEORY, THEME, TOPIC, TARGET)

2.1 CONCEPTUAL APPROACH
TO CROSS EXAMINATION

Too many lawyers approach cross examination either with no game plan whatsoever, or with the game plan of "fight, yell, accuse, be indignant." It simply does not work. You cannot expect to simply smash an opponent without a plan.

Conceptualizing—meaning having a plan or intention to prepare and present—cross examination is the only way to approach properly telling the story at trial. In this book, the Five Fundamentals of Cross Examination are introduced as a fool-proof way to plan, prepare, and deliver a winning cross examination.

Starting with the overall case theory—the answer to "why are we here?"—the trial story is set through themes (sub-plots), topics (scenes), and target facts. The concept is akin to storyboarding a movie.

A. USING THE FIVE FUNDAMENTALS

As discussed in Chapter 1.4, "The Five Fundamentals of Cross: Theme, Topic, Target, Tone, Tempo", these tools help you structure the cross examination in a way that is both complete and solid, but also flexible and malleable. In fact, sticking to these fundamentals is wise when also structuring direct, and in turn opening and closing. The fundamentals give you the ultimate control over the story you are presenting and the witness you are using to present it.

In this chapter, you will learn how to approach arriving at your overall case theory, and how to paint the story across time through witnesses. Those witnesses will, one after the other, take the stand and, just like in a movie, lay out your target facts for you through carefully scripted and directed sub-plots (themes) and scenes (topics).

Remember, this is what it looks like:

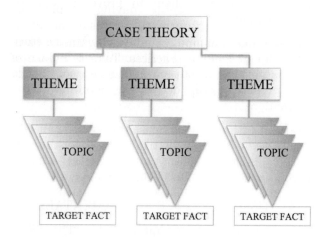

2.2 CASE THEORY

Figuring out the theory of your case goes well beyond identifying the cause of action or charge. It's actually beyond a generalized recitation of the facts.

The case theory is the most provable AND persuasive version of your client's story. Remember, you have to infuse this story through the case from pre-trial motions, through jury selection, in openings, in directs, and especially in cross examination. If you wait to present the case theory until getting up to deliver a closing argument, you have waited too long.

Developing the case theory is accomplished by developing the story. Lawyers forget that trying a case before a jury is in many respects no different than telling a story to a friend or relative. You take the good parts, highlight them to make the story interesting, and use them to prove a point or illustrate an idea.

For example, imagine a civil case against a bank for fraudulent lending practices. Take a "breach of fiduciary duty" cause of action. That's a pretty heady set of words for a jurors to get their heads around— they don't speak "legalese". If the cause of action stems from a bank misusing a customer's funds for its own benefit, that's a basic vanilla version of *how* it happened, not *why* it happened. Why is not persuasive, *how* is.

What's the *theory* behind why the bank did what it did? What was the motivation? Pure greed? Desperation caused by financial problems? Something as simple as accounting problems? The one-word "hooks" can be the gateway to an explanation as to *why*, and perhaps can summarize a case theory, but "hooks" or "grabbers" are not in and of themselves sound, persuasive theories upon which to build a case.

You have to develop a theory from large to small—from all the pieces, down to a word. In the Exercise section (2.8), you are tasked with taking a movie or a real trial and writing out the story in a page. Then you take that page down to a paragraph, then the paragraph to a sentence. Once you have that final sentence, you find one word that encapsulates the sentence. This is "fact-to-theory reduction", to coin a phrase.

In the bank example above, the story could be that the bank was under an audit, and had too much money loaned out, and used a borrower's funds "creatively" to cover other older debt that was on the street. The theory could be similar to "robbing Peter to pay Paul." Or more simply, *greed*.

As the real-life case develops, the facts can change, and more facts can come to life. The reality of trying any case is that sometimes you want a case theory to be one way, and the facts that come out simply will not support that theory. You would love for a witness to say he or she knew about the rip-off scheme, but most of the time people will not admit wrongdoing and expose themselves to legal liability like that. The days of honor are sadly behind us—today, it's all about self-preservation. Witnesses that you know were in on it will likely not admit it (or even close to it). Emails disappear, documents go missing. However, even the holes in the story—the "what's missing"—can be powerful storytelling tools for presenting your case theory. In the example above, if there were never a letter from the bank to the borrower explaining how the money was being used, that omission is a pretty good indicator of a cover-up of theft (see Chapter 2.5.G, on using what's not there in cross—negative impeachment).

Never underestimate how important having a solid case theory is to your success.

A.   WHAT'S THE STORY?

What's the story? How do you tell the story? Not like a lawyer, that is certain. Tell it like a *person*, or a *writer*, or a *movie director*. Infuse *life* into an otherwise dull, legalistic story. In doing so, you will have a much more believable and persuasive story for the jurors to accept and believe.

Gather facts. In Chapter 3.4, we discuss where the target facts come from. Remember that until you know all the facts, and what facts are missing, then you cannot tell the entire story.

Good facts. Your good facts are priceless, and will guide what theory you select for your case. Investigate your good facts, be sure they are unquestionable and cannot be attacked. Preparing your cross examination will focus largely on these good facts.

Bad facts. Bad facts cannot be ignored. Jurors will latch on to bad facts, and punish you for ignoring them or worse, trying to illogically spin them into an absurd position. Marshall the bad facts just as you do the good facts. Bad facts can be explained or neutralized during your cross examination—but they cannot be ignored.

What's the other side's story? Knowing your opponent's case theory allows you to prepare to attack it. Not only should you scour the pleadings, all reports and statements, and depositions, but *talk* to the other attorney. While settlement negotiations are not admissible at trial, pay close attention to what is said, as the other side will often reveal their theory against your client.

Remember, sometimes your opponent will surprise you. Think of alternate theories, and also alternate ways to present a theory. Discuss your case with your co-workers. Maybe even prepare openings, closings, and cross examinations as if you were your own opponent.

Is there some common humanistic theme? The power of persuasion comes in attaching your story to a basic, innate, resounding human emotion or moral. Love, hate, justice, sorrow, greed, pain, lust, etc., are all things virtually every juror will know and share with each other and with you and your client. As a nationally known political huckster recently said about a foe, "I like living rent-free in his head." He knew that his story had connected on a visceral level and resonated soundly with his audience (his opponent).

If you can get your story to live in the jurors' heads and hearts, you will succeed.

B.   THE ESSENCE OF THE CASE, IN A SENTENCE OR A WORD

Love.

Hate.

Truth.

Trust.

Corrupt.

Dishonest.

Unfair.

These are words that describe morals and mores—things that are at the center of what drives us as humans. As I always say, we all know truth . . . love . . . fair . . . unless you're a sociopath. But for the rest of us, there are universal things that we all get.

The word that describes your case theory should not simply be your "hook" for opening or closing—it should be the case theory "glue" that binds the story together.

Themes, topics, and target facts should in some obvious way to the theme of your case. Always bear in mind the theory of the story you tell, all the way through every part of your case, and you will create a cohesive story that unfolds throughout the trial. The jury will appreciate it, understand it, and—if you do it correctly—reward you with the verdict you want.

2.3 THEMES (PLOTS)

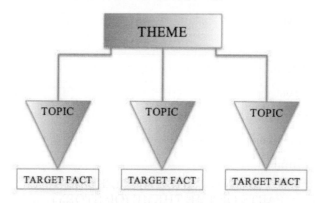

With the overall theory of the case settled, you can begin to devise the storyboard and how the facts will be presented to tell your story. This is an important concept that is lost on so many trial lawyers. The story is not simply what you say in opening, and then what you say in closing. The story is the journey you take the jurors on, going through all parts of the trial. It has to be easy to understand and follow, and be interesting so the jurors *want* to be involved in it— especially how it resolves. Remember, the jurors write the last part of the story—*the verdict*.

You can control how that last part is written. You do that through controlling the stories presenting during the trial. You have objections to use on direct to control the witness and opposing counsel (see Chapter 5, "Evidentiary Objections). On cross, *you* tell the story (see Chapter 2.3.C, "Using Cross

Examination to Explain the Subplots and Move the Story") and control how the story moves.

Each part of the story you want to tell can be capsulized into a *theme*. Themes are not limited to how a contract was breached, or the motive for a murder. Themes can also be the lack of credibility of a witness, told though cross examination of bias and prejudice.

As you identify the parts of the story, you will have an easy time plotting the themes into the cadence of the overall story.

A.   IDENTIFYING THE DIFFERENT PARTS OF THE THEME (OR STORY)

Imagine a case where the defendant is charged with a crime, but claims he is being framed. Law enforcement on the scene of the crime did not collect critical evidence for testing, that could have proved the defendant did not do it, and/or that someone else did. Further, there is only one lay witness, who hates the defendant and will testify that the defendant committed the crime.

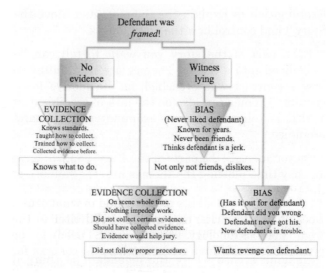

Elements of a theme. A theme is something important the story tries to tell us—something that might help us in our own lives. As discussed above, it could be a moral, or a more, or an ethical consideration. In the example above, being accused of something one did not do is a really, really horrible thing to happen to a person. So the theme of embarrassment, anger, and fairness would color the story and cross examination.

Plot. What are the main events and players in the case? How did the facts of the case unfold while it was going on in real life? What was the sequence of events? How will you present that to the jury over the course of a day, days, weeks, or even months of trial? Loping facts into a presentation is reckless and unpersuasive. If I tell you what I did last Friday, but don't put it into a logical sequence, then you have no context as to how my day was.

In the "framed" example, the plot is how the charges came to be, with no evidence and a witness with a motive to fabricate. In effect, you almost tell the story in reverse, starting with being in the courtroom and working back through the lies and insufficient evidence until arriving at the conclusion that someone else committed the crim.

Story structure. Related to plot, a story's structure is how it all fits together and in what order. Does one set of facts, maybe discovered later in the "real life" chronology of the story, need to be presented to the jury early so there is context for everything else? In a murder case, the discovery of the victim's dead body (ostensibly at the END of the crime) sets the scene for everything that lead to his or her demise. In a contract breach case, the damages caused to the plaintiff set the tone for just how bad the defendant's actions were, and how they were foreseeable. As mentioned above in the "framed" example, the structure might actually be told backwards.

Characters. Who are your players? Who are the "good guys" and who are the "bad guys"—the "heroes" and the "zeros"? Who are innocent bystanders? Who has baggage that will impact credibility? *How do these characters tell your story?* You should always think of witnesses in terms of what their characters add to the story.

In the example above, two characters have their own thematic material: one is incompetence, the other is vindictiveness. Within those themes, there are topics for each, and clearly defined target facts for closing argument.

Setting. I always go to the scene of where the crime occurred, if I can. I like to walk around, look at it from different angles, check out any places described by the witnesses (intersections, etc.). If there is a video of the incident, I stand where people stood, try to see how they said they saw it.

When you are in a cross, you become more effective if you know the actual setting or stage upon which your story plays out:

Q. Let's talk a little about the scene. You have lived in that neighborhood your whole adult life, right?

A. Yep.

Q. Bought your home in 1980?

A. Yes, June of 1980.

Q. Living there for 27 years now, if my math is correct?

A. It is, 27 years.

Q. As you enter the subdivision, your home is the tenth one down on the left?

A. [Pauses to mentally count] Yes, that's right. I've never counted it before, believe it or not.

Q. You may have never counted that, but certainly you know about "the" magnolia, right?

A. Oh yes, everyone knows Big Girl.

Q. Now, when you enter the subdivision and round the corner, Big Girl is the tree on the right, correct?

A. Yes.

Q. And she's a big one, isn't it?

A. Yes, it is pretty big. Very big—huge.

Q. The leaves on that tree are really big, too?

A. Yes, it's an old tree.

Q. A tall old tree?

A. Yes.

Q. A dense old tree, meaning you can't see through the leaves, can you?

A. No, it's pretty thickly packed together.

Q. Now, Big Girl is really close to the road, too, isn't that right?

A. Yes, it is.

Q. In fact, it's between the sidewalk and the roadway, correct?

A. It is.

Q. Tell us, when you bought in there in 1980, was Girl already big?

A. Pretty much—they didn't want to cut her down, so they kind of built around her.

Q. That curve in the road—it's for Girl?

A. Yep, and the sidewalk, too.

Q. So, as you drive into the subdivision, you cannot see around Big Girl, can you?

A. *Kinda, but it's hard.*

Q. *You can't see your house because of her can you?*

A. *No, not until I pass her.*

Q. *As you drive in, you can't see your house through her, can you?*

A. *Not at all.*

Q. *So, as you drive into your neighborhood, you cannot see down to your house?*

A. *No, I cannot.*

**TARGET FACT: Clearly, then, one would not be able to see someone coming in or out of his house from down the street.

Because you were out there and saw this for yourself, you can much more effectively paint the scene for the jury.

In our "framed" example above, think of how you would walk the police officer through the crime scene, stopping to mention each opportunity to examine and impound each item of evidence. Setting a calm and controlled setting helps the jury understand the officer's missed opportunities to give them the evidence the need to resolve the case. Certainly, photos and diagrams can assist you with setting the scene.

Style and tone. *See* Chapter 4, infra. How you present the story through cross examination is important, as you as the storyteller of the facts can signal to the jury what you want them to focus on. Remember, these jurors are in a new situation, and group dynamics will dictate how they respond to that situation. Most will look for cues from a leader—that leader is you. You can summon emotions and reactions by your speed, cadence, tempo, and tone of voice. Your mannerisms and gestures will also impact your presentation.

B.   GETTING THE SUBPLOT PLOTTED

Consider the importance and potential use of every fact. Use the following checklist to figure out where your facts go:

Fact:

Witness(es) giving fact (indicate dir or cross):

Is the fact a *positive* (does it exist?)

Is the fact a *negative* (is the fact that something important that is absent, or not present)?

Is the fact a *constant* or a *variable* fact?

    If a variable, who interprets it, and how?

    What are the varying interpretations?

Is the fact in fact even a fact, i.e. is it indisputable?

Is the fact a *target fact* (see Chapter 2.5)?

    Is it a core, case related fact?

    Is it an impeachment fact?

Is the fact a *supporting* fact?

    Does the fact set a scene?

Does the fact explain a predicate action?

Does the fact develop a character or witness, whether for good or bad?

Is the fact a spoken fact, or an implied fact?

Does the fact come from a witness or a document?

Careful examination and analysis is critical. Not only will you begin to discover the overall story (case theory), you will see where the fact fits in to the overall story, and how you will use the fact on cross examination.

C.   USING CROSS EXAMINATION TO EXPLAIN THE SUBPLOTS AND MOVE THE STORY

This might be the most important chapter in this book—the most important part of the message here. Your chance as an advocate to tell the story on cross is the most valuable part of the trial.

Remember the flow of information: on direct, the facts are coming from the testifying witness. *On cross, however, the facts are coming from you, the advocate, and the witness is simply confirming those facts for the jurors.* That is not to say that you will "testify" or become a witness; rather, you will present the facts in the order you want and simply have the witness affirm or deny as you go. It is often said that the best cross examinations are the ones where the witness simply says only "yes" or "no" to the questions (*see* Chapter 4.1 on "The Ideal Cross").

This is why using lists of questions simply does not work. Using Cross Exam Sheets (see Chapter 3.5) keeps your story together yet provides the flexibility required of a trial. A long list of questions does not. Organizing all the subplots, the breaking them into scenes, not only keeps you in control, it keeps the jury involved and understanding the story. Remember, the one who tells the best story, wins.

2.4 TOPICS (SCENES)

This is the meat of the coconut. The theory is the "why", the themes are the "what", and the topics are the "how"—how you tell the story. The scenes are carefully scripted, put together in a purposeful and persuasive manner, and played for the audience.

It is in the topics that you find the target facts, and all of the question sets that lead to those goal facts.

Topics and target facts could almost be synonymous. The difference is that a topic (scene) may have more than one target fact.

For example, a topic may be the witness' credibility regarding a particular thing, such as the ability to see/hear/act, or a bias/prejudice that may disqualify the witness' account. There could be more than one target fact, i.e. that she lied about A, she lied about B, and she lied about C. It's too easy to say "she lied", and much more effective to point out that she lied about three different things at three different times. And, in each case, set up the target fact's "pow" impact through development of the scene leading up to the lie.

A.   NARROWING THE TOPICS FROM THE OVERALL STORY ARC

Rarely are stories started with the conclusion. Jokes do not begin with the punch line. You have to set up the story or the joke—that is human nature. We relate to stories because of our familiarity with the journey the characters are on. We feel for them, we emote with them, and we come to understand them through their backstory. With jokes, the punch line is made funny because of our familiarity with the setup—but the twist or unexpected insertion of a dissonant fact is what gets the laugh.

The narrowing of facts is really applicable to any presentation. Think about it—a salesperson is not going to start with the price of the house . . . he or she is going to talk about the town, then the neighborhood, then the schools in the district, then the comparable sales nearby, then show the exterior, the interior, then finally the details of any electronics or fancy trim work. After the broad-to-narrow presentation is finished, the buyer has a complete picture—and is ready to accept the target fact: the sales price.

So, topics (and themes)—and their target facts—should be presented to the jury in the way they most easily ingest information—from broad to narrow. While this is true of both direct and cross, it is most helpful in cross. Narrowing as you go will figuratively trap the witness into a corner. Admitting, admitting, admitting . . . nowhere to go as the walls close in.

B.   USING CROSS EXAMINATION TO PAINT EACH SCENE

To reiterate, the most important thing for you to remember about, and implement during, cross examination is that *you are the storyteller*. The facts come from you. You control what facts come out, the order, and the amount of focus and importance placed on each fact.

Don't waste the opportunity by blasting aimlessly through the cross examination. Choose the right tempo to paint each scene and maximize the impact on the jurors. Remember that persuasion is getting your listener to come to the conclusion on his or her own.

Here's how not to do it, when trying to nail down a defendant into admitting that he stole money from his employer:

Q. You stole the money, right?

A. No.

Q. You were there and you took it, didn't you?

A. Nope.

That can go on all day. It does not work because this line of questioning goes right to the ultimate factual question and misses the story behind the ultimate factual questions. Setting the scene lets the listener follow the story to its undeniable conclusion.

But painting the scene requires you to tell the story—take the time to set up the who, what, when, where, why, and how. Maybe one of these "W's" is missing from your affirmative target facts. No worries—that missing piece is the conclusion that the jury will come to if you set the scene correctly. For example:

Q. Mr. Defendant, as an employee of EmployeeMart, you were given several responsibilities?

A. Yes.

Q. And you were trusted to perform those responsibilities?

A. I was.

Q. Your bosses didn't look over your shoulder?

A. No.

Q. They allowed you to work unsupervised, correct?

A. Yes.

Q. You knew they trusted you?

A. Yes, I gave them no reason not to.

Q. Now, your duties included making the bank deposits each morning, right?

A. Yes.

Q. *You were trained how to do that?*

A. *Yes.*

Q. *You were supervised at first?*

A. *Yes.*

Q. *But eventually you began to do it all by yourself?*

A. *Yes.*

Q. *The deposits are prepared by you before anyone else gets in, correct?*

A. *Yes.*

Q. *There are EmployeeMart policies for preparing the deposit, right?*

A. *Yes.*

Q. *You are familiar with those policies?*

A. *I am.*

Q. *One of the policies is that when there is a discrepancy between the previous night's final audit, and the money in the safe the next morning, you are to notify the general manager immediately?*

A. *Yes.*

Q. *On June 6, you went in as usual?*

A. *Yes.*

Q. *You got the money from the safe?*

A. *I did.*

Q. *And you compared it to the previous night's audit?*

A. *I did.*

Q. And you testified on direct that there was $2500 missing?

A. That's right—there was cash missing from what the register receipts and the night manager's count said there should have been in there.

Q. As a side note, you know that the EmployeeMart policy for the final night audit is that it has to be confirmed by both the manager on duty as well as an assistant manager?

A. It's supposed to be.

Q. And on June 6, you saw that the previous night's deposit had in fact been confirmed?

A. Yes, it looked like it had been.

Q. But it was $2500 short.

A. Yes.

Q. At no time did you notify the general manager?

A. I was looking for the lost money, so I forgot to call her.

Q. Well, that the money was the missing was not discovered until the end of the month, right?

A. That's when I was notified that the bank deposit did not match the audit.

Q. That's over three weeks later.

A. Whatever the math is, yes. A couple of weeks.

Q. Despite knowing the money was missing all that time, you never notified anyone?

A. No, like I said, I was looking for it.

Q. You're telling this jury that you found a light deposit, went ahead and put what was there in the bank, and told no one?

A. I was looking for it.

Q. You did not enlist help in looking for it, did you?

A. No.

Q. You did not question anyone about where it might be?

A. No, I was trying to keep things "as usual" until I solved the mystery.

Q. You didn't make a report?

A. No.

Q. You did not document your investigative efforts?

A. No, I remembered everything.

Q. But you were the only one who knew the money was missing.

A. Yes.

Q. You were the only one who knew for three weeks?

A. Like I said, I was working on investigating the issue.

Q. Was part of your investigation buying a new car?

A. I'm sorry, what?

Q. You bought a new car on June 6, right?

A. Uh, yes, I had already been looking at a car and already made the deal. I don't see what that has to do with anything.

Q. Right—you had told everyone at work you were going to buy a new car, remember that?

A. Yes, I talked about it.

Q. You talked about it quite a bit, didn't you?

A. Pretty much.

Q. You even took a selfie of you and the car, and showed it to everyone?

A. I did—it was a nice car. People wanted to see it.

Q. You'd already picked it out, and the afternoon of June 6 was the day you went into sign and make the down payment?

A. Well, yes, but I was a little late because I was trying to figure out what happened to the deposit money.

Q. Speaking of deposits, you had to put down money on the car when you financed it, right?

A. What does that have to do with this?

Q. Let me ask my question again, perhaps you didn't understand it. You had to put money down on the car, correct?

A. Yes.

Q. And that amount you had to put down was . . . . $2500.

A. I don't really remember.

Q. Would seeing the sales contract refresh your recollection?

A. No, I think that's right, I'm not really sure.

Q. You talked about that new car all the time, you're telling this jury that you don't remember a major detail of getting it?

A. [mumbles something]

Q. No further questions.

Here, there is no reason to get into the whole back and forth about the defendant having stolen money from the business to pay for the deposit. He will never admit that, as it will convict him. He wants to make the jury think this was a mystery he had valiantly undertaken to investigate, and his car purchase was merely a coincidence.

In this cross, the scene is painted that (1) he was the only person there when the "discrepancy" was discovered, (2) he did not report the missing money, and (3) he made a large deposit on a very important purchase with an equivalent amount of money the same day. You don't need him to admit it. 2+2 . . . the "4" is that he took it. The jury gets it, and you get your conviction.

In real life, the facts may not line up for you quite as serendipitously. But there is always a way to set the scene such that the jury comes to the only logical conclusion.

2.5 TARGET FACTS

Target facts are the entire reason you open your mouth on cross examination. They are the pillars of your case. Target facts are the foundations upon which your case is built.

Target facts are not necessarily *ultimate* facts. They can be ultimate facts, but don't have to be ultimate facts. Usually, ultimate facts are for the jury to decide (liability, guilt, etc.). For instance, having a confidential informant admit that he did not buy drugs from the defendant, but rather bought them from someone else, is an ultimate fact. How might that fact come out? A confidential informant is not simply going to admit, "I lied to the cops and falsely accused someone." So how do you think it would go?

While the ultimate fact is the overall target of the case, other important (but not ultimate) target facts can set the foundation for the jury to make its own conclusion about the ultimate fact. In the example above, the target facts that were established along the way leaves the jury with the conclusion that the employee stole the money. It's certainly nice when the witness admits liability, or guilt, or whatever ultimate fact. But the advocate should never, ever bank on that happening. Instead, a good cross examination will set the pillars of target facts that paves the way for an unavoidable conclusion—the conclusion the advocate wants.

A.   CRITICAL IMPORTANCE OF TARGET FACTS

If there is one thing that you should take away from this book, it is how incredibly important target facts are in cross examination.

Target facts are the facts that you stood up to get out of the witness. They are the facts you will argue to the jury in closing summation. They are the pillars of the story you are trying to tell.

A target fact is something the jury will talk about. It is a fact that makes your story believable. Sometimes it is the ultimate fact (who the killer is; who lied; who is at fault in the accident; etc.) that is the target. Other times, target facts are on topics such as bias, prejudice, impeachment issues, credibility issues. Whether an ultimate or a supporting issue, a fact that qualifies as a "target fact" deserves special attention.

That is not to say that foundation questions—those that lead from the broad theme down through the topics to the target—are not important. They are, but not as important as the target facts. It's not as important *how* you get there, as it is *that* you get there.

Examples:

- Witness Smith really hates my client (shows bias).

- The contract was never countersigned and accepted (shows no breach).

- The email was sent *and* received on Monday (shows timing and knowledge).

There are probably an unlimited amount of target facts, based on the vast number of different factual scenario, charges, causes of action, and witnesses. It's impossible to make a definitive list. You as the advocate have to work with your client to review the statutes, pleadings, and jury instructions to know what facts quality as "golden egg" target facts.

B.   THE DOMINO EFFECT

The "domino effect" is often used to describe a chain of linked events, one based on another, that perpetuate to a conclusion. If you have ever seen dominoes set up and knocked over, you can visualize the event.

In cross examination, the domino effect is the linking of target facts together to (1) tell your story, and (2) create a rift in the opponent's case.

When thinking of the target facts, think of how they link together to tell the story.

For instance, regarding the thieving employee mentioned above, once it is established that he has lied about something, the rest of his testimony is going to be suspect. Establishing the next lie with the jury may come easier than exposing it from the witness—in other words, he may not admit the next lie, but the jury will certainly think he's lying. The more he talks, the more that first lie is going to come back to haunt him. Finally, he is rendered uncredible and unbelievable.

C.   IDENTIFYING TARGET FACTS

Target facts can come from anywhere. They can be a part of the elements—what you have to prove. The ultimate *issue*, so to speak. Target facts can also come from the ultimate *question*.

Do not forget that target facts can also be facts that attack the witness' credibility, or bias or prejudice, or memory. That an opposing witness is not to be believed is a part of your story—dig to get the facts that tell (illustrate or prove) that part of your story.

1. Ultimate Factual Question

The ultimate issue is a *factual* issue. Was the defendant the person who pulled the trigger? Did the defendant divert the funds from the company account to his own? The list goes on and on. Think of the ultimate factual question as the question or questions that the jury must answer in order to be able to render a verdict.

To find target facts that go to the ultimate factual question, look at the elements of the cause of action or crime. Then look at defenses (consent, self-defense, etc.). What's the story you need to tell?

2. Ultimate Legal Issue

The ultimate is just that—not necessarily a factual question to be answered, but one of a legal nature. For example:

- Was self-defense legally used?

- Was the defendant sane at the time of the offense, or what should he be found not guilty "by reason of insanity"?

- Does the statute of limitations apply?

- Was there consent (which certainly could be a factual issue, too)?

- Was there contributory negligence, and if so, how much?

The list goes on, as there are always statutory defenses and issues that must be resolved.

Target facts in this area can be based in fact, but they have to be clearly isolated and presented in order for the law to resolve the matter.

D.   DOES IT HELP, DOES IT HURT . . . DOES IT EVEN EXIST? POSITIVES AND NEGATIVES

This section may be perceived as "overthinking", or even overkill. Understanding your target facts is one thing . . . *realizing their place in the overall persuasion process is another*. To understand where to put the target facts (including whether that place is the garbage can), you must break down each fact and look carefully at it to see what it really is. Don't take anything for granted—look at every fact, no matter how "obvious" you may think it is. So while this may seem to be over-analysis, this is in fact what a trial attorney must do with every fact.

Target facts fall into one of four categories. Keen attention must be paid to each target fact. For cross examination purposes, a target fact can be an *actual fact* (some that happened—a positive), or it can be an omission (something that did not happen or of which there is no proof—a negative). Graphically, think of it like this:

	POSITIVE (Helps your case)	**NEGATIVE (Hurts your case)**
POSITIVE (Fact exists)	Constant, existing fact Positive, Affirmative Directly supports your case theory Goes to an element of proof Goes against an affirmative defense	Constant, existing fact Lack of anything hurtful to your case Absence of any infirmity of your case
NEGATIVE (Fact missing)	Constant, non-existent fact Positive, affirmative Denial of any attack on your case	Constant, non-existing fact Positive, affirmative Hurts your case No way to mitigate or spin

I like to call these "positive/positives", "positive/negatives", "negative/positives", and "negative/negatives". That is a lot of parsing down to the finest degree, but is helpful in concluding what is the best way to deal with the fact. Figuring out how best to use the fact is critical to how you will present the case.

Remember, for cross purposes, that something does not exist or cannot be proved, *is in itself a fact*. Think of it as an "empty set" in math—an empty set is a unique set that has no elements (https://en.wikipedia.org/wiki/Empty_set). That there are no elements does not mean there is no set—the set is simply empty. Much like an empty glass is still, in fact, a glass.

Missing facts are established by *negative impeachment*—the skill of accentuating the missing. See Chapter 2.5.H, below.

Below are examples of how facts might end up being categorized. Again, think about the impact of the fact in relation to your causes of action and defenses. Where to use the fact? How to present the fact? These are all going to factor into how you develop your target facts, and subsequently the themes and topics that will contain those facts.

1. Positive/Positives

Positive positives are affirmative constant facts that are completely and undisputedly favorable for your client and that support your case. Example:

Q. Officer, my client is clearly not the person who committed the crime, right?

A. That is right.

OR

Q. You were at your office across town when the murder occurred at your house?

A. Yes.

2. Positive/Negatives

Positive negatives are affirmative (constant) facts that hurt your opponent's case. Example:

Q. Officer, your investigation revealed that the accuser in this case was lying, correct?

A. That is correct.

OR

Q. Mr. Defendant, you definitely were not home when the murder occurred at your house?

A. No, and I was not.

The second example is a reversal of the positive/positive above—the negative fact is that he was *not* at his house (as opposed to the positive fact of where he actually was at the time of the murder).

3. Negative/Positives

Absent or missing/unavailable facts that help your case. Example:

Q. Officer, you dusted for fingerprints inside the burgled house?

A. I did.

Q. And you found fingerprints of ten different people?

A. That is correct.

Q. And my client's fingerprints were not in that set, were they?

A. That's correct, they were not.

That there are no fingerprints for the jury to consider *is a fact*. It is a negative fact—like the empty set from math, it is a thing but the thing is important because of its non-existence.

Why there are no fingerprints for analysis and consideration is another theme and/or topic.

4. Negative/Negatives

Absent or missing/unavailable facts that hurt your case and help your opponent's case. Example (it does not get worse than this):

Q. Ma'am. You're telling this jury that the only person in the world who had access to your missing jewelry was my client?

A. Yes, I am. She is the only one that could have stolen it.

No one saw the defendant take the jewelry—the lack of eyewitness testimony is a *negative*. However, that she alone had access creates the negative fact that she alone took it.

The bottom line with negative/negatives is that they are not good for you. As they are constants (as opposed to variables, that are open to interpretation), then there is not a whole lot you can do about it. If your client is seen on video stealing the company's trade secrets from the vault, that is about as negative/negative fact you can get.

From a cross examination standpoint, and to state the obvious, you do not want to incorporate negative/negatives into your target facts. In fact, you want to identify them in order to steer clear of them when structuring your cross examination. Use other target facts, relating to credibility and impeachment, instead.

5. Does It Even Matter?

Discretion is the better part of valor, is the old saying. In cross examination, there are times that the question, or the questioning, is just not a part of the story.

Consider your story. Is there are target fact you need a witness to give you? If not, what does the witness add to your story? Can the witness detract from your story?

Ask yourself, does it even matter? *Why am I asking this question about this fact?*

a. Insignificance

After you identify your positives and negatives, be sure to rethink and re-analyze whether the thing even matters. If it doesn't, it is not a target fact. Insignificant facts may be relevant but they bog you down. Get rid of them, and focus on telling your story concisely and succinctly.

b. Lack of Controversy

If there is no controversy over a particular target fact, consider simply mentioning it and moving on. There is really no reason to go through a broad-to-narrow question set if the witness will readily admit the target fact. Certainly there are times you will need to set some context or history for where you are going. But, if you can get there immediately with a stipulation, do it.

> *Q. Mrs. Witness, based on what you said on direct examination, you do not have any first-hand knowledge of what happened?*
>
> *A. No, I do not.*
>
> *Q. Thank you. Let's move on to the business records you brought here today, okay?*
>
> *A. Okay.*

E.   TARGET FACTS ABOUT THE WITNESS

In addition to target facts arising from ultimate factual questions and ultimate legal issues, there are issues related to the opposing witness that you will cross examine. We want to get good facts from the other side's witness (that always looks good—why in the world would the other side help you *unless it were true*?). But in the event there are no really helpful facts the witness is willing to give you, attack the witness' credibility and believability. Look for target facts to bring out *about* the witness.

Bias, prejudice, memory problems, lying, being a convicted felon are all target facts *about* the witness. Using those as a theme—*this witness cannot be believed*—and developing topics under each area will allow you to design question sets that bring out deadly target facts. Breaking down the other side's storyteller only strengthens your story and your case.

1. Bias

Bias is a human trait, or perhaps frailty. We all have biases for and against things, from the trivial (sports teams) to the profound (religion). Our biases for and against things impact how we see them, remember them, and relate them later. Two football fans of rival teams will surely have very different versions of a game-deciding penalty call. The winner will have seen it, remember it, and relate it one way; the loser will have quite the opposite version of events.

In litigation, bias is

a term used in the 'common law of evidence' to describe the relationship between a party and a witness which might lead the witness to slant, unconsciously or otherwise, his testimony in favor of or against a party. Bias may be induced by a witness' like, dislike, or fear of a party, or by the witness' self-interest. Proof of bias is almost always relevant because the jury, as finder of fact and weigher of credibility, has historically been entitled to assess all evidence which might bear on the accuracy and truth of a witness' testimony.

United States v. Abel, 469 U.S. 45, 51, 105 S.Ct. 465, 469, 83 L.Ed.2d 450 (1984). Think of bias as one of the themes (sub-plots) of your story—every story has a villain. The biased witness is that villain.

Clearly, the evidence code broadly permits examination into bias:

Rule 607. Who May Impeach a Witness

Any party, including the party that called the witness, may attack the witness's credibility.

Courts have held that exposing a special motive to lie is not a collateral issue. *See e.g. United States v. Harvey*, 547 F.2d 720, 722 (2d Cir.1976). Bias is a broad term that may refer "both to a witness' personal bias for or against a party and to his or her motive to lie." *McCloud v. United States*, 781 A.2d 744, 752 (D.C.2001).

Some examples of bias in litigation are:

- There is other pending litigation between the parties.

- Long-standing bad blood between neighbors, co-workers, family members, etc.

- Witness has an interest in the outcome—related to a party, stands to get money or not go to jail, immigration issues upon conviction, etc.

- Witness has or has had his or her own pending charges or lawsuit based on the same facts and circumstances.

- Witness has lied at some other point in the case but has been given immunity from a perjury prosecution.

- Co-defendant or uncharged co-conspirator has or will likely receive leniency or other favor from the government.

- Witness has some romantic interest or familial relationship (son, daughter, etc.).

- Witness delayed in getting involved for no good reason.

- Expert is being paid to testify favorably.

- Refusal to participate in the pretrial discovery process.

While the overall theme is "biased witness", the reasons for the bias (as in one of those listed above, for instance) are the topics—and there can be more than one reason someone is biased. The topics will then funnel down to the unspoken target fact—which is simply that the witness cannot be believed. Remember, the witness will not admit he or she cannot be believed . . . but by using "2+2 . . ." the jury will conclude the "4" all on their own. Then you argue it in closing—the witness is *unbelievable* and all of her or her testimony should be wholly rejected.

Remember that any line of questioning must pass the test for relevance and probative value versus prejudice. F.R.E. 401, 403, and 404.

2. Prejudice

Prejudice is something beyond bias. Bias is the way a witness feels about a subject, for or against it, and impacts that person's partiality. While taken from a discussion of jurors (not witnesses), the following definition is on point:

> Bias, in its usual meaning, is an inclination toward one side of an issue rather than to the other, but to disqualify, it must appear that the state of mind of the juror leads to the natural inference that he will not or did not act with impartiality. Prejudice is more easily defined, for it means prejudgment, and consequently embraces bias; the converse is not true.

Hyundai Motor Co. v. Vasquez, 189 S.W.3d 743, 751 (Tex. 2006) (internal citations omitted).

Prejudicial attitudes go beyond bias—like the examples above, a witness exhibiting such biases has a "bent", or a "leaning." Prejudicial attitudes are *fundamental* problems—views about a particular race, age, gender, religion, sexual orientation can cause prejudice. People may or may not act on their prejudices; your discovery process may uncover that the witness has in fact mistreated your client because of prejudices. That becomes huge fodder for cross examination. Exposing prejudice, as with bias, tells the jury that the witness is *unbelievable*, and the testimony should be rejected.

As with bias, prejudice shapes the way we perceive things and events, remember those things and events, and relate them later.

Note, a witness' prejudice against your client or your cause is different that the prejudicial effect of certain evidence. As a reminder, if prejudicial material starts to come out while the witness is still on direct, object as to the relevance. Remember Federal Rule of Evidence 403:

> The court may exclude relevant evidence if its probative value is substantially outweighed by a danger of one or more of the following: unfair prejudice, confusing the issues, misleading the jury, undue delay, wasting time, or needlessly presenting cumulative evidence.

When assessing the probative value of evidence under Rule 403, a court must consider both whether the evidence was offered to prove an issue that was in genuine dispute, and whether the evidentiary point could have been made with other evidence that did not present a risk of unfair prejudice. *United States v. Bain*, 874 F.3d 1, 27 (1st Cir. 2017).

3. Memory Problems

Along the way, I came across the technique wherein the cross examiner begins the cross examination by confirming that the witness has no memory issues:

Q. Good morning, Ms. Witness.

A. Good morning.

Q. You feeling OK today?

A. I am.

Q. And before we start, let me ask: your memory is not giving you any problems today, is it?

A. No, it doesn't seem to be.

The witness would have a hard time later in the cross examination trying to cover the revelation of bad facts by claiming not to remember.

If the witness does continue to have memory problems, your target fact is that the witness is simply not *reliable*, and therefore the jury should not put much (if any) stock in that person's testimony.

4. Lying—Prior Inconsistent Statements

The classic and most prized score in cross examination is to catch a witness in a lie. Impeachment by prior inconsistent statement is the best way to accomplish proving a witness has lied. This is because the jury has two of the witness' own statements to compare. Federal Rules of Evidence 607 and 613 cover impeachment and prior inconsistent statements:

Rule 607. Who May Impeach a Witness

Any party, including the party that called the witness, may attack the witness's credibility.

* * *

Rule 613. Witness

(a) Showing or Disclosing the Statement During Examination. When examining a witness about the witness's prior statement, a party need not show it or disclose its contents to the witness. But the party must, on request, show it or disclose its contents to an adverse party's attorney.

(b) Extrinsic Evidence of a Prior Inconsistent Statement. Extrinsic evidence of a witness's prior inconsistent statement is admissible only if the witness is given an opportunity to explain or deny the statement and an adverse party is given an opportunity to examine the witness about it, or if justice so requires. This subdivision (b) does not apply to an opposing party's statement under Rule 801(d)(2).

There is a proper procedure that must be followed. This is called the *foundation*, and is achieved through using a litany of questions to establish both statement and their consistency.

A prior inconsistent statement is any statement made before trial (oral or written) that departs from the witness' direct testimony at trial. For example, witness "A" said in a deposition the traffic light was red. At trial, "A" testifies that the light was green. The deposition is the prior inconsistent statement.

The keys to effective impeachment are "The Three Cs": *Commit, Credit, and Confront*. Charles Rose, *Fundamental Trial Advocacy*, 2nd ed. 2011.

The cross examiner must first *commit* the witness to the critical direct testimony. This orients the witness, court, and jury to the subject matter. This should be done so that the answer that the witness is now committed to is exactly the opposite of what he or she said in his or her prior statement. Start the "commitment" by using his language and then move the witness to the language that is the mirror image of what was said before.

[*Commit* the witness to what was just said in court]

Q. You stated earlier today that the light was green.

or

Q. You told us on direct examination that you saw the accused in the bank before the robbery?

[*Credit* the prior statement, thus enhancing its reliability and trustworthiness. Do this with a series of short leading questions directed to the circumstances of the prior statement.]

Q. Let me take you back in time for a moment— you gave a deposition in this case?

Q. A court reporter was present?

Q. Before answering any questions at that deposition, you took an oath?

Q. Just like the oath you took here today?

Q. That oath was to tell the truth—the whole truth?

Q. You were given the opportunity to review the transcript of that deposition for accuracy? (note: this would not apply if the witness "waived reading" of the transcript before trial.)

In this example, the questions are designed to credit the validity of a prior statement given in a deposition. Your "credit" questions may vary depending upon the type of prior statement used to impeach the witness' testimony.

Another example would be of using a prior written statement (not necessarily a deposition) in the "credit" and "confront" parts of the impeachment:

[Credit]

Q. You made a statement about this case on [date]?

Q. And the events were fresh in your mind at that time?

Q. You swore to tell the truth before you gave your answers or wrote your statement?

Q. Just like the oath you took here today?

Q. That oath was to tell the truth—the whole truth?

Q. You initialed each page?

Q. You read it over?

Q. You signed the statement?

Q. You were given the opportunity to make corrections or changes?

Q. You were given the opportunity to review the statement before you testified here today?

Finally, you reach the dramatic (but not necessarily hostile) moment of *confrontation.* This can be done two ways. The traditional method is for the cross examiner to read the witness' own words to him.

[Confront]

*Q. I am calling court and counsel's attention to
page ___, line ___, in (witness' name)
deposition / statement. Mr. Witness, when I asked
you the question "what color was the light when
the car entered the intersection?" you answered,
"the light was red."*

Q. "You said that, didn't you?"**

**Don't forget this!! This is the actual
impeachment!

In performing this method of impeachment, you
would not show the written statement to the witness
unless the witness denies making the statement.
Perhaps the witness will deny making the prior
statement, in which case you will then approach the
witness with the prior statement and get an
admission from the witness that the prior question
was in fact asked and that the witness' answer was
in fact what you read, i.e., "Mr. Witness, you were
asked (read question) and your answer was (read
answer)." The jury will thus have also observed the
witness denying under oath ever having made the
statement—sort of doubling the effect of the
impeachment.

Most importantly, never ask the witness to explain
the inconsistency or tell the jury which statement is
the truth. These are the "one question" too many and
will undermine the effect of the impeachment as the
witness will make every effort to explain or at least
minimize the inconsistency.

5. Prior Convictions

As with any impeachment that is governed by a rule, strict adherence to the proper procedure for impeaching a witness with a prior conviction is imperative. This is not a treatise on evidence, and the coverage of the rule contained herein is in the context of planning a cross examination. *Careful attention should be paid to the rules and cases interpreting the rule in your state or jurisdiction.*

The rule. The rule regarding prior convictions:

Rule 609. Impeachment by Evidence of a Criminal Conviction

(a) In General. The following rules apply to attacking a witness's character for truthfulness by evidence of a criminal conviction:

(1) for a crime that, in the convicting jurisdiction, was punishable by death or by imprisonment for more than one year, the evidence:

(A) must be admitted, subject to Rule 403, in a civil case or in a criminal case in which the witness is not a defendant; and

(B) must be admitted in a criminal case in which the witness is a defendant, if the probative value of the evidence outweighs its prejudicial effect to that defendant; and

(2) for any crime regardless of the punishment, the evidence must be admitted if the court can readily determine that establishing the elements

of the crime required proving—or the witness's admitting—a dishonest act or false statement.

(b)   Limit on Using the Evidence After 10 Years. This subdivision (b) applies if more than 10 years have passed since the witness's conviction or release from confinement for it, whichever is later. Evidence of the conviction is admissible only if:

(1)   its probative value, supported by specific facts and circumstances, substantially outweighs its prejudicial effect; and

(2)   the proponent gives an adverse party reasonable written notice of the intent to use it so that the party has a fair opportunity to contest its use.

(c)   Effect of a Pardon, Annulment, or Certificate of Rehabilitation. Evidence of a conviction is not admissible if:

(1)   the conviction has been the subject of a pardon, annulment, certificate of rehabilitation, or other equivalent procedure based on a finding that the person has been rehabilitated, and the person has not been convicted of a later crime punishable by death or by imprisonment for more than one year; or

(2)   the conviction has been the subject of a pardon, annulment, or other equivalent procedure based on a finding of innocence.

(d)   Juvenile Adjudications. Evidence of a juvenile adjudication is admissible under this rule only if:

(1)   it is offered in a criminal case;

(2)   the adjudication was of a witness other than the defendant;

(3)   an adult's conviction for that offense would be admissible to attack the adult's credibility; and

(4)   admitting the evidence is necessary to fairly determine guilt or innocence.

(e) Pendency of an Appeal. A conviction that satisfies this rule is admissible even if an appeal is pending. Evidence of the pendency is also admissible.

Proper procedure. The proper procedure for *initially* questioning a witness about his or her prior convictions is as follows:

Q. Mr. Witness, have you ever been convicted of a felony?

A. Yes.

Q. How many times?

A. Three.

[IF YOU BELIEVE THERE ARE NON-FELONY CRIMES OF DISHONESTY, CONTINUE]

Q. Other than that, have you ever been convicted of a crime of dishonesty?

A. Yes.

Q. How many times?

A. Once.

If the witness lies or equivocates about the convictions, most jurisdictions will permit you to ask about the actual convictions. The rules are complicated, and suffice it to say you will be permitted to ask about convictions you have a good faith to believe exist—meaning you have a certified copy of the conviction from the clerk of court *in your hand.*

If the witness tries to explain away the conviction, that may open the door to your being able to get into the substance of the conviction (charge, sentence, other circumstances).

Again, know the local rules and judge's procedures before undertaking this procedure. Going so far can result in a sustained objection, censure before the jury, or even a mistrial.

F. THE DIFFERENCE BETWEEN THE TARGET FACT AND THE "ONE QUESTION TOO MANY"

You have to know when to stop. When you have made your point. You have to be able to control yourself and resist the urge to keep going when you have given the jury "4". There are times you just want to solve the quadratic formula for the jury . . . but you don't have to. They have already arrived there.

Recall from Chapter 1.2.A (Persuasion) the power of the inference, and having the jury get the point on their own. It's a human nature thing—to come to a conclusion organically, based on personal experience. It is so much more lasting and impressive than simply being told the answer.

Target facts are no different. Remember, target facts can be actual or implied (see Chapter 2.5.A). Regardless of actual or implied, once the jury has the fact, your mission is accomplished. The point of the topic is made and your story has both longevity and persuasiveness.

But then there are the times the advocate just wants to keep beating the horse long after its demise. The target fact has been neatly and succinctly established, and the jury completely understands the target fact and its correct place in the story. But the advocate continues. What ensues is generally not helpful, and is in fact often harmful.

This old example that every law school advocacy student has heard demonstrates the point:

Q. You did not see my client bite the nose off of the victim?

A. No, I did not.

Q. So you don't actually know whether he bit it off, do you?

A. I'm pretty sure I do—I saw him spit it out!

How do you recover from that?

Remember that credibility is an incredibly hard thing to earn in a courtroom, and a very easy thing to lose. Also remember that credibility is the foundation for your story—your client's story. Once you lose credibility, your story is soon to follow.

I have long said that a person who has something to hide will give you facts one through nine, but will never give you fact ten no matter what. It is human nature to want to seek acceptance of one's story by being agreeable, and in so doing try to become a reliable and credible source of information. And, the malfeasant hopes, in becoming credible then the listener will surely believe the total swerve in logic right before the damning final fact. In other words, if I give you a credible story that goes one through nine, then you should also believe me about ten no matter how absurd my denial sounds.

Remember, if you have established one through nine in your favor—you don't need to fight with the witness about ten. The jury knows, and that is all that matters.

And a final thought about the "one question too many": *good advocates never ask a question to which they do not already know the answer.*

G.   MAKING SURE THE JURY KNOWS THE TARGET FACT

There are subtle ways to cue the jury that the target fact has arrived. I suggest a movement, a well-placed and well-timed pause, and a look at the jury. Nothing dramatic, nothing to try to improperly influence the jurors' decision-making.

Review Chapter 4.5 ("Conducting" cross examination by using gestures during cross).

H. WHEN THE TARGET FACT IS "MISSING"— THE TARGET FACT AS NEGATIVE IMPEACHMENT

As explained above, for cross purposes, that something does not exist or cannot be proved, is in itself a fact. Think about the instance of a report is missing a crucial fact that the witness wants to discuss on the stand at the time of trial. The missing fact is a negative—the fact is the *absence* of the fact in the original report. That negative is a positive for your case, as you can impeach the witness by his or her omission.

"The theory of impeachment by omission is that 'if [a] former statement fails to mention a material circumstance presently testified to, which it would have been natural to mention in the prior statement, [then] the prior statement is [considered] sufficiently inconsistent' to be admitted to impeach the present testimony." *United States v. Useni*, 516 F.3d 634, 651 (7th Cir. 2007) (citing *Moylan v. Meadow Club, Inc.*, 979 F.2d 1246, 1249 (7th Cir. 1992) (quoting 1 John W. Strong, McCormick on Evidence § 34 at 114–15 (4th ed. 1992)) (first alteration in original)).

1. The Power of Highlighting the Missing

Movie makers know that the scariest monster is the monster you cannot see. Think about all those movies where the monster is out there, and everyone is running (or swimming) around scared to death— but you don't even see the monster.

Why is that monster so scary? Because of the power of the listener's mind and imagination. That the main antagonist from the story is not actually there is incredibly powerful.

What is missing holds great value, and great importance. The same holds true in cross examination—which is called negative impeachment.

> The fact that the question included so-called negative evidence should not have barred the impeaching question. Pertinent is a statement by Professor Wigmore: 'A failure to assert a fact, when it would have been natural to assert it, amounts in effect to an assertion of the non-existence of the fact. This is conceded as a general principle of Evidence. * * *' 3 Wigmore on Evidence § 1042 (3rd Ed. 1940), p. 733.

United States v. Standard Oil Co., 316 F.2d 884, 892 (7th Cir. 1963).

Negative impeachment is the art of highlighting what is missing—what should be there, but is not. That it cannot be seen, heard, tested, analyzed, or confronted creates a "unseen monster" in your story.

The effect of negative impeachment is that is forces the jury to consider whether the witness is fabricating, nor not. There are two types of negative impeachment.

What is said in court appears nowhere else. Some witnesses will try to sneak in testimony that has never been heard before the moment it is said in trial.

Good pretrial preparation will give you command of what evidence and testimony is available. When something comes up that has never been said before, be prepared to inquire as to *why*. Simply asking "why didn't you mention that before" has no impact, and allows the witness to be able to make up a reason (whether believable or not) as to why the omission occurred. But remember that you are telling the story, and have to advantage of control.

2. Using Negative Positives

Here is an example of how to set up a powerful impeachment by omission from a written document. This made-up example might be what you'd find in a product liability or employer liability tort claim, where the employee was inadvertently exposed to toxic level of lead.

Q. You testified today that Mr. Plaintiff was advised about the dangers of lead used to make plastic toys your company produces?

A. That's right, it was discussed with him during his entry interview on his first day.

Q. And you are saying he was told to wear protective gear when in Production Room 2 where the lead is stored, is that what you are telling this jury today?

A. Yes.

Q. As the human resource coordinator, you personally open every employee's file, correct?

A. Yes.

Q. *You personally speak with each new employee on day one?*

A. *Yes, that is my job.*

Q. *And you personally advise them of the rules and regulations of employment at the toy factory?*

A. *I do.*

Q. *Now, you memorialize all of that in a memo, right?*

A. *Yes.*

Q. *You prepared a new employee for Mr. Plaintiff?*

A. *I did.*

Q. *The first part of that memo is a checklist of items to be reviewed with the new employee?*

A. *It is.*

Q. *And the second part of that memo is a narrative, where you document what you discussed in the meeting?*

A. *Yes.*

Q. *You made the checklist as you went through the meeting with Mr. Plaintiff?*

A. *As I went through everything, yes.*

Q. *The narrative you made right after the meeting, right?*

A. *Yes.*

Q. *And everything from the meeting with Mr. Plaintiff was fresh in your mind with you made it?*

A. *Yes.*

Q. Nowhere in this memo did you note that you had advised Mr. Plaintiff about the lead?

A. I did not check it off, but I know I had to have mentioned it.

Q. Nowhere in your narrative did you record that you had told Mr. Plaintiff about the lead?

A. No, I did not specifically note that.

The target fact is the negative/positive of the missing entry—which is argued in closing as an attack on the credibility of the witness.

Next, consider a hypothetical witness in a generic criminal theft trial, who has just testified for the first time on direct examination that the defendant admitted to taking the stolen items. Nowhere else does that statement appear—not in the police report (her oral statement) and not in the witness' oral deposition. She never made a report, but was spoken to several times and never mentioned the fact.

Q. Miss Witness, your testimony on direct examination today was that Mr. Defendant admitted to you that he took your property?

A. Yes.

Q. No other specifics, just that he said he took it?

A. Yes

Q. Now, you have been involved in this case over a year, correct?

A. I was the victim of the incident.

Q. The incident was June 17 of year before last, correct?

A. Yes.

Q. And that is over a year ago?

A. Yes.

Q. So the answer is, yes, you have been involved for over a year?

A. Yes.

Q. After the incident, you met that same night with the police officers?

A. Yes.

Q. They were helpful to you?

A. Yes.

Q. They made you comfortable?

A. Yes.

Q. They did not rush you?

A. No.

Q. They asked you to tell them everything that happened?

A. Yes, I answered their questions.

Q. And some time after that, you met with the prosecutor?

A. I don't know who that is.

Q. You met with Mrs. Jones over here?

A. Yes.

Q. And you know her to be the prosecutor handling this case?

A. Yes.

Q. So let me ask again—after meeting with the police, you met with the prosecutor?

A. Yes.

Q. And that was only two days after the incident?

A. Yes, I think so.

Q. It was within a few day after, would you say?

A. Yes.

Q. You understood that Mrs. Jones was there to help you?

A. Yes.

Q. And she was helpful?

A. Yes.

Q. And she wanted to know everything about the case?

A. Yes, I answered all of her questions.

Q. And you came to a deposition here at the courthouse about six months ago, right?

A. Yes.

Q. I was there?

A. Yes.

Q. Mrs. Jones was there?

A. Yes

Q. We treated you professionally?

A. Yes

Q. And you were asked to tell us everything about the case?

A. I answered all of your questions.

Q. You recall the question, "Is there anything we have not specifically asked you about this case that you think we should know?"

A. Yes.

Q. And your answer, "no, nothing that I can think of."

A. Yes.

Q. And while this case has been going on, there have been court hearings?

A. Yes, I came court.

Q. Right—you came to court many times?

A. I don't recall how many, but several, yes.

Q. Miss Witness, prior to taking the stand today, you have never told anyone that Mr. Defendant admitted to taking your property?

A. I was never asked.

Q. You never told the police he said that?

A. They never asked.

Q. You never told Mrs. Jones, the prosecutor that?

A. She never asked.

Q. You never told us in deposition, even when given the chance to say anything you wanted, that Mr. Defendant said that?

A. No.

Q. A person admitting to a crime is a pretty big deal, don't you think?

A. I suppose.

Q. But not until Mr. Defendant entered a plea of not guilty and demanded a trial, did you finally decide to come out with this?

A. [who cares what she says—the jury gets the "4"]

The "unseen monster" in your story—this oddball admission by the defendant to the crime for which he is on trial—is now favorable to you. She had every opportunity to put forth what could be the biggest fact in the case, yet she did not. The negative impeachment—her omission—is a huge credibility issue.

Similarly, things that could have been done, but were not, can create an "unseen monster" effect in your story. This is especially effective in criminal cases, where the standard of reasonable doubt controls the jury's decision.

Things that are omitted that can come up and bite a witness at trial come in many forms. Failure to get consent, failure to look for other evidence (DNA, fingerprints) or other suspects, and failure to investigate other witnesses are just a few.

Be creative, and think in 3D (see Chapter 1.6) when looking for points of negative impeachment where the information or evidence is simply missing.

2.6 TRANSITIONS AND SIGNPOSTS

No one likes to listen to some speaker drone on and on. No one likes to watch a two hour play with no scene changes. Opera—I *like* opera, but most folks

don't. That's probably because while there are
different scenes, it's all in a different language and
sung—not spoken—to boot. Opera can be difficult to
sit through simply because most people do not know
what is going on . . . and on . . . and on . . .

Because of how we are as humans, we need time to
stop and process. Smaller bites are easier to chew
than big ones, and there's less risk of choking. We
take schedules breaks at work, at school, in long
movies . . . psychologically, we crave processing time
and mental health breaks.

Segue (pronounced "SEG-way") is a musical term,
that describes the movement from one part of a song
or piece to another. It is best described as a seamless
transition, without any noticeable or protracted
pause.

A.   THE IMPORTANCE OF SIGNPOSTS
IN CROSS EXAMINATION

Signposts along the highway deliver a lot of
information—most importantly of which is *where you
are*, and what is coming up. In cross examination,
having a transition or segue as a signpost serves two
purposes. First, it marks the end of one theme (or
topic) and the beginning of the next. Second, and
more importantly, it gives the jurors a road map of
where you are and what is coming up. Your jury and
your witness know where you are and where they are
expected to be. And, most importantly, you control
the witness.

When preparing and delivering an excellent cross, be sure to leave room for your jurors to process, decompress for a second, and reset for the next act.

Words as signposts. In the next sections, you will find examples of words, phases, and questions that serve as transitional signposts. Be sure to use them boldly so it is absolutely clear that the jury knows where you, and that the jury knows that you know where you are.

Movement as signposts. We will discuss the importance of gestures when asking questions in Chapter 4. Equally important is your movement about the courtroom to accentuate transitions. If you are allowed to move freely about the courtroom, you have more room (pun intended) to be creative. Once you get to the target question that closes the topic and theme, relax, turn to the left or right, perhaps look at your jurors to see how they are doing, move to your new spot a few feet away, and start with the next topic.

Some judges will require the advocates to stay directly behind or at least within reach of the podium (or even as counsel table, where there is no podium). In that case, you still have movement available to you. At the end of the target fact, you can simply make a purposeful physical pause. Take a moment to deliberately turn to your next cross sheet, perhaps take a few seconds to jot (or pretend to jot) a note on your pad, take a look at your jurors. Whatever it is, make it look as if you are doing it on purpose. Looking at the jury always creates a personal connection, and signals to them that (1) you care about them and (2) you care about them getting the information.

B.   TRANSITION STATEMENTS

When moving from theme to theme and topic to topic, a well-placed transition statement works wonders to signal what is coming next. As discussed previously, it is a nice break that allows the jurors to reset the brain.

Transition statements should be:

- Neutral (not in any way *improper*)
- Non-argumentative
- Non-testimonial
- Short
- Fact-free
- Not editorial

Examples of transitional statements are:

Q. Let's talk about [theme or topic].

Q. Let's talk about June 6.

Q. Let's talk about your plea deal.

It's not a bad practice to get agreement from the witness: "Let's talk about June 6, is that OK?" Of course the witness will agree. If he or she says "no, that's not OK", see that as your opportunity to pounce. Be sure to look at the jury before you do—they will tell you with a look that they want to know *why does this person not want to talk about June 6??*

Q. *I would like to move on to [theme or topic].*

Q. *I would like to move on to discuss June 6.*

Q. *I would like to move on to your plea deal.*

Again, a "is that OK" locks the witness in so they cannot later pretend to not know what you are asking about. Some other transitions or segue statements:

Q. *Let me turn your attention to [theme or topic].*

Q. *Now that we have established ___, let's talk about ___.*

Q. *Since you mentioned ___, now would be a good time to talk about that.*

Q. *Let's move on to . . .*

Q. *Can we talk about ___?*

I have heard the lock-in question of "*is that OK?*" posed more stiffly as "*do you understand?*" Certainly there are errant witnesses that deserve the strong-arm treatment, but use tough tactics sparingly.

C.   TRANSITION QUESTIONS

Like transition statements, transition questions can turn the exchange to a different topic while giving the jury a little break and a new direction. It is difficult to design a leading transition question that is fact-specific, so think more generally.

Some examples:

Q. *Now, can we talk about ___?*

Q. *Would you mind us discussing ___?*

Q. *Let's tell the jury about ___?*

D.   TRANSITIONS OR SEGUES AS "SAFE HARBOR" QUESTIONS

In Chapters 5.5.E and 6.4.B.1, we will discuss "safe-harbor" questions. Segues can get you back to a safe-harbor, and bail you out of a tough spot. Some "safety segues" are:

- I understand you want to discuss that, and you can with [Mr. or Mrs. Name of Opposing Counsel], but I need you to answer about ___.

- Can we go back and establish a few basic facts?

- So it's clear to the jury, let me take you back to ___.

Much like the safe-harbor questions, these transitions should become part of your "advocacy muscle memory" and ready for use at all times.

2.7 TAKEAWAYS

When structuring your cross examination, remember:

- Solidify your overall case theory.

- Think about what target facts you need from the witness to tell your story.

- Themes—large parts of the story.

- Topics—scenes within the themes.

- Lay out the theme-to-topic-to-target questions in a logical, story order.

- Remember that the jury has to understand your story.

- Look for target facts not only in the elements and defenses, but in impeachment and credibility issues.

- Are the target facts *actual* facts, or the *absence* of facts?

- Does the target fact you are considering even matter to the story?

- Use signposts and transitions, so everyone knows where you are in the story.

2.8 EXERCISES

Exercise 1:

Rent, download, or pop in the DVD of your favorite movie. Ask yourself these questions:

What is the overall theory of the movie, i.e. what is the writer/director trying to get across? Some movies are serious and sentimental, others are shoot-'em-ups . . . but they all have an overall message. Some are complicated (love is a misunderstood flower that blooms only once in a lifetime . . . blech) and some are simple (the guys in the white hats always win). Think carefully about it, and write down your thoughts.

What are the themes—subplots—used to tell the story? Like *Star Wars*, there are always layers of themes (or, at least there should be). Goods constant struggle over evil; budding love; loyalty; etc. In your favorite movie, what themes are used? How do the sub-plots spell out these themes and use them to tell the overall story?

What are the "a-ha" moments? These are the target facts—the points that, once they are revealed, change the complexion of the story. That a witness did not see something he or she once claimed to see, or the revelation that the witness has lied, and the like, are those special moments when you can feel the tide of the trial change in your favor.

Exercise 2:

Go watch a *real* trial. Youtube does not count for this. Go watch a real trial. Unless you live on a deserted island and they've yet to build a courthouse out of palm trees, there are trials going on in your county every day. Find one—call the court administrator, the judicial assistant, or the prosecutor or public defender's office. Watch the news. There are constantly opportunities for you to see others practice the craft you are studying. While he was in college, Tiger Woods taped the broadcasts of every golf tournament on TV, so that he could study the courses and how others played them. Worked out for him, didn't it? Get to the courthouse and camp out.

Start with jury selection. Can you tell from what the attorneys are asking what the case will be about? The theory of the case? What about themes and topics? If so, write them down.

Do not be afraid to ask the attorneys or the judicial assistant for access to documents. The complaint, depositions, police reports ... whatever they will share. Read it over before the trial. *Think about what theory, themes, topics, and targets you would weave into the story.*

Watch the trial, and observe this one thing: *what is the story?*

As you listen for the story, look for a logical theory, well-organized themes (sub-plots), topics that set the scenes, and clearly delineated target facts.

Exercise 3:

Consider this ...

Why do attorneys not tell stories like movie directors?

How hard is it really to approach as trial case like a story or a movie?

Do you think it is important for jurors to hear trials in story format?

Is how people listen to and process information important to a trial lawyer?

True or false: *whoever has the better story, wins.* Why?

Can you be an effective trial lawyer without being a raconteur?

Exercise 4:

Taking one of the movies or trials you observed in the exercises above, do the following:

A. Boil the story of the movie or case down to a typed page.

B. Boil the typed page down to a paragraph.

C. Boil the paragraph down to a sentence.

D. Use one word to describe the story you have conveyed in the sentence.

Objection! It's unfair! Opposing counsel has Joseph Bodiford's "Cross Examination In a Nutshell."

CHAPTER 3

PREPARING FOR CROSS

3.1 PREPARING FOR CROSS

What story are you trying to tell?

As discussed in Chapter 2, the singular most important thing you can remember when preparing for cross examination is that you, the advocate, have the chance to tell the jury your story from your lips. What a powerful tool.

Think about it—you don't have to rely on anyone else to remember all the facts. You don't have to hope that a witness gets the story out in an understandable order. You control the flow of the facts—you tell the story. *You* are stating the facts, and the witness is merely there to agree with the undeniable.

Q. *You graduated from high school?*

A. *Yes.*

Q. *That allowed you to enter college?*

A. *Yes.*

Q. *You graduated from college?*

A. *Yes.*

Q. *That allowed you to enter law school?*

A. *Yes.*

Q. *You graduated from law school?*

A. *Yes.*

Q. *You applied to be a member of the state bar?*

A. Yes.

Q. That allowed you to sit for the bar exam?

A. Yes.

Q. You passed the exam?

A. Yes.

Q. You passed the bar background check?

A. Yes.

Q. You met all the other requirements for bar admission?

A. Yes.

Q. And you were admitted as a member of the bar.

A. Yes.

Q. That admission has not been revoked?

A. No.

Q. You have not resigned or gone inactive?

A. No.

Q. You registered an LLC with the secretary of state?

A. I did.

Q. And that was for Witness Law, LLC?

A. Yes.

Q. You are the sole owner of that LLC?

A. Yes.

Q. When a LLC is registered, a statement of purpose is filed?

A. Yes.

Q. And the stated purpose of the LLC is the practice of law?

A. Yes.

Q. And you filed that, correct?

A. I did.

Q. You obtained a tax ID number from the IRS?

A. Yes.

Q. You have a law office?

A. Yes.

Q. You take on clients and cases?

A. Yes.

Q. You render legal advice to those clients?

A. Yes.

Q. You file motions?

A. Yes.

Q. You draft documents?

A. Yes.

Q. And your clients pay you to do that?

A. Yes.

Q. You are a practicing attorney at law.

What have you concluded about this witness? What has the jury concluded? What if the witness answers, "no, I am not a practicing attorney?" Does that change your mind as to whether he or she is a practicing attorney? No, of course not.

Remember, counsel does not actually testify. You cannot introduce facts that are not in evidence, or mischaracterize or "spin" facts. You can, however, possess such a command of the facts and their importance that you can use a witness to confirm or negate the narrative that you establish. In the "practicing attorney" example above, the facts are undeniable and lead to the conclusion that the person is actually practicing law. Even if he or she denies it, the facts say otherwise and the listeners (the jurors) can draw their own conclusion. The method works for any factual scenario.

So when you begin to prepare for cross, be sure to remember and embrace the power you have as the storyteller. Your theory, your themes, and the topics you cover, and the order in which you reveal and lay out your target facts will present your story, and you will be on the center stage directing the action.

3.2 WHY ARE WE HERE?

Why are we here? What has brought all these people to this courtroom today? Your story depends on you knowing the answer to that question. Once you know, you then tell the story to the jury.

As discussed in Chapter 1, the basics of persuasion and storytelling revolve around a moral, more, or ethical theme that will resonate with the listener.

Basically, if *you* do not know why—*really* know why—you are in court, then you cannot convince a jury of that.

Here are some considerations to work on when preparing for cross:

- **Know your *cause*.** I use the word "cause" but "winning" is not necessarily a cause. Are you in a civil case, and seeking to be vindicated totally from any liability, or are you trying to limit your client's exposure to only 20%? There is a big difference. Same with criminal cases—are you shooting for a "not guilty" altogether, or are you trying to get the jury to convict only of a lesser charge? Conceding some guilt to avoid other is a very common tactic, as opposed to "swinging for the fence" with an across the board acquittal. Knowing and fully understanding your *cause* will really impact the story you tell during your cross examinations, as well as your approach to the whole case.

- **Know your case theory.** You can know your cause, but you still need to understand how to accomplish the goals for your cause. The cause is the what, the theory is the *why* and *how*. You can easily understand that the cause is to recover for your injured client. You will fail at that endeavor unless you have a clear theory of why and how the injury happened, and consequently who is at fault.

- **Case theory: boil it down to a word.** Again, not necessarily a fancy "hook" or grabber—rather, a word based in emotion or morality. Think *essence*. Once you know your cause, and know the theory of your case, go through the exercise of expressing the essence of your case in a single word. You can start with a paragraph, then pair it down to a sentence, the work to find the word that embodies why you are in court. Remember to look at the common moral, more, and ethical words—greed, lust, trust, anger, etc. What word describes your case? That word should resound in every sentence of your presentation to the jury. Weave it into voir dire, opening statement, and certainly in cross examination, where it will become most vibrant to and resounding with the jury.

- **What you want to achieve on cross: boil it down to a word.** Just like the essence of the case, your goal for the cross can be boiled down to a word. Certainly, the word can be different than the overall case theory descriptive word, but it has to be a word that furthers the telling of the overall story. How does this witness fit into your story? Is your goal to use the witness to confirm your story? Affirm. Corroborate. Demonstrate. Is it to totally discredit the witness? Impeach. Discredit. However you are going to use the witness to help tell your story, know exactly how. Of course, a witness can be more than jury one thing in your story. Just be sure to identify the witness' usefulness or danger that needs containment.

3.3 WHAT'S THE STORY?

Finding the story in the case is difficult for most attorneys to do, mostly because it is not usually the focal point of litigation. Advocates worry about court dates, meeting pretrial order deadlines, issuing subpoenas, trying "one last time" to negotiate an eleventh hour settlement, writing out an opening, writing out a closing, writing a list of questions for direct and cross exam (again—*do not do this!*) . . . basically doing everything except for finding a way to persuade the jury.

Think of a call to a parent, or a casual conversation with a friend. One may ask you, "hey, you are going to trial next week, what is the case about?"

What comes out of your mouth next defines who you are as an advocate.

If the story is, "two guys got into a contract to buy a business, and one of the guys somehow made off with the money and the first guy is suing him", that's a pretty lousy story. You would never encapsulate your clients plight and all of your hard work into a statement like that!

Here is how the story would go:

My client worked for forty years to build an autopart supply store. It's over on Main Street, across the street from the park. He built it up to one of the biggest supply houses in this part of the state—he was really doing well financially. His kids were through college and he was ready to kick back and enjoy life. He figured that he could sell the business, buy that fishing boat he'd always wanted but never let himself buy, and retire. Then he and his wife could be together in their golden years.

Well, all that was a great American dream until he met the defendant. The defendant offered to purchase the store, and they went through all the due diligence to get the project to contract. All the references checked out. The defendant had good credit and the bank was helpful in getting the sale closed. Everything seemed great—my client would have chunk of money at closing, and would have a monthly income for many years. That chunk of money went to pay off his kids' college debts, and to buy that little boat. That was the retirement he'd always dreamed of— until this nightmare started.

The defendant never paid a single monthly payment. He would stall, he would make up excuses, he would duck and dodge my client's request for information. Come to find out, the defendant had a secret debt to a bookie in Las Vegas, and was under a lot of pressure to get him paid . . . "or else". The defendant took over the business, liquidated the on-hand supply of parts, and paid the bookie. Then he simply let the forty year old business die. Meanwhile, Mr. Defendant changed the books to look like sales were slow, and blamed the whole thing on customers not liking the "new management."

The bad news for my client is that he had to go back to work when he should have retired. He had to sell the boat to make ends meet. His health has declined out of sheer stress. The defendant, meanwhile, has gone on to open another auto supply store in a different city, using my client's business model and trade secrets. Meanwhile, my client is now having to work an hourly job for his old cross-town rival, as a stocker in the parts department.

In this story, which can be told in a minute or two, I infused several emotions and morals to which people can relate: pride, hard-work and perseverance, immorality (gambling, to some, is an immoral act), greed, pain, embarrassment, and callousness. Of course all stories are different, but all good stories should paint a clear picture with the colors of life and life experience.

How would the cross examination of the defendant go in this case? Perhaps something like:

Q. You knew Mr. Plaintiff before you bought his business?

A. Yes.

Q. You knew how long he had owned it?

A. Yes.

Q. You knew that Mr. Plaintiff had borrowed money to start the business?

A. Yes.

Q. You knew that Mr. Plaintiff had paid those debts off over several years?

A. Yes.

Q. You knew that Mr. Plaintiff's family had worked in the business over the years?

A. Yes.

Q. You knew the time they invested?

A. Yes.

Q. *You knew the pride they had in their family business?*

A. Yes.

Q. *You knew how much they valued their reputation?*

A. Yes.

Q. *And how much they valued their customers, right?*

A. Yes.

Q. *That business meant everything to them, didn't it?*

A. Yes.

Q. *And you took it from them.*

A. *I bought the business.*

Q. *But never paid them.*

A. No.

It doesn't matter what the next answer it—the jury feels the emotion of pride of ownership, the American Dream, families taking care of families, small-town America. Those are deeply rooted emotions and feelings for most people; those that take unfair advantage of Mr. & Mrs. America quickly become pariahs.

How you tell your story is the key to your success as an advocate. Here are some things you can consider when figuring out your case's story:

- **Does your cause of action in and of itself incite emotional, moral, more, or ethical**

feelings? There is no case that does not evoke some emotions or feelings. Boredom is a feeling—and you don't want that one.

- **Does any particular fact of the case stir any of the basic humanistic feelings?** In the example above, pride, love, fairness, and honor are some that come to mind. What others can you think of? Does the questioning above stir *you*? If so, why? If not, why not? What would you do differently.

- **Does any particular witness bring an emotional, moral, more, or ethical issue (positive or negative) into the case?** In the family business example above, the basic moral issue of only taking what is yours is prominent. Another one is living up to your word; as a more, it would be honoring a binding contract. What others?

- **Is there another story similar to yours— something from literature, movies, or current events, that evokes strong emotions, morals, mores, or ethics?** Think of the "#metoo" movement of 2017 if you were trying a gender discrimination case—your case may not have the abhorrent sexual abuse component of #metoo, but there are similar themes from which you can build your story. In the family business example, Bernie Madoff comes to mind—he callously ruined people's lives by taking their life savings. Granted, some of those that invested so much with him were likely motivated by greed themselves, but they did not exhibit the evil he did. So the themes play off of each other.

- **Is the story one that people have heard before?** Injuries after a car accident, fallout after being ruined financially, being falsely accused or arrested, and other common situations. Talk to people you know have been in that situation, and ask them about their feelings and emotions. Build your own client's story on those fundamental emotional blocks.

- **Does your story make sense?** Missing pieces of logic, or lapses in the "flow" will totally destroy a story. We have talked about "2+2"—now think "A, B, C, ___, Z". If you are missing D through Y, the story is not going to make sense.

- **Is your story believable?** As a criminal defense attorney, I have heard many tall tales told to me by people charged with crimes. Most people are comfortable relaying the truth to their attorney. Others feel it necessary to lie and make up unbelievable stories. When I hear these things, I tell my client to imagine he or she is a juror—and ask them would he or she believe the story as I tell it back to them. Most say "no"—I tell them that is what we are up against with 6 or 12 jurors. Simple believability comes from the credibility of the story, as well as of the characters that tell it. On cross examination, you can use the witnesses to establish that the story.

3.4 WHERE ARE THE FACTS COMING FROM? DISCOVERY—AND MORE!

Trial lawyers often say, "we don't build 'em, we just fly 'em." In other words, we cannot make up the facts, we can only use the ones we have.

But what we can do is *find* facts. Never, ever expect all the facts to jump out at you. You have to find them, and you have to know where to look for them.

Discovery is supposed to be the exchange of information. In criminal cases, *Brady* mandates that the government *must* turn over all exculpatory information. In many states, the government must turn over all evidence in its possession. One would think that because a criminal case is brought *after* an investigation, all the facts would be easily available. That's not always the case, and sometimes motions to compel have to be filed.

In civil cases, where the advocates can be anything BUT civil, it's never that easy. It seems that files are full of ugly letters and emails, full of demands for overdue discovery. Court dockets seem to always have hearings where one side is accusing the other of delay, or being incomplete, or some sort of shenanigans. *Don't be this litigator.* Know the local rules, know what is required by the judge's pretrial order—*and comply.* The other side is going to get the discovery—be the professional that sends it timely and completely. Work with opposing counsel to exchange information. These words seem so hollow in a system where the advocates seem to thrive on making each others' lives miserable.

Generally, whether in a civil or a criminal case, you will have these major sources of discovery information available:

- Sworn statements (affidavits, pleadings)
- Unsworn statements (reports, emails, notes, letters, social media posts)
- Depositions
- Public records
- Witnesses

In both types of cases, having an investigator available is always advisable. An investigator can get out and do things that you do not have time for, such as chasing down witnesses. Investigators can access information databases to which you may not have access, to look up criminal records and relevant financial information (deeds, judgments, etc.). Most importantly, an investigator can serve as a source of a prior inconsistent statement if the witness changes his or her statements later on. You cannot become a witness, so it is better to have investigators interview witnesses than you doing it yourself or alone.

Review the rule on impeaching a witness with extrinsic evidence of prior inconsistent statements:

Rule 613. Witness

(a) Showing or Disclosing the Statement During Examination. When examining a witness about the witness's prior statement, a party need not show it or disclose its contents to the witness. But the party must, on request, show it or disclose its contents to an adverse party's attorney.

(b) Extrinsic Evidence of a Prior Inconsistent Statement. Extrinsic evidence of a witness's prior inconsistent statement is admissible only if the witness is given an opportunity to explain or deny the statement and an adverse party is given an opportunity to examine the witness about it, or if justice so requires. This subdivision (b) does not apply to an opposing party's statement under Rule 801(d)(2).

In other words, you can always ask the witness about a prior statement, whether oral or written:

Q. So you're saying here today that Mr. Defendant committed the crime?

A. Yes, he did.

Q. But you told the police that some other dude did it, right?

A. Huh?

Q. You told Officer Ferguson that some person other than Mr. Defendant committed the crime, didn't you?

A. I don't recall that. Did he write a report?

Q. Yes, he did. Would you like to see it?

You show it to the witness and opposing counsel, per the rule, and re-ask the question. If the witness still denies making the statement, you can call Officer Ferguson and admit the statement through him.

A.   UNSWORN STATEMENTS AND SOURCES

There are many sources of information that can be considered "unsworn" statements. Remember, at this point you are looking for facts, not preparing for impeachment. And this chapter is about being creative and brainstorming—not a primer on the admissibility of evidence.

Culling information is like panning for gold. It can be tedious, but the rewards can be amazing. I once tried a case wherein my client was charged with battery on several detention deputies in the jail where he was incarcerated. He maintained that he was targeted by the guards because he was so vocal about inmates' civil rights. His defense was that he was beat by the guards so badly that he had to go to the jail hospital, and they in turn charged him with battering them to cover up their own misdeeds.

We listened to seemingly hundreds of hours of jail phone calls relevant to his incarceration, and came across one of my client's wife speaking with a classification officer, who agreed that he was being targeted by the guards and that he would be moved to a different jail pod for his safety. To say the least, that phone call saved the day—but we would not have known about it without painstakingly going through the tedious process of looking. *See Mateo v. State*, 932 So. 2d 376 (Fla. Dist. Ct. App. 2006).

Here are sources of information for you to use when building your story. While this is not a complete treatise on trial advocacy, or discovery, it is important to point out the sources.

- **Pleadings.** Facts are contained in pleadings. Remember, *you were not there.* As an advocate, you are usually playing a game of catch up. Review the complaint, answer, interrogatory responses, admissions, indictment, arrest report, release report, etc. Depositions are probably the greatest source of cross examination material.

- **Correspondence.** Letters, and more commonly, emails and text messages are rich sources of information. So long as they can be authenticated, you can use them to get admissions of favorable facts during cross examination.

- **Business records.** Businesses keep all sorts of records. Be sure to get a records custodian subpoenaed for trial.

- **Medical records.** Medical records are rich with personal factual data, but are also protected by privacy laws. Your jurisdiction will have specific statutes and/or rules on how to obtain and use medical records.

- **Public records (public record requests).** The Federal Freedom of Information Act and the individual states' public record laws allow access to the public records of governmental agencies. We all deal with governmental agencies on a regular basis, so there is a record of every contact. Emails to and from public officials and government workers. Filings, payments, and other interactions. All

of those paint part of the picture of who we
are.

- **Bank records.** As with other records, bank
  records are a wealth of usually undisputable
  facts—when, where, how much . . . and if you
  get the ATM or lobby videos, *who*. And as
  Federal prosecutors like to say, *follow the
  money*.

- **Corporate records.** State governments keep
  records about the legal entities operating
  within its borders. Those are usually easily
  available online, and contact facts about who
  may be involved with an action, as well as
  important filing dates.

- **E-discovery and metadata.** Remember that
  the backend of electronic data is rich with
  facts. An email's contents are one thing; the
  metadata as to when it was sent, from where,
  who was copied, and other things are facts
  that can lock in the "who, what, when, where,
  why, and how" facts you need. Photos taken
  with electronic devices have GPS location
  data. Webpages that are accessed have not
  only information about where and when it was
  accessed, but also can be traced to storage
  locations on computers, and documents that
  may have been access and downloaded. Be
  sure to consult and expert in this area so you
  don't miss anything!

- **Social media.** People live their lives on social
  media—be sure to investigate their pages and

posts. Be careful not to (1) tamper with a witness by trying to "friend" or otherwise connect with the witness, or (2) tamper or destroy evidence by advising a client to remove or delete posts. Every social media company has a legal division that will deal with record subpoenas. Be sure to look closely as you may find gold.

- **Case law.** While not a source of specific facts relevant to your case, case law is a great way to see how other similar cases have played out. Reading about similar cases will let you know where to look for sources of facts, and how those facts have been used in cases like yours. Do your research.

- **Witnesses.** Perhaps the best place to look for facts—the actual witnesses and what they will say (or have said). You are allowed to talk to any witness that will talk to you, and depositions are most always an option. **NOTE: use an investigator to interview witnesses; if a witness changes his or her story, you cannot become a witness to the prior inconsistent statement. You call your investigator.

- **Prosecutor's files (*Brady*).** Prosecutors have disclosure duties pursuant to Federal and state criminal court discovery rules. If there is *exculpatory* information, the prosecutor must disclose it. *Brady v. Maryland*, 373 U.S. 83, 83 S.Ct. 1194; 10 L.Ed. 2d 215 (1963).

- **Other lawsuits and cases.** One of the great aspects of clerks offices around the country moving to an electronic format is that you can search the databases from your desk. No more trips to the courthouse to look at microfiche (you young lawyers should ask someone what that is, and the misery of using it) or microfilm (same thing). Now, all you have to do is have a computer and you can see everyone's litigation history.

The bottom line is that you are only limited by your imagination, creativity, industriousness, and the rules of your jurisdiction. An effective cross examination depends on your complete preparation for the witness. Your preparation for the witness will drive what facts you get out. The facts you get out will fuel the persuasiveness of your story—and the verdict the jury gives you.

B.   SWORN STATEMENTS

Sworn statements provide the most powerful source of information for preparing to cross examine a witness. The power and solemnity of an oath is not lost on most people—especially when deciding whether someone else violated another the other person took. Criminal cases have many such statements, taken on-scene by law enforcement. Notarized affidavits are also common in both criminal and civil cases. Be sure to inquire if any have been made, and get copies.

C. DEPOSITIONS

Probably the best source of information in discovery. Why? Because you already know the story, and the story you want to tell. The deposition is the time to make sure you have the facts available to tell the story, and that there are no facts that will destroy your story.

Preparation for the deposition is important. Before the deposition, you should:

- Re-read all information

- Meet with your client and your witnesses

- Look into the witness' background

- Have an investigator look into the witness' background

- Prepare any exhibits you want to discuss with the witness

- Organize all notes, target documents, and other information on the deponent into a folder (so everything is handy during the deposition)

I have taken many depositions, defended many depositions, and had my own deposition taken several times. I have seen many different techniques, and have my own. This is not a treatise on deposition techniques, nor an attempt to be all-inclusive as to the almost infinite different tips and tricks there are for taking a deposition. But some pointers for taking the deposition with any eye toward cross examination are:

- **Let the witness talk.** Ask open-ended questions that call for a narrative, and let the witness give as much as he or she will.

- **Don't argue.** Don't try to make the witness agree with you or your theory of the case. Just get information, don't give any.

- **Don't reveal your story.** Again, just listen and asked open-ended questions. The less you give of your position, the better.

- **Lay some traps.** Set up any impeachments by asking about issues the witness would otherwise deny on cross—bias, prejudice, etc.—give them the chance to deny it in deposition so you can further prepare for the in-trial impeachment

- **Shut down opposing counsel.** Do not let opposing counsel coach, interrupt, disrupt, guide or "coach" the witness. Ask your opponent to stop, and if he or she persist, you may need to certify the question, or even go find a judge on the fly to compel the witness' answer. Be professional, no matter what the other attorney does.

- **Do NOT let the witness agree to waive pretrial reading of the deposition, and completion of an errata sheet.** This is a practice commonly used, wherein the witness is asked if he or she "reads or waives". I do not let witnesses do that, and make them agree to read it and make any errata notes before taking the stand. Think about it: you later try to impeach, and the witness defends my saying, "well, I don't remember what was said in the deposition, and I have never seen a transcript, so I can't tell you if this is right or wrong." Your impeachment is shot—*unless* there is an on-the-record request by you for the witness to review it, and an on-the-record agreement by the witness to do so. That then becomes part of the cross examination, and fodder for the jury to use when weighing credibility—*why wouldn't the witness read his or her own deposition? Why doesn't he or she remember?*

- **Don't argue with the witness, or with counsel.** Ask your questions, and get your answers. If you don't get answers, use the proper remedies available in your jurisdiction. Don't let the witness think he or she has gotten one over on you, because that will set the tone for the cross examination at trial.

Deposition practice is a skill in and of itself. However, following these guidelines will help you set up your cross examination of the witness.

D.   OTHER SOURCES (WITNESSES, ETC.)

Fuel for cross examination themes, topics, and target facts are not found just in prior statements. Undisputed facts can come from any place, including other witnesses.

Think about that for a second. You know from your client and your witnesses what happened—that becomes *your story*. You want to tell your story on cross examination. Therefore, you want to use the opposing witness to confirm your facts. So use facts from other sources to set the cross. Take the following example, wherein you know that your witnesses are going to say they were present when a physical assault occurred, and will say Mr. Defendant did it unprovoked:

Q. Mr. Defendant, when the incident started, there were several people there?

A. Yes, a bunch.

Q. A bunch—many more than just you and Ms. Victim?

A. Yes, a bunch, like I said.

Q. John was there?

A. Yes.

Q. Mary was there?

A. Yes.

Q. Warren was there?

A. Yes.

Q. You have discussed the case with them since then, haven't you?

A. We have talked about it a little.

Q. You are aware that they saw what happened.

A. Yes, they saw it.

Q. They are your friends, right?

A. They were.

Q. Close friends, almost like family, right?

A. They were. Not any more.

The "2+2" here is that the defendant knows his own friends (or former friends) think he is guilty—that is why they no longer associate with him. He can play it off like it is he who does not want to be with them, but the jury gets it. And no hearsay was elicited—but rather their knowledge of the situation. Using the opposing witness, you have added credibility to your own story.

3.5   CROSS EXAM SHEETS

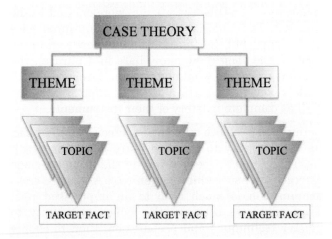

This chart, from Chapter 2, is the blueprint for the organization of cross examination. The Cross Sheets (below) are the bricks and mortar.

It is probably clear by now that the author uses movie and other analogies to teach advocacy. That comparison stops when we get to the concept of a fixed *script*. Great movie roles are brought to life by actors memorizing and interpreting the lines on the scripts. But truly memorable on-screen moments are those that are improvised by talented actors who are able to get the idea and expound from there (think Robin Williams, Larry David, Tim Conway and Harvey Korman, and Bill Murray).

The same is true of jazz—great jazz musicians improvise solos on the spot. All of the legendary jazz solos in history, those of Dizzy Gillespie, John Coltrane, Oscar Peterson (if you don't know these musicians, YouTube them!), etc. were created in the moment. The musicians don't read the printed solos off the page, but they have intimate knowledge of the form of the song (how many bars in a phrase), the chordal structure, what notes are in the chords, what scale modes fit on certain major or minor scales—as well as complete mastery of their instruments.

Improvisers, both on stage or screen and in music, have the ability to combine years of training with reacting the exact perfect way in the moment. Done correctly, this exhibits genius. A good cross examination is much akin to an improvised role. Trial advocates all have the same opportunity to master techniques and preparation, then to couple that with reacting in real time. The problem is that most do not, and cross examinations fall completely flat.

Using the Five Fundamentals, and the Cross Exam Sheet method (see below), the advocate can combine all the training and preparation with the ability to act and react as the cross unfolds. The Cross Exam Sheet method assists the cross examiner in keeping on-track, organized, flexible, and in control—all while continuing to tell the client's story.

A.   FORGET THE LIST OF QUESTIONS (THINK HORIZONTALLY, NOT VERTICALLY)

The title is not misleading . . . I know the sheet I am about to introduce is in a vertical format. That's not the point. The point is that all the sheets—all the *target facts*—are organized horizontally in a storyboard format. That is how your client's story will unfold before the jury. Scene one, scene two, scene three and progress . . . just like in a movie.

Remember, your cross is going to be organized by theory, then themes, then topics, all leading to target facts. Recall this diagram from Chapter 2:

TOPIC

BROAD QUESTIONS

NARROWER QUESTIONS

NARROWER QUESTIONS

NARROWER QUESTIONS

NARROWER QUESTIONS

TARGET FACT

When organizing the themes and topics and target facts, simply use the Cross Exam Sheet:

CASE: WITNESS:	THEME: TOPIC: TARGET FACT:
FOR CROSS	Notes from direct
Page _____ of _____	

You can use this form, devise your own on a computer, or simply use sheets of paper or a legal pad. Just stick to the organizational format, and have plenty of them available. Don't feel compelled to put all the witnesses on one Cross Sheet. The method is by theme/topic/target, not simply "per witness".

Witness information. In the top left, identify your case and more importantly, the witness. As above, *print as many sheets as you need for each witness.* More is better—before trial you have the calm, collected opportunity to thoroughly engage all aspects of what the witness brings to the trial, and identify target facts you need to present to the jury. Have extra blanks in trial, ready for things that come to light or need further inquiry.

Theme and topic information. In the top right is where you will keep yourself organized. Identify your theme (sub-plot), and the topic (scene). Keep those sheets together. Each target fact will have its own Cross Exam Sheet (maybe more than one sheet, but try to avoid long lists of questions).

Target fact. This is the thing you need to get out of the witness. Remember, it may be some fact that the witness admits, or it may be an inference you are getting the jury to draw from your questioning. A target fact may have several pages, all going to that fact.

A target fact can be as dramatic and a "a-ha" moment, such as the admission to a crime, or to liability in a civil case. It can be subtle, like a date or time. It can be a negative—an omission, or the lack of an important part of the puzzle.

The point of a target fact is that it is important, and you and the jury need to know it.

Outline of cross examination. The bottom left is for your cross examination *outline*—not a list of questions, but an outline of the facts, from broad to narrow (see section 2.6., below) that get you to your goal fact.

If you think in 3D, you have the ability to question on a topic without a set of specific notes. If you think in 3D, you don't need a list of questions, rather, just a starting place and a target fact. Perhaps there are some keywords you need to list, to help you remember critical facts (dates, scientific words, etc.). Other than that, this section of the Cross Sheet is solely for a *guideline*, not a list of questions.

Remember, if you are glued to a list of questions, you have effectively paralyzed yourself.

Real time notes. The bottom right is for your notes during direct. Remember, your job as a cross examiner begins when the opposing side calls that witness to the stand. The direct examination contains gold to be mined (see Section 1.72, "The Cross Examiners Job on Direct"). Note all inaccurate statements, puffery, lack of memory—anything that you know you can use. Uses range from impeachment (attacking witness credibility) to telling your side of the story (making sure the opposing witness plugs in facts favorable to your story).

Cross Exam Sheets can be used to prepare *direct* examination just as easily. There really is no overall difference in the witnesses: both are there to offer factual proof and support to the case. The difference is in how the facts are retrieved from the witness and presented to the jury. Using Cross Exam Sheets to organize and present a direct examination assists in the overall organization (see section 3.5, below).

Page numbers. I like to use a system wherein I have the topics (scenes) grouped together: Topic 1 are pages 1, 1.1, 1.2 etc.; Topic 2 are pages 2, 2.1, 2.2, etc. Because the pages are not to be stapled or otherwise attached together, this helps keep you in some order. Remember, we are not creating a list of questions, rather, a fluid and flexible system that can be moved around to adjust for any situation.

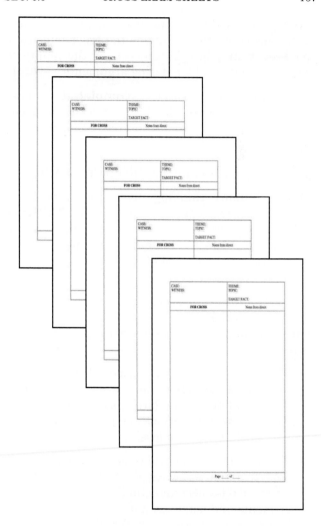

How easy is that? Lists of questions are static; Cross Sheets are fluid. Change the order mid-cross, and keep your place. You also have the ability to change them around for closing arguments.

Example of some completed cross examination sheets. See Chapter 8.2.B, for some actual sheets that I used in a trial, along with the transcript.

B. ORGANIZING FROM BROAD TO NARROW

When initially thinking about the case, think about the issue from broad to narrow. This first triage of the issues will lead you through the essential elements, the defenses, the main factual issues, and a general idea of who the players are in the case.

Whatever the case, preparing for the cross requires you to identify the story and break it down. There are many ways to do this, and some of the points to work on are:

- **The elements and defenses.** Look at the jury instructions, read the statute, and look at the pleadings that have been filed. The elements will be very clear—prove them and win, neglect them an lose!

- **The legal issues.** Legal issues weave into the story in a couple of ways. First, there are those overt legal issues that actually impact proof of elements and defenses, and that the jury will know about and consider. Whether a statute was complied with . . . whether a deadline was met . . . whether a local law's procedures were followed, are examples. Further, there are those cases with implied causes of action, such as civil rights violations based on illegal police conduct.

Second, there are "behind the scenes" legal issues that gatekeep facts and can severely impact the ability to tell the story. The evidence code and rape shield statutes are examples. Dealing with those issues early will tell you what you can and cannot plug into your story.

- **The factual issues.** Beyond purely legal considerations, such as that a contract wasn't formed, or some other legal condition precedent did not occur, there are actual factual issues that permeate litigation. That a particular conversation did or did not happen, that a person was or was not at a particular place. Be sure to analyze whether the factual issue is a subset or topic of a larger legal issue.

- **The players.** Unless it is a purely white collar case, the witnesses will undoubtedly be a major part of the story. I was involved in a two-month federal trial wherein 99.9% of the story was the categorization of a small amount of mortgage interest under the Medicare reimbursement system. There were 1800 banker boxes of documents, and the deluge of digits was overwhelming. However, there was on tiny little fact let out by one witness—that there was a suggestion that the government's Medicare auditor that was causing the problem for the company, and a suggestion that she simply be hired away from her government job to solve the problem—that was the "smoking gun." That part of the two-month trial took about 5 minutes of testimony.

There is almost always a point of impeachment to use on a witness—from the severity of prior convictions, to the slight of potential bias. Prior inconsistent statements imply liar. Lack of memory implies unreliable. Telling your story requires you to make sure your witnesses are as protected as possible, all while using the other side's witnesses to tell your story on cross.

- **The jurisdiction.** Remember the discussion about using themes that connect with jurors. Morals are universal (unless someone is a sociopath), but mores and local customs vary from locale to locale. Notwithstanding the universal nature of morals and ethics, the amount of value those things have can vary from locale to locale.

- **THE STORY.** Of course, all of this should be geared toward telling the story to the jury. Your story, as told on cross, should be logical and easy to follow. Use transitions and signposts (see Chapter 2.6) to make it even easier for the jury to follow along.

Once you have the broad-to-narrow analysis of the fact, begin to organize your cross. Theory of the case, then themes, then topics, then target facts.

Write them down. I like to use a pencil—to me, there's something primal yet almost artistic about the feel of graphite on paper. You can use what makes you comfortable, but I strongly suggest that your memory should not be that tool. Writing (or typing) memorializes and gives you the ability to come back to and change your thoughts over time. Trust me, write it down. Or type it. Whichever.

I like to "bubble"—I get a blank sheet of paper and start with my case theory in the middle. That is the broadest you can get. I write it down, and draw a circle around it, and it keeps growing. Here are a couple of examples from a real trial, on the charge of felonious possession of a firearm, dealing with gunshot residue, blood, and DNA on the weapon, tying it to my client:

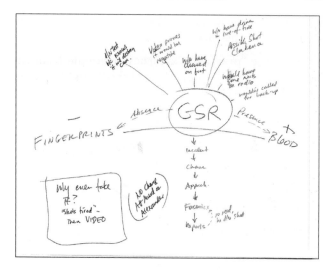

Of course, the case theory can be dynamic. It can change completely, and it can change minimally (rather, it can *adapt* to a situation). Seeing the case theory keeps you grounded as the case progresses to trial.

Draw out your thoughts. I cannot overstate the fact that *a list of questions will not work.* As discussed in Chapter 3.5.A, a list of questions simply paralyzes you and your ability to adapt and react.

Drawing out, or mapping, your thoughts is the beginning of the process that will ultimately result in your themes, topics, and targets—not only the actual themes, topics, and targets, but how they are connected and work together to tell your story. Be free and do not edit yourself—you can pick and choose later. Be honest with bad facts. The only way you will find the story is to be open and honest about all aspects of the case.

Using the "practicing attorney" example from the beginning of the chapter, some of the thought bubbles might look like this:

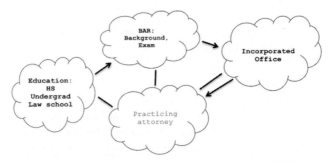

Some bubbles become the epicenter of the story. Others get crossed out. Some that are crossed out get brought back later. The point is *fluidity* and *inclusion*—getting it all out there and into the realm of consideration.

Track your thoughts. Usually, by the time of trial, my paper is ragged, has red pen, purple pen, highlighter, sticky notes, and other pages stapled to it. It is my road map; I have a bad habit of repeatedly coming back to and rehashing a point that has already been decided, and forgetting we nixed it. When I look at my "bubble sheet", I easily know where all my thoughts have been.

As I shape my cross examination, all the thoughts are there for me to choose from—and nothing is left out of consideration.

Write a lot, but don't erase. It is fine to cross out (what I call "popping" one of my bubbles), but do not erase or delete it. That point that is bad for your, or does not work, may very well be the case theory of your opponent. At a minimum, it could be a rabbit hole that your opponent may go running down. You know it, you have thought about it, and you are ready to deal with it if it comes up. You are not stuck wondering where the other side's case is headed—you know how and why that popped bubble fits into the overall scheme of the case.

Turning bubbles into themes, topics, and targets. Think about the points you have pulled out. Are they larger, thematic material? Are they actual narrow, target facts that create those final "gotchas" that we all want?

Theory. As discussed in Chapter 2.2, your overall case theory is the "why" you are in court. Don't lose sight of that.

Themes. You will begin to figure out which target facts need what treatment. In other words, some target facts will really need you to start broadly and work your way in. As with the "practicing attorney" example, we started way back with high school and went forward, to show that the path was long and deliberate, all with the intention of—and actually—practicing law. The themes we see are:

- Education
- Bar admission process
- Setting up an office

- Acting like an attorney

Topics. Similarly, the topics go on to set the scene for each target fact. In the "practicing attorney" example, the topics were:

- Education
  - High school
  - Undergrad
  - Law school
- Bar admission process
  - Application
  - Background check
  - Exam
- Setting up an office
  - Incorporating
  - Getting a tax ID number
- Acting like a lawyer
  - Seeing clients
  - Filing motions, etc.

Target facts. What are the actual facts you need to use to put your story together? Carefully identify them, where they come from, and how and in what order you will bring them out at trial. Note them on the cross sheet.

The target facts here are simple:

- Witness has a law degree
- Witness is a member of the Bar
- Witness has a law office
- Witness practices law (the "4")

While this might be over-simplistic, it demonstrates the way you have to think about preparing your cross examination, of whatever witness comes before you.

C.   ORGANIZING FROM NARROW TO BROAD

Perhaps a target fact can make the whole case. One target fact only. It's possible. What then? Do you sit and wait for cross, then just ask about the one target fact, and sit down with whatever answer you get?

Perhaps you could do that, and there may be those times that such a tactic is a good one. But the experience of countless trial lawyers tells us that nothing in a courtroom ever comes that easy. One target fact can be the basis for the entire story, but it is up to you as the advocate to set that story up and weave it into the trial.

So, in preparing, there are cases where you can start with the narrow target fact, and work back out to the broad. Identify the target fact, and script the scene in which it comes out. Take that scene, and place it within the story and with the other themes that will make highlight the target fact. Remember, if the witness does not actually give you or admit to the critical target fact, the jury can always infer it and give it to you in the form of a favorable verdict.

D.   SEQUENCING THE CROSS TOPICALLY

The fun begins when you start to think about how you are going to get the cross witness to help you tell the story. What goes first? How do you end? It is exciting to think of how the story will come out, and to watch the jury look at you and nod as they follow your story (and your case).

Initial organization. "Primacy and recency" is a good way to organize—the really important target facts go at the front and as closers. People tend to remember what they hear first and last when listening to a sequence of information. Thus, one way to tell the story is to tell the important parts where the jury is most likely to receive them.

If you want to stick to the story format, which I believe is the stronger way to compose a cross, then think of how the target facts will unfold.

Storyboard your cross. Tell the story by lining up the target facts, and see if they tell a logical and persuasive story, of if they are a jumble of facts. Bubble it, or use note cards, or simply draw it on a piece of paper—but be creative. *Think* carefully about what fact goes where. The concepts of primacy and regency (how people retain and recall information) can guide you. Sometimes the chronology of the case in and of itself dictates the order of your cross. Sometimes you want to get the best target fact out *first*, and then loop back to it as you unfold the story on cross.

Start writing target facts on your Cross Sheets. Line them up—what fact goes where? Do the facts fall under one topic? Do the topics fall under a particular theme? As you begin to move around your Cross Sheets, you will have a storyboard (and it may look like a game of Solitaire!).

BE FLEXIBLE. This might be the biggest point of this chapter, and the whole reason the Cross Sheet system works—it allows the ultimate in flexibility.

You may ask, *if I spend all this time identifying and organizing my themes, topics, and target facts— WHY ARE YOU TELLING ME TO BE FLEXIBLE?*

Easy. For the same reason you don't want to use a list of questions. If a gold nugget gets dropped on direct, you need to be able to take advantage of it without sacrificing the rest of the cross. If something gets out of place on your cross, you want to be able to adjust. If an adverse ruling hits you, you can easily remove and replace and rearrange such that you still have an effective cross.

Lists of questions require you to circle, strike out, draw arrows, frantically write yourself notes and directs . . . it just adds to the anxiety of trial.

Using Cross Sheets, all you have to do is rearrange the physical order of the papers. It doesn't get easier than that.

E. USING CROSS SHEETS (TOPICS AND TARGETS) FOR CLOSING ARGUMENT

It is often said in advocacy training "you should write your closing argument first." I agree only to the extent that drafting the closing can help the advocate flesh out (or storyboard) the basic story. But it seems unlikely that the story would be any good, without the "storyboarding" process of case analysis, identifying target facts for direct and cross, and finding the essence of the story by living with the case through that process.

However, I disagree to the extent that the closing must be argument about what was actually heard by everyone in the courtroom during the trial. Closing is a time to connect the facts and the inferences from those facts. It must be based on what the jurors heard, so it has to be flexible.

The Cross Exam Sheets are designed for the most efficient and effective organization and delivery. After the evidentiary portion of the trial is over, the Cross Exam Sheets are ready with all the important facts neatly organized by their topics and themes. Many times in a trial, there is no overnight or lunch break in which to practice a closing argument. With pre-trial preparation and the Cross Exam Sheets, the advocate can quickly (within a matter of minutes) organize the entire trial and be ready to argue to the jury.

Remember that Cross Sheets are also perfectly useful for direct examinations. Having all of your facts on these sheets allows you to easily lay out your closing—actually lay it out on your desk, target fact by target fact, witness by witness. Putting it all together is as easy as organizing your wallet, notebook, or coupon book.

How it works is simple. Your Cross Sheets already contain your thoughts. Since you did not write out a list of questions, you have an outline to refer to as you argue. Since *you* provided the facts, you already know them, and how they fit into the themes and topics.

You also have the "live" direct notes section on the Cross Sheet, which you can refer to in arguing specific things the witness said on direct. As you get to the theme and topic you want to argue to the jury, simply pull up that Cross Sheet.

Remember, the idea is flexibility and to not look like a robot. A memorized or unprepared closing argument does not connect on any emotional or other level with your jurors. Your Cross Sheets *assist* your argument, they do not *make* it for you.

3.6 ORGANIZING

So, where to start? Organization starts with having all the tools to tell the story: reports, statements, photos, interview recordings, impeachment materials, charts/graphs . . . anything that contains information that has to go to the jury.

- Organize yourself.
- Organize your file.

- Organize your facts.

- Organize your cross.

A. ORGANIZING YOURSELF

How do you learn—auditory, visual, or tactile? How do you remember things? What is your notetaking style? You must know how you *intake* information. More importantly, you must know how you best *relay* information. What is your speaking style? Do you even have a style? How do you argue points? Are you more surgical, or more confrontational?

If you are going to be a trial lawyer, you need to figure it out. Having a comfortable system in which to prepare and present will make you more comfortable and effective. An *organized* you is a *controlled* you. And you have to control yourself before you can control a witness on cross examination.

B. ORGANIZING YOUR FILE

Each witness to be cross examined is uniquely important to the trial. Therefore, each witness must be treated as if he or she is uniquely important. Each witness must have his or her own file, and certain mandatory information must be in that witness' file—even if duplicated somewhere else, for two reasons. First, so that all the target documents containing target facts stay with the witness through preparation. Second, so that all the sources of the facts stay with the witness through trial.

Each trial lawyer differs as to how he or she likes to organize. A preferred method is to have one folder for each witness, or a folder with a series of inner folders for each witness. Other attorneys like a binder or notebook, with all of the target documents behind a labeled tab. Some attorneys—to their detriment—simply take a large folder or a banker's box with everything in it, and hope for the best.

When preparing for the cross examination of a witness, there are mandatory things you have to have readily available in that witness' file:

- Reports and other documents prepared by the witness

- Depositions

- Investigative reports pertaining to the witness

- Prior record and certified copies of supporting judgment and sentences

- Your preparation notes

- Cross examination sheets

- Photos, diagrams, maps, and other exhibits to be used during the cross examination of the witness

- Case law and bench briefs supporting arguments on anticipated evidentiary issues pertaining to the witness

The file has to be at your fingertips during the cross examination, in case you need to refresh or impeach. You never, ever want to be searching for something while the jury is waiting. The life gets sucked out of your cross examination when then happens.

C. ORGANIZING YOUR FACTS

A major point of this book is realizing and understanding just how essential the facts are to telling the story. Mastery of the facts and evidentiary issues cannot be stressed enough. You have to know everything before you can decide what to put in what to leave out. Thus, a careful review of all facets of a witness, place, situation, document . . . whatever it is, is how to start.

Once all the facts are identified, and all of the evidentiary issues worked out, then and only then can one begin to organize the cross folders, and themes and topics.

When putting the puzzle together, use this checklist as a start:

- Overall chronology of facts
- Characters
- Who said what
- Who wrote what
- Positive/positive facts
- Positive/negative facts
- Negative/positive facts
- Negative/negative facts

- Case theory

- Critical target facts

- "What happened" facts

- Impeachment facts (bias, etc.)

Don't skip over anything. Write it all down. Use Cross Sheets for your target facts. It's better to have too much than not enough.

D.   ORGANIZING YOUR CROSS—
USING THE CROSS SHEETS

Once you know how you work, have your file organized, and have your facts organize, you can get to the task of organizing your cross. This is where the Cross Sheets are worth their weight in gold.

Theme. First, the theme. What is the sub-plot you are looking to shape? In a criminal case, perhaps reasonable doubt. In a civil case, perhaps causation. Remember, the sub-plots are all woven together to form the full movie. So the advocate must think about how to identify the individual themes and each theme's importance and placement in the cross.

Topics. Next, the topics. The individual scenes that tell the story through the sub-plots. In a criminal case, under the theme of reasonable doubt, it might be the training of the case detective; another may be the detective's collection of evidence on the scene of the crime. In a civil case, under the theme of causation, it may be the defendant's failure to perform maintenance on his car.

Target facts. Finally, and most importantly, the target facts. What fact in each topic is most important? What fact do you have to have your opponent's witness admit, so you can argue it in closing?

Let's look at an example. For the civil "causation" case mentioned above, we may have:

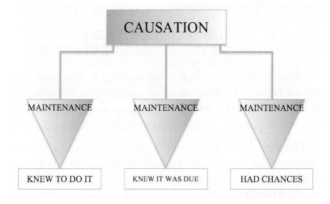

Each target fact supports the negligence of the defendant that led to his brakes failing and causing the car crash that injured your client.

3.7 MOTIONS *IN LIMINE* AND OTHER PRETRIAL MOTIONS

Pretrial motions are a great source of material for cross examination, and roadmap as to how to structure the cross. It is also a great way to test issues that you may have planned to use in cross examination. First, they can be an extension of discovery, meaning that facts that were not discovered before may come out in pretrial motion practice. If you file a motion to dismiss a particular claim, or a motion for summary judgment, the opposing party may defend by revealing facts they might otherwise have been trying to save for trial. This is likely to occur more in civil cases, due to *Brady* and other mandatory disclosure rules in criminal cases. But certainly motions can shake loose facts in any type of litigation.

Second, a hearing on a pretrial motion can reveal strength and weaknesses *on both sides*. It will tell you about your opponent's preparation, and possibly the other side's own case theories. It will tell you about the judge's feeling about the issues and the case. You may come to learn what works for you and what doesn't, all before trial.

Motions in limine usually go directly to issues that the litigants anticipate coming out from a witness on the stand. I always encourage litigating evidentiary issues before you start your cross examination—you may be counting on facts coming out that end up getting excluded on an objection. Then you are in trouble. If at all possible, bring the issue up in advance.

An additional bonus is that pretrial motions are another control tool for cross examination, used to control the story and flow of information (for example, through motions *in limine*). For example, you may encounter a witness in a deposition who wants to discuss superfluous and irrelevant—yet salacious—information regarding your client. A limiting order from the judge carries with it the possibility of contempt—and if effective is silencing the "noise" from a runaway witness. The witness will certainly know you filed the motion, and you muzzled him or her. You have exerted control before the witness even takes the stand.

Evidentiary hearings, where witnesses are required to testify, provide the chance for additional sworn testimony as well as the chance to test a witness in cross examination. You also get more testimony to use against the witness at the actual trial down the road!

If the opportunity arises for pretrial motion practice, be sure to follow this checklist:

- Research the motion carefully, and cite current authority

- Look for evidentiary issues that can be dealt with before testimony starts (irrelevant issues, hearsay, authentication issues)

- File only if you can do so in good faith

- Request a hearing

- Subpoena witnesses you need for the hearing—do not rely on opposing counsel to supply them for you

- Get a court reporter

- Order the transcript afterward

- Add the transcript to your discovery disclosure, witness/evidence list, and follow any local rules about filing a copy with the court prior to trial

- Prepare cross themes, topics, or target questions off the transcript

- Have the transcript and a copy available at trial in case the need to refresh or impeach arises

3.8 PREPARING YOUR OWN WITNESS FOR CROSS

Preparing your own witness for cross examination cannot be emphasized enough. One easy way to do it would be to take everything in this book, and assume that all these techniques will be used on your witness.

The witness has to know that opposing counsel, if prepared, is going to try to control the narrative and tell her or his story through the "yes" and "no" answers the witness should give. That's one of the main points of this and every other book on cross examination.

The witness also has to know that he or she does not have to agree with opposing counsel. Explain why "you would agree" types of questions are improper, as it is not the attorney's opinion that matters. Advise the client to answer, "*I don't need to agree with you, the fact is the fact. And the fact is ___.*" Be sure to object, too, if you hear this question.

Further, the witness must be advised that he or she can explain their answer, if the question is nebulous. Remember, if the question is phrased correctly, is a leading question, and deals with only one particular fact—the yes or no answer should suffice and not require further elaboration. But when counsel gets to aggressive, wants to jump to the target fact (or beyond), then the cagey witness will qualify: "yes, but . . ." or "no, but . . ." and will be allowed to explain the answer.

3.9 TAKEAWAYS

- Find all the facts—never stop looking, and be creative where you look.

- Know your facts cold.

- Free yourself to think through all aspects of your case.

- Write down *everything* you think of—you'll use it at some point.

- Use Cross Sheets to marshal your target facts.

- Storyboard your target facts.

- Find a system of organizing that works for you.

- Use motion practice when you can.

3.10 EXERCISES

Exercise 1:

Take a case you have already worked on, and go back to the drawing board. If you have never worked on one, find a mock trial case file at your law library.

What are the target facts you need to tell the story of your cause of action?

How can you storyboard those facts—lining them up, moving them around, and rearranging them to best tell the story?

Who are the characters?

Exercise 2:

Take your favorite movie, and "reverse engineer" it into Cross Sheets. What are the target facts? Topics (scenes)? Themes (sub-plots)? See if you can storyboard the plot using only Cross Sheets.

COUNSELOR, NO NEED TO GET UGLY
WITH THE WITNESS.

CHAPTER 4

DELIVERING CROSS EXAMINATION (TONE, TEMPO)

4.1 THE IDEAL CROSS EXAMINATION

From time to time, we all find cross examination nirvana. That happy place as an advocate where every favorable fact is admitted, our story is told, no one interrupts, and we look like the greatest trial lawyer ever to walk the face of the Earth. We walk out of the courtroom, calling colleagues to tell them about the *perfect* cross examination.

If you follow the teachings and recommendations of this book, and approach cross examination as a surgeon intend of a sumo wrestler, you can find that nirvana. A ritualistic approach to preparation and delivery will leave you in control and allow you to reach a higher level of understanding *for your jury*.

A. LEADING QUESTIONS, YES OR NO ANSWERS

Exactly what you want as the storyteller   for you to get the facts out in the form of a question, and for the witness to simply say yes or no. The importance of using exclusively leading questions on cross examination cannot be overstated—it is the ultimate control of the flow of facts.

Remember, a leading question is one that suggests the answer. *See* Chapter 1.5.A.

Example, in a case where a police officer missed getting a statement from a driver involved in an accident:

Q. Now, you had the chance to speak to the driver of the car, right, officer?

A. Yes.

Q. But you did not, did you?

A. No.

Or, of a plaintiff in an assumption of the risk defense to a tort claim:

Q. You had played basketball before, right?

A. Yes.

Q. It is a very physical game, right?

A. Yes.

Q. Part of the game is to try to take the ball from your opponent?

A. Yes.

Q. Players wrestle over the ball?

A. Yes, not wrestle, but struggle, maybe.

Q. You have struggled over the ball with other players before, right?

A. Yes.

Q. And while that struggle is going on, bodies twist back and forth while pulling?

A. Yes.

Q. Elbows are flying everywhere?

A. Yes.

Q. And if you are standing behind this struggle, you may get hit by an elbow?

A. Yes.

Q. Doesn't mean the player meant to hit you, right?

A. Well, no.

Q. But when you take the court, you know that it is a part of the game that you could get an elbow in the nose?

A. You don't really think about it.

Q. While you may not think about it, you know it, right?

A. Yes.

Q. And on the day you say Mr. Defendant hit you and broke your nose, you knew physical struggles are a part of the game?

A. Yes.

Q. But you joined the game anyway, didn't you?

A. Yes.

It's pretty simple to formulate a leading question, isn't it? It's hard to remember to do it every time, right? You know *how* to do it? You know *to* do it? So when is the last time you ended a great series of leading questions with an open-ended question?

See what I did there? All the questions in the proceeding paragraphs were leading, except for the last one. In the first four questions, I supplied the fact, the questions called for either a "yes" or a "no". The last question is open-ended, meaning that I have asked you (the questionee) to supply the fact. You cannot answer a "when" question with "yes" or "no".

In a perfect cross, the flow of information is from the storyteller—the advocate. The questions are designed to contain a fact: *the car was blue? the engine was warm? the payment was never made?* All the witness is doing is affirming the positive and negating the negative—either "yes" or "no"—as asked by the storyteller. The jury gets the facts almost directly from the lawyer, not the witness.

B.   LOGICAL, EASY-TO-UNDERSTAND AND FOLLOW ORGANIZATION

As easy as it sounds. The themes are clear. They flow from one to the next in a logical, building manner. The topics are concise and stack up like cinder blocks of a building, supporting a roof. The target facts pop out without a fight and you can see the satisfied expressions on the jurors faces as your story unfolds before them.

Recall the ideal structure for your cross examination:

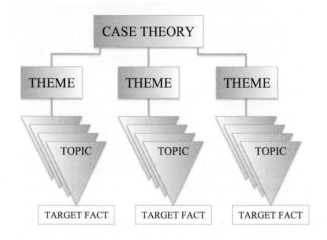

The outline is a logical, easy to follow story, as told on cross examination. The organization of the cross makes the story come alive. It's like a well-written book or movie. Using the assumption of the risk example, the story may look like this:

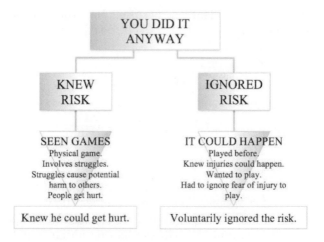

If this flow of cross examination were to come out like this, you would have no problem telling your story and having the jury flow right along with you.

C.   COOPERATIVE WITNESS

The witness smiles at you as you approach the podium. As you ask questions, she gives you the "yeses" you want, and the "nos" you want. She or he doesn't "ad lib" or try to explain the answers. She waits for you to finish you questions before she answers. And, best of all, she looks at the jury to agree with you on the important points, just to make your story stronger and more believable.

Believe it or not, this does happen. Mainly when the other side has called a witness favorable to your client on direct, and you get to cross examine her— which happens. It's a glorious few moments ...

delivering a pile-driver to the opposing side by throwing out favorable fact after favorable fact to a witness more than happy to go right along with you.

This sublime scenario is pretty infrequent. Keep using the Five Fundamentals and the "housetraining" techniques in this book, you can make it happen by controlling the witness and the flow of information.

D.   NO OBJECTIONS

As you deliver your cross, your opponent sits silently . . . your topics and themes flow, your questions have a deliberate and meaningful tempo and tone . . . and the witness has no option but to comply. Your target facts are obvious, and the jury nods with approval. The only thing that makes it better is when you get to the target fact, and the witness looks to opposing counsel's table, with the "help me" or "I'm sorry I'm about to say this" face on full display to the jury. That is often coupled with the lack of response from the attorney, who is busy reading a deposition and preparing for the next witness. What's even better is when you are delivering a masterful cross and your opposing counsel is *totally* paying attention and not getting in the way because he is so mesmerized with your story and delivery.

Note, even when you encounter a bump-on-the-log opposing counsel, you cannot go crazy. The rules still apply, and you are all the more powerful delivering a cross that is as intriguing as it is ethical.

E.   THE JUDGE THAT LETS
YOU TRY YOUR CASE

At the time of writing this book, I have been a trial attorney for almost twenty-two years. I have been before plenty of judges in all kinds of different trials, in both state and Federal courts. I like to think they all pay rapt attention to the entire case, and are spellbound by my brilliant cross examinations. But, whether they are or not, I am most happy when they stay out of my way and let me do my job.

It seems there are three types of judges:

- those that expect that both advocates will know the rules, and follow the rules, and so he or she sits and intently watches, simply calling balls and strikes as objections are raised;

- those that are overly involved, looking either to train lawyers by interjecting *sua sponte* corrections and admonitions—or those that want to exert control over lawyers not held in high regard;

- those that are out to lunch and are not involved, or do not know the law and evidence code and make horrible rulings

During the "perfect" cross, the judge sits attentively, listening and following along with your story . . . happy he or she is hearing a logical, well-prepared objection-free cross examination.

F.   HOW THE FIVE FUNDAMENTALS KEEP IT CALM AND COOL

Preparation, organization, and delivery skills are the key to your cross at least having the chance to go completely right. As they say, *people don't plan to fail, they fail to plan.* Being prepared the correct way is the best starting point you can have.

Preparing ensures that you have everything covered—better said, that you are not going to miss anything important. As we saw in the previous chapters, as well as above, you want to have an identifiable, easily understood structure. This is really important the further into your cross examination story you go:

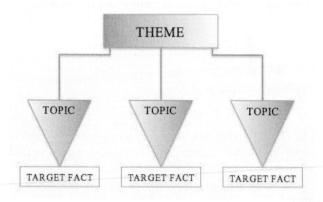

Organization (theme, topic, target) ensures that you have the story straight and can tell it from "Genesis to maps" in the most understandable and persuasive way.

Coupling your organization skills with your delivery skills (tone, tempo), you have self-confidence and erode the confidence of the witness.

Now, let's look at how cross examination can go painfully wrong.

4.2 FRENETIC CROSS

It is a painful thing. It is a scene that makes skilled advocates squirm in their seats, and purse their lips with impatience and frustration. It is a situation where judges will intervene to impose an unwritten judicial "mercy" rule, just to stop the insanity.

The frenetic cross. Where the witness runs amuck, the advocate is being anything but, and the whole point of the story (and sometimes the trial itself) is lost.

A.   OPEN-ENDED QUESTIONS

Q. Why did you . . . .?

Q. Where were you . . .?

Q. Well, then, please explain . . .

If there is one sin of cross examination that is worse than all others, it is to ask open ended questions. If you do so, unless it is for a specific reason at a planned time, then you have relinquished control of the witness, and of the story.

Open-ended questions are for direct. They invite the witness to take over and tell the jury his or her version of what happened. You are no longer telling your story—you have yielded the floor to the opponent's story. You are simply standing there, conducting another direct.

Another problem with open-ended questions, is that they give the witness a chance to not only reiterate damaging points from his or her direct, but to clarify any issue that may have not had the intended impact on direct. Why give the witness the knife and let him or her cut *your* throat?

Avoid open-ended questions—*lead*. It's not only permitted, it is encouraged!

B.   OBSTINATE WITNESS

Just when you think you have structured your cross examination perfectly, and prepared all the facts to fit into your story, you run into a witness who has another idea of what is going to happen during cross examination. Sometimes you know from discovery or pretrial proceedings what to expect. Other times, you will be met with complete resistance from the stand. You will have encountered the obstinate witness.

The lawyer witness. The witness who knows the law and is prone to dropping legal terms. Or even an actual lawyer, who wants to prove he or she knows more than you. This witness wants to quibble and try to match wits with you, or try to out-flank you. Some will even tell you, "*I know what you are trying to do . . . you're trying to___.*"

The instant expert. The witness who has an air of superiority, wants to let the jury know the he or she knows everything about everything. Also wants to quibble with you, and play word games when the matter is otherwise clear and straightforward.

The "fire hose" witness. You ask a leading, "yes or no" question, and the witness spews everything on his or her mind before you can say "don't do it". Takes every opportunity to ramble and narrate.

The clueless witness. The witness was there, has given a deposition and a sworn written statement, yet cannot recall or relate a single fact. You ask simple, one-fact leading "yes or no" with obvious answers, and the witness responds with equivocation, ambiguity, or outright absentmindedness. This witness also asks for clarification of your simple, direct, easy-to-understand question.

The victim witness. The witness never misses a chance to tell the jury how hurt, injured, inconvenienced, embarrassed, upset, crushed, or heartbroken, he or she is because of your client. Cries, asks for breaks, pretends that you are confusing him or her and that is because your client is a horrible person.

The cutesy witness. The witness who plays word games, splits hairs, and generally wants to never directly answer the question. When you ask if the shirt was "blue", he or she wants to have a discussion about whether the shirt was royal blue of French blue. Thinks he or she is clever, and wants the jury to think so, too. This witness will also ask for clarification where none is needed. The cutesy witness also likes to answer your question with a question.

In Chapter 4.6, below, you will learn control techniques for dealing with these witnesses. If you have those techniques committed to "advocacy muscle memory", you can control any witness.

C.   OBJECTION AFTER OBJECTION

As discussed in Chapter 5, evidentiary objections are a great way to control opposing counsel. However, that same technique can be employed—or at least attempted—*on you*. Watch out!

The scenario is annoying and frustrating: you ask a question, opposing counsel makes an objection. Repeat. Repeat. Every question is met with an objection.

One school of thought says to let it happen, and to draw the jurors' attention to the theme or topic by them wondering what the other side wants so desperately for them to not hear.

The better tactic is to *listen* to the objections, and if they are valid, adjust. Stop asking the witness to speculate. Don't—facts not in evidence. Stay within the evidence code. If you have prepared, these problems should be at a minimum, or better yet, non-existent. If you are in an improvised cross situation (see Chapter 6), you may have more problems but you can still stay in the parameters with just a little discipline.

If the objections are baseless and merely designed to throw you off, there is a remedy. Ask for a sidebar or to approach the bench (whatever the custom is in your jurisdiction). Place on the record the amount and pattern of objections (i.e., every question has been objected to) and note that they are being overruled because they are in fact baseless. Point out the opposing counsel is being obstructionistic, and impugning your client's right to a fair trial and to contest the evidence and witness. Conclude by stating that objections made in bad faith are violates of the Bar ethical canons.

But suffice it to say, you will encounter the jack-in-the-box opponent who will rise to object to every question you ask. It's frustrating, but you can handle it.

D.   JUDGE SHUTS YOU DOWN

Q. INSERT LUCID, INTELLIGENT, WELL THOUGHT-OUT LEADING, ONE-FACT QUESTION HERE.

OBJ.   Objection, relevance.

J.   Sustained.

Q. INSERT ANOTHER LUCID, INTELLIGENT, WELL THOUGHT-OUT LEADING, ONE-FACT QUESTION HERE.

OBJ.   Objection.

J.   Sustained.

Q. [Wants to bury head in sand]

We have all had those moments, and they are not fun nor entertaining. Maybe the judge is missing the point. Maybe the judge does not like the case, or your, client, or even you. Whatever it is, you are clearly not winning the battle.

Stay calm, be professional, and keep asking questions. If it gets bad, ask for a sidebar and discuss the issue with the judge.

E.   IMPEACHMENTS DON'T WORK

The main reason impeachments do not work is not because of the witness, but because of *you*—the attorney. In twenty-two years of courtroom experience, which counts for seeing and participating in hundreds of trials and thousands of hours in court, I have seen countless attorneys completely ruin great impeachments.

You know the witness made another statement, or has a prior conviction, or whatever point of impeachment, and because you do not approach the impeachment with technical perfection, you are shut down. If your client loses, then you must consider whether the impeachment you missed contributed to that—not a fun analysis.

Be sure to see Chapter 2.5.E regarding impeachments.

F.   YOU FINALLY SIT DOWN IN SHAME

Admitting defeat, you finally utter, "no further questions", in a tone that smacks of agonizing surrender rather than triumphant conclusion. Not daring to look at the witness or the jurors, you quickly gather your documents and practically run to your table. You sit down and begin to look for your briefcase under the table—not because you want to access your briefcase, but because you want to be under the table with it.

More cross examinations are suicidal than homicidal. United States Attorney for the Southern District of New York Emory Buckner uttered in 1920 those words that are still so very painfully poignant. Without planning, you will fail. With an impotent list of questions that you don't deviate from, you will fail. Without thinking in 3D, you will fail.

Go to any courthouse in America on any given day, walk into any trial, and sit there for a while. Sadly, you'll see this very scenario play out.

4.3 TONE

Tone is the mood you set for the cross examination, which is really the mood you are setting for this part of your story. There are many moods that can be set in a courtroom. Moments of levity can be found in some of the ugliest of cases. Profound sorrow can be found in many cases. Anger, sadness, nonchalance, and every other emotion can set a mood in a trial.

As the cross examiner, it is up to you to choose a tone that is proper for the case, the witness, and the mood in the courtroom. Is this a blasé witness, who needs no further scrutiny? Then be matter-of-fact, get in, and get out. Is the witness sympathetic—a victim, particularly young or old? Does the nature and severity of the crime or cause of action make the witness more sympathetic? A sexual battery victim, or elderly victim of fraud (think Bernie Madoff) needs very special care. That type of witness is very different that someone who picked a fight, got bested, and is not suing for damages.

The tone you set will not only provide the backdrop for the questions you as on the way to your target questions, but it will determine how you as the storyteller is received.

A.   KNOWING YOUR AUDIENCE

Great performers play to their audiences. They sense, and they respond. They feel, and they emote. They perceive, and they deliver. As a trial lawyer, you must have that same connection with the jurors.

Your connection with your jury should being long before your cross examination of the first witness. Jury selection is the *only* opportunity to converse—enter into a dialogue with—your potential jurors. If you pay attention, you will see some of their individual personalities come out. Some jurors will hide and be totally silent—it is up to you to connect with those silent jurors. While this is not a treatise on jury selection, it is important to mention. You can't play opera at a rock concert, and you can't play baseball at a football game. You have to know the field upon which you play—or your game will be for naught.

You also have the ongoing opportunity to *watch* the jurors—in opening, during objections, while witnesses are testifying, while they are coming in and out of court.

What does their body language tell you? What do their expressions tell you? How are they carrying their items? How do they sit and stand? Do they look at you? Do they whisper among themselves?

This is no treatise on kinesic or paralingustic communication. But being a trial lawyer requires all of your faculties and senses. After all, you are not trying to persuade a brick wall ... you are persuading *human beings*. Being sensitive to how you are coming across will be critical to success in conveying your story.

Is the topic sensitive?

Is the witness sensitive or sympathetic?

Is the jury tired or bored?

What other testimony has come out that you are now competing against?

Whether any of these things apply, or other issues apply, know what they are and approach your cross examination—your story—appropriately.

B.   READING YOUR AUDIENCE IN REAL TIME

People communicate, both verbally and also with their body language. In daily life, talk less and watch/listen more. You will be amazed what you learn about people by watching their non-verbal cues.

Do not be so involved in note-taking that you miss the action in the courtroom. On direct, look at the jury. Watch *people*—their eyes, their expressions, how they sit. Are they moving about or squirming? Do they look at the witness, or away? Do the jurors make noises—sighs and other paralinguistics can reveal a lot. And by watching and listening, you can adjust your presentation as discussed below.

C.   CHANGING TIDES . . .

The key to the Cross Sheet system is flexibility. The system allow you to move things about, add and subtract on the fly, and adapt to every situation.

That being said, you cannot *deliver* the cross with blinders on. You have to watch your jury. They may really like what you are doing, and really dislike the witness and her or her position. But the jury may not like *you* and *your questions*. The jurors may have a very different attitude about the witness than you do. You job is to tell the story—but a story only has impact and import if the listener is listening and absorbing, and thinking about your point. If you develop a hostile relationship with the jury, you may as well sit down.

What to look for in jurors. Most jurors will look at you for the question, and to the witness for the answer. There are times they will linger on you or the witness, out of nothing more than just thought and attention. Don't think anything about that.—

- *Kinesic communication.* Arms crossed, tapping fingers, twiddling thumbs, head on hands, etc.

- *Looking around.* Jurors who are not paying attention are clearly a problem. What is going on while they are zoning out? Do you need to pick up the pace? Cover new ground? Take a pause, move to a different position, use a transition. Bring the jurors back to the story.

- *Not looking at you at all.* Not just boredom, but angst at you or something you are saying or representing. What was it? Figure it out quick. If it is sensitive materials, you had better have talked about that in jury selection—both as a warning, and to find out who would be upset by it.

- *Glares.* You don't have to be an expert in non-verbal communication to know when someone is aggravated at you. Glares, pursed lips, shakes of the head, and the like are very powerful forms of communicating to you that you have crossed the line. You need to bring them back, and fast.

- *Sighs, other noises (paralinguistic communication).* A non-verbal sign of exasperation. Sighing, throat clearing, smacks, blowing out breath, and the like. You know it when you hear it. If you hear it, adjust what you are doing. Move on, get to the point, or maybe finish up.

- *Whispering to each other.* Once the jurors are talking to each other, "normality" or juror protocol has been thrown out the window. The whispering jurors have come to the point where they are bonding with each other over what is going on in front of them. Usually, it's a train wreck. If you were under the train, you have a problem.

How to right the ship if you start losing ground with the jurors. Jurors are not unforgiving. Sometimes you and the witness get off on the wrong foot unintentionally. You can right that with certain phrases that will make you seem professional, while not giving up your planned tenacity and line of questioning.

Q. I'm sorry, I did not understand. Let me start over.

Q. That's my fault, please let me start over.

Q. I did it make myself clear—allow me to ask it this way . . .

Even if the tides change, your job is to *control* and to change them back. Showing your professionalism is far more important to your credibility than is showing your ability to yell at or embarrass a witness. Do not be satisfied to leave the witness and the jury both in a smoldering pile on the courtroom floor. Your verdict will reflect how the jurors feel about that!

Another thing: *watch your opponent.* Is he or she cuing the witness? Is he or she frustrated or impatient with the witness' testimony? What does that tell you? It could tell you that the witness is prone to going off script. On cross, a witness who may go astray from the planned testimony can give you lots of great information, or be one who needs extra control. Opposing counsel's actions with the witness can also cue whether the witness was properly prepped or not. An unprepared witness can give you gold on cross, because he or she will not have been told what to try to avoid or how to answer certain questions. Be vigil.

4.4 TEMPO

The pace you set for the cross examination will depend on the subject matter, the case theory, the jury, and the witness. Think of tempo as a measure of intensity—how you push the witness forward, or reign the witness in to a slower pace.

Law enforcement officers are usually experienced witnesses. You can push them harder as they are accustomed to it. If a lay witness is not being forthright, you can push that witness as if to break them. More frail or innocent witnesses need a slower tempo, so as to not appear to be nasty with them.

Whatever you choose, choose before you start. Plan on making the witness work by firing questions in rapid succession. Or, plan on forcing a witness you know will be trouble to work at your pace. Whatever you choose, use tempo to control the witness.

A. CADENCE

Tempo is a measure of intensity—slower, faster. Cadence is entirely another creature. Think of a drumline in a marching band, playing as the band marches into the stadium. The rhythmic flow of the beats creates a cadence—a pattern. It may be fast, or it may be slow. Whichever, it is sustained at that level.

In cross examination, you want to avoid bursts of questions unless it is part of your attack on the witness. If you chose a rapid tempo, then have your questions such that you can sustain that cadence and there is a rhythmic flow. The flow of question-answer-question-answer helps you tell your story. Think of it as a rhythmic flow of your facts.

The best part about creating a cadence of questions is that when it is broken, it is usually because the truth is not apparent. The witness is searching for the answer. The break in the rhythm will be attributed—negatively—to the witness by the jury.

Be on your toes, think ahead, and have your questions ready!

4.5 "CONDUCTING" CROSS EXAMINATION USING GESTURES

Gesticulation is a real thing. Learning how to be comfortable with your own body/hands/expressions in a courtroom can help you tell the story and control he witness.

A.   INTRODUCTION TO GESTURES AND FACIAL EXPRESSIONS

"Put your hands down."

"You're waving your hands around too much."

"Don't point."

As an advocacy teacher, I have heard and, regrettably, said these words to students. The thought behind the admonition seems to be that hands distract from the spoken word. We have all seen people that "talk with their hands"—those that go mute if you tie their hands behind their backs. Truly, useless flailing of the hands, stabbing the air, or gestures repeated *ad nauseum* for no reason are distracting.

On the contrary—hand gestures accentuate and complement our words. We were designed to use our hands to communicate. It is inherent in all of us— gestures (and facial expressions) go right along with the words to help convey the message. As humans, we "communicate" whenever word or act influences someone else. The key word is "influences." We can influence a word with a word, or and act with a word.

Q. How are you?

A. I am fine.

or

You better run, I'm going to kill you. [Runs]

In the former, words have influenced another to reveal feelings (words). In the latter, words have influenced action (flight).

Similarly, we can influence an act with a word, or an act with an act. Think about the last time you met someone at a door at the same time. You both could not go through at the same time. You, being the nice person you are, offered to let the other person go first. You could have done that a number of ways:

- Simply stopping and waiting.

- Saying, *please, you go first.*

- Stopping, and indicating the other person's passage by holding your hand, palm up, toward the door.

That hand gesture is called *gesticulation*—communicating with gestures—(https://www.merriam-webster.com/dictionary/gesticulation).
What other gesticulations can you think of? My father could control me with a mere facial expression (my brother and I refer to it as when "Dad would give you that look.") How about a look of love? Disgust? If someone pinches her nose with one hand, and rapidly fans the air away from her face, what does that tell you? How about the "face palm" that we see so often—someone who face-palms himself is probably not having a great day.

If we all are capable of communicating with gestures, then why not strategically incorporate the most basic human communication skills into the examination of a witness? Controlling yourself in opening and closing from gesturing wildly is one thing . . . controlling a witness by gesturing strategically is entirely another. That key word—*influences*—becomes even more important. It is important to note that as the cross examiner, you are not trying to influence the witness to lie, but to the contrary—to tell the truth, and to tell it as you direct.

Using the Five Fundamentals of Cross Examination (theme, topic, target, tone, and tempo) are critical to effective trial advocacy. But other than tone, the fundamentals focus on *the words* that create influence—highly effective communication is not just about *what* you say, but *how* you say it.

Understanding that one can influence and in turn, control with hand gestures and facial expressions, to conduct the witness' responses, is important to effective cross examination. *Learning* to use specific gestures at specific times is critical. It will not only control the witness, but also control the questioner—you. It's just a matter of incorporating strategic gestures into your litigation repertoire, or "quiver of arrows."

Think of the conductor of a symphony orchestra. No words at all are used in a performance. Gestures alone summon intensity, passion, quiet, brilliance . . . the list of emotions and moods goes on and on. You can "conduct" a cross examination in a similar manner by the use of practiced gestures.

B.   IMPORTANCE OF ADDING GESTURES TO THE WORDS

You have an advantage over the silent orchestra conductor—you can strategically combine a gesture and a word or sentence. The result is powerful.

Why do gestures work in witness influence control? Because of how we as humans intake and interpret information. Facial recognition is an emotional response for the brain—it sees something it knows, and is pleased, disgusted, scared, etc. Thus, a strong gesture or facial expression that accompanies a question is likely to get a true response from a witness who is otherwise prepared and practiced to try to get around your questions.

Remember that one the most influential forms of communication is silence. Silence speaks volumes: "I'm not interested", "I'm mad at you", "I'm thinking of something more important", "you're not worthy of a response" . . . Gestures emphasize the silence. Remember the "talk to the hand . . ." retort that was popular several years ago? The rest of the implied saying was ". . . 'cause the face ain't talking back!" Now, all people do is hold up the hand to the person to be ignored, and the point is made. That gesture has become that recognizable.

C.   WHAT GESTURES AND WHEN TO USE THEM

One cannot imagine that there is an exhaustive list of gestures or movements that can influence or control others. But having a "go to" list of gestures that work for your advocacy style is as important as having an extra pen and writing pad. When you need it, you don't have to go looking for it.

Here are several basic gestures that can help a cross examiner conduct the flow and exchange. As discussed at the end of the chapter, practice makes perfect. Know which one (or a variation of which one) works for you and how you best deliver it. The last thing you want to do in a cross examination is to look contrived, silly, or to make a spectacle of yourself.

These are some of what work for me—feel free to use them, or come up with what works for you. But don't just stand there like a bump on a log—*take control!*

1. "Don't Speak" or "It's My Turn, Let Me Finish"

Witness View

Jury View

I find this gesture is effective to prevent a couple of problems. First, to prevent the witness from interrupting you. Second, to stop the witness from "free styling" and going beyond a yes or no. Remember, optimal cross examination is getting a series of yes or no answers without the witness editorializing in between.

This is asking to "talk to the hand" in that whatever is being said by the witness is being met with total and unconditional opposition. You are demanding that the witness shut up immediately.

If the witness is trying to interject or talk over your question, this is the gesture to use. A persistent witness may require two hands. How forcefully you project are matters of comfort and practice.

If the witness goes on a long narrative answer, this gesture will telegraph to him/her and the jury that this is not how the process works and he/she needs to get back in line.

There are at least three methods of implementation while using this gesture: (1) to simply continue your question, (2) with silence and (3) repeating the witness' name with the gesture up . . . "Mr. Jones . . . Mr. Jones . . . Mr. Jones . . ." When the witness stops and looks at you, regroup with "I'll repeat my question. You left the door unlocked, yes?"

2. Speak, or "It's Your Turn"

Witness View

Jury View

Much like cuing the trumpet players (who are always willing to blare away), this gives the witness the green light—"it's now your turn."

The trick to using "speak" is to do it with some easy "yes" and "no" leading questions at the outset of the cross examination. Biographical or constant facts are good topics to get yes and no answers flowing. Coupling those questions with the "speak" gesture conditions (or trains) the witness to respond when he or she sees (recognizes) the "speak" gesture. It also conditions the jury that you are both in control and fair in letting the witness respond. When the witness gets cagey and goes on a verbal run, your use of both the "don't speak" and "it's your turn" gestures will remind the jury that this is not how the process works and that the witness is not playing by the rules—and that goes to the jurors' assessment of the witness' credibility.

3. I Don't Believe You

Witness View

Jury View

A simple gesture that indicates disbelief serves two purposes. First, it reinforces with the jury that there are others in the courtroom that are not buying it. Second, it lets the witness know that no one is buying it, and it's a good time to stop talking. Or, to keep talking, trying to explain the lise and making it worse.

This gesture is a work-around to statements or remarks by counsel, even in the form of a question, that could draw objections to "counsel testifying" or "argumentative". And while the "I don't believe you" gesture is not intended to substitute for an impermissible argument or comment, it is a powerful was to influence the witness to stop whatever offending behavior he or she is exhibiting.

4. We Don't Believe You

Witness View

Jury View

Similar to "I don't believe you." This gesture should only be used when it is clear that the jury is not buying what the witness is saying. As my friend

Professor Charles Rose says, "never cut the witness' throat unless the jury hands you the knife." Once you see that the jury is beginning to disconnect (eye rolls, lack of eye contact with the witness, shifting and looking around, frowns, audible sighs, etc.), then you can gain credibility and support by for your case by gesturing. Use this gesture from as close as you can get to the jury box, looking at them first, and then to the witness. You assume the position as impromptu spokesperson, and you join and become a member of the jury's little community.

5. And of Course the Answer Is . . .

Witness View

Jury View

Witness View

Jury View

Much akin to "speak", this gesture is very effective when you get to the witness to admit the target fact. When you reach the target fact, if you have done it correctly the jury will be right there with you. The target fact answer will be obvious. Highlighting that obviousness with a gesture is, again, like cuing the cymbal to crash. If the cue is given and nothing happens, the silence is deafening.

The top pose is the *wind-up*: I am asking the target question, and wanted to get the witness' attention and concentration—and silence—all to control the big moment.

Then, the target fact gets *cued* with some flair. The witness may or may not admit it . . . but your gesture to "speak" cues the jury—who is following along and knows what the target fact it—to watch the witness either wither in submission or continue to squirm and lose credibility. Either way, the target fact is hammered home.

In my example, I have given you both my one-hand and my two-handed "punches"—I use the one hand for "so the answer is . . ." and the two hand version for "*of course* the answer is . . ." That's what works for me—you will have your own approach.

6. We Are Not Listening to You Babble . . . .

Witness View

Jury View

Not so much a gesture, as a physical manifestation of total disregard. My favorite technique in this regard is to turn to (not just look at) the jury, take a step toward them and then take off my glasses and clean them with my handkerchief (or my tie). I still look at the jurors (although they are blurred without my specs on), who by then are looking at me, and just continue looking. Sometimes I smile, other times I look bored—I try to mimic what I sense they are feeling. I am conveying to them, "hi, I know we are all in this together and I hate that you have to sit through the garbage coming from this witness' mouth . . . but we'll get through it. Hang on while I go back to work."

There are several "blah blah blah" gestures or activities. Walking back to your counsel table to look at (not for, but purposely at) a document, pouring some water from the courtroom carafe or your water bottle, and even running your finger over the top of the podium and checking it for dust are all examples. Another is taking off your watch and winding it— that carries the added implication of "time is wasting." The jury will note your absence from the fray and look for, and ultimately at, you. The babble from the witness stand is properly put in its place of unimportance.

Whatever the gesture, be sure the gather yourself up before the witness, and restart with, "thank you for all of that, but let me turn you back to my question." Then repeat *exactly* the question you asked before the witness' prattling on and on.

7. Large, Medium, Small

Witness View

Jury View

My advocacy teacher, the legendary Professor William Eleazer of Stetson University College of Law, taught the importance of manipulating time during an examination. Things that are bad for your that took 30 minutes to do in real life, should only be discussed for a second. Things that are good for you but only lasted a few seconds, he said, you should discuss for five minutes.

Accentuating, or diminishing, a witness' testimony by using gestures is a powerful psychological and nonverbal communication tool. Every time you talk about how quickly something happened, make the gesture above ("short" or "small"). Whatever the time or size you are accentuating, make the gesture several times and the impact on the jury will be great. Do this in all phases of the trial so the impact is consistent and even more powerful and lasting.

This technique is to use your body to shorten or lengthen, or enlarge or reduce. Don't be outrageous, and remember that over-selling can impact your credibility (the *ethos* part of Aristotelian rhetoric, and arguably the most important one).

8. Listing

Witness View

Jury View

If you have several points you want to drive home, list them with your fingers: one, two, three . . . This is particularly helpful when you circle back to discuss the witness' testimony in closing. As you discuss the great points you got from that witness, you hold up the corresponding finger. Of course, one should be reasonable with the listing, and stick to no more than three points. Jurors will not remember what point *ten* was, but they will remember how silly you looked with that many fingers in the air.

The idea is to be able to use this in argument, especially if one of the most important target facts is in the middle (say number three). In closing, you can use the "three" gesture to bring the jury back to that very important target fact. This works well with elements of causes of action and crimes.

9. Believe Me . . . Hear Me . . . Understand Me

Witness View

Jury View

Probably just as much for the jury as for the witness, this gesture personalizes the message and the messenger. Whatever the assertion, when the "believe me" gesture is used it accentuates it as having come from the heart, or that you are taken aback by what you are hearing. It adds sincerity and emotion to the message.

Remember in Aristotelian rhetoric, the credibility of the messenger (ethos) is as important as the message (logos). Jurors can spot false sincerity a mile away. However, when connecting on a personal and emotional level, gestures are critical. In opening statement and closing argument, you do not put your hands behind your back or in your pockets. In cross, when you as the advocate assume to role of storyteller, your hands become part of the story. Use them in a manner that accentuates your sincerity.

There are likely as many gestures that can relay sincerity and believability—figure out what yours is, and use it sparingly.

D. IMPLEMENTATION

Don't practice in front of a mirror—*mirrors lie to you*. Use video to record your delivery. Watch it later. You'll be surprised.

Ask those that know you what they know about your gestures. When you do a certain movement, what are you conveying? When you are conveying a thought, is there a gesture that you use without thinking? Is there a thing you do when you are mad? Do you have a "tell" (to borrow from the poker players) that lets everyone know you are being less than candid? Is there something that people see when you are really, really serious about something?

Try this exercise. Set up a video recorder on you and get in a debate with someone. Pick a sore spot topic that will have some meaning and generate some "heat". You can also use a fact pattern from your trial advocacy skills or mock trial case file, and deliver a cross or a closing. Be yourself, use your normal gestures and facial expressions.

Later, watch the video. Note how you deliver each of these gestures. Note which ones "feel" easy and normal. Note which ones do not come easy. Compare your own gut reaction to using them with what you see on the video. Adjust from there.

Create your own list of ticks and tells. List what your friends or coworkers say when they assess how you look when employing certain gestures. Some are universal while others are more personal to the individual. Try to incorporate gestures that are easily and precisely understood.

Question	Gesture	Assessment

E.   FINAL THOUGHTS ON GESTURES AND CROSS EXAMINATION

"Gesticulation" is a practiced and specific skill that compliments the Five Fundamentals of cross examination and allows you to conduct the witness in telling the story you want told. It controls the witness and the substance of what is coming from the stand, and also controls the questioner. Having several specific gestures in the repertoire will have a significant impact on influencing and controlling the witness and persuading the jurors.

4.6   TOOLS TO CONTROL "THOSE" WITNESSES (WE'VE ALL SEEN THEM)

While a great degree of what happens in a courtroom is spontaneous, trial advocates should have solid fundamentals ("trial advocacy muscle memory", as I call it). Having perfect and practiced fundamentals keeps you in control and gives you a move in those cases where you think you are boxed in.

Difficult witnesses present the hardest advocacy situations of all. Wrangling with a difficult witness is unlike anything else in life. Think about it the scene: you alone, in front of a bunch of people, trying to get another person who is clearly against you (and may even dislike you) to agree with you—all for the purpose of your livelihood and career and your client's life. No pressure, right?

Yet this all-too-critical part of the trial is where we see the least amount of skill. Yelling does not work and judges will not permit it—yet we see attorneys simply repeating the question at a higher pitch and louder volume. Just taking the answer does not work, yet that happens all the time when the lawyer simply moves on.

There are a few solid techniques that the cross examiner can have in the quiver of arrows, or toolbox, that are easy to remember and use, and will produce results.

The following are tools and techniques to have at the ready in order to keep the questioning from derailing.

Composure, listening, navigating the situation. Always listen and think ahead. Where are you going? Where is the witness going? What did he or she just say? The witness is being a jerk—what do I do now? What is the jury thinking about this—and the witness—and *me*?

Asking the witness if he/she understands the question, or needs clarification. While we have some great control techniques listed below, sometimes you might ask a confusing question. That's okay—it happens to all of us. If you see the witness struggling, be the professional and ask the witness if he or she understands. If not, clear it up. Everyone will appreciate it. If the witness is being "that witness" and pretending not to understand, ask a time or two and clear it up a time or two. Then turn it on the witness by asking *"what part of my question did you not understand?"* Usually they cannot explain it, so you return to your original question and continue.

Cross Exposition. Remember from Chapter 1.6.B that there are times you need to stop, take a detour for a minute, clear some things up, then get back to the story.

What does not work. There are some things that simply do not help you in a bad cross examination or with a tough witness. Yet you see them all the time. Avoid:

- Arguing
- Yelling
- Asking the judge for help
- Asking untrue questions or somehow falsifying facts
- Losing your composure and professionalism
- Attacking an honest witness

There are certain objections that the advocate can use to control the speaker on the witness stand. See Chapter 5 for a discussion of controlling the subject matter, the witness, and opposing counsel.

No doubt that all advocates, no matter how prepared and polished, will encounter an obstreperous and contumacious witness. It is not unusual for witnesses to want to wiggle, if not outright revolt—most people do not want to be told what to say or to have words put in their mouth.

When the witness becomes uncooperative or combative, there are tools and techniques that will help the advocate. One must be (1) skilled and able in the art of witness control, and (2) have enough wits to deal with the situation in real time. Simply becoming argumentative or combative with the witness is ineffective.

A.   HOUSETRAINING A WITNESS— THE BASICS (LEAD AND LIMIT)

The basics discussed in Chapter 1.5 are leading and limiting. You cannot deviate from these fundamentals. There is not a more basic witness control method than to use leading, one-fact questions.

There are times that you may need to ask an open-ended question. A preferred technique is to ask a "why then . . ." or "please explain . . ." once the witness is backed into a corner where there is no explanation. The point of an open-ended question in that situation is to get a fact from the witness who is being confusing. It can also expose the witness as a liar or that the contention he or she is making is absurd. The answer to the open-ended question, however, should lead to more leading, limited questions.

Q. You watched as the accident happened?

A. Yes. Well, I wasn't watching.

Q. You testified on direct that you were watching the intersection as it happened, no?

A. No. I said was as looking.

Q. You were looking as the accident happened, then?

A. No.

Q. You were not looking at the intersection as the red car hit the blue truck?

A. No.

Q. Tell us what you saw.

A. I was looking in that direction, but then I looked the other way. I heard the screech of brakes, so I glanced over and saw that the red car had hit the blue truck.

Q. Okay. Can we go through it, then?

A. Sure.

Q. You were looking at the intersection?

A. Yes.

Q. And then you looked away?

A. Yep.

Q. You heard tires screech?

A. Yep.

Q. You looked back toward the intersection?

A. Yep, now you've got it.

Q. And the red car had already hit the blue truck.

A. Yes, sir.

Q. So you did not actually see the initial impact.

A. Well, no.

In this scenario, the witness was not being clear, and finally asking the open-ended question allowed the cross examiner to back up and get another run at it—and get the admission that the witness had actually not seen the initial impact.

B.   THAT WAS NOT MY QUESTION

After the first nonresponsive answer, pause and then state respectfully, "Perhaps you didn't understand my question. My question to you is . . . (restate the question), listening respectfully and attentively to the answer.

If you get a second nonresponsive answer hold up your hand as they are being nonresponsive. When they stop say, "*Thank you, but that was not my question. Let us try this a third time. My question to you was . . .* (restate the question again)."

Note: If the witness will not stop when you hold up your hand then you should drop your hand, turn away, go to counsel table and look through your notebook. Once they finish, count to three silently, look up and say, "*Thank you, but that was not my question. Let's try this a third time. My question to you was . . .* (restate the question yet again)."

If you get a third nonresponsive answer then turn and face the judge. State the following, "Your honor move to strike the witness's testimony as nonresponsive"—wait for the ruling.

C.   HAVE YOU FINISHED? LET'S GET BACK TO THE FACTS (OR MY QUESTION)

Some witnesses will run like a hooked tuna. As much as they can, as fast as they can. These witnesses like to talk, and to oversell to the jury:

Q. Sir, you were the CEO of ABC Corp at the time the contract was signed?

A. I was the CEO at the time when your client breached the contract, swindled me, and cost my company revenue and jobs.

Ouch. That does not seem good. This witness is either truly aggrieved or looking for an acting award. If he is truly aggrieved, truly injured, and none of it was his fault, then you have to be a little more delicate in correcting his behavior on the stand. If he is overselling and pandering to the jury, then you can snap the collar back much harder.

For the really injured victim:

Q. Sir, you were the CEO of ABC Corp at the time the contract was signed on January 17?

A. I was the CEO at the time when your client breached the contract, swindled me, and cost my company revenue and jobs. We had to hire an outside—

Q. Hold on. Let's get back up a little, to my question.

Q. We're talking about January 2017?

A. Yes

Q. There was only one CEO of ABC Corp at that time, is that correct?

A. Yes, just me.

Q. Okay . . . and the contract was signed in January 2017?

A. Yes, on January 15.

Q. So we are clear, the answer to the original question is simply "yes", you were the CEO of ABC Corp at the time—January 17—when the contract was signed.

A. Yes.

The idea is to back up a little, add some soft facts using an easier tone and a moderate tempo, and make the questioning less confrontational from your angle. Most witnesses will back down and participate, because they either get or merely sense what you are doing. They do not want to look like a jerk, so they tone it down.

Then there is the witness who just cannot resist being either the martyr or the showboat. Witnesses will cry, add irrelevant facts, and do and day other improper things. These witnesses can annoy jurors—watch the jurors, they will let you know.

Here is how the "let's get back to my question" controller would work with a blabbermouth witness:

Q. Sir, you were the CEO of ABC Corp at the time the contract was signed?

A. I was the CEO at the time when your client breached the contract, swindled me, and cost my company revenue and jobs.

Q. Thank you—now, let's return to MY question. You were the CEO, yes?

A. Yes.

Q. Of ABC Corp, yes?

A. Yes.

Q. Thank you.

This type of control can be preceded by a "perhaps you did not understand my question", as set forth in Chapter 4.6.G. It is an openly-stated redirection, and a bit condescending. But, there are times that it is needed, and works.

D.   THE FLIP TO THE OPPOSITE

There are times that the witness will not admit to something blatantly obvious. Sometimes it is to overtly lie, other times it is to play games and not admit *exactly* what is asked (even when everyone understands the question).

For example:

Q. Officer, you arrived on scene at 7PM, correct?

A. I didn't arrive "on" the scene. I arrived "at" the scene.

Really? This witness wants to play a game of semantics? Correction must ensue:

Q. Officer, you arrived on scene at 7PM, correct?

A. I didn't arrive "on" the scene. I arrived "at" the scene.

Q. So you did not arrive at 123 Elm Street at 7PM?

A. No, I did arrive at that address.

Q. You understand what "on scene" means?

A. Yes.

Q. So, my question again, you arrived on scene at 7PM?

A. Yes.

The correction comes in the form of taking the undeniable, finding its opposite, and asking the person if the opposite is true—which it is not, and would be absurd for the witness to admit.

Q. You saw a tall man?

A. I can't say what specific height the man was, so . . .

Q. He wasn't average height?

A. No.

Q. He wasn't short?

A. No.

Q. The opposite of short is tall, correct?

A. Yes.

Q. He was tall, right?

A. Yes.

It's not a terribly powerful correction tool, but it trains the witness to stop with the word games, or hiding the answer, and to just come out with it.

E.   THE WEED-OUT GAME

Dodgy witnesses do not like to admit the obvious. They like to play semantics games and get cute in front of the jury. Certainly, there are times when the attorney is either the one playing games, or the issue is so narrow that it requires precision. In those cases, the witness is correct to hold the questioning attorney to the specifics.

The weed-out game is a strong way to lock a witness into a specific answer. It is the process of going through every possibility, eliminating one after the other, and arriving at the only real or true answer/fact. For example, in a breach of a construction contract, where the contractor is on the stand and being cross examined by the plaintiff's attorney:

Q. Mr. Witness, you entered into a contract with Ms. Plaintiff to remodel her kitchen cabinets, right?

A. I enter into lots of contracts.

Q. The contract with Ms. Plaintiff was not to remodel a living room, right?

A. No.

Q. Or to build an addition on to a garage, right?

A. No.

Q. It was to replace her kitchen cabinets, right?

A. Yes.

Q. So you remember this contract, don't you?

A. Yes.

Q. She contracted with you to take out her old cabinets and put in new ones?

A. Yes, as I recall—whatever the contract says is what it says.

Q. She paid you in advance?

A. Yes, in full.

Q. The cabinets you were to put in were to be oak?

A. Again, whatever the contract says.

Q. You have read the contract, correct?

A. Yes.

Q. You heard it read here in court today?

A. Yes.

Q. The contract did not call for maple cabinets, did it?

A. No

Q. The contract did not call for pine cabinets, did it?

A. No.

Q. The contract did not call for birch cabinets, did it?

A. No.

Q. The contract did not call for poplar cabinets?

A. No, it was for oak cabinets.

Q. Right. And you installed particle board cabinets, didn't you?

A. I am not sure what was installed.

Q. You saw your cabinet supplier's invoice here in court, right?

A. Yes.

Q. And that is your signature on it?

A. Looks like it.

Q. You signed it the day you received the cabinets?

A. *It was signed that day.*

Q. *And that receipt clearly says the cabinets are made of partible board?*

A. *It appears to say that.*

Q. *You read and signed this invoice, didn't you?*

A. *It appears that I did.*

Q. *Are you telling this jury you did not read and sign the invoice from the cabinet supplier?*

A. *No, I signed it.*

Q. *And you read it.*

A. *I may have, I don't recall.*

Q. *Are you telling this jury you sign things without reading it?*

A. *I trusted the guy, so . . .*

Q. *Now, you have been installing cabinets, what, twenty years?*

A. *Yes.*

Q. *It took you, what, two full days to install these cabinets?*

A. *Yes, about that much. We did not work non-stop for forty-eight hours, if that's what you are getting at.*

Q. *You didn't work for just an hour on this project?*

A. *No.*

Q. *You didn't work just one morning?*

A. *No.*

Q. *You didn't work just one work day?*

A. No.

Q. You were there both Tuesday and on Wednesday?

A. Yes.

Q. And on both of those days, you didn't work just an hour?

A. No, we worked a full day.

Q. You yourself actually installed the cabinets?

A. I had an assistant.

Q. The assistant did not do it all by himself, did he?

A. No.

Q. You handled the cabinets?

A. Yes.

Q. You handled the doors?

A. Yes.

Q. You installed the door hardware?

A. Yes.

Q. The installation called for you to drill through the cabinets and doors to install the hardware, didn't it?

A. Yes, you have to drill holes and stuff.

Q. You know from experience that hard oak is very different to drill into than particle board?

A. It's all about the same.

Q. Particle board is pieced together from lots of little pieces, isn't it?

A. Yes, it's all glued together.

Q. It is softer than pine?

A. I suppose.

Q. It is softer than maple?

A. I guess.

Q. It is softer than poplar?

A. I guess.

Q. Softer than birch?

A. I guess.

Q. And particle board is softer than oak, isn't it?

A. I guess.

Q. By "I guess" do you mean to tell this jury you do not know the difference between cheap particle board and expensive oak?

A. No.

Q. You do know the difference, don't you.

A. Yes.

Q. Please tell this jury—you noticed before the installation, when you signed the invoice, that the cabinets were not oak?

A. I told you, I don't recall specifically looking at the invoice.

Q. Tell them—certainly you noticed during installation that the cabinets were not oak, didn't you?

A. Well, I don't . . .

Q. And you went ahead an installed them anyway?

A. I installed what she ordered.

Q. *She ordered oak, right?*

A. *Yes.*

Q. *And those cabinets are not oak, are they?*

A. *No.*

In this scenario, the witness clearly knew that the cabinets were not what the homeowner ordered. In fact, he likely tried to swindle her by ordered the cheaper cabinets and passing them off. First, he tried to play cute with the fact that he did not remember the terms of the contract. Eliminating the things that he did not contract for narrowed it down to the cabinets. He also pretended to not know that the cabinets were inexpensive. With there being many different types of wood for comparison, it is easy to be able to compare the cheap material to the many available luxury woods. Each time, weeding out the impossibilities left only the true target fact.

The bottom line is that by thinking in 3D, you can present enough non-viable alternatives to the witness until the witness has to concede what you want. This technique prevents wiggling and equivocating, and reminds the witness that you are in control.

F.   THEN THE ANSWER IS YES (OR NO)

An easy corrective tool is to make the witness say yes or no. That is provided, of course, that you have *asked* a question that calls for a yes or no answer.

This is sometimes a game of repetition, of training of the witness. If you do it enough, the witness may finally resort to simply saying yes or no.

Q. On December 23 at noon, you were at the intersection of Capital Circle and Apalachee Parkway?

A. I was running all my holiday errands that day.

Q. Then the answer is "yes", you were at that intersection, yes?

A. Yes.

Q. And you saw Mr. Defendant's red car?

A. I think it's more of a maroon.

Q. But the answer is "yes", you saw Mr. Defendant's car approaching?

A. Yes.

Q. And your light was red?

A. I was stopped, so . . .

Q. So the answer is "yes", your light was red?

A. Yes.

Q. And you turned in front of Mr. Defendant's car, didn't you?

A. Yes.

Consistency is the key to training the witness. It's like correcting a dog—you have to do it at the moment of the bad behavior, otherwise the dog doesn't connect the correction to the bad behavior. You have to win the battle with the witness, exerting dominance and establishing the understanding that you will never, ever let them get away with not saying yes or no.

Note, there are judges that will permit witnesses to explain their yes or no answers. I submit that there is no room for explaining on cross examination—the flow of facts simply calls for yes or no. Re-direct is a chance to clean up answers and or expound upon facts. The argument is that when a witness is permitted to go beyond yes or no, and get into explaining why he or she answered yes or no, that witness becomes an advocate. By explaining yes or no, the witness gets to chose why and what the explanation is without prompting. That requires advocacy, and takes the witness out of the proper role of witness and improperly permits advocacy.

For more on judges limiting your cross examination, see Chapter 9.1.A.

G.   YOU DIDN'T UNDERSTAND MY QUESTION

This control technique makes you look like the nicer person. If the witness does not give you a contextually appropriate answer, consider using this technique.

Understand and remember that witnesses will not always give you an answer that you like. There is a difference, however, in the witness answering your question not to your liking, and not answering the question at all. The distinction is important to know and understand, as re-asking the same question when it has in fact been answered will draw a sustainable objection.

H.   RE-ASK THE QUESTION (WITH OR WITHOUT A CONTROL TAG)

This technique is good when you need to get a little more "stern" with the witness. Tags such as "right?" are colloquial, and not necessarily good and proper form. But it's nice. Just asking the question point-blank connotes *I mean business* when it is coupled with a no-nonsense tone.

Q. After the report was made, you had a chance to review it, right?

A. I had a chance, you know, I went in, and I was given a copy of what was filed, and. . .

Q. [Slower, more deliberately, and in a stern tone] You reviewed the report?

A. Uh, yes.

Q. Thank you. Now, turning your attention to . . .

I.   WE'LL GET TO THAT IN A SECOND . . . THIS QUESTION IS ABOUT _____

It can also be used with a slight variation when the witness jumps ahead, and wants to begin a narrative answer. When that happens, cut him or her off after your question is answered:

Q. The car traveling behind the red truck was a blue car?

A. It was a blue car, yes, and it hit the back of the red truck, which was—

Q. Excuse me, we'll get to that in a second. My question was simply about the color. Now, moving on, the make of the blue car was BMW, right?

Be sure to come back to the point the witness was about to make, or when getting to it, use a short preface phrase such as *"now, regarding what you were going to tell us, what you saw the red truck do . . ."*

J. INTERRUPTION

If you have control of the courtroom, interrupting a witness is not hard. In other words, if you are delivering a well-thought out objection-free story of a cross, both the judge and opposing counsel will have little to interrupt or complain about.

Q. Miss Witness, you did not come in the office on the day of the fire?

A. Well, no, because I had to—

Q. Let me stop you there. You were not there to see who might have been there when the fire started?

A. No.

However, if you interrupt a witness, the judge can call you down with the admonition that the witness should be permitted to explain his or her answer. If that happens, you should re-evaluate your questions—most likely you are asking non-leading, open-ended compound questions that *require* the witness to explain. In the example above, it is likely completely irrelevant where the witness was, so she should not be allowed to explain. That's especially true if she were someplace such as chemotherapy or a funeral, which would cause the jury to feel sorry for her. No place for that in a trial, either.

If you sense the witness is about to say something that will cause a mistrial, stop him or her.

Q. Mr. Witness, you did not know Mr. Defendant prior to that day?

A. I did not.

Q. Never seen him before?

A. Well, I had seen—

Q. Let me stop you there. You had never seen him in person, correct?

A. Correct.

If the answer was "[w]ell, I had seen his face on the sexual offender list up at the post office", then you would have had a mistrial. Interrupting the witness would be appropriate. Of course, you want to make sure that the witness is instructed not to mention things that may have been prohibited by the court in pretrial motions.

K.   SIMPLIFYING THE QUESTION, AND "PLAYING DUMB"

When you get the first nonresponsive answer hold up your hand and apologize: *"I'm sorry, perhaps I wasn't sufficiently clear, let me ask it a different way"* and ask a simpler version of the same question. It works better if you can ask an even more black and white question. This method asserts control as it forces the witness to play along and by "dumbing it down" for you, and so limits the answer.

If you get a second nonresponsive answer you should remain calm, wait the witness out, allowing them to answer completely and then state, "*I appreciate that you said* (or *felt the need to say*) *that, but my question to you was* (simplest version possible for the question)."

If you get a third nonresponsive answer you should stay calm but be firm, stating the following:

Q. *Sir/Ma'am, we can at least agree that you are the witness?*

A. *Yes.*

Q. *I am the lawyer?*

A. *Yes.*

Q. *We are in a court of law?*

A. *Yes.*

Q. *In a trial?*

A. *Yes.*

Q. *And you just testified on direct in response to Ms. Opposing Counsel's questions?*

A. *Yes.*

Q. *Now I am asking you questions?*

A. *Yes.*

Q. *You are supposed to give answers?*

A. *Yes.*

Q. Thank you. Please answer this question: [re-ask question]

I freely admit that one of the most difficult aspects of cross examination and witness control revolves around balancing the need to be in charge while not appearing unfair, rude, or unethical. Unlike other aspects of trial advocacy, these particular skills are very much dependent upon the situation. Our own sense of self and power in the room are challenged when witnesses refuse to answer. Our need to be 'in charge' can keep us from clearly seeing the right question in the right moment. It is important to keep your head about you when this happens. Slowing down, focusing on the moment, and listening critically are all skills that stand each of us in good stead when this happens.

What real life situations have you experienced? How did you handle (or wish that you had handled) it?

L.   USING THE JURY TO HELP CONTROL THE WITNESS (HAMMER PHRASES)

As Professor Charlie Rose of Stetson Law says, *you should not cut the witness' throat unless the jury hands you the knife.* Great advocates are in tune with the jurors, and know how they are doing against the runaway witness. The jurors' expressions and body language tell it all. When they are looking at you, they are with you. When they look down, perhaps with arms folded, they are tired of the witness and have shut the witness and his/her waning credibility out.

You can take advantage of jurors' moods when controlling a witness.

Tell these folks . . . When you get to a target fact, or to a critical question or two before the target fact (whether the target fact is an actual fact-fact, or a point of impeachment), incorporate your jury into the process by having the witness look at them and give his or her testimony.

> Q. *So, please tell these folks* [gesturing toward jury, moving closer to the jury box], *you knew the gun was loaded.*

Tell these folks again . . . Stepping slightly aside, pausing while looking at the witness, look at the jury. Then look back to the witness and ask him or her to repeat what he or she just said or said on direct. This is a safe open-ended question, you want them to hear again, so that you can really accentuate the impeachment you are about to do based on that statement.

> Q. *Mr. Witness, you recall discussing—on direct examination?*
>
> A. *Yes.*
>
> Q. [Pause, look at jury] *Please tell these folks again what you said about—.*

The idea is to reiterate the questionable testimony, to reinforce that it is in fact not credible. Listen carefully to hear if the witness changes the story in any way. If it does change, confront:

Q. Ok, but on direct examination you told this jury that you were standing behind the car when the shots rang out, didn't you?

One of two beneficial things will happen: (1) the witness will claim not to recall, or (2) the witness will agree to saying the first statement.

You're telling these jurors that ... To really emphasize a target fact, again, whether an actual fact or a point of impeachment, you can preface your question with *"you're telling these jurors that you did not know the gun was loaded?"*—the implication is that there is no way this witness is really sitting up there lying like that. The witness will likely squirm!

Don't tell me, tell them ... When a ridiculous explanation is coming out, make the witness try to convince the jury—it forces the witness to confront an already disbelieving jury. Point to the jury, maybe add a *"please, look at them and tell them ..."* for effect.

All of these approaches combine well with the gestures discussed above.

M.   I'M THE ONE ASKING THE QUESTIONS

You will at times get witnesses who want you to answer questions they what to ask, in an effort to throw you off.

When a witness answers questions with questions, you have a great phrase to derail that tactic: *I'm sorry, but the rules of evidence don't let me answer your question. Let me ask mine again.*

It's a great control technique, and effective because the witness now knows that asking questions breaks the rules. The stigma of not playing by the rules is generally enough to prevent further question back at you from the stand.

4.7 EXPERT WITNESS CROSS

The preparation for the cross examination of an expert is really no different than that of any other witness. You should use the Five Fundamentals to shape and sculpt the overall cross to tell your story. That being said, there are a few extra issues to consider when cross examining experts.

Target documents will be more extensive. The witness will be very polished. In all probability, the witness will be very prepared. Do not shy away from the chance to discredit the expert on cross examination, and make that a part of your story—*the other side is so desperate, they hired a quack!*

Be prepared to pick apart the expert's resume or curriculum vitae. The qualifications of an expert to even *be* an expert are a ripe area. Are there "honor societies" he or she is in, upon which membership is based on peer selection/ recommendation? Or, is the expert just paying an annual fee to be in the society? How are the expert's schools ranked in relevant national polls?

Investigate the expert. Find everything you can—scour the internet, check Lexis and Westlaw, ask other attorneys in the area, ask insurance adjusters. You will be amazed at the amount of information you can amass.

Be prepared to go through every detail of the expert's report or findings. Target facts can be found in the report, such as:

- The overall absurdity of the opinion

- Lack of or incomplete testing

- Failure to follow standards in the field

- Not following up if additional work or analysis is required

Know and use the standards and opinions of other experts in the area. It is said that lawyers become experts in their own rights in many different areas. This is simply because of having to know so much about an area in order to depose and cross examine the witness. For your cross examination, you have to know whether the witness is really, really good, or simply a "hired gun" willing to say anything for a buck. You have to know the terminology and the procedures. You have to know what prior analyses have revealed, and why those opinions are accepted or not. In other words, you have to be able to know everything the expert knows in order to boil it down for the jury to understand your cross examination.

Acknowledging that your expert is qualified and respected. Perhaps this starts at deposition. Ask the expert if he or she knows your expert. If not, why not—and would the witness be willing to familiarize him—or herself with your expert before the trial. If so, what is his or her opinion of your expert? On cross examination, you have fuel to work with either way:

Preparation for testimony. Experts are infallible, just like any other expert. Explore how long he or she worked on the case, how many hours were spent, whether there were meetings with the attorney and/or the client, etc.

Credibility issue: prior court experience. You must know if the expert witness is a regular in court. Is he or she someone who will say whatever, if the price is right? Has the expert has ever been disqualified, or not permitted to testify—especially if on the specific area you are crossing on. What an amazing point of cross examination! See Chapter 8 for a real-life example of this type of expert cross examination.

Q. Mr. Expert, you were once disqualified as an expert?

A. I am not sure what you mean.

Q. On this specific issue of _____, a judge in this courthouse refused to let you testify as a witness—don't you recall that?

A. What do you mean?

Q. Judge Smith, down the hall—you know who Judge Smith is?

A. Yes.

Q. And you remember the Jones case from last month?

A. Yes.

Q. You were hired by the plaintiff to testify about _____?

A. Yes.

Q. Exactly like you were hired by the plaintiff in this case to testify about the same topic?

A. Yes.

Q. And Judge Smith made a ruling that you were not qualified as an expert in that area, didn't she?

A. Yes.

With a cross examination like this, you have neutralized the expert witness, and have amazing material to support your story!

Credibility issue: dealings with opposing counsel. Lawyers and experts tend to run in packs, especially when both are local. I personally called a particular psychologist as an expert in more cases that I can remember—he was local, he was reputable, and he was good. That was mostly at sentencing, so there was no real issue with a trier of fact. The judge understood that the psychiatrist was there to present findings in support of a lesser sentence, and either accepted or rejected the mitigators when deciding the sentence.

But when the expert is called in a trial to assist the trier of fact—*the jury*—in deciding an issue, the close relationship between the expert witness and the lawyer is important. If the expert is making a living testifying for one particular lawyer, his or her credibility becomes an issue. Think about it—in order to keep the cases and cash flowing, the expert witness needs to give the lawyer opinions that the lawyer likes. That sets up some great cross examination:

Q. *Mr. Expert, you are being paid to be here?*

A. *I am.*

Q. *You make your living testifying at trials like this one, right?*

A. *Partially.*

Q. *You're not saying you have income other than being a witness, are you?*

A. *Well, no, but it involves more than just testifying.*

Q. *You* only *do expert work, don't you?*

A. *Yes.*

Q. *And being an expert means you have to do an analysis, right?*

A. *Yes.*

Q. *Form on opinion?*

A. *Yes.*

Q. *Possibly give a deposition?*

A. *If asked, yes.*

Q. *And testify at trial, right?*

A. *If asked, yes.*

Q. *All of that is what you do as an* [makes quotation fingers in the air] *expert witness?*

A. *Yes.*

Q. *And you get paid to do that.*

A. *I do.*

Q. You get paid hourly, right?

A. Yes.

Q. For reading, reviewing, analysis, and that, you get paid?

A. Yes

Q. For that you get more than one hundred dollars per hour, right?

A. Yes

Q. More than two hundred dollars per hour, right?

A. Yes.

Q. You get paid even more than three hundred dollars per hour, don't you?

A. Yes.

Q. And that's not in-court work, right?

A. Correct.

Q. For non-court work, you get three hundred and fifty dollars every hour?

A. Yes.

Q. Now, once you get to court, that rate goes up, right?

A. Yes.

Q. That rate goes to five hundred dollars per hour.

A. Yes.

Q. You have been on the stand for two hours so far today, right?

A. Yes, I believe so.

Q. [Turning to jury] *That means you have earned one . . . thousand . . . dollars . . . while these people have been sitting here listening to you?*

A. Yes.

Q. And that amount is paid by that man over there, right? [pointing]

A. Yes.

Q. And his attorney, Mr. Lawyer, hired you, right?

A. Yes.

Q. This is not the first time you have testified for Mr. Lawyer?

A. No, it is not.

Q. He hires you quite regularly, doesn't he?

A. Yes,

Q. He hires you for five cases or so a year, right?

A. Yes.

Q. And your average billing to his clients is about ten thousand dollars, right?

A. Yes, as an average.

Q. So Mr. Lawyer give you fifty . . . thousand . . . dollars per year of work?

A. Something like that.

Q. Your relationship with Mr. Lawyer is important, isn't it?

A. As it is with all my lawyer clients.

Q. And that is because without a good relationship, you do not get hired?

A. I would assume not.

Q. Without Mr. Lawyer hiring you, you would lose fifty thousand dollars a year from his cases?

A. Yes.

You do not have to go any farther—the target fact is clear to the jury.

Credibility issue: extent of witness willingness to testify for anyone who pays. Much like the above, get out of the witness how many times he or she testifies for pay. If you can adduce instances where he or she has testified for the same side as yours, even better.

Credibility issue: opinion contradicts prior opinions in similar cases. Finding out about other opinions is not too hard, if you just look. Ask other attorneys about the witness, pull transcripts, look for publications. Jurors are very keenly interested to know if witness is a hired gun or a real analyst. The difference in credibility assigned by the jury between the two can make or break your case.

Credibility issue: objectivity. Playing off of the "keep the hiring lawyer happy" theme, bring out any evidence that the analysis or opinion is not based on any objectivity. Compare to your own expert, especially if they are far apart in their opinions, to show the opposing expert's opinion is simply not reasonable—and therefore should be rejected as it is not objective but subjective based on the paying side's position.

A final note about expert witness cross examinations: knowing where you are—and knowing who the jurors are that are listening to the expert. Regionalism is a real thing in trial work. Big city, fancy suit wearing lawyers are not welcomed with open arms in rural communities. We would be kidding ourselves to think that race and gender do not continue to play a role in how people are accepted in some parts of this country. All that to say that there are reasonable "—personal—" issues that can be exploited before the jury. Imagine an expert from a large city, with a big practice in an urban area. How he or she conducted his or her review, and how he or she testifies in a small Southern town could be an issue. Urbanites tend to be busy folks, accustomed to the fast pace of city life. They do not get offended by short, direct, even curt responses. Southerners might revile such a presentation, and not trust the expert— that is wholly within their purview.

If the witness is an older, established, kindly person with a good reputation, don't attack him or her. If he or she is of another national origin, be careful that the jury doesn't think you believe the expert to be a lesser person because of that—never be thought of as racist, sexist, or otherwise.

However, if the witness is talking down to you and the jury, exploit that:

Q. The initials DNA stand for deoxyribonucleic acid, right?

A. [Sighs] *I'd assumed you wouldn't know that, but yes.*

Q. Really. You also assume that these folks in the jury box don't know it?

A. No.

Q. You assume they we are not smart enough to know what DNA stand for?

A. No.

Q. Do you think you are smarter than the folks here?

A. No, that's . . . that's certainly not it.

Q. You don't know who in this room knows what, do you?

A. No.

Q. So you should not assume anything, should you, doctor?

A. No, I'm sorry. DNA stands for deoxyribonucleic acid.

Q. Thank you.

Perhaps a far-fetched example, and maybe a little argumentative, but know that experts will test you, and will try to exert superior knowledge on you. You have to control them.

If the witness is unprepared and uncredible, but has that "aw-shucks" likability, be super nice and just as endearing—all while getting the witness to agree that he or she did not analyze or consider certain things, did not fully prepare—and generally cannot be believed.

Q. Hey, I was looking at your report, and looks like you didn't take any measurements of the other's car's tire skid marks?

A. Where you looking at?

Q. Page three—under the third paragraph.

A. Well, let me look.

Q. Sure, take your time.

A. You know, I thought I took those measurements, and put it in there.

Q. You probably had a lot going on at the time, right?

A. Oh, sure, I have quite a few clients.

Q. And you do your best for them, of course?

A. Absolutely.

Q. But sometimes we all miss something, right?

A. I suppose we do, because that other car's skid mark measurement sure isn't in this here report!

You don't pile-drive the affable witness. Your point is made and preserved. You have established a key deficiency in the expert's work, but done so with a nice tone. The jury will respect that you were nice to the nice, and take the witness' concession of error as honest. You didn't have to beat it out of him, which makes it genuine. What great material for closing argument!

Using the Five Fundamentals gives you the ability—watch the jury as to the tone and tempo you chose.

4.8 COURTROOM POSITIONING

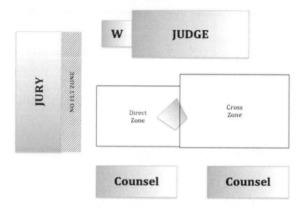

This diagram depicts the layout of most courtrooms—the scale may differ, as may the placement of counsel tables and the judge's bench. Counsel tables are assigned either by the judge's preference, or "first come, first served" (also known as "you snooze, you lose" for those who actually want to be by the jury box). Most of the time the plaintiff or prosecution is closer to the jury box—for no other reason than to prevent the jury overhearing conversation between counsel and the defendant. I prefer to have my client away from the jury box for that reason.

On direct examination, ensuring that the witness tells the story to the jury is key. Direct witnesses are trained to look at the jury while answering. I instruct my direct witnesses to look at the jury, and if they are looking at me *I* will look at the jury during his or her answer, as a cue to look at the jury. Thus, the *direct zone* is where the examining attorney will usually want to stand while questioning.

On cross examination, *you* are telling the story. So you do not want the witness looking at the jury, but rather looking at you as he or she affirms the story you are telling with yes and no answers. By standing in the *cross zone*, you can keep the witness looking at you and not at the jury.

Note, some witnesses (experts, experienced law enforcement) will know to always turn to the jury box to answer. If that happens, try slowing your tempo. Try pausing before you ask you question to attract the witness' attention. If the witness is looking at the jury, and the question doesn't come, it gets uncomfortable and the witness will eventually look at you. Try it—it's instinctual to look to see what is going on. When the witness looks, fire off your question.

Another technique works by using the opposing of the pause, which is to increase your tempo. Speed things up by immediately asking the next question as soon as the witness' answer is finished. Rapid fire questioning does not give the witness time to keep turning to the jury.

A.   BE CAREFUL WHEN MOVING AROUND!

Note, some judges require you to remain within arm's reach of the podium. That is especially true in federal court. Be sure to know if you are free to move about "the well" (as the area inside the bar is known).

You do not want to get called down by the judge and sent back to the podium.

There is a "no-fly" zone in the courtroom: the area immediately in front of the jury box. There are hard and fast rules about remaining physically removed from the jurors, and violations are punished quickly and severely. You cannot "invade the province of the jury" with your questions, arguments, or with your body. Remember:

- *Do not* under any circumstance go too close to the jury box.

- Don't touch it.

- Don't lean on it.

- Don't try to go and sit down next to the jurors.

- Do not address the jurors directly (ask the judge, "*Your Honor, would you please inquire as to whether all the jurors can see?*" or similar).

- If something has to be handed to the jurors to view, do not hand it directly, but give it to the clerk or bailiff to hand to them. Similarly, have one of the court personnel retrieve it.

As a final note, be sure not to talk over the witness. Ask your question, get your answer, ask your next question. If the witness is talking over your, hold your hand up (see Chapter 4.5) to stop them. If that does not work, state *"let me ask my question before you answer, ok?"*. If that doesn't work, and it is hurting your case, ask the judge to admonish the witness to wait for the entire question before answering.

4.9 TAKEAWAYS

- Always lead, always limit. You can almost never ask and open-ended question on cross and keep control of the witness. To control the narrative, you have to ask about one fact at a time.

- Stay calm, stay cool, stay focused. Don't get flapped up by the witness, or opposing counsel, or the judge. You are there to help the jury—they need you to stay composed.

- Always be in-tune with the jury, and sensitive to how the jurors are feeling about the case. Adjust as necessary.

- Don't rush through like a robot—ebb, flow, feel the rhythm of the cross. Don't let the witness set the tempo. If you need to stop and fish, drop anchor.

- Use your eyes, mouth, arms, and body to direct the witness. Add some flair to what you do—no one wants to see a lifeless fish at the podium.

- Memorize your control techniques, practice using them. Pull them out on witnesses who need to be snapped back into line.

- Be careful of your positioning—maximize witness control without making the judge or jury uncomfortable.

• Don't talk over witnesses.

4.10　EXERCISES

Exercise 1:

Find a sparring partner. Think of a topic as in Exercise 1 or 2 in Chapter 1, and come up with a cross examination. Have your witness be a little obstinate, and practice control techniques.

Exercise 2:

Do the exercises in Exercise 1 in an actual courtroom. Use different positions to find what you think is comfortable. Ask your practice cross witness how he or she felt about your positions and movements. Video and review.

Exercise 3:

Try out the gestures in this chapter. What works, and what doesn't. Have your cross examination sparring partner, and others who know you, take a look and comment. Find some willing strangers, and have them watch a mock cross wherein you use control techniques. Have the strangers comment on what they think works for you, and what does not.

Exercise 4:

From a mock trial case file, have an "opposing counsel" join you and your cross sparring partner. Have "opposing counsel" make any and all objections that can be made in good faith. Practice responding, regrouping, and resuming. If you can find a judge, evidence professor, or practicing attorney to "preside" and rule on the objections, that will make the exercise even more effective.

I HAVE NO FURTHER QUESTIONS OF THE WITNESS.

CHAPTER 5
EVIDENTIARY OBJECTIONS

5.1 INTRO TO EVIDENCE, OUR "TECHNICAL MANUAL"

Advocates must always be in control. Control of the witness, opposing counsel, the testimony, and the record.

The evidence code is our technical manual. NASA cannot launch a rocket without a technical manual. Well, perhaps they could launch one, but bringing it back without a technical manual would be an entirely different task. The military uses technical manuals, industry uses technical manuals . . . specialties of every type use technical manuals. Why? Because in every one of these scenarios someone figured out the best way to perform a task and memorialized it.

I find it interesting that we Americans tout the fact that we have the best justice system in the world, bragging with self-effacing admiration that there is nothing better than our jury system. We trial lawyers spend ridiculous time and effort studying jury persuasion and psychology. Yet, we have an evidence code designed like a sieve to carefully filter what evidence we allow the jury to receive. I suppose the reason behind that is that we (or those in charge of "we") can't trust the common sense of the jurors that make the system so great.

Why trial lawyers refuse—or simply fail—to have an intimate understanding of the evidence code is beyond me. It's malpractice. Knowing what the rules of the game are is paramount to winning. Knowing what the rules are is having the ability to stop the opponent in his or her tracks. By overlaying the facts onto the evidence code, and alternatively the evidence code onto the facts, the advocate can begin to shape the opposing witness' testimony before rising to begin the cross.

Some attorneys think that objecting will aggravate the jury, and make the attorney look bad. Courts around the country regularly instruct the jury that it is the job of the attorneys to make objections, and to not hold that against the attorneys:

(1)   There is one more general subject that I want to talk to you about before I begin explaining the elements of the crime charged.

(2)   The lawyers for both sides objected to some of the things that were said or done during the trial. Do not hold that against either side. The lawyers have a duty to object whenever they think that something is not permitted by the rules of evidence. Those rules are designed to make sure that both sides receive a fair trial.

(3)   And do not interpret my rulings on their objections as any indication of how I think the case should be decided. My rulings were based on the rules of evidence, not on how I feel about the case. Remember that your decision must be based only on the evidence that you saw and heard here in court.

United Stated District Court for the Sixth Circuit Pattern Criminal Jury Instructions 1.09 (Lawyers' Objections).

There are rules that control what can be received into evidence. When a lawyer asks a question or offers an exhibit into evidence, and a lawyer on the other side thinks that it is not permitted by the rules of evidence, that lawyer may object. This simply means that the lawyer is requesting that I make a decision on a particular rule of evidence. You should not be influenced by the fact that an objection is made. Objections to questions are not evidence. Lawyers have an obligation to their clients to make objections when they believe that evidence being offered is improper under the rules of evidence.

United States District Court for the District of Rhode Island, Model Civil Jury Instructions for the District Courts of the Third Circuit 1.5 (Preliminary Instructions—Evidence).

Sometimes the attorneys will disagree about the rules for trial procedure when a question is asked of a witness. When that happens, one of the lawyers may make what is called an "objection." The rules for a trial can be complicated, and there are many reasons for attorneys to object. You should simply wait for me to decide how to proceed. If I say that an objection is "sustained," that means the witness may not answer the question. If I say that the objection is "overruled," that means the witness may answer the question.

When there is an objection and I make a decision, you must not assume from that decision that I have any particular opinion other than that the rules for conducting a trial are being correctly followed. If I say a question may not be asked or answered, you must not try to guess what the answer would have been. That is against the rules, too.

Florida Standard Jury Instructions in Civil Cases 202.2 (Explanation of the Trial Procedure).

Florida is serious about making sure lawyers are not themselves put on trial:

Remember, the lawyers are not on trial. Your feelings about them should not influence your decision in this case.

Florida Standard Jury Instructions in Criminal Cases 3.10 (Rules for Deliberation)

So do not be afraid to protect and control. If done appropriately and professionally, the jury will respect you—and in turn, perhaps give you and your story the benefit of the doubt or a second consideration.

The following is a *basic* (and in no way exhaustive) list of objections that must be mastered—what to listen for, when and how to interpose "objection!", the technical legal objection, the rule, and the argument. This has to be advocacy muscle memory. Commit this list to heart. There are 3 main categories of objections: to control counsel, to control the witness, and to control the substance.

As you listen to a direct examination, and are waiting for your cross examination, there are three points where you should be attentive: *to the question asked and who asked it, to the answer, and to the witness who provided the answer.*

**NOTE, there are more objections available for use in opening and closing, such as "misstatement of the law". This section focuses on objections to use during direct and cross.

A concise, accurate, and inexpensive evidentiary objection guide is available from the author through eLEX Legal Publishers LLC at www.eLEXPublishers.com.

OBJECTION GUIDE

Your objection to evidence must be timely and specific. If not, your objection may be waived unless a definitive ruling on the record has been made (Rule 103). Make your objection succinctly and in a clear, firm voice.

EXAMPLES: "Objection, Your Honor, the question calls for hearsay." "Objection, leading." While you generally voice your objection in front of the jury, do not argue your objection in front of the jury. If argument is required, request permission to approach the bench, then present your argument. When the judge sustains your objection you may "move to strike" and request that the judge instruct the jury to disregard the question and/or the

answer. Use the Federal Rules of Evidence to bolster your argument.[1]		
Legal objection	*What to listen for*	*What to argue (if needed)*
5.2 - CONTROLLING THE SUBSTANCE		
Hearsay Sec. A *Also: hearsay within hearsay*	Counsel asks for, or the witness states, something that was SAID out of court. Requires knowledge of the exceptions	Counsel is asking for, or the witness is testifying to, an inadmissible out of court statement
Relevance Sec. B *Also: irrelevant*	The testimony has nothing to do with a material issue	The testimony does not have a tendency to make a fact more or less probable; the testimony has no consequence in determining this action
Authentication Sec. C	Counsel is trying to put in evidence without passing	Counsel has not laid the proper foundation (or

---

Also: lack of authentication; lack of foundation	the most basic test of whether the evidence is what it purports to be	predicate) for the admissibility of this testimony/ evidence
Best Evidence Rule Sec. D	The witness is testifying about a writing, recording, or document without the item (or a permissible copy) being at the trial and available for the jury	The best evidence of the thing the witness is trying to testify about is the thing itself.
Rule of Completeness Sec. E	The evidence is only a part of a writing or recorded statement	Fundamental fairness requires that the entire writing/ recording be presented to this jury for consideration
Privilege Sec. F	The substance is about communications that are privileged under the Construction, a statute, or rule	This testimony/ evidence violates the attorney-client (or other) privilege

5.3 - CONTROLLING THE WITNESS

Narrative Sec. A	Witness is going on and on, beyond the subject of the question asked, and/or adding irrelevant facts or opinions	The witness is simply going on and on, not in response to a proper and specific question
	TYPE 1: Counsel asked question so broad that it will let the witness go on and on (objection would be "calls for a narrative")	**TYPE 1:** Counsel is asking the witness to control the flow of information, which is improper. Counsel should be instructed to ask a series of questions so that the witness does not go on aimlessly, and potentially into inadmissible and perhaps mistrial areas.
	TYPE 2: The question was OK but the witness is rambling on and on	**TYPE 2:** The witness is not responding to questions, but is

		simply talking on and on.
Speculation Sec. B *Also: lacks personal knowledge; improper opinion; call for a conclusion*	Witness does not know the answer or fact asked for, but is clearly just guessing or opining	The witness is not providing a fact in response to a proper question, but it guessing/ opining.
Nonresponsive Sec. C	Question is on point, but answer is on a different point	The witness is not directly answering, or has nor directly answered, the properly asked question
Hearsay Sec. D	Counsel asks for, or the witness states, something that was SAID out of court; requires knowledge of the exceptions	Counsel is asking for, or the witness is testifying to, an inadmissible out of court statement

5.4 - CONTROLLING OPPOSING COUNSEL

Leading Sec. A	Question calls for a yes or no as the answer	Counsel is suggesting the answer in his/her question, which calls for a yes or no instead of being open-ended and asking the witness to provide the facts.
Counsel testifying Sec. B *Also: facts not in evidence*	Opposing counsel is bringing up specific facts in the question, instead of asking "who, what, when, where, why, how" open-ended questions that ask the witness to provide the facts; counsel is the one putting the fact into evidence, not a witness or item of evidence	Counsel is injecting facts into this trial as if he/she were a witness. Counsel should be admonished to simply ask and open-ended question without suggesting facts, so that the witness may do his/her job and provide the facts

Arguing with the Witness Sec. C *Also: "badgering the witness", improper, inflammatory*	**TYPE 1:** Anything that attacks the witness, or comes across overly confrontational; listen for tone of voice and common argumentative statements **TYPE 2:** Making an argument to the jury guised as a question to the witness	**TYPE 1:** Counsel has resorted to arguing with this witness, which is not proper or permissible cross examination **TYPE 2:** Counsel is arguing the ultimate facts to the jury in the form of a question, by asking for a conclusion or opinion that invades the fact-finding province of the jury
Calls for . . . Sec. D • *Conclusion* • *Opinion* • *Hearsay* • *Speculation / opinion* • *Narrative*	Opposing counsel's question asks the witness to do something other than provide an admissible fact	Counsel is asking this witness to do something other than provide an admissible fact, in the form of [conclusion, opinion, etc.]

		Counsel should be instructed to ask a series of questions so that the witness does not go on aimlessly
Improper Sec. E • *Ambiguous* • *Asking witness to comment on another witness' testimony* • *Improper character evidence* • *Bolstering* • *Violation of a pretrial order* • *Improper impeachment (prior statement, prior record, etc.)* • *Antics (sighing, eye-rolling, etc.)*	There are several things opposing counsel can do that are improper; listen for anything that is not asking for a relevant, admissible fact; for this objection, it is advisable to add "may we approach?" or "may I be heard at sidebar" to your contemporaneous legal objection, so you make a proper record Watch for opposing counsel making facial expressions, or getting to close to the witness in an	Counsel is attempting to: • ask a question that can be interpreted different ways, counsel should be more specific • have this witness comment on another witness • place improper and inadmissible character evidence before this jury • bolstering this witness which invades the

• *Injecting personal beliefs* • *"Golden Rule" violation*	intimidating manner Asking the witness to put him-/herself in the place of another witness, victim, the defendant, etc. (the "Golden Rule")	province of the jury • violating a pretrial order regarding ____ • conduct an improper impeachment • acting inappropriately and pandering to the jurors • improperly stating his/her own person beliefs, which are irrelevant • violate the Golden Rule by asking this witness to put him/herself in the place of the victim, etc.
Misstating the Evidence Sec. F *Also: improper characterization;*	A poorly worded question that can lead to the witness misunderstanding the question and potentially giving an innocent, well-	Counsel is misstating the testimony of Mr. Witness, or the facts, and in so is misleading and/or confusing

misleading; confusing	intentioned answer that could lead to an impeachment; the witness does not understand the question but doesn't ask for clarification; counsel is putting his/her own "spin" on the facts	this witness and the jury. I ask that the jury be instructed to disregard that last statement from counsel, and to rely on their own recollection of what the evidence was, and counsel be instructed to not misstate the facts
Beyond the scope Sec. H	On re-direct examination, opposing counsel asking questions about irrelevant issues not addressed on cross examination	The question goes beyond the scope of what was asked on cross examination, and the door has not been opened for this line of questioning
Compound question Sec. I	Listen for compound questions that ask for multiple facts or different	Counsel is asking for two separate factual answers, and in so is misleading

	answers or discussion of different topics	and/or confusing the jury
"You'd agree with Me" or "Isn't It True" Sec. J	Any phrase that essentially asks the witness to agree or concede to opposing counsel's version of the facts	Counsel is attempted to have this witness agree with his or her own personal opinions of this case, which are irrelevant, and this line of questioning is entirely improper
Asked and Answered	The same question over and over, even in slightly various incarnations	Counsel has asked for a fact, and a fact was given. Asking for the same fact over and over is improper, cumulative

5.2 CONTROLLING THE *SUBSTANCE*

Remember—whoever tells the better story, wins. To have the better story, not only do you have to be the better storyteller, you have to have better *substance*. The substance comes from the facts—the substance of what the jury hears and considers comes from *controlling* the substance. The jury will hear both stories, and human nature will cause the jurors to gravitate to the version that has the more believable, more persuasive, more easily understood facts. Substance matters to jurors.

So, when you can control the substance, the better chance you have of controlling the outcome. Plus, if you anticipate a certain cross examination, you do not want the other side to impede your cross by adding in superfluous and irrelevant testimony, or improperly propping up and bolstering the witness' credibility. Controlling that is the essential to your success on cross.

Controlling the substance is done through imposing the right evidentiary objections at the right time. The code mandates that evidence (either testimonial or tangible evidence) has to pass muster—in other words, be relevant, not be hearsay (an out of court statement) or be admissible hearsay with a valid exception, be capable of authentication, be the best evidence of the statement or item, and that it be complete. All counsel have an ethical duty to adhere to court rules (including and especially the rules of evidence). When that doesn't happen, you have the opportunity to shut it down.

A.   HEARSAY

The scope of this book is to give an introduction on the art and skill of cross examination. That, by design, does not attempt to undertake a treatise on what hearsay is, what it isn't, and the many exceptions to hearsay. However, this is a good place to discuss the tactics of making hearsay objections as the cross examiner listening to a direct examination.

Two initial reminders: (1) know the evidence code and interpreting case law, and (2) work through the witnesses and statements *before* trial to anticipate what may be hearsay. *See* Chapter 3.4 (Where are the facts coming from? Discovery!).

The rule. Rule 801 tells you what hearsay is, and what it is not. Every law school graduate should be able to recite in his or her sleep that hearsay is an "out of court statement that goes to the truth of the matter asserted." Rule 802 tells you what is not excluded from trial under the hearsay rule (alternatively stated, what's "exempted" from the rule against hearsay). Rules 803 and 804 tell you what exceptions there are that make certain hearsay statements admissible. These rules, along with rules 805, 806, and 807 create a Gordian Knot of how a particular hearsay statement fits into a particular factual pattern in a trial—and many sleepless nights in preparation for the Bar exam.

Oversimplified analysis: just about anything that was said or stated outside of the courtroom during trial is hearsay if it plays a part in the issues to be decided by the jury. Do not take for granted that you will be able to simply waltz a witness on the stand and have out of court statements come ringing out. Know the rule; find case law that discusses the type of hearsay you are objecting to or defending; be prepared to fully discuss every aspect of the application of the rule and case to your facts.

Finding hearsay. Your pretrial preparation has to include thorough research into the substance of the statements, and into the rules and case law that interpret hearsay. If it is going to come into evidence, you need to know what it is, and have analyzed all the ways it can impact your story.

Remember Chapter 3.4—where are the facts coming from? Just about anywhere. Statements from witnesses, in the form of interviews, investigate reports, depositions, videos, audios . . . just about anything in which someone has given a historical account of an incident, will contain hearsay statements. Remember, Rule 801 defines "statement" as "a person's oral assertion, written assertion, or nonverbal conduct, if the person intended it as an assertion." Do not forget to look at social media posts!

Documents—contracts, memoranda, and the like—can contain hearsay as well. Take a look at all the discovery production to find objectionable hearsay.

Depending on the complexity of the hearsay, consider a pretrial motion in limine and/or a bench brief with case law on the issue. *See* Chapter 3.7 (Motions in Limine).

Making the objection to hearsay. Probably the easiest to recognize, yet surprisingly the most missed objection is hearsay. Relating something in the past—which is what a witness does—is usually a free-flow of information. Lay witnesses are not accustomed to monitoring and editing themselves for out-of-court statements. You as the advocate should not miss them. Remember, the control you exert on direct will shape your themes and topics for cross.

DIRECT:

Q. What happened when you arrived home?

A. I saw my neighbor, Laura, and she said that John Smith had broken down the door and gone inside.

OBJ.   Objection, hearsay.

J.   Sustained.

That's pretty easy.

Be careful with two things: (1) judges of the disposition that "meh, what someone saw is going to come out anyway when they call the witness who really saw it"—in other words, "what's the harm?", (2) and those questions that do not explicitly call for hearsay but let a witness testify as to hearsay indirectly.

As to the former, keep objecting where there is a valid legal objection to be made. You are the advocate, so it is up to *you* what objections to make. You can't control the judge's temperament or decision-making, but you can control making a proper record. *See* Chapter 5.7 (Contemporaneous Objections). Give up making objections, and you give up control.

The latter commonly encountered is when the direct examiner gets out hearsay under the guise of having the witness testify what he or she did in response to the hearsay, without actually stating the hearing. It comes in the form of the jury filling in the missing yet obvious hearsay. Here are some examples:

Q. Officer, how did you become involved in this case?

A. I heard a "be on the lookout" come across the radio.

Q. Based on that, what did you do?

A. I went to Winfield Forest Drive to look for a white van.

Q. What happened next?

A. I saw a white van speeding out of the Winfield Forest subdivision, and I immediately stopped it.

If the homeowner has just testified that she lives in the Winfield Forest subdivision, and she came home to see a white van pulling out of her driveway, and immediately found that her home had been burglarized, and that she placed a call to 911 . . . then everyone can figure out that the hearsay statement contained in the "be on the lookout" was for a white van in that subdivision. Frankly, most jurors could do that *without* the homeowner's testimony—just reading the exchange above you can guess what the hearsay statements of the homeowner and in turn the 911 dispatcher. Did the officer just happen to stop a white van? No. This is difficult and almost impossible to get a sustained hearsay objection on, as there was no actual out of court statement offered.

Similarly:

Q. Mr. Coens, when you walked in the room where your wife and the defendant were, what happened?

A. My wife said that the defendant has just . . .

OBJ. Objection, Your Honor, hearsay.

J. Sustained. Don't say what someone else said.

Q. Without telling us what she said, can you tell us what you did?

A. I walked over to the defendant and punched him in the face.

Of course, the proponent of the wife's statement could try to lay the foundation for the excited utterance exception, but without that, her statement is inadmissible hearsay. Yet even without it, it is not hard to figure out that the wife told the husband that the defendant had just done or said something inappropriate to her. Again—*does this missing hearsay give you a topic for cross examination?—if so, how to get it in??* See Chapter 2.5.G.

To object or not to object? So do you object? Perhaps not—but you may have a topic for cross examination based on the "insinuated" information. It's accurate to say some things are just too trivial to matter. Does the hearsay statement *hurt* your case? Do you want it to come into evidence because it *helps* your case? Does it matter?

Whatever the decision, be sure to make timely objections—*object before the question ends or as the witness is giving the hearsay statement*: "Objection,

Your Honor, hearsay." Have the rule ready, and if it is complicated, case law and maybe even a bench brief. *See* Chapter 5.7 (Contemporaneous Objections).

If the issue is complicated and obvious (meaning not something you think your opponent has missed), consider a motion *in limine* to have a meaningful motion, hearing, and argument. See Chapter 3.7 (Motions in Limine).

A final reminder. *Listen.* You must listen to the direct examination and react. You cannot be caught up in your notes, or looking through transcripts, or daydreaming. *See* Chapter 1.7.B (The Cross Examiner's Job During Direct). If you hear anything that sounds like an attempt to elicit hearsay, or a witness about to make a hearsay statement, be on your feet and *object.* It's better to object, and withdraw it, than to miss it altogether.

B.   RELEVANCE

The rule. Relevance objections seem to be in the eye of the beholder—very subjectively applied by most judges. *See* Chapter 9.1.D (Other Common Issues).

Federal Rule of Evidence 401:

Evidence is relevant if:

(a) it has any tendency to make a fact more or less probable than it would be without the evidence; and

(b) the fact is of consequence in determining the action.

Making the objection to relevance. In the following example, the case at trial is a shareholder dispute, where Plaintiff is suing Defendant for falsely inflating the value of the stock.

DIRECT:

Q. Did you buy stock in a company?

A. I did—I bought 1000 shares of stock in WidgetCo.

Q. Why did you purchase stock in that particular company?

A. Well, I have used those products for years, and find them so great that I wanted to invest in the company.

Q. What other products did you use besides those of Widget Co?

A. We used Clean and Gleam, as well as SoapySoap.

Q. Which one smelled the best?

OBJ. Objection, Your Honor, relevance (or irrelevant).

That's overly simple, but it explains the objection. There is nothing about other product use that goes to proving a material fact in dispute. The objection becomes more complicated when the fact in dispute is more difficult to prove, or perhaps emotional. Consider this example, in a sexual battery prosecution:

DIRECT:

Q. Miss Witness, how did this attack impact your family?

OBJ. Your Honor, respectfully, I must object to relevance.

Due to the sensitive witness on the stand, the tone of the objection changes just a little—you don't want to appear to be insensitive to the victim of such a horrendous crime, even if you are representing the accused. The testimony may be relevant for sentencing, but not for deciding guilt or innocence.

As you listen to direct and prepare for cross, controlling and limiting the substance will allow the jury to focus only on what is important. You can keep out the fluff—they will thank you for doing that, and also have fresher memories about what was actually said about the important facts.

C.   AUTHENTICATION

One of the main substantive considerations with tangible evidence is making sure it is what it is, and that it can be authenticated. You may need or want to cross examine on a document or other item of evidence, and not object to any lack of authentication. Otherwise, you may be able to keep evidence out of the purvey of the jury by objecting—and again, control the flow of information on direct.

The rule. As is usual, knowing the rule is the start of being able to become the keeper the evidentiary gateway:

Rule 901. Authenticating or Identifying Evidence

(a)   In General. To satisfy the requirement of authenticating or identifying an item of evidence, the proponent must produce evidence sufficient to support a finding that the item is what the proponent claims it is.

(b)   Examples. The following are examples only—not a complete list—of evidence that satisfies the requirement:

(1)   *Testimony of a Witness with Knowledge.* Testimony that an item is what it is claimed to be.

(2)   *Nonexpert Opinion About Handwriting.* A nonexpert's opinion that handwriting is genuine, based on a familiarity with it that was not acquired for the current litigation.

(3)   *Comparison by an Expert Witness or the Trier of Fact.* A comparison with an authenticated specimen by an expert witness or the trier of fact.

(4)   *Distinctive Characteristics and the Like.* The appearance, contents, substance, internal patterns, or other distinctive characteristics of the item, taken together with all the circumstances.

(5)   *Opinion About a Voice.* An opinion identifying a person's voice—whether heard firsthand or through mechanical or electronic transmission or recording—based on hearing the voice at any time under circumstances that connect it with the alleged speaker.

(6) *Evidence About a Telephone Conversation.* For a telephone conversation, evidence that a call was made to the number assigned at the time to:

(A) a particular person, if circumstances, including self-identification, show that the person answering was the one called; or

(B) a particular business, if the call was made to a business and the call related to business reasonably transacted over the telephone.

(7) *Evidence About Public Records.* Evidence that:

(A) a document was recorded or filed in a public office as authorized by law; or

(B) a purported public record or statement is from the office where items of this kind are kept.

(8) *Evidence About Ancient Documents or Data Compilations.* For a document or data compilation, evidence that it:

(A) is in a condition that creates no suspicion about its authenticity;

(B) was in a place where, if authentic, it would likely be; and

(C) is at least 20 years old when offered.

(9) *Evidence About a Process or System.* Evidence describing a process or system and showing that it produces an accurate result.

(10) *Methods Provided by a Statute or Rule.* Any method of authentication or identification allowed

by a federal statute or a rule prescribed by the Supreme Court.

Making the objection to a lack of authentication. Make a timely objection (usually when the item is being offered into evidence): "Objection, Your Honor, authentication" (or "lack of authentication", or "lack of foundation").

- The best tactic is to simply state the objection—nothing more. If the judge is paying attention, the objection will be sustained. You will not have tipped off opposing counsel as to the deficiency in the foundation and not given the other side a chance to correct the error. The item is not in evidence.

- If the judge overrules you, and is about to admit the evidence, ask to approach. If the judge refuses your request, readdress it at the next available time court is outside the presence of the jury to perfect your argument for appeal.

- If you get to argue the objection at the bench, cite the evidentiary rule and simply state that the foundation has not been laid. Try not to tip the other side off. If the judge pushes you, then you have to reveal it. Either way, your objection is preserved, or you have at least controlled the flow of evidence.

Attack on direct. It may be too late to attack authentication once you begin your cross—once an item of evidence has been entered into the record, judges will be reluctant to remove or exclude it. Plus, the jury has already seen or heard about the evidence, and one cannot "unring a bell".

If there is a question about the authentication (say, a witness is not sure about making a document, or that an item "is what it is"), then attack the witness' credibility on cross. Make the uncertainty a target fact, and design a question set that leads to establishing the target fact that the evidence and witness are simply to unsure to be believed.

Attack on cross examination. While the legal standards for authentication may be met and the item admitted, you can still explore all of the authentication issues on cross examination.

Q. You were not there when this item was made/created/found/recorded/etc.?

Q. You have no idea who made/created/found/recorded/etc. this item?

Q. You have never received a letter or note from the writer?

Q. You have only ever seen the writer's handwriting once before this?

Q. You never spoke with the speaker in the audio/video?

Q. You can't pick the speaker's voice out of a line up, could you?

And so on. Think in 3D (*see* Chapter 1.6, "3D Cross Examination), and think of all the reasons the witness is not attached to the item. Then create topics that lead to the target fact that the item may not actually be what it is, or that the witness has no knowledge of it, or it is not as important to the other side as your opponent wants the jury to believe.

D.   BEST EVIDENCE RULE

The rule. The best evidence of what is contained in a document, or photograph, or video or recording, *is the thing itself*. The contents are the substance and the fact or facts. The witness should not be able to get on the stand and talk about what something depicted or contained—it's hearsay (or in the case of a photograph, "seesay", to coin a term) and improper.

In today's highly technical world, people are connected to technology in ways never imagined. As discussed in Chapter 3.4 ("Where Are The Facts Coming From? Discovery!), this is the technology age, and the courts know it. The digital world most folks live in can be captured and brought to court. Trials in this era are beginning to have almost as much documentary evidence as testimonial evidence. Think of all the things you have in your cell phone— which the United States Supreme Court has said is a misnomer:

> The term "cell phone" is itself misleading shorthand; many of these devices are in fact minicomputers that also happen to have the capacity to be used as a telephone. They could just as easily be called cameras, video players, rolodexes, calendars, tape recorders, libraries, diaries, albums, televisions, maps, or newspapers.

Riley v. California, 134 S.Ct. 2473, 2849 (2014).

That is in addition to all the traditional items of evidence, such as lab and medical reports, and the like.

Take a look at the rule:

Rule 1002. Requirement of the Original

An original writing, recording, or photograph is required in order to prove its content unless these rules or a federal statute provides otherwise.

Making the objection with the Best Evidence Rule. "Objection, Your Honor, Best Evidence" or "Best Evidence Rule." See the example below for what can happen when you make the objection.

Example. Remember, if the witness *sees* the thing or event, the witness can relate what he or she saw.

Q. Mr. Witness, were you present when the accident happened?

A. Yes, I was on my bicycle with my GoPro camera, recording my ride.

Q. Did you see the accident as it happened?

A. I did.

Q. Do you know if the GoPro captured the accident?

A. I do, and it did.

Q. Thank you, that was going to be my next question.

Now, the questioning can go one of three ways, without objection: (1) the witness can either testify as to what he saw, or (2) he can be used to lay the foundation for the admission of the recording into evidence, or (3) both—he can testify as to what he saw, then the video can be played for the jury. What *cannot* happen, is this:

> Q. *Mr. Witness, were you present when the accident happened?*
>
> A. *Yes, I was on my bicycle with my GoPro camera, recording my ride.*
>
> Q. *Do you know if the GoPro captured the accident?*
>
> A. *I do, and it did.*
>
> Q. *Please tell us what is on the GoPro video?*
>
> *or*
>
> Q. *What does the GoPro recording show?*
>
> OBJ. *Objection, Your Honor, Best Evidence Rule.*

The best evidence of the recording is the recording. Alternatively stated, the best evidence of what the recording depicts, is gleaned by watching the recording. Similarly, a photo speaks for itself. The witness can describe the scene, or lay the foundation for the admission of the photograph—but he or she cannot describe the contents of the photo. "The best-evidence [sic] rule does not apply to testimony relating to the *existence* of a document, as opposed to its contents." *United States v. Iverson*, 818 F.3d 1015, 1023 (10th Cir. 2016) (emphasis in original).

**NOTE, duplicates are sometimes acceptable: "[a] duplicate original or originally executed copy of a written instrument is generally considered to be an original within the meaning of the best evidence rule; and appellee testified that his original copy was missing and could not be found after a diligent search. The primary reason the original of a writing is preferred to a copy is that the copy is always subject to errors on the part of the copyist. *See* 4 Wigmore, Evidence § 1179 (3d ed. 1940)." *Sauget v. Johnston,* 315 F.2d 816, 181 (9th Cir. 2963).

Using the Best Evidence Rule when defending a direct and preparing to cross. The Best Evidence Rule is a great control tool to make sure the witness does not elaborate or make an item of evidence be or depict more than it really is, or embellish. One tactic is to shut the witness down completely, using the objection to prohibit any "free styling". Another tactic is to let the witness embellish, then cross examine on the actual item *using* the actual item (*see* Chapter 8.2.C, "The Cross", where I used the video to impeach an embellishing witness).

When original is not available. Rules 1001 through 1008 deal with originals, copies, and summaries, as well as who makes the determination as to certain aspects of admissibility and authenticity. If the original is not available, that is a topic and potential target fact that you can explore on cross. *See* Chapter 8.6 (Cross Examination of a Law Enforcement Officer in a Criminal Case), where I cross examined an officer about why a video was no longer available for the jury. It goes to the credibility of the witness—if something is important enough to be mentioned in a trial, it is certainly important enough to merit care in preserving and maintaining it. *Why* it is not available is a very important issue for the jury to consider.

E. RULE OF COMPLETENESS

The rule. Subject to mistrial implications, the whole of any document or statement has to be admitted if any part is admitted. This is the Rule of Completeness:

Rule 106. Remainder of or Related Writings or Recorded Statements

If a party introduces all or part of a writing or recorded statement, an adverse party may require the introduction, at that time, of any other part— or any other writing or recorded statement—that in fairness ought to be considered at the same time.

The Rule of Completeness applies to *written* statements via Rule 106, and to *oral* statements through Rule 611(a) ("The court should exercise reasonable control over the mode and order of examining witnesses and presenting evidence so as to: (1) make those procedures effective for determining the truth; (2) avoid wasting time; and (3) protect witnesses from harassment or undue embarrassment.) *See United States v. Pacquette*, 557 F. App'x 933 (11th Cir. 2014).

Controlling the substance of the evidence by using the Rule of Completeness requires the advocate to actually *know* all of the substance of the evidence. Too many times attorneys miss a critical addition to a statement by not having read and closely studied the source of the statement.

Making the objection. "Objection, Your Honor, Rule of Completeness."

Example. Consider a breach of contract action where the contract is not available:

Q. Mr. Witness, what were the terms of the contract?

A. Well, my company was to receive payment in the amount of $100,000.

Q. Did the other company pay that amount?

A. Yes, it did.

Q. Let's move on to . . .

OBJ. Objection, Your Honor—Rule of Completeness.

J. What is missing?

A. The witness has described the performance of the plaintiff, but has not described the obligations of his own company. The contract has an offer and acceptance, and requires performance by both sides. So, to be complete, this witness should also testify as to his company's obligations and its performance, or lack thereof.

J. Sustained. Counsel, please make sure you discuss the entire contract.

In this over-simplified example, opposing counsel was trying to skirt the issue of the breach of contract by the witness' company. Ask to approach if necessary, or if the judge overrules you. Have the document handy, and be sure to point the court and opposing counsel to the appropriate spot in the statement. Be careful to make a record as to the missing part of the statement, and proffer the document (see below). And, be sure to point out the prejudice to your client in only part of the story being told.

If the entirety of the statement is not admitted on direct, clarify with the court as to your ability to address it on cross. Most judges will permit this, as an impeachment by omission. If that is not permitted, be sure to proffer a complete copy of the statement so that the appellate court has access to it.

F.   PRIVILEGE

The rule. Federal Rule of Evidence 501 states:

Rule 501.   Privilege in General

The common law—as interpreted by United States courts in the light of reason and experience—governs a claim of privilege unless any of the following provides otherwise:

> the United States Constitution; a federal statute; or rules prescribed by the Supreme Court.

But in a civil case, state law governs privilege regarding a claim or defense for which state law supplies the rule of decision.

Rule 502 pertains to the attorney-client privilege and work-product protections. Otherwise, the available privileges come from the common law in the state where the trial is held. Many of the states have adopted specific privileges. To be sure, the way Rule 501 is written makes it a complicated issue, but the most notable privileges that *may be available* based on the venue of the trial are:

- Marital (husband-wife) privilege

- Informants

- Physician-patient

- Accountant-client

- Clergy (priest-penitent)

- Journalist/reporter

- Psychotherapist

- Protecting political votes

- Trade secrets

- Secrets of state and other official information

**NOTE: Be very careful to research the evidence code in your jurisdiction as to what privileges may apply.

Making the objection to a privilege. "Objection, Your Honor, privilege." Going beyond that is probably a speaking objection, but if asked by the judge, simply state "attorney/client" or "pastor/penitent" or "clergy" or "husband/wife"—whatever it may be. You may want to ask to approach the bench or for a sidebar to further explain. Of course, this is best handed by a pretrial motion in limine. Don't forget the Fifth Amendment right against self-incrimination when thinking about protected statements.

Example. The following example is just one (that of the clergy) of the several privileges recognized under the common law.

Q. Reverend Witness, when is the last time you saw the defendant?

A. Before his arrest, he came to the church and asked me to meet with him in the sanctuary.

Q. And when you met with the defendant, what was his demeanor?

A. He seemed very upset.

Q. Did he tell you why he was upset?

OBJ.   Objection, Your Honor, privilege.

J.   Approach the bench.

[AT SIDEBAR]

J.   Why is this privileged?

Q. I believe Reverend Witness will say that Mr. Defendant was there to confess that he had just murdered his co-worker, and wanted forgiveness and spiritual guidance. It was made completely within the relationship for the pastor and penitent, and is protected by the common law privilege and Rule 501.

J. Sustained.

5.3 CONTROLLING THE *WITNESS*

Recall Chapter 1.7.B ("The cross examiner's job during direct"). You can't just sit there while the witness takes over the show and starts being the main storyteller. I believe that jurors fully expect lawyers to defend their clients and not sit like a bump on a log.

Controlling the witness takes on two dimensions. First, you have to try to control the substance of what the witness is saying (as discussed in 5.2). Second, you have to control *how* the witness presents the story. Controlling the "how" comes in the form of fighting a witness' attempts to talk about what someone else said, speculating about things the witness did not witness, and just sitting there and rambling away.

You will find two types of witnesses: those that innocently violate the rules, and those that intentionally violate them. Lay witnesses are not skilled in the rules of trial combat, so they tend to run afoul of them but immediately back off. There are those that are of the personality that they will just run wild in any setting. Those witnesses are easier to snap back into place.

The intentional violators are the seasoned witnesses—law enforcement and experts. They know when to take the direct question and run with it, and they know how to sneak in an inadmissible statement here and there. And they do it. You have to be prepared to fight that witness and corral him or her back into submission.

A. NARRATIVE

The rule. Rule 611(a) is the catchall rule and authority for the judge to manage the trial, including how a witness testifies. The advisory committee notes tell us that the court's authority includes "such concerns as whether testimony shall be in the form of a free *narrative* or responses to specific questions."

One court had to deal with a *pro se* defendant taking the stand and attempting his own direct examination. The problem that was created, and trial court's solution, is applicable to any narrative situation:

[The defendant will] have to ask himself a question and then answer the question, and the reason for that is the evidence is presented in a question-and-answer format. It allows the opposing party to object to the question because it may be an improper thing for the jury's consideration—you've seen that throughout this trial—so obviously the defendant is not allowed to do any different from any other witness. He can't just get up on the witness stand or where he is now and make a narrative statement to you—he can't do that. So it may be a little awkward, but we'll get through it.

United States v. Beckton, 740 F.3d 303, 306 (4th Cir. 2014) (applying the abuse of discretion standard to trial management matters, and affirming the conviction).

Making the objection to narrative. Remember that direct is the time when the questioner asks an open-ended question, and the witness responds with a factual statement. When a witness goes on a long, un-directed diatribe, it's a "narrative" and objectionable response. This objection can be interposed nicely, or in a non-aggressive manner, to politely remind the witness that he or she must listen for a question, then give a direct answer. You have to be really vigilant and intuitive to know when the witness is "going rogue" and jump in with the objection at the right time.

Example. Believe it or not, this can happen:

Q. Mr. Witness, please introduce yourself to the jury by stating your name.

A. Hello, my name is John Doe, and I am the victim in this case because Mr. Defendant is a so-and-so who has continually harassed me and threatened my family for the last five years, even following me to work where I am a master postman with twenty-five years of service and where I am respected and have received several commendations and this is impacting my retirement as I want to move to Montana and raise chicken because I love to eat fricassee and Buffalo wings, which I can't really do as much anymore as I am on a diet—I've lost about thirty pounds . . . but, yeah, I'm John Doe.

In the example above, the "objection, Your Honor, narrative" should come after the word "victim."

Expert witnesses and narratives. Highly technical testimony is not "Q&A friendly", and often impossible to accomplish in the usual flow of questioning for direct examination. So while you may impose a narrative objection during this type of expert testimony, the judge will likely use his or her discretion and allow it. This could be one of those times you don't make the objection, and just prepare normally for the upcoming expert cross examination.

B.   SPECULATION

The rule. The Federal Evidence Code (and in turn, most states) require that the witness have the ability to testify to something about which they know:

Rule 601.   Competency to Testify in General

Every person is competent to be a witness unless these rules provide otherwise. But in a civil case, state law governs the witness's competency regarding a claim or defense for which state law supplies the rule of decision.

This is most commonly applied to someone who has no knowledge about a topic or subject and *per se* is not competent to testify to it, and is therefore merely speculating.

Sometimes the question itself calls for speculation—such a question is usually found in asking someone to opine as to why something happened or someone did something.

Making the objection to speculation. "Objection, Your Honor, speculation." As with all objections, whether to make it depends on the topic and its impact on your case. You can also use "Objection, Your Honor, lacks personal knowledge", or "improper opinion" or "calls for a conclusion." Remember, most judges prefer the "formal" legal objection and not what could be considered a speaking objection.

Some judges will not sustain your objection, but give the witness the easy out by turning and asking the witness, "if you know, you can answer." The witness then states, "I don't know" and that is that.

Remember, if the witness is allowed to pontificate beyond his or her personal knowledge, you must cross examine on that lack of personal knowledge. If goes directly to the witness' credibility.

Example. First, an example of someone who has no knowledge of the fact:

Q.   What time did the police arrive at your house?

A.   Well, I was not home yet, so I would have to guess it was around . . .

OBJ.   Objection, Your Honor, speculation.

J.   Sustained. Please only answer if you actually know the fact.

A question that is poorly designed and inappropriately asks the witness to "fill in the blanks":

Q. Why do you think Mr. Defendant signed the contract two weeks late?

"Why do you think" implies that the person does not know, but is going to guess. Guesses, even educated guesses, are not permitted.

C.   NONRESPONSIVE

**NOTE: This is an objection that you can use on direct *as well as on cross examination*—you can use it to control the witness on direct *and* on cross. It forces the witness to answer a properly asked question.

The rule. Some answers simply do not answer the question that was asked. As we know, Rule 611 mandates that the trial judge should exercise reasonable control over the mode and order of examining witnesses and presenting evidence. . ." and the rule covers "such as concerns as whether testimony shall be in the form of a free narrative or responses to specific questions . . ." Rule 611; *see also* Notes of Advisory Committee on Proposed Rules, Subdivision (a).

The traditional view of the "nonresponsive" objection is that only the advocate asking the question can use it. As stated above, I disagree. As discussed in Chapter 1.7.B, your job on cross begins during direct. You have to control the witness and protect your case and your client.

That you can use the objection as the opposing party to a direct (i.e. the cross examiner listening to the direct) is based on case authority. The main reason is to prevent the witness from blurting out prejudicial statements against your client. For example, in *Brooks v. State*, 868 So. 2d 643, 644 (Fla. Dist. Ct. App. 2004), the victim of a crime was asked by the prosecutor (on re-direct) about a prior domestic violence incident between her and the defendant, where she shot the defendant:

> Q. *Did the police investigate this?*
>
> A. *Yes. I was never arrested, never had a mug shot taken, never fingerprinted. I had to give a statement, and the police brought me back home.*
>
> Q. *Okay. Did the defendant get charged in that case?*
>
> A. *A few months later, he was sent back to prison.*

Brooks' own defense attorney promptly made an objection to the nonresponsive answer, and moved for a mistrial. The appellate court held that the answer was in fact a nonresponsive answer to the prosecutor's redirect question, and reversed the conviction because it was improper and unduly prejudicial.

Making the objection to a nonresponsive answer. "Objection, Your Honor, nonresponsive." You may also want to ask at a sidebar to identify why the answer is inadmissible (irrelevant, prejudicial, etc.). You may also ask for the witness to be admonished to listen to and directly answer the *specific* question asked.

Be sure to prepare your own witness to prevent this from happening and your own witnesses looking bad. See Chapter 3.8 (Preparing your own witness for cross).

Examples. There are a couple of situations you must be wary of—some on direct, and some on cross.

The basic nonresponsive answer:

Q. On what date did you meet Mr. Defendant?

A. On the worst day of my life, when everything I ever worked for began to spiral down the drain and he ruined my life.

That is entirely improper, not responsive to the question ("on what *date*"), and the witness must be corrected.

Consider this nonresponsive answer:

Q. What did the defendant tell you about the missing jewelry?

A. He said he took it—which I already knew because he had just gotten out of prison for grand theft when he moved in next door.

Oops. There is not a lot you can do to fix that statement on cross. A mistrial is probably in order.

Granted, some nonresponsive answers are mistakes and unintentional. However, those loaded against your client are telling. Those substantive, material nonresponsive answers can present one of two problems:

- The first is in the form of a witness who wants to be the center of the show, provide more information than being asked, editorialize, taint the jury, and generally say as many hurtful things as possible (the "obstreperous witness").

- The second is in the form of critically damaging information getting before the jury . . . and causing a mistrial

The obstreperous witness. When dealing with the obstreperous witness, you have to take control immediately. Lodge and continue to lodge objections: "Objection, Your Honor, nonresponsive." The judge may or may not sustain on the first one, depending on what the nonresponsive statement was, and its potential impact. If it continues, object and ask to approach. Ask the court to remove the jury and admonish the witness. Most judges will during this time take control of the witness and stop the nonsense.

If none of these things work, prepare for a hostile cross (*see* Chapter 4.2.B, "Obstinate witness") and to use your control tools (*see* Chapter 4.6, "Tools to Control "Those" Witnesses—We've All Seen Them).

Motion to strike, disregard damaging information. If the statement is from an obstreperous witness but the substance is not that bad, consider letting it go. Observe the jury—do the jurors think the witness is credible, or being a jerk?

If necessary, when at the bench, ask the court for an immediate instruction to the jury that it disregard the previous statement and not consider it in deliberations. That adds a little more authority to your control of the witness.

Motion for mistrial. If the information is fatal to your ability to have a fair trial, then you must move for a mistrial. You must to it timely— contemporaneously to the objectionable statement. *See* Chapter 9.1.C (Mistrial Standards).

D.   HEARSAY (AND PRIOR INCONSISTENT STATEMENTS)

As discussed in Section 5.2.1, above, hearsay is pervasive in every trial. Lay witnesses are not accustomed to editing themselves to not repeat "out of court statements." And forget trying to have a lay witness explain "the truth of the matter asserted" or anything close to a hearsay exception.

When controlling witnesses on direct in preparation for cross examination, be sure to consider the following points:

- Is the hearsay statement intended as an "assertion"?

- Do you need the hearsay statement in order to cross examine?

- Keep objecting until the witness or opposing counsel get it

- If harmful, be sure to ask to strike the hearsay, the question calling for hearsay, the

for a curative instruction to the jury to disregard the hearsay

Witness' hearsay as point of impeaching credibility. Don't forget that controlling the witness includes attacks on the witness' credibility. Prior inconsistent statements are a huge issue when impeaching a witness. Thus, you may want some hearsay to come out so that you can compare it to other, inconsistent statements during your cross examination (see Chapter 2.5.E).

Here are the witness-related hearsay rules regarding impeachment with prior inconsistent statements:

Rule 806. Attacking and Supporting the Declarant

When a hearsay statement—or a statement described in Rule 801(d)(2)(C), (D), or (E)—has been admitted in evidence, the declarant's credibility may be attacked, and then supported, by any evidence that would be admissible for those purposes if the declarant had testified as a witness. The court may admit evidence of the declarant's inconsistent statement or conduct, regardless of when it occurred or whether the declarant had an opportunity to explain or deny it. If the party against whom the statement was admitted calls the declarant as a witness, the party may examine the declarant on the statement as if on cross-examination.

* * *

Rule 801. Definitions that Apply to This Article; Exclusions from Hearsay

. . .

(d) Statements That Are Not Hearsay. A statement that meets the following conditions is not hearsay:

(1) A Declarant-Witness's Prior Statement. The declarant testifies and is subject to cross-examination about a prior statement, and the statement:

(A) is inconsistent with the declarant's testimony and was given under penalty of perjury at a trial, hearing, or other proceeding or in a deposition;

(B) is consistent with the declarant's testimony and is offered:

(i)   to rebut an express or implied charge that the declarant recently fabricated it or acted from a recent improper influence or motive in so testifying; or

(ii) to rehabilitate the declarant's credibility as a witness when attacked on another ground; or

(C) identifies a person as someone the declarant perceived earlier.

5.4   CONTROLLING OPPOSING COUNSEL

Controlling the substance of what comes out in court is critical, and a great part of accomplishing that control is making sure opposing counsel sticks to the rules in questioning on direct.

To control opposing counsel, you must listen carefully to the questions and be ready to object at the exact moment the question is finished but *before* the witness has a chance to answer it. The timing is important, as the judge cannot rule on the question until it is formed. Premature objections will draw an admonition from the judge to let counsel finish the question. For instance:

Q. Ms. Witness, as you were in your yard, what did your neighbor—?

OBJ. Objection, Your Honor, calls for hearsay.

J. Well, let me hear the question first.

You have not only highlighted the testimony, you have lost the objection you likely would have won had it been a hearsay question (thus either confusing the jury or simply having them think you are incompetent), and opposing counsel gets another stab at getting out the hearsay statement. This is assuming, of course, that the statement is in fact hearsay and there is no valid exception under the rules.

Otherwise, get your timing down by being on your toes:

Q. Ms. Witness, as you were in your yard, what did your neighbor say to you about the prior owners of the property?

OBJ. Objection, Your Honor, calls for hearsay.

J. Sustained.

The witness has no time to answer before your valid objection is interposed. You have stopped your opponent's attempt to circumvent the rules.

In the event you miss the objection, and the hearsay comes out, as discussed above in Section 5.3.4, interject over the witness. Try to cut it off. If all of the hearsay comes out before you can make the objection, and your objection is sustained, consider asking for a curative instruction to disregard, to strike the hearsay, and an admonishment to the witness not to do that again. As always, keep objecting.

As with all objections during direct, if you hear something that is objectionable, think about whether to object or to let it in—but have a valid reason for not fighting the objectionable testimony or tangible evidence. Perhaps you want to set up an impeachment on cross, or perhaps the objectionable evidence *helps* your case. But whatever it is, do not simply miss your opportunity to object. Remember, you know you're themes, topics, and targets long before trial starts. You have plenty of time to anticipate the direct questions and what the other side may try to get before the jury. So, be wise and be vigilant.

A. LEADING

Probably the most prolific violation opposing counsel will commit is leading. This is especially true if opposing counsel is unprepared, has not prepared the witness, or is simply not skilled or experienced.

The rule. "Leading questions should not be used on direct examination except as necessary to develop the witness's testimony. Rule 611(c). The notes of the Advisory Committee explain what "develop the witness's testimony" contemplates:

> The rule continues the traditional view that the suggestive powers of the leading question are as a general proposition undesirable. Within this tradition, however, numerous exceptions have achieved recognition: The witness who is hostile, unwilling, or biased; the child witness or the adult with communication problems; the witness whose recollection is exhausted; and undisputed preliminary matters.

So that means that there are some leading questions that are not harmful—those that lead the witness through some biographical or background information, or simple transition questions. Opposing counsel may be trying to control a hostile or a "bucking bronco witness", perhaps to avoid a mistrial—you should recognize this, and give him or her some latitude. Objecting in those situations is not necessary and could ingratiate you to the jury. Remember, jurors are not stupid and they know what is going on—you do not want to be considered an obstructionist.

But when counsel is simply unprepared or has not prepared the witness, and is leading as to substantive matters, then correction must be imposed. You have an obligation to represent your client—not to passively watch as opposing counsel wanders as a "tipsy coachman" into proving his or her case when you could have shut it down.

Example.

ON DIRECT:

Q. The defendant touched your vagina, right?

A. Yes.

Q. And he touched inside your vagina, right?

OBJ. Objection, Your Honor, leading.

J. Sustained.

I did not chose this example to be intentionally graphic. I chose it because in most states, there is a difference between sexual contact and sexual penetration. The prosecutor has led the victim into the contact crime; he was attempting to lead the witness into the penetration crime. The reason for the objection is that on an open-ended question, the witness may not have testified as to penetration. The difference could equate to years in prison.

B.   COUNSEL TESTIFYING

Remember that what the advocates say is not evidence. Consider [Pattern Jury Instruction B4 11th Circuit]:

> As I said before, you must consider only the evidence that I have admitted in the case. Evidence includes the testimony of witnesses and the exhibits admitted. But, anything the lawyers say is not evidence and isn't binding on you.

The law of the case, so to speak, is that what the lawyers say is not evidence. So when an attorney injects a fact into the case, *that fact is not evidence.* Thus, the jury cannot consider it—legally. But how does one un-ring a bell? Once the fact is stated in court and planted in the mind of the jury, can a lay jury really isolate it and omit it from consideration of the facts properly admitted into the record? What if that fact is an essential and material part of the case?

You must be ready to counter the improper flow of facts. If on direct your opposing counsel states a fact that has not come from any witness, then the objection is "counsel testifying."

Example, of the testimony of the first witness at a trial:

Q. Please tell the jury your name.

A. Willie Witness.

Q. Mr. Witness, when you worked at WillieWorld, what was your job?

OBJ. Objection, Your Honor, counsel is testifying.

The testimony is in the form of where Willie worked—the attorney supplied that fact, not the witness. The proper question would have been, "were you working on June 6, 201x?" and then after an affirmative answer, "where were you working?" The answer from the witness: "WillieWorld." We have arrived at the fact from the proper source.

This example is, like most in this book, a simplistic one. Opponents will sneak in a fact when (1) the witness is having trouble relaying the facts at trial, or (2) the attorney knows that if the fact comes from the witness there could be an issue with perjury. *Neither are valid ethical reasons for counsel testifying.*

If the point is immaterial or simply biographical, one may consider not making the objection and letting the trial progress. However, you can control your opponent by forcing him or her to stick to open-ended questions and making the witness provide the facts. You will know the time and situation in which to do this.

C.   ARGUMENT, HARASSING

Many cross examinations turn into an arguing session. That is because they are not carefully planned, the advocate does not have any control, and because the counsel does not protect his or her own witness.

These objections is really designed to be used by the direct examiner during cross examination for the direct examiner's own witness. Just like the job of the cross examiner does not start on cross (but rather while listening to direct), the direct examiner's job does not end when the cross starts.

In defending the witness from the cross examiner, the advocate must listen for certain key terms, or behavior.

Argumentative. There are two times that the "argumentative" objection can be used. First, when the cross examination has devolved into an actual argument, back-and-forth between lawyer and witness. For example,

- No, you didn't.

- That's not correct.

- You're wrong.

- Stop trying to avoid the answer.

- I'm not going to let you get off so easily, so answer me.

- You don't like me, do you?

- Why are you lying?

Second, remember that the question can be argumentative in and of itself—even when asked in the most professional and non-aggressive way. This happens when the question is making legal argument, instead of presenting a fact to the witness to confirm or deny. For example:

- In a DUI case: Mr. Witness, the defendant was legally under the influence?

- In a fraud case: Mr. Witness, the defendant intended to cheat you out of money?

- In an injury case: Mr. Witness, the defendant was driving negligently that day?

The distinction can be found in the concept that the question pertains to an essential element of a claim or defense, and is asking the witness to either opine or substitute his or her judgment for that of the jury.

Such a question takes the ultimate issue out of the province of the jury.

Harassing the witness. Yelling, eye-rolling, getting to close to the witness, laughing at the witness' answers, and other such actions are improper and designed solely to bully a witness. Harassing a witness for the sake of trying to intimidate the witness for opposing your case or your client is patently unprofessional. Harassment can come in the form of trying to confuse a witness on a point that is otherwise clear and not subject to impeachment. It can be in the form of asking irrelevant and embarrassing questions, designed solely to hurt the witness' psyche or reputation— again, for no relevant and admissible point of legal impeachment. It can come in the form of simply being obnoxious and rude. All are improper. If you use the tools and techniques in this book, you do not need to resort to schoolyard bullying to try to sink a witness.

If the questions serve no legitimate purpose, and could (or are) causing emotional distress to the witness, it is harassment.

Some jurisdictions refer to this as "badgering the witness"—whatever you call it, you must defend your witness. If you don't, the jury will wonder why.

D.   CALLS FOR . . .

A very effective way to shut down the advocate *and* the witness at the same time is to perfectly time an objection to a question that asks the witness to do something inappropriate. The most frequent violations come in the form of asking the witness to speculate or provide hearsay. Both are prohibited, and the advocate should know that. Whether the question is intentional or inadvertent, objecting can prevent the answer.

And, objecting controls the flow of information, and the narrative of the case.

For example, if the question calls for hearsay and there is no exception that would permit its admission, shut it down. Why wait until the hearsay statement is out there and then make a straight hearsay objection? It should be handled like this:

Q. Mr. Witness, what did the lady next door say to you?

OBJ.   Objection, Your Honor, calls for hearsay.

J. Sustained.

Similarly, if someone lacks personal knowledge of a situation, that person cannot be allowed to simply opine as to what may or may not have happened. In this example, assuming that in deposition it was discovered that Ms. Witness did not have direct personal knowledge of the source of funds used in a transaction, but knew the defendant's parents were wealthy and may have given the defendant the funds:

Q. Ms. Witness, do you know where the money came from that Mr. Defendant used to purchase the car?

OBJ. Objection,   Your   Honor,   calls   for speculation.

J. Sustained.

**NOTE, the "calls for speculation" objection is similar to "lacks personal knowledge". Either way, if you know the witness does not know, object.

As with all objections, use your discretion. Sometimes it is not worth the effort on an unimportant collateral issue. Other times the evidence is going to come out one way or another, and there is no point in drawing more attention to it by fighting about it in front of the jury. Remember, jurors don't know the technical fineries of legal objections and evidence, but they understand that if you are objecting to something, it probably hurts your case. With practice and experience will you learn to make these decisions on the fly. It's like reading a pitch in baseball.

E.   IMPROPER

An objection to "improper" can come from a variety of different questions, techniques, and behavior. As the objection covers a broad array, the discussion here about what to look and listen for, and what to argue, covers the objection's use on both direct and cross examination.

Sometimes, there is not an exact legal objection that covers what is going on. As can be gleaned from the list below (which is by no means exclusive), there are just some things that cannot be otherwise identified other than that they are simply *improper*.

Making the objection to something improper. "Objection, Your Honor, improper, _____". What you have to fill in, to the best you can, is what is improper:

argumentative, personal attack on counsel or the witness, vague, calls for hearsay or other inadmissible evidence, etc. Sometimes, with blatant and egregious violations, "improper" is enough and the judge will already be aware of what is going on. Watch out for speaking objections, and ask to approach if necessary to get time at sidebar to argue out of the hearing of the jury.

Violations by the person. The advocate him—or herself can *act* improperly, and you must shut him or her down. Examples of improper behavior are:

- Pretending to have impeachment

- Pretending to know something bad about the witness

- Implying has committed or is about to commit crime (i.e. perjury)

- Arguing or name calling

- Speaking directly to opposing counsel

- Insinuating opposing counsel did something illegal or unethical

- Moving too close to the witness or jury

Violations by the question asked. While counsel may *act* totally professionally, there are entirely improper questions that simply cannot be asked, and questioning techniques that are not permitted. They include:

- Violating pretrial orders

- Discovery violations

- Violating motions *in limine*
- Blatantly asking for narrative, or for irrelevant or inadmissible testimony
- Not laying proper foundation for certain testimony, or using an item of tangible evidence or demonstrative without laying the proper foundation
- Asking a question about privileged matters (Fifth Amendment; attorney-client and other privileges protected under the applicable rules; settlement negotiations, remedial measure, offers to pay medical bills (Rules 407, 408, 409, 410))
- Using improper refreshment documents that might confuse or mislead
- Asking compound, overly broad or ambiguous questions
- Asking a witness to reenact a crime, etc.
- Asking a witness to admit bad yet collateral behavior
- Continuing to go into areas that have been asked and answered, simply to highlight some point ("asked and answered")

Remedies. There are several remedies you can ask for, in addition to making the objection to try to halt the behavior. Other remedies, in ascending order of severity, is:

- *Ask jury be instructed to disregard.* Let the jury know that what was done was not right and to hold counsel accountable by not considering what was said or done.

- *Ask for sanctions.* Ask the court to admonish the attorney before the jury; depending on the severity of the malfeasance, it may rise to contemptuous behavior, which you might suggest to the court.

- *Ask for mistrial.* No one wants to have to start over, and spend more time and money, but sometimes the bell was rung so hard that there is no other option than to get a new set of untainted jurors. Think carefully about this, because it gives the other side a chance to correct any mistakes it made in the first trial.

- *Consider reporting conduct to the Bar.* Most state bar associations have a rule that requires attorneys to report unethical conduct of other lawyers. It is said that it is the most violated rule of all. No one wants to mess with another's meal ticket and livelihood. But there are rules, a no one of us has the right to violate the rules we all share. The good of the order and of the profession demands it. So, depending on how bad it was, the issue may be one for the bar.

F.   MISSTATING THE LAW/FACTS

When you have prepared for a cross, and anticipate the testimony of a witness will be a certain way, be sure you do not let opposing counsel mess that up on direct. Make sure your opponent is accurate and not misleading.

Inadvertent misstatements. When opposing counsel misstates the law or the facts, you may find yourself in a quandary. If the misstatement is inadvertent or a simply misspeak, and everyone knows it, then let it go. If it's inadvertent but merits correction so that the record is clear, or so the witness does not get confused, then make an objection—but do it in a constructive manner:

Q. Mr. Witness, which way was Mr. Plaintiff driving?

A. He was driving north.

Q. Which way was Mr. Plaintiff driving [clearly meaning to say, "Mr. Defendant"]?

OBJ. Your Honor—to clarify, is counsel referring to Mr. Defendant?

Q. I'm sorry, yes, thank you—which way was Mr. Defendant driving?

A. He was driving south.

Note that the word "objection" was not used as to not be confrontational. We like to think of this as being helpful and not being adversarial. Most judges will appreciate the gesture.

Purposeful misstatements. There may be a difference between purposeful misstatements based on underhanded tactics, and those predicated upon a lack of understanding of the facts. One is perhaps ethically worse than the other, but you cannot permit misstatements to stand when they can (1) unduly confuse the jury, or (2) hurt your cross examination.

Whether to object or not. As sadly as it is, you will see attorneys that simply do not know the facts. I tried a case a couple of years ago, wherein my client's actions spanned the period of a couple of hours over the "spring forward" part of Daylight Savings Time, from Saturday night until Sunday morning. He testified in his own defense about the time period, telling the jury that it was the "spring forward" weekend, hence the disparity in the officer's report about the time. The prosecutor was busy doing who knows what, but was not paying attention to his testimony. When she began her cross examination, she lit into him about where he had been for an extra hour before being stopped (which was not really relevant anyway, as there was no allegation of drinking or drug use). She would not let the issue go, even when he explained it to her again—he looked at me, the jury looked at me, and I just shrugged at them. Everyone in the courtroom thought she looked like an idiot. Rather than correct her (and them!), I let it stand as it really hurt her credibility. Needless to say, the client was acquitted.

G.   FACTS NOT IN EVIDENCE

To understand this objection, one must bear in mind the flow of information during trial examinations. On direct examination, the facts come from the witness, not the advocate. Cross is the opposite. When listening to a direct, be sure to listed for who is supplying the facts—if the attorney is injecting facts, object.

Take for example a case where the issue is when a fire occurred at a factory. The following questioning is of the first witness in the case:

Q. Mr. Witness, what time did you arrive at work on June 6?

A. About 8:25 in the morning.

Q. Was the fire already burning at that point?

OBJ. Objection, Your Honor, facts not in evidence.

J. Sustained.

Another improper line of questioning would be, still assuming this is the first witness and no one has talked about the fire yet:

Q. Mr. Witness, what time did you arrive at work on June 6?

A. About 8:25 in the morning.

Q. Did you notice anything unusual upon arriving?

A. No, not at that point.

Q. What time did the fire start?

Q. Was the fire already burning at that point?

OBJ. Objection, Your Honor, facts not in evidence.

J. Sustained.

The proper way to handle the questions is as follows:

Q. Mr. Witness, what time did you arrive at work on June 6?

A. About 8:25 in the morning.

Q. Did you notice anything unusual upon arriving?

A. No, not at that point.

Q. Did something unusual happen at work that day?

A. Yes, in fact, it did.

Q. And what was that?

A. There was a fire in the factory part of the building.

Q. Do you know what time the fire started?

A. Not exactly, but I the fire alarm went off at 8:35am. So it would have had to have started sometime after I got there at 8:25 and when I heard the alarm ten minutes later.

Linking it up later. Counsel may introduce a fact for the limited purpose of trying to put some context into the surrounding questions. While technically objectionable, it is not entirely improper. For instance, a set of introduction or biographical questions may allude to the not-yet-introduced fact, but as the questioning will ultimately get the fact from the witness, it will be linked up.

Using the same scenario, suppose the plaintiff first calls the owner of the factory, and asks the following questions:

Q. Ma'am, how are you involved in this matter?

A. I am the owner of Factory.

Q. Is it still in business, after the fire?

The direct examination questioner did not get the fact that there had been a fire from the owner or any other witness, so technically it is still assuming a fact not yet in evidence. Any objection would likely be resolved like this:

OBJ. Objection, Your Honor, facts not in evidence.

Q. Your Honor, I will link this up is just a bit. This witness has direct knowledge of the fire, as she was the owner and present at the factory when it happened, and will explain all that very shortly. If I could just be permitted some latitude to get through the background information.

J. Overruled, so long as you are representing you will and can link it up later.

The issue is good faith, and that the question can be asked at all.

Be very aware of and vigilant for opposing counsel attempting to "smuggle" in extrinsic facts that will likely not get admitted under any legal theory. *Principles of Evidence*, Graham C. Lilly, Daniel J. Capra, and Stephen A. Saltzburg, West 2012 (sixth Ed), section 9.3, Techniques of Impeachment. This type of question would be one where a question about a relevant topic contains some irrelevant or otherwise extrinsic fact. Using the factory fire scenario, we find this example:

Q. When you arrived at 8:25, was anyone else there?

A. A few people.

Q. Was John Smith there, the guy who had been fired the day before?

OBJ. Objection, Your Honor, facts not in evidence.

J. Sustained.

The question was pertaining to who else was present that may have seen, or even been responsible, for the fire. Adding in the description of John Smith as having been fired the day before is probably not relevant, but is smuggled into the question to paint the picture that John Smith may have had a motive for arson.

Of course, whether the fact is relevant or extrinsic (and inadmissible) is driven purely by the cause of action and defenses, and the facts. If it is John Smith's criminal arson trial, it may in fact be relevant—but this witness may lack the personal knowledge about John Smith's status with the company. In that case, opposing counsel is still testifying to a fact not in evidence. But what if it is a bad faith claim against the insurance company?

Listening carefully to the question, and forcing opposing counsel to stick only to asking questions and not giving facts, is a powerful control tool.

H.   BEYOND THE SCOPE
(ON REDIRECT EXAMINATION)

This objection is one that is constantly misunderstood and misused. To understand it, we must look at Federal Rule of Evidence 611(b):

(b) Scope of Cross-Examination. Cross-examination should not go beyond the subject matter of the direct examination and matters affecting the witness's credibility. The court may allow inquiry into additional matters as if on direct examination.

It's pretty clear from existing case law that the courts have wide latitude in permitting cross examiners to go into some matters that were not covered on direct.

The cross examiner must be very careful to watch for the same thing from opposing counsel when the questioning swings back to redirect.

If opposing counsel is permitted to go beyond the scope of your cross examination, you are entitled to confront and cross examine on the new topics. Be sure to ask for cross, and if denied, make a record. There are times—especially in criminal cases, where re-cross examination is mandatory under the Sixth Amendment's confrontation clause. A blanket "no re-cross" prohibition will likely be reversed. "When material new matters are brought out on redirect examination, the Confrontation Clause of the Sixth Amendment mandates that the opposing party be given the right of recross-examination on those new matters." *United States v. Jones*, 982 F.2d 380, 384 (9th Cir. 1992), as amended (Apr. 6, 1993).

I.   COMPOUND QUESTIONS

A compound question is one that asks for two different facts at one time. For example, from what might be an employment discrimination case:

Q. Can you please tell us your employment history, and what you did upon learning you had been terminated?

There are two significant parts to that question. The first part calls for an answer that supplies facts pertaining to interview dates and processes, hiring date, training, on the job experience, duties, salary, promotions, and the like. To be sure, it could be broken down into many narrower questions that would prevent the witness from simply rambling on and on.

The second part gets into the cause of action—a claim of employment discrimination. Depending on the facts, the facts surrounding "what you did upon learning you had been terminated" could have a large number of facts.

The point of forcing opposing counsel to break down the questions is so that you have a clear and concise slate of facts to dissect and use on cross. Remember:

- Direct questions call for direct answers

- No ambiguity in the direct answer means the witness understood it

- Direct answers offer no wiggle room for the witness on cross

- Single-fact questions control potential hearsay and other irrelevant comments

J.   "YOU'D AGREE WITH ME THAT . . .", "ISN'T IT TRUE . . ."

Tags, editorials, and other random statements are prevalent among untrained cross examiners. Words matter. Adding a "and" before every question, or a "okay" at the conclusion of every one of the witnesses response is simply bad discipline. Those taglines are not necessarily objectionable (perhaps improper bolstering) but make you sound awful. I have seen it so bad that the jury completely stops listening to the substance of the exchange, and starts counting the word "and" to see if the lawyer will really do it before every single question. Not good.

A very common direct examination tagline evolves from asking the witness to agree with the advocate. The direct examination witness is not there to agree with the advocate—the witness is there to provide facts. A witness can agree that a particular fact is what it is, and still not agree with the position of the advocate. So asking a witness "wouldn't you agree with me that . . ." or "wouldn't you agree . . ." is improper. "Isn't it true that . . ." is similarly improper.

An excellent reasoning as to why these types of questions are improper was set forth by the Florida Supreme Court, who dealt with a prosecutor in a murder case asking "isn't it true" questions about something he could not back up with facts:

> This Court recently held that "[i]t is impermissible for the state to insinuate impeaching facts while questioning a defense witness without evidence to back up those facts." . . . We recognized that this principle held true regardless of whether the State insinuated impeaching facts and never had proof of those facts or whether that evidence did exist, but was not later proved. . . .

> The Third District Court of Appeal has explained why such insinuation is impermissible without later presenting proof of the underlying facts:

> > The reason that such proof must be forthcoming is because the predicate question—e.g., 'Didn't you tell me . . .?' or 'Didn't you say to so-and-so'—is itself testimonial, that is, the question suggests that there is a witness who can testify that such a statement was made. When this suggested witness is not actually called to give the impeaching testimony under oath, all that remains before the jury is the suggestion— from the question—that the statement was made. When that occurs, the conclusion that must be drawn is that the question was not asked in good faith, and that the attorney's purpose was to bring before the jury inadmissible and unsworn evidence in the form of his questions to a witness.

Evans v. State, 177 So. 3d 1219, 1232 (Fla. 2015) (internal citations omitted). This admonition also holds true on direct, where these types of questions can improperly bolster the witness' testimony—the attorney's belief is irrelevant and inadmissible, and the jury is the finder of what is true or not. The witness cannot opine as to truth.

On cross, be careful yourself: simply ask the witness whether the fact is the fact, yes or no. Again, the witness is not there to agree with your position, just how you present the fact.

5.5 BEING ON THE RECEIVING END OF A SUSTAINED OBJECTION

There will be those times where you get shut down—rightfully, or maybe not so rightfully. We all ask just bad questions from time to time.

Don't give up. *Think* about where you are and what you are doing. There should be no surprises in your cross examination, as you will have thought through your themes, topics, and target questions. You should not have any issues come up that you have not anticipated and are prepared.

If, however, you do find yourself in a jam, do the following:

Never, never, never lose your cool. Stay professional. Stay focused on why you are there—the client—and what your story is, and what your goals are in the courtroom. I have seen too many attorneys roll eyes, blow out huffy frustrated sighs, and some even accuse the judge and opposing counsel of somehow ganging up on the attorney. Just stay calm and *think*. Think before you speak.

Ask for a moment. When the objection comes, stop and think about the objection, and if there is any ruling, what it was. Does it apply—is the judge right or wrong? Have your evidentiary objection guide (such as the one the author uses found at www.eLEXPublishers.com) handy—pull it out and take a look at the rule. It is better to take a second to recompose, than to continue to ask the bad question over and over.

Confer with co-counsel. You should have a trial partner, who should be paying attention. When you ask the judge for a moment (which you may even phrase as, "Your Honor, may I have a moment to confer with co-counsel?"), purposefully walk to your counsel table, and have a discreet conversation with your partner.

Re-phrase the question. Take another stab at it, and carefully reword your question to narrow it to the exact and precise. If you need a second, take it. Jot down the question so you do not trip up again.

Ask to approach. If you think the objection was improvidently sustained against, you, ask to approach or for a sidebar. Or ask, "may I be heard?" Whatever the custom in your locale, be sure to get the judge's attention so you can expand your legal argument outside the earshot of the jury.

Make a record. Sometimes the judge is just wrong and will not have any of your attempts to be heard. At the next break, when the jury is not in the room, as to be heard again. If the judge still refuses, ask that you be able to proffer the question and answer for the record. Some judges will let you, some won't. Those that won't like to get reversed. If that does not work, then make careful notes and file the appropriate post-trial motions (just in case you do not win your trial).

When to give up. You must know when you are beat, and make a professional retreat. As stated above, there are times when the judge is just going to have to make your life miserable and not budge. If you continue to fight in front of the jury, *you* look bad—not the judge. Be respectful, make your record, and move on. You might be able to recall the witness as your own, so at the end of the cross examination and re-direct examination, ask the judge to have the witness remain.

A. POTENTIAL OBJECTIONS AND RESPONSES

Every objection discussed herein is susceptible to use against you during your cross examination.

There are some "advocacy muscle memory" responses you can use if you are not otherwise already prepared for the objection (*see* Chapter 5.5.B, below). They are:

- *Yes, Your Honor*. Always a good one! Be sure to show deference to the trial judge's rulings, and adjust accordingly.

- *Your Honor, may I be heard (at sidebar)?* Signals to the judge that you have a longer and more complicated reason for asking the question, and you do not want to argue it within the earshot of the jury.

- *Your Honor, may I briefly respond?* Same as asking to be heard, but signals that the response may simply be a short response, like "best evidence" or "statement of party opponent", which is not really a speaking objection that could improperly influence the jury somehow.

- *Your Honor, may I have a moment?* As above, do not be afraid to take a moment to gather your thoughts before your respond or move on.

- *May I rephrase, Your Honor?* A good, general, transition statement wherein you are showing deference for the sustaining of the objection, but signaling that you are going to fix the problem and for the judge to pay attention— so the next objection is overruled.

Above all else, *stay cool and professional.*

B.   ANTICIPATION OBJECTIONS

There is absolutely no reason for any trial attorney with any modicum of skill to not anticipate objections. It is a simple matter of knowing the facts and knowing the Evidence Code.

There are many sources for evidentiary objections (such as the one available from the author through www.eLEXPublishers.com), so not knowing the code is no excuse. That, and the fact that any trial lawyer has by definition taken evidence in the accredited law school that led to his or her admission to the state bar. Simply stated, ignorance is not an excuse. It is malpractice.

In looking at the source materials, it is not hard to anticipate the objections you will draw and the ones you will make.

If you know you will draw an objection, you must first ask yourself if you can ethically ask the question in good faith. Is there a hearsay exception? Is the evidence self-authenticating? Then have the rule number noted and ready for the bench conference.

If you know you can make an objection, weigh whether to even make it, and if you have to, have the rule and case law ready to back your argument.

Motions *in limine* are an excellent way to control the admission of evidence (see Chapter 3.7). The good part of motions *in limine* are that they are outside the heat and tempo of the trial, and can get more time and attention from the judge. The bad side is that (1) you tip your hand to objections that may otherwise catch your opponent unawares, and (2) the judge may not have enough context in the pretrial setting to be able to render a ruling—any may defer until the actual testimony is happening. Even then, you have cued the court in on a potential problem he or she will have to address later.

At my firm, we enjoy writing "bench briefs"—short memos on the topic. We usually limit them to a page or page and a half, and have the case law attached. In the case law copies, we highlight the pertinent text in both the court's and opposing counsel's copies. The bench brief is very handy for arguing complicated or very important issues. I have found that judges will even take a short break to go in chambers and read the bench briefs—or give them to a clerk to quickly confirm the research. Some even consult other judges. Not only that, but having taken the time to not only identify the issue, but also to brief it, is polished and professional.

Remember, too, that a contemporaneous objection is required to preserve any appellate review—even if a pretrial motion is filed and denied, an objection has to be made in real time when the objectionable evidence or testimony is presented.

Follow this checklist:

- Is this piece of evidence or testimony objectionable?

- If so, what is the objection?

- Is this piece of evidence or testimony critical and material?

- Is the issue clear on its fact, such that can be argued on the face of the rule?

- If the issue so complicated that it requires case law authority in order to properly argue it?

- Should a motion in limine be filed?

- Should a bench brief be prepared?

- What is the proper legal objection to be contemporaneously made in trial?

C.   DESIGNING NON-OBJECTIONABLE QUESTION SETS

As we know, one of the best ways to make a smooth, zen-like cross examination is to design (and deliver) questions and question sets that are not objectionable.

Analyze the facts. Then ask yourself, "if I were my opponent, what would I argue is objectionable about this fact?" Think about whether it is relevant, whether it is hearsay, is there a better source of "best evidence" . . . is it cumulative, or does any other evidentiary rule apply that could impact the admissibility of this fact?

Evidentiary issues *must* be dealt with and resolved before trial starts—long before the propounding of the question to the witness in your very important cross examination. There is no excuse for not having the issues identified and researched prior to trial.

When looking at themes and topics, use the following process chart to plot out each fact. In doing so, if you can answer "yes" to each question, then the fact is admissible. This process can be used to deal with themes (broad), topics (narrower), and target facts.

FACT	Relevant?	Not hearsay or exception?	Best evidence?	Authentic?	Not privileged?	ADMISSIBLE
	Y/N	Y/N	Y/N	Y/N	Y/N	
	Argument:	Argument:	Argument:	Argument:	Argument:	✔

You may deduce that this is a version the old law school mnemonic "BARPH" (**B**est evidence, **A**uthentic, **R**elevant, **P**rivilege, **H**earsay), which has been reordered here to reflect the most often lodged objections over evidence to the least. However you look at it, this is the only way to prepare questions—while keeping in mind the rest of the evidence code, as well as any statutory provisions that may apply.

It is important to note that this analysis can be applied by any advocate during any part of the trial—if in trouble, use your "advocacy muscle memory" and stick to the basics.

Recall that you may only ask questions for which you have a good faith basis in asking. See Chapter 7.4 regarding ethical issues in cross examination—always be the most professional advocate in the room.

Remember, that there is always an opportunity to test the admissibility of your questions (at least your topics and themes) through motions in limine (see Chapter 3.7).

D. JUDICIAL LIMITATIONS ON CROSS

As noted earlier in the chapter, judges do have the authority to control all aspects of a trial. When dealing with the negative impact of that authority on your ability to try your case, remember two things. First, if the judge does not understand what you are doing or attempting to do, he or she may not rule in your favor and that's your fault. Second, the limiting authority is not absolute, and is subject to review on appeal, *if properly preserved*.

Explain yourself. If you are being shut down unnecessarily, *get the judge's ear*. Ask for the sidebar, or to approach the bench. Let the judge know that it is critical to your case that you be allowed to be heard on the issue.

Make a record for appeal. As previously discussed, you have to put your proposed questions on the record if you want an appellate court to help you. If the judge will not permit you to make your record at the time of the question, you need to at least make as much of a contemporaneous proffer as you can. Later, at the first opportunity outside the hearing of the jury, you must ask again to argue why you should be permitted the proposed cross examination. Be sure to clearly state the question and what you believe the answer would be.

Be sure to see Chapter 9.1.A for case law on judicial limitations on cross examination, and Chapter 5.6 on how to make a proffer.

E. SAFE HARBOR QUESTIONS

There will be times when you have been beaten back into a corner. Try as you might, you cannot get the question out without drawing an objection that is sustained. The witness is running away. Whatever it is, you are losing control and need a place to go.

Never ask a question to which you do not already know the answer. I remember learning this maxim long before I went to law school. A lawyer simply does not ask a question to which he or she does not know the answer. Building on this, you can find safe harbor questions.

Safe harbor questions are designed to be so vanilla and harmless that it gives you time to get back to your game plan and back on tempo.

Examples. Here are some examples of "always (usually) safe" questions:

- *You volunteered to be here today, didn't you?* Goes to bias *for* the party for which witness is testifying, goes to credibility.

- *You are aware of the charges you/the defendant is facing?* Goes to the severity of "trouble" the party for which the witness is testifying (which could be him—or herself), and goes to credibility.

- *You testify all the time, don't you?* Experts and law enforcement officers, and perhaps some snitches, can be categorized as someone who makes a living—or at least an avocation—out of being on the stand. That begets the argument that this is not a pure, innocent bystander—rather, it is someone who has an interest in the outcome. The argument for closing is that this witness has to substantially contribute to the verdict for his or her client, so that he or she will continue to be called. Or, job performance and promotions can be a part of how well someone does on the stand.

- *You trained on how to testify?* As a criminal defense lawyer, one of my favorite areas. Jurors always seemed amazed that the witness has training on, essentially, how to hoodwink them! Usually only the lawyers are thought of as "sleazy"—getting the jury to understand that witnesses have something to gain or lose is important to getting the jurors to question the witness' credibility.

- *You were paid to be here today, right?* Similar to "you testify all the time", experts are very vulnerable to this, and if you have done your homework, you will know how much. Think in 3D and explore all the things associated with the cross of an expert—reputation, livelihood depends on successful cases associated with, money earned, etc.

- *You met with the attorney for the [other side]to prepare for today?* If "yes", casts some doubt on whether the testimony is pure, or was coached. If "no", makes the other side look unprepared and nonchalant. Either is fodder for closing argument—the topic being lack of credibility.

Don't forget the basic of impeachment as "safe harbor questions":

- *You were there?*

- *You had a clear view?*

- *You saw what happened?*

- *You heard what happened?*

- *You have had every opportunity to give a statement?*

- *At no time prior to today have you ever told anyone about what you saw?*

- *You'll make over $25,000 for your work on this case, right?*

- *You have two prior felony convictions, true?* (if already elicited on direct; otherwise, follow the proper procedure for impeachment by prior convictions.)

- *All of this happened very fast, right?*

If you cannot remember these "safe harbor" topics, *write them down* and take them to the podium with you when you begin your cross examination. Better to read than to stand there like a bump on a log.

Finally, remember what legendary advocacy professor William R. Eleazer of the Stetson University College of Law, my friend and mentor, taught: *you never sit down on a sustained objection.*

There is always something you can ask that will get you a "yes" or "no" answer. For example:

OBJ.   Objection, Your Honor, relevance.

J.   Sustained.

Q.   Mr. Witness, all of this took place in Leon County?

A.   Yes.

Q.   No further questions.

If you sit down after the judge sustains an objection against you, there is a sense and feeling of defeat. Safe harbor questions avoid that problem.

F.   REDIRECTION

A very good control tool is redirection. Redirection is correcting the subject area of the witness' statements. The basis for redirection is making sure that you are in control—if you get off topic, then what is expected of the witness? Remember your control techniques (see Chapter 4)—and *lead* and *limit.* Questions that call for yes or no *only* answers (no room to freestyle) and questions that only ask about one fact at a time.

Redirection is similar to "back to my question" but is a little broader. And, perhaps, a little nicer.

Q.   After you left the scene, Officer, you went to interview the victim?

A.   I did, but before I could, there were several cars that needed to be moved. So I called Officer

Sawicki to come to the scene. He arrived a bit later.

Q. Thank you, but let's focus on the victim interview for now, okay?

A. Okay, yes.

G.   THE DEAD END

There are times when you are not going to get what you want. Even the most experienced of us get stuck, and need an out. Remember, you can argue the *demeanor* of a witness in closing:

Members of the jury, let's talk about Mr. Witness. Recall my questioning of him—everything I wanted to discuss, he wanted to talk about something else. I would ask a question, he would talk about what he wanted to talk about. He was not interested in answering questions about his involvement in the conspiracy. He was quick to change the subject. You saw how he acted. The law says you may judge his demeanor and whether he was forthright in answering my questions. Please do—and if you do, you will find that he is not at all credible about his assertions of innocence.

5.6 MAKING A RECORD BY PROFFER

If you have a line of questioning that the judge will not permit, you must preserve it and your objection/motion for review on appeal (just in case).

A proffer is merely a prevention, or offer, of proof that is made on and for the record but is outside the purvey of the trier of fact. A proffer gets the information into the record when that information is otherwise not in evidence.

You cannot forget to make a proffer, nor can you leave before putting something on the record. If you do not make a record, then the appellate court has no idea what the issue was and cannot make a ruling. On the other hand, if you have made an objection, or tried to present some evidence that the judge has excluded, and you have a full record of what the missing testimony or evidence is, then the appeals court may be able to bail you out in the even you lost the trial.

A.   EXAMPLE OF A PROFFER

Virtually any situation in cross examination may be subject to a judge intervening and closing down the questioning. Some are truly collateral or irrelevant—if you properly prepared, you should not encounter that problem.

When faced with a judge excluding critical questioning, be sure to get the questions on the record. Take this cross examination, for example:

Q. Mr. Witness, have you ever been convicted of a felony?

OBJ. Objection, relevance and improper impeachment.

J. Sustained.

Q. Your Honor, may we approach the bench for a sidebar?

J. Yes, please approach.

[SIDEBAR]

Q. Judge, impeachment with prior convictions is permitted under Federal Rule of Evidence 610, and the credibility of this witness is a critical component of this cross examination in the defense of my client.

A. Judge, this is a minor witness, so his criminal record is of no relevance.

J. I agree, I do not see why we have to embarrass this witness.

Q. Your Honor, this is the accuser, the victim— there could not be a more important witness. He is claiming my client stole from him—I have the right to challenge his credibility under the rules.

J. No, I don't see why this poor victim has to be put through any further discomfort. Sustained.

Q. Your Honor, may I quickly proffer what the anticipated testimony would be?

J. Quickly.

Q. My question would be, "have you ever been convicted of a felony?", and I anticipate the response would be yes. In fact, Mr. Witness has three separate prior convictions for fraud. Those convictions were in 2010, 2012, and 2016—all of which involved convictions. And for the last conviction he has been on probation on the entire time from when the allegations in this case occurred until now.

J. Opposing counsel, do you agree with that?

A. Oh, clearly, judge, Mr. Witness has those three convictions.

J. OK. I'll maintain my prior ruling, and sustain the objection. You have made your record, and the appellate court will decide if I have made the right call. Please step back, and move on to your next question.

This situation may not be as absurd as you would think, as there are times when the judge may just make a mistake. You cannot compound the matter by making the additional mistake of *not* making a record. In this example, if you lose the trial, the appellate court now has a complete picture of what happened, and why the error is reversible.

B.   MAKING A COURT EXHIBIT

If the excluded evidence is in the form of a document, or other tangible piece of evidence (an audio or video recording, a photo, etc.), then you should include it in the record for appellate review.

Taking the above example from Chapter 5.6.A, if someone has been convicted of a crime, there will be a court document memorializing that conviction. In fact, most jurisdictions will not let you even ask the question unless you have the good faith to ask it based on having possession of a certified copy of a judgment of conviction. See Chapter 2.5.E.4 for a discussion of impeachment with prior convictions.

Here is how you would make a proffer of the documents:

Q. *My question would be, "have you ever been convicted of a felony?", and I anticipate the response would be yes. In fact, Mr. Witness has three separate prior convictions for fraud. Those convictions were in 2010, 2012, and 2016—all of which involved convictions. And for the last conviction he has been on probation on the entire time from when the allegations in this case occurred until now.*

J. *Opposing counsel, do you agree with that?*

A. *Oh, clearly, judge, Mr. Witness has those three convictions.*

J. *OK. I'll maintain my prior ruling, and sustain the objection. You have made your record, and the appellate court will decide if I have made the right call. Please step back, and move on to your next question.*

Q. *Yes, Your Honor. I have certified copies of the judgment of conviction in each of those cases, and I would like to have it included in the record as a court exhibit.*

J. *The court will receive as Court's Exhibit 1A, 1B, and 1C the certified copies that counsel has just handed to me. I will give those to the clerk for inclusion in the record, but direct that they not go back with the jury in deliberations. They are not evidence in this trial at this time. Both counsel will refrain from making reference to them before this jury.*

Q. *Yes, Your Honor.*

A. *Yes, Your Honor.*

It's that simple. Remember, in the event that the judge does not permit you do proffer the documents at that time, do it at the first recess outside the presence of the jury. If the judge will not hear that, then do a separate *Notice of Filing* and file them with the clerk, making note as to why they are being included.

Again, do not give up. If you don't win at trial, your success on appeal could depend on making a proper record for the appellate court to review.

5.7 CONTEMPORANEOUS OBJECTIONS

As the big shoe company says, "just do it." When you have an objection, you have to make it *as the action is happening.* This cannot be stressed enough. If you do not object at the time of the offending question/comment/etc., you may forfeit appellate review.

5.8 TAKEAWAYS

- Know the evidence code better than anyone in the courtroom.

- Know your available evidentiary objections.

- Identify and prepare to address any hearsay, relevance, and other objections.

- Listen on three levels: to the substance, to the witness, and to counsel.

- Have prepared responses for standard objections ("advocacy muscle memory").

- Have prepared "safe harbor" questions.

5.9 EXERCISES

Exercise 1:

Get a copy of an evidentiary objection guide. For example, eLEX Publishers' *Trial Guides* (www.eLEXPublishers.com) is the oldest and most widely used, and is updated every year. Read it. Practice reciting the "go to" laser responses to hearsay, relevance, and other major objections. Consider making your own list, and having it laminated and hold-punched for your trial folder.

Exercise 2:

Go back to a direct examination you have done. It can be from actual practice, or mock trial team, or trial advocacy/trial practice class. *Rewrite it* to be as objectionable as possible. Looking at the other side of an issue will deepen your analysis of why your argument is good or bad.

Exercise 3:

Find a factual pattern, from real life or from a mock trial package. Prepare a cross examination of one of the witnesses. Find a friend to play the witness, and another to play opposing counsel. Find a place and conduct a mock direct and mock cross examination. Make objections and discuss. Ask the friend to also prepare an objectionable direct (as in Exercise 5.9.2, above) and make objections. Discuss.

Exercise 4:

Go watch a real trial, and take notes as to objections made that you also would object to, those that are made that you miss, and those that are *not* made that you would have made. Ask if trial counsel, or the trial judge, will discuss with you after the verdict.

I HAVE NO MORE QUESTIONS OF THIS WITNESS.

CHAPTER 6

IMPROVISING CROSS EXAMINATION

6.1 IMPROVISING CROSS EXAMINATIONS

To be honest, choosing the right term for an unplanned spur-of-the-moment cross was difficult. "Blind" was somewhat insensitive. "Spontaneous" captured the surprise, but didn't capture the seriousness of the skill. "From the hip" connoted both "gunslinger" (which has both a "killer" feel to it—and that is *not* what I have tried to teach in this book) and "unprepared."

Improvised means something entirely different to me. As a life-long fan, student, and performer of jazz, I can attest that much is required of a jazz soloist. The whole point of jazz is improvisation. Think about it, before a concert, *the soloist has no idea what he is going to play!* Classical musicians practice for perfection, then take that work and execute it flawlessly on the concert stage. Jazz is an entirely different experience. It is entirely based on the improvisation of music in real time before the listener.

In jazz, *improvisation* is the culmination of mental acuity, physical dexterity, emotional connection, experience, and mood. The mental acuity is the in-depth knowledge of complicated jazz music theory, understanding of the relationships between notes and chords, the soloist and the rhythm section, and the structure of the song the soloist is playing. Every instrument requires years and years of laborious practice in order to obtain the mastery of the physical dexterity required to play without boundaries. Knowing the song and what it is about, and infusing one's own life experiences give the soloist the ability to draw the listener into the emotion and mood of the song and the solo. And, all of that is happening at the same time between several musicians.

To be sure, the same can be said of modern rap artists—they have a framework of beats within which to work, and material about which to express all sorts of sentiments, and an audience. It is then up to the rap artist to improvise the rap—to weave together words, thoughts, sounds, jokes, taunts, social issue call words, and the like—to move and evoke certain passions in the listener.

Improvised cross examinations are much the same. You are not absolved of your obligation to tell your client's story. You are not relieved of your duty to use the witness to your advantage—whether to actually get favorable facts from the witness, or to discredit the witness. Prepared or not, you have to use your mental acuity, physical dexterity, emotional connection, experience, and mood and not get lost or give up.

A. WHEN YOU MIGHT ENCOUNTER AN IMPROVISED CROSS

When might you conduct an improvised cross? Criminal cases and civil cases present different problems and situations. Administrative hearings can be different as well.

In a criminal case, there are many times in which a cross examination of a witness may be conducted without prior preparation, or even prior knowledge of the witness. There are first appearance hearings, probable cause hearings, bond hearings, sentencing hearings, and many other fast-paced, quickly scheduled hearings.

In a civil case, it would seem that the opportunity to cross examine a surprise witness may come fewer and further between.

My students have made it clear to me: the most dreaded advocacy moment is having to conduct a cross examination on a surprise witness.

I have made it clear to my students: there are few times that an advocate would be asked to conduct an unprepared cross examination. And virtually no time that the advocate is unprepared. Practically speaking, an advocate who finds him or herself in that position is well-advised to not proceed lest he or she be charged with incompetence.

Nonetheless, we all find ourselves in a position, from time to time, in which we have to jump into a cross examination. I liken it to sightreading music, or, as above, taking a solo in a jazz setting. In sightreading music, there are things a musician can do to be prepared. Mastery of the instrument is certainly the first priority. One practices hour after hour to learn how to handle the instrument in every way, or to sing in proper voice. A great musician will look at and play or sing through as much music as possible to be exposed to as many different rhythms, intervals, meters, and other musical gymnastics as is possible. A master musician knows that in order to perfectly perform a piece of music that he or she has never seen before, the first time seeing it, he or she must have complete mastery of the instrument or voice. That command, muscle memory, and reaction allows the musician to perform anything.

The advocate as the same opportunities throughout his or her career, in which to practice over and over.

It should go without saying that there are times where a surprise witness makes the entire process come to a screeching halt. The system favors fairness. If a witness is credible, and has the potential to devastate your case, then you have the duty to your client to (1) discuss that witness' testimony with the client and make good decisions that are in your client's best interest, and (2) not proceed unprepared if there is any way possible to prevent that terrible situation. Judges will give you time to prepare.

Settling or negotiating a plea is not a sign of weakness or being afraid to go to trial; proceeding with a trial just because you think you can handle a witness without preparation or just want the experience of handling a surprise witness in real life could be malpractice.

6.2 WHO IS THIS WITNESS, AND HOW DID I GET HERE?

The first thing to do is *do not panic*. Alternately stated, the first thing to not do is to panic. However you want to say it, *remain calm and keep crossing.*

If the person has no relevance to the case, or no knowledge of the case, that will be exposed pretty quickly on direct. You may stand and say "no questions, Your Honor."

If the witness is there to do your case damage, you have to think quickly about what to do. The game plan set forth herein will allow you to remain in control of yourself, your story, and the witness.

6.3 WHY IMPROVISED CROSSES ARE REALLY NO DIFFERENT THAN PLANNED CROSSES

Think about it—fundamentals are the same. A baseball player addresses the plate and gets in hitting position the same way no matter the day, the time, the ballpark, the opposing team, or who the pitcher is . . . fundamentals remain the same.

For trial lawyers, it is *advocacy muscle memory*. Advocacy muscle memory is the complete command of the fundamentals of trial advocacy. The fundamentals of cross are in this book; the fundamentals of direct are always asking open-ended questions, using the correct litanies for the admission of evidence (remember, there is a difference between "reasonably represent the scene" for a photo and "same or substantially the same condition" for an item of tangible evidence!), and proper objections and responses.

You know the case, you know the story. You know why you are there. Don't lose sight of that just because you have a new witness in front of you.

Using the techniques in this book, and having solid fundamentals, you can easily walk into any cross situation and get from the witness what you need to win.

6.4 QUICK PREP

Improvised crosses are going to happen. If you plan on a life in litigation, you have to accept that and know that you can effectively handle them with poise and professionalism.

Don't be nervous or freak out. You have your fundamentals and control skills at your disposal. At a minimum, you will be able to get through the improvised cross without looking like a rookie.

Don't ever hesitate to ask for time to get ready. Fundamental fairness and professionalism dictate that both sides should be on even ground and surprise should not allow one advocate to get and unfair advantage over the other.

If you are not given much time, ask the trial judge to have opposing counsel give a reason for calling the witness and a short proffer of what the substance of the testimony will be from that witness. Most judges will be curious enough themselves to want to know why the witness is going to take the stand.

Pull it together. With whatever time you are allowed, pull it together and get your target materials ready.

- **Pleadings—stay with the obvious.** Not only will that keep you grounded, it will keep your listener tuned in to the story you've been telling all along.

- **Reports referencing what the witness is discussing**—have the reports ready in case you hear a contradictory date, time, place or other fact. Don't rely on your memory, go to the paper. Ask opposing counsel for any and all documents, reports, notes, memos, *anything* he or she has on the witness.

- **If rebuttal, the substance of the testimony of the witness being rebutted**—go back to what the other witness said, look at your cross sheets (or direct examination), and focus on the subject material at issue.

- **Blank cross sheets**—as you hear themes and topics emerge, start a new cross sheet. *This will be a fluid situation, and develop rapidly*. Keep track of what you want to cover on cross with your cross sheets. Take a moment before you start your cross to organize your sheets into a comfortable and sensible order. *Use them* on cross.

- **Think about whether to cross or not—** rebuttal witnesses can be called in response to something major, like you having opened the door to otherwise inadmissible evidence. They can be called as a desperate measure by the other side, to simply try to prop up some untenable position or is otherwise not hurting your case. Think carefully about which category the witness falls into. If you have opened the door, you have a bigger problem than facing an improvised cross. What's more, you should already know why the evidentiary door was closed to begin with, and what the witness is going to say. After all, it was most likely your objection or motion in limine that prohibited it in the first place. Your cross of that witness should already be prepared.

If the witness doesn't hurt, why give him or her any more time. If the jury gets that the witness is immaterial, validate that by simply saying "I have no questions for this witness."

As you experience more improvised cross situations, you will become less fearsome and more aggressive. While new to you, an improvised cross may simply be getting out an obvious bias or credibility target fact. Later, you will feel more comfortable using your intuition and skills to actually dig deeper into the cross, just like it was the cross of a witness you'd known about all along.

A.   OBJECT TO THE WITNESS AS PREJUDICIAL

In most situations where you may be called on to spontaneously cross a witness, it may be that the witness has just been sprung on you. Surprise witnesses are, sadly, not uncommon. At times, it is the result of opposing counsel playing dirty, or succumbing to the overwhelming workloads and not being prepared, or simply because the opposing client did not timely give the name to the attorney. At times it is the sheer nature of the proceeding (an emergency injunction hearing in a civil case, or a first appearance hearing in a criminal case). Whatever or whenever, it happens.

In making an objection as to prejudice, be sure to argue not only that the witness is a surprise, but *how* the late disclosure prevents you from being able to effectively cross examine the witness (prejudice). Not being able to investigate the witness' background and criminal record, other cases the witness has been in, who else knows about this witness' character for truthfulness, and the like. To make a proper record in the event the judge makes you go forward, explain *how* this witness is prejudicing your ability to represent your client.

B. POLE POSITIONS—FIND YOUR FOOTING

You will never cross examine in a vacuum. In other words, there is always a context for why the witness is before the tribunal. There will always be an arrest report, or a complaint, as a guide star. If you have no idea what the case is about, you have no business trying to litigate it!

Gather what documents you can, and if time permits, jot a few notes on a separate sheet of paper for each document. Alternatively you can use stick-on notes—just don't go crazy. Too many notes is just as ineffective as no notes, and a lot more confusing.

Make a Cross Sheet on whatever you have handy. A legal pad is nice, but not always available (we are in the days of paperless files!). One of my old prosecution buddies would rifle through the file and pull out an inconsequential pleading (an old hearing notice, for instance), flip it over to the blank side, and start making notes. It worked for impromptu preparation, and at least he had something to keep him organized. There is always paper in a courtroom—docket sheets that are not really needed, old pleadings, whatever you can find will work.

Burn a time out! Tell the judge the witness is a surprise, and you need a continuance (see section 6.4.1 regarding objecting to the witness as prejudicial)—or at least a break in the proceedings to be able to speak with the witness prior to him or her taking the stand. Opposing counsel can be present but cannot impede your access to the witness. ABA Ryle 3.4(f) states that a lawyer shall not request a person other than a client to refrain from voluntarily giving relevant information to another party, unless the person is a relative or and employee or other agent of a client, AND the lawyer reasonably believes that the person's interests will not be adversely affected by refraining from giving such information.

When speaking to the witness, it is a best practice to have someone from your camp (other than your client, if at all possible) to witness what the witness tells you. That way, you have an inconsistent statement witness and you as the lawyer do not become a witness. At a minimum, if you are alone, then use the voice recorder on your smart phone, with the witness' knowledge and consent.

1. Safe Harbor Questions = Base Camp

"Safe harbor" questions always give you a place to start, and to return to if things get out of hand. Remember you always have a base to use with safe harbor questions. While perhaps seemingly obvious, safe harbor questions can be used to reinforce your position and your story.

Times, places, dates, names, and other constants are always safe to use to help establish your story.

Common moral and ethical issues are usually safe.

Remember, do not sit down on an objection. Similarly, do not sit down after a chaotic cross (which should not happen if you stick to your fundamentals). Think of a safe question to have on hand at all times. I like, "and all of this occurred in Leon County?" or something similar. Something so safe that even the most surly witness will give you the yes or no you seek.

For an expert (which should NEVER be an improvised cross), you could ask "You were paid to be here today?" and other safe harbor questions.

2. Recall What Your Case Is About

Contract breach. Unlawful touching (battery). Breach of a duty owed. Remember the essence of your case, and what your story is—don't get caught up in something else that may sideline your flow.

Think in 3D—think about all the case law you have read on the issues in the trial. Think about the scene you went to, and think about sitting through all of those depositions. Think about what the witnesses have said in the courtroom. Think about the reaction your friends and family had about the case when you told them you were going to trial and what it was about.

If you keep yourself in the moment, and don't panic, you can make it through any surprise witness.

3. Recall and Use Your Fundamentals

So many times I have seen good advocates get lost in the hoopla and forget how to admit an item of evidence, or forget the basic tenets of hearsay, or some other basic skill.

We discuss "advocacy muscle memory" in this book. Those skills must *always* be present. In the event you have an improvised cross witness hand you an impeachment, you have to be able to execute it flawlessly. If done correctly, it may be the highlight of your cross and the thing that discredits the witness. If you struggle through it, and your opponent makes sustained objections, the witness wins the credibility war and your case is dealt a blow.

Always remember when starting any cross examination, how to:

- Impeach a witness

- Refresh a witness' recollection

- Lay evidentiary foundations (predicate questions)

- Using exhibits for demonstrative purposes

If you think you will not remember your basics in the heat of the moment, *put them in a trial notebook and take them to the podium with you.*

4. Remember Your Control Techniques

It may not be a bad idea to take this book with you to trial, in your box or briefcase. When in trouble, pull out Chapter 4. Otherwise, have your own cheat sheet of control techniques that you can use to at least keep the witness from running amok.

C.   IDENTIFY TARGET FACTS

Just like remembering what your case is about, grab the Cross Sheets you used with other witnesses and start identifying target facts relevant to this witness. The witness has some connection to the case, otherwise he or she would not be called. So, you know right off the bat there has to be some common target facts.

Once you identify those target facts, quickly set them in topics that pertain to the new witness. The, cross examine as usual.

Remember, target facts can be substantive facts (who, what, when, etc.), or they can be point of impeachment. Isn't a great target fact for a surprise witness that he or she cannot be believed because of overwhelming bias against your client? That's a point for closing, and a very important target fact.

D.   THINK IN 3D

As discussed in Chapter 1.6, you always have to consider every angle, every aspect, and every permutation of an issue of a witness' testimony. The freer you think, the more adaptable and effective you will be.

As the improvised cross witness is testifying, *listen*. Think about how this witness fits into the case.

We all learned the basic elements of information gathering when we were in elementary school. Who, what, where, when, why, how. These questions call for *factual* answers, not simply yes or no answers. Do not stray from the basics.

- **Who—who is this person?** Does he or she, by the very nature of who he or she is, have a bias or prejudice that can be exploited to your advantage? Mother, father, brother, sister, significant other, co-worker, friend, or someone with an emotional or financial stake in the outcome?

- **What—*subject matter*—what does this person know about the significant issues?** Again, this witness has some connection to the case, or he or she would not be called at trial. How is the person relevant? How can you make him or her *not* relevant?

- **When**—think not only about when the incident occurred, and whether the improvised cross witness was there or somewhere else, but also think about *when* the witness became involved in the case. Is this someone who allegedly had knowledge early on, and waited to come forward—why did he or she wait? Is there a possibility or fabrication based on the delay? Is there a likelihood that his or her testimony is influenced by things he or she may have heard during the time from the incident at bar until the time he or she got involved in the case. Timing is everything, as they say. Quickly creating a timeline to establish that the witness is a latecomer and subject to disbelief can become part of your story.

- **Where—is there anything you can glean from the scene of the incident?** If something happens to someone at their home, it is more likely than not that the witness has intimate and detailed knowledge about the surroundings. What about someone simply driving down a street who witnesses something? He or she does not know the buildings, trees, traffic pattern, or other things that could have influenced his or her perception. Bringing out on cross that the witness is unfamiliar with those aspects of the "where" can cast doubt on whether he or she is to be believed. Having courtroom access to an online map service will help you significantly with this line of questioning.

- **Why**—the "why" of a case is subject to two considerations. First and foremost, "why" usually begs the question of motivation—which is an operation of the mind and not something another person can assert personal knowledge over. Perhaps a statement from the defendant can be put before the jury so they can draw their own conclusion as to motive (or why someone did something), but the witness cannot opine as to why. That is speculation and invades the province of the jury. Another consideration is why the witness him—or herself has acted a particular way. As with the "who", "why" can open an avenue for you to explore the witness' own motivation for testifying—bias or prejudice for or against a party, or an expert being paid to testify. Be sure to think of the "why" in 3D, so you don't miss an opportunity to discredit a witness.

- **How**—how something happened is subject to a detailed factual analysis, and something you can really attack on the cross of an improvised cross examination witness. This comes not from the witness spelling out factual details that are favorable to you, and the ability to give the whole (or at least complete a part) the story you are telling. It also comes through also exploiting other aspects of the total story that the witness does not know about but that the jury has heard—asking about obvious holes in the surprise witness' story is powerful when everyone in the courtroom *except* the witness knows what it missing.

Be sure to note your questions on your cross sheets, to stay organized!

6.5 OBJECT ON DIRECT
(USE KEY OBJECTIONS)

Recall that an improvised cross examination is really no different than a prepared cross examination—and you have the same responsibilities during the direct of an improvised cross witness. Be sure to listen for common objections.

More so than ever, controlling the substance, the witness, and controlling counsel is essential to having any success in the improvised cross scenario.

Remember the basics (see Chapter 5):

- Control the subject matter
- Control the witness
- Control opposing counsel

Relevance is going to be a main objection. If you and the judge are not familiar with the subject matter or the witness (or both), then both of you will be on more alert. Both of you will be listening more carefully and more critically and analytically. Therefore, you have a golden opportunity to use a "plugged in" judge as a gatekeeper. Raising relevance objections, coupled with a sidebar or conversation at the bench will force the opposing counsel to explain the line of questioning. When the explanation is provided in defending the objection, you have just forced your opponent to reveal his or her motive and in turn case theory (or theme or topic, or even target fact). Once revealed, you can not only start thinking of cross points, you also have the ability to anticipate additional objections.

It is important to note again the circumstances in which improvised crosses are encountered—most of which are evidentiary hearings, and not jury trials. Hearings can come at any time in a case; trials come after all discovery is conducted and closed and a lot of preparation has occurred. The most notable distinction is that hearsay is allowed at many, perhaps even most, evidentiary hearings. If it is allowed, why object? You never know what you may hear, plus it's coming in anyway.

Due to the timing of evidentiary witnesses and improvised cross witnesses mostly being early in the case, you will usually have an opportunity to depose the witness later. As the following objections are discussed, bear in mind that you are not shutting the witness down forever—make a note of the question and your objection, and revisit it in a deposition later. If it is in fact inadmissible, then file a motion *in limine* prior to any subsequent hearings or the trial.

Be sure to object to best evidence, as some documents may be known but may not be available at an emergency hearing.

Your opposing counsel may be as surprised by the witness as you are—and consequently may lead the witness on direct to try to control him or her—so object to leading. Make the witness tell facts on direct—you may not use them on cross, but you will have the witness under oath giving a version of the facts. That locks that witness' testimony in—it cannot change later, lest it be subject to impeachment and the witness subject to a prosecution for perjury.

Surprise witnesses are, in my experience, prone to giving irrelevant information. Many are brought in by clients because the client is looking for any advantage. Be sure to continue to limit the witness by objecting to relevance.

In these situations, again, because the proponent of the witness (your opponent) is not familiar with the witness, the direct may contain broad, probing questions. Those questions may call for the witness to speculate—object to that.

6.6 DELIVERING THE IMPROVISED CROSS

Remember, if you apply what is in this book, *you can cross examine anyone at any time.* My friend, trial lawyer, and fellow trial team coach Stacy Sharp likes to say, "always ready, never prepared!" Of course he is always prepared. That is his tongue-in-cheek way of saying *I have the skills, knowledge, and confidence to engage any witness at any time—bring it on.* You, too, can have that swagger, if you simply follow the Five Fundamentals and exercise your advocacy muscle memory.

A.   ORGANIZATION

Organize yourself. REMEMBER THE FIVE FUNDAMENTALS. Take a minute (or as much time as the judge will give you) to pull it together. Don't freak out! Do not rush, be methodical and deliberate. Ask for a moment or a short recess. It is not unprofessional to be prepared—but it is to be unprepared.

Write it down. Thoughts come up—write them down *neatly*. Use sticky notes to add the surprise witness' notes to already existing Cross Sheets.

Organize your file. Have your target documents for the witness with you and organize them best you can. Ask the clerk or bailiff for sticky notes or paperclips. Jot notes on the top of the documents as to what they are, perhaps ever number them. Stack things neatly.

Organize your facts. Quickly figure out what you need to get out of the witness—*what is your target fact or facts?* CLEARLY note them so you do not forget anything.

Organize your cross. Take the time you need—resist the urge to please the judge by rushing along. As quickly as you can, improvise a Cross Sheet (if you don't have any with you) and map out:

CASE THEORY (OVERALL STORY TO BE TOLD): _____

THEME 1: _____

TOPIC 1: _____

TARGET FACT: _____

Do the same for Theme 2, Topic 2, etc. *This will keep you organized.* It will also give an improvised cross some structure that the listener can follow. Remember, if the witness follows, you are telling your story.

B.   COMMON GROUND ISSUES (BIAS, CREDIBILITY, ETC.)

Shoot for any "safe harbor" questions, such as about having a chance to have come forward sooner, being paid to be at the trial, dislike for your client, etc. When you have nothing else, you can hit the obvious.

C.   CONFRONT WITH OTHER EVIDENCE FROM THE CASE

As mentioned earlier in the chapter, surprise witnesses usually come after everyone has heard a lot of evidence in the case. In rebuttal, the jury is already completely familiar with the facts. They may have even made up their minds. You can use facts that are already in evidence to test the witness, but asking leading questions to test the witness' knowledge of the case. The less he or she knows, the less likely he or she is to be believed.

D.   EXPLOIT STANDARD WEAKNESSES IN A SURPRISE WITNESS' TESTIMONY

Bias.

Prejudice.

Lack of personal knowledge.

Lack of preparation.

Lack of investigation or action.

Coaching by opposing side.

Unfamiliarity with other witnesses and evidence in the case.

E.   CAREFULLY NOTE SURPRISE WITNESS' MANNERISMS, DISPOSITION, TICKS AND TELLS

Always be vigilant to questions that strike a chord. A shift in a chair. Letting out a slow breath. Waiting longer than usual to answer a question. Looking at opposing counsel (perhaps for help?). Asking to look at a report or memo or deposition, perhaps more than once.

Don't go too fast. If you see there is a weakness, stop and probe. Think in 3D or all the facets of the issue. What is bothering the witness? Is there a prior inconsistent statement out there? Is there a big gap in the witness' knowledge that you can exploit? Does the witness simply hate your client?

6.7 HOW TO ARGUE THE SURPRISE WITNESS IN SUMMATION

If the witness is one that has never come forward before, making an argument as to lack of credibility is fairly simple. *The witness had plenty of time to tell the truth, but did not until today. Why not? Members of the jury, what does that tell you about this witness?*

If the witness is one that you did not anticipate, but is otherwise not a newcomer to the case, simply use the target facts gleaned from that witness as you would facts from any other witness. Use them to tell your story. *The witness did not add anything to the other side's case, and is only an attempt to influence you with quantity, not quality.* Or, *the witness clearly does not like my client—what does that tell you about his/her motivations to testify?*

Whatever the witness, your cross examination should fit right in to the rest of the story you came to court to tell. Keep it consistent, and remember why you are there!

6.8 TAKEAWAYS

- Always remember your why you are there— case theory, themes, topics.

- Always use the Five Fundamentals to the extent that you are able.

- Gather any and all available target resources.

- Improvise Cross Sheets if you don't have any pre-prepared sheets on hand.

- Look for common areas of impeachment— think in 3D!

- Stay calm, and stay ahead of the witness!

6.9 EXERCISES

Exercise 1:

Improvising a cross examination may be one of the hardest things anyone can attempt in life—you are matching your skills against another human being, not for fun or laughs, in a public setting, where it really means something big. That's daunting. Knowing if you have what it takes to do that is important.

Self-analysis is key. Think about the following things.

What are your strengths in general everyday arguments? If you have litigated any cases (no matter real or mock, civil or criminal, court or administrative), think about what you did well. What are your weaknesses?

How well do you know the evidence code? Can you recite the standard language used for a hearsay or relevance objection? Do you know the difference between "not hearsay" and the hearsay exceptions?

How do you, and how *well* do you, take notes? How to you organize on the fly? What triggers do you use to remember to go back and mention or discuss something—in an argument, or even a conversation, what do you do to make mental notes about things the other person says, so you can go back and talk about them?

Do you get scared of confrontation? Are you afraid of public speaking? How do you control your nerves and emotions?

Make a list of to help identify what fundamental skills you can improve upon before your next cross examination.

Exercise 2:

Find an advocacy training book and look for mock trial case files. Most will have an instructor manual, or at least a summary or synopsis for the instructor. Have a colleague learn on of the witness roles before you read the case file or summary/synopsis. Once in the room with your "witness", quickly read the critical parts of the file or the summary/synopsis. Then cross the witness.

Exercise 3:

As in Chapter 1, have a friend select inanimate objects, or characters from TV show or movies, to cross examine. This practices thinking in 3D. Look for any and all aspects of the thing or person to ask about.

Exercise 4:

If he or she is willing, broach a sore subject with an acquaintance. Sticking to politics or sports is wise; getting into religion may get really sore; past issues in relationships are only for the faint of heart. But what does not kill us only makes us stronger. Have the person make a statement about the issue. Take notes and cross examine your friend. But, please be careful—this is someone you like, not an opposing witness in a trial!

Exercise 5:

Watch a trial on TV or in real life, or interviews on cable TV. Pay close attention to the witness' or speaker's ticks, tells, expressions, mannerisms. What do they tell you? Is the witness truthful? Assured? Skeptical and duplicitous?

"I OBJECT TO THIS LINE OF CROSS-EXAMINATION!"

CHAPTER 7

REMEMBER. . .

7.1 THINGS TO REMEMBER: ADVOCACY MUSCLE MEMORY

Trial skills are like any other repeated skill, especially sports or musical instrument skills. You don't practice them until you get them right. *You practice them until you can't get them wrong.* Swinging a golf club. Throwing a football or baseball or javelin, or scales on the piano. Even rote daily tasks like properly brushing your teeth or combing your hair are done so often that you can do them correctly without thinking about it.

In trial advocacy, the "advocacy muscle memory" are found in the repeated tasks associated with properly participating in a trial. They have to be done the same way, every time. Deviation from the proper way to do trial tasks results in either not getting the objection sustained, the evidence admitted, or looking like unprepared and unprofessional to the judge and jury.

Making an objection. Stand. "Objection, Your Honor, [state legal objection]. If it is obvious on its face, that should suffice. If it is complicated, follow the legal objection with, "may I be heard?" If the judge wants to hear more, he or she will direct you to the bench or sidebar. Do not assume you can simply approach the bench or sidebar, but "may we approach?" will properly ask permission. I have heard some advocates say only "sidebar"—as a

command, not a question—which I find offensive and
not something a polished professional would do. Of
course, it never hurts to ask the court's preference
before the trial starts.

Refreshing a witness. There are times on cross
that you will need to get the witness in the right place
before commencing the questioning. Any hesitation,
and lapse in memory, any equivocation about the
facts, all lead to the witness being able to upset your
version of the story. How can you get a pattern of
"fact—yes/no—fact—yes/no" when the witness keeps
saying *I don't recall* or *I'm not certain*?

Review Federal Rules of Evidence 612 (Writing
Used to Refresh a Witness), 803(5) (Recorded
Recollection) to refresh your own recollection of the
rules.

Refreshing a witness' memory is different than
impeachment, and many attorneys do neither with
any precision. It is even more different in the
adversarial context of cross examination. The proper
predicate for refreshing recollection on cross
examination is as follows (in this example, by using
a deposition):

- Establish that the witness in fact does not
  recall a fact. Having asked the question, and
  the witness indicating lack of memory, state:
  You do not recall _____?

- Once the witness confirms lack of memory,
  state: *You gave a deposition on _____, 2018?*
  You did remember at that deposition, didn't

you? Seeing your deposition would refresh your memory?

- Once the witness admits that seeing the deposition would help his or her memory, ask: *May I approach the witness with an exhibit?*

- Before approaching, show the deposition to opposing counsel.

- Approach the witness, and state as showing the deposition to the witness: I am showing you what has been previously marked as *State's Exhibit 1 for identification. This is a copy of your deposition taken on _____, 2018. Please read the deposition to yourself, specifically looking at [paragraph][lines]. Let me know when you are finished.*

- When finished, take it back from witness, and ask: *Now that I have taken the deposition back from you, is your memory refreshed?*

- Once the witness confirms, repeat the exact cross examination question.

If the item is admissible under Rule 803(5), use the predicates below.

Impeachment by prior inconsistent statement. There are different types of impeachment, but the one that requires the most technical accuracy is impeaching with a prior inconsistent statement. Impeaching a witness with a prior statement, say a deposition, is different from refreshing.

My friend and colleague, Professor Charles Rose, advocates using the "Three Cs"—*commit*, *credit*, and *confront*. Charles Rose, *Fundamental Trial Advocacy*, Chapter 10 (Impeachment), 2d Ed. 2011 (West). The foundation and predication questions/actions would be like this, which is adapted from materials I used in teaching advocacy at the Stetson University College of Law:

Commit

Q. You stated earlier today that the light was green.

or

Q. You told us on direct examination that you saw the accused in the bank before the robbery?

Next, you want to credit the prior statement, thus enhancing its reliability and trustworthiness. Do this with a series of short leading questions directed to the circumstances of the prior statement.

Credit (with deposition)

Q. You gave a deposition in this case?

A. Yes

Q. A court reporter was present?

A. Yes.

Q. Before answering any questions at that deposition, you took an oath?

A. Yes.

Q. Just like the oath you took here today?

A. Yes.

Q. That oath was to tell the truth—the whole truth?

A. Yes.

Q. You were given the opportunity to review the transcript of that deposition for accuracy? (note: this would not apply if the witness "waived reading.")

In this example, the questions are designed to credit the validity of a prior statement given in a deposition. Your "credit" questions may vary depending upon the type of prior statement used to impeach the witness' testimony. Another example would be of using a prior written statement (not necessarily a deposition):

Credit (with written statement)

Q. You made a statement about this case on [date]?

A. Yes.

Q. And the events were fresh in your mind at that time?

A. Yes.

Q. You swore to tell the truth before you gave your answers or wrote your statement?

A. Yes.

Q. Just like the oath you took here today?

A. Yes.

Q. That oath was to tell the truth—the whole truth?

A. Yes.

Q. You signed the statement?

A. Yes.

Q. You initialed each page?

A. Yes.

Q. You read it over?

A. Yes.

Q. You were given the opportunity to make corrections or changes?

A. Yes.

Q. You were given the opportunity to review the statement before you testified here today?

Finally, you reach the dramatic (but not necessarily hostile) moment of confrontation. This can be done two ways. The traditional method is for the cross examiner to read the witness' own words to him.

Confront

Q. I am calling court and counsel's attention to page ___, line ___, in (witness' name) deposition. Mr. Witness, when I asked you the question "what color was the light when the car entered the intersection?" you answered, "the light was red."

A. Yes.

Q. "You said that, didn't you?" [Don't forget this!!]

A. Yes.

Asking the witness if he or she made the statement is the impeachment. You cannot leave that out, and can certainly follow up with "and that is different *than what you said here today, isn't it?"* The jury will ask itself, without you having to ask, *was the witness lying then, or he is lying now?* The impeachment is done, and you can move on.

To be clear, sometimes you have to refresh a witness with an item before you impeach him or her with the item. In the example above, if the witness did not admit giving a deposition, you would stop and refresh his or her recollection of having given the deposition with the deposition transcript.

Entering a piece of tangible evidence (foundation or predicate). The foundation or predicate questions for entering a piece of tangible evidence must be memorized and capable of perfect recitation at any time. *Tangible evidence* is an item such as the murder weapon, or the contract. It's the *original* item—the thing itself.

The procedure is simply authenticating the item as required by the evidence code. In other words, *the thing is what the thing is.* This is done by the witness testifying about his or her familiarity with the item, and explaining how he or she came to know about it, and generally establishing that it is the same item as was taken into evidence.

**NOTE: some jurisdictions do not permit you to enter an item into evidence during your opponent's case in chief. In those situations, you will have to discuss with the judge how to discuss cross examining a witness with the item. Some suggestions on how to deal with this are:

- Ask opposing counsel whether he or she objects to your admitting the item on cross examination. Most attorneys will understand that an otherwise admissible item will be coming in to evidence, and will not put up a fight simply to keep the trial moving. In other words, it's going to happen so why fight it.

- Ask the judge for leeway in admitting it as your exhibit during the other side's case, and explain why.

- Offer to lay the foundation with the cross examination witness, use the item, and simply enter it into evidence after the other side rests and you open your case. Form or substance, but it is a technically proper option.

- Simply call the witness in your own case, and ask that the witness be treated as a hostile witness and that you be permitted to confront the witness on direct by leading the witness.

Whatever the resolution, anticipate the issue and do not wait until the middle of your cross examination to figure it out! You will lose momentum, confuse the jury, and lose credibility with everyone for not being prepare.

Before entering the exhibit, properly *prepare* it:

- Prepare an exhibit list pursuant to any local rules, and timely disclose to opposing counsel. Some items are rebuttal and their use may not be anticipated. In that case, be prepared to explain *why* the item was not previously disclosed.

• Be sure, to the extent possible, to have the witness look at the item before the trial, and review with the witness the questions (below) that he or she will answer regarding authenticating the item.

• Prepare any anticipated argument against the item's admission into evidence, in other words, be prepared to fend off any attack that the item is not authentic.

• Be sure to know the judge's preference for numbering—whether it's 1, 2, 3, or A, B, C. Ask during pretrial proceedings or check with the clerk.

• Premark the item, using an evidence sticker or tag (usually available from the clerk) or one similar to this one, used by the Federal Middle District of Florida:

- If the item is dangerous, be sure to secure it and notify court security of its presence in the courtroom.

- Keep the item ready for use during trial; some courts require all items to be placed with the clerk or in another special place prior to its use at trial.

- Do not show it to the jury before authenticating it with the witness or witnesses (if establishing a chain of custody is required).

Memorize and follow this set of predicate actions/questions:

Do not show the item to the jury

- Show the item, as discreetly as possible, to opposing counsel.

- State: *I am showing to opposing counsel (or Mr./Ms. ___) what has been premarked as Plaintiff's Exhibit 1 for identification purposes.*

- Before showing to the witness, ask: *Your Honor, may I approach the witness?*

- Once permitted, carefully take the item to the witness, again, being careful not to let the jury see it.

- State: *I am showing you what has premarked as Plaintiff's Exhibit 1 for identification purposes. Do you recognize it?*

- After witness acknowledges recognizing it, ask: *How is it that you recognize it?* [Note, be sure to have the witness explain any distinct features, circumstances, etc., that make it recognizable.

- After witness explains his/her knowledge of the item, ask: *Is it in the **same or substantially the same condition** as when you last saw it?*

- After the witness affirms the item is what it is, state: *Your Honor, I move Plaintiff's Exhibit 1 for identification into evidence as Plaintiff's Exhibit 1.*

- After dealing with any objections, and the item is received, state: *May I publish it to the jury?*

- After receiving permission, show the item to the jury. Be sure to follow instructions of courtroom security if the item is or could be considered dangerous.

Once the item is in evidence, and has been published, you may question the witness about the item. ***The witness may not write on or mark the item once it is in evidence! Ask permission to use a copy or photo of the item for the witness' markings.* You can quickly authenticate the duplicate by asking the witness what it is, and is it a fair and accurate copy (see foundation, below).

Be sure to return it to the clerk after you are finished using it.

Remember, business records have their own foundational litany of questions under Rule 803(6).

Entering a photo or copy (foundation or predicate). The foundation or predicates for a photo or copy are similar, *but not the same.* Many attorneys use them interchangeably and they simply are not. The difference is that the witness has to establish familiarity with the original item or depiction in the photo (for example, the crime scene). Then the witness has to establish that the copy or photo fairly and accurately depicts the original or subject of the photo.

- Do not show the photo or copy to the jury

- Show the item, as discreetly as possible, to opposing counsel

- State: *I am showing to opposing counsel (or Mr./Ms. ___) what has been premarked as Plaintiff's Exhibit 1 for identification purposes.*

- Before showing to the witness, ask: *Your Honor, may I approach the witness?*

- Once permitted, carefully take the photo or copy the witness, again, being careful not to let the jury see it

- State: *I am showing you what has premarked as Plaintiff's Exhibit 1 for identification purposes. Do you recognize it?*

- After witness acknowledges recognizing it, ask: *How is it that you recognize it?* [Note, be sure to have the witness explain any

- After witness explains his/her knowledge of the photo or copy, ask: *Does this photo **fairly and accurately represent** the scene as it looked on the date the photo was taken?*

OR

*Does this copy **fairly and accurately represent** the original document?*

- After the witness affirms the photo or copy is what it is, state: Your Honor, I move Plaintiff's Exhibit 1 for identification into evidence as Plaintiff's Exhibit 1.

- After dealing with any objections, and the photo or copy is received, state: May I publish it to the jury?

- After receiving permission, show the photo or copy to the jury. If the item is illegal or protected (child pornography, trade secrets, etc.), ask that the item be placed under seal at the end of deliberations.

Once the photo or copy is in evidence, and has been published, you may question the witness about the item. ***Remember, the witness may not write on or mark the item once it is in evidence! Be sure to return it to the clerk after you are finished using it.*

This procedure also works for audio and video recordings. The witness was present for and familiar with the event that is depicted in the video, or heard the conversation on the audio, and can testify that the recording fairly and accurately represents what was recorded.

Again, be sure you have *both* versions in your "advocacy muscle memory."

**NOTE: if you item is not admitted into evidence after an objection, be sure to make it a court exhibit so that it is preserved for appellate review.

Demonstrative exhibits/aids. Demonstrative evidence is something that helps explain the evidence or other exhibits, but will not be admitted into evidence. Demonstrative exhibits or aids must be relevant. Examples are:

- Enlargements of photos, X-rays/MRIs, etc.

- Charts

- Diagrams

- Maps

- Graphs

- Anatomical diagrams

- Models

- Computer animations

Blow-ups or enlargements of photos are an example. The actual photo will be in evidence; the enlargement is used by the witness to explain what he or she saw or did.

To use the demonstrative, follow this predicate/ foundation:

- Prior to trial, prepare the witness to use the exhibit to the extent you can. Always disclose to opposing counsel as timely as possible.

- Do not show to the witness, but approach the witness with it.

- State, *please take a look at this, and tell me what it is.*

- Once witness identifies it, state: *would this assist you in explaining your story?*

- Once the witness agrees that it would help, ask the court for the witness to be able to step down and make use of the exhibit.

- Ask questions about the exhibit.

For cross examination, the witness may be more reluctant to assist you. In that case, you may ask the court for some leeway in establishing the witness' knowledge of the scene. In other words, you essentially lead the witness through the predicate questions. Consider this example:

Q. Mr. Witness, you were not in a position to see the accident, were you?

A. No, I saw what happened.

Q. Your Honor, may I approach with a demonstrative exhibit, an enlargement of an overhead photo?

J. You may.

[Shows to opposing counsel]

Q. Mr. Witness, you have lived on that street for twenty years, right?

A. Yes.

Q. And before that, you lived one block over since birth?

A. Yes.

Q. You are very familiar with this area, then?

A. I am familiar with it.

Q. Your street is a cul-de-sac, right?

A. Yes.

Q. And the street curves back from the intersection to your house, right?

A. Yes, the street is kind of like an S or a snake.

Q. You have to go through the intersection where this happened every day?

A. Yes.

Q. Leaving your home to go anywhere, you go through it?

A. Yes.

Q. And returning from wherever you went, you go through it?

A. Yes.

Q. I am showing you a map of the area, please take a look at it.

A. Okay.

Q. Do you see your street here [indicating]?

A. Yes, and there is my house [indicating].

Q. And the intersection where the accident was is here [indicating]*?*

A. Yes, that is where it happened.

Q. You were on your front porch when the accident occurred?

A. Yes.

Q. Would you take this marker, and draw a line that represents your line of vision, from your porch to the intersection?

A. [Draws line] *Okay.*

Q. And you claim you saw the accident as it happened?

A. Yep, I saw the whole thing.

Q. [Indicating] *Right here on this photo, your line goes through this dark area, do you see that?*

A. Yes.

Q. That's a stand of trees, isn't it?

A. Yes.

Q. That's a thick stand of trees, isn't it?

A. Well, it's kind of thick.

Q. And that stand of trees is between your front porch and the intersection, isn't it?

A. Well . . .

Q. So back to my original question, you were not in a position to see *the accident, were you?*

A. I was on my porch when I heard *the crash.*

Leading the witness through the exhibit not only discredits the witness, but also empowers the jury by giving them a detailed description of the scene.

For a more detailed and pragmatic discussion of exhibits, please see Charles Rose, *Fundamental Trial Advocacy*, Chapter 7 (Exhibits), 3d Ed. 2015 (West).

7.2 SAFE HARBOR QUESTIONS

In case you get stuck, there are common, general cross examination questions that you can ask to get you back on track.

You should always, *always*, have safe harbor questions at hand. They should be as engrained in your memory as is the foundation for refreshing recollection. If you can't remember them, then print your list and take it with you to the podium with your target documents.

Some safe harbor questions are simply questions that do not hurt you, and give you a moment to get back on track. Those questions, which are *constants*, have an obvious known fact that you can use to reestablish a foothold by which to move forward. Others are such that can lead to further questions, depending on the answer. Those questions, *variables*, can be open-ended, and give you a starting (or start-over) place by which to move forward.

A.   WHAT'S SAFE IN CROSS?

Safe areas are those that are known, non-arguable *constant* facts, or safe *variable* facts. They may seem simplistic, and may even come across as "stupid questions". But when you are in the mire of a cross examination, and in intellectual spar with witness, opposing counsel, the judge, and your own nerves, you have to reestablish control. When you get bogged down and need to regroup, go to safe harbor questions.

B.   CONSTANTS

Constant safe harbors include:

- Age
- Date
- Names
- Contents of photos
- Contents of videos
- Contents of audios
- Contents of documents (signatures)
- The unexplained presence of fingerprints
- The unexplained lack of fingerprints
- The unexplained presence of DNA
- The unexplained lack of DNA

In civil cases, safe harbors can be things like dates, names, moral issues like truth, accountability, duty, etc.

Think of facts that cannot be argued or equivocated. Ask a few questions that will get you back on track, then recommence your prepared themes and topics.

C. VARIABLES

Remember, variables are just that—the answer may be yes, it may be no, it may be "I don't know". Depending on what you hear, you can move forward with some effective cross examination.

Variable safe harbors include:

- Preparing for testimony
- Speaking with attorneys
- Reviewing documents
- What the witness brought with them to court

Variable safe harbors are areas that you know will yield information that will not get you into too much trouble. As discussed below, depending on what you find, a Cross Exposition (see Chapter 1.6.B) may be used to further flesh out impeaching or discrediting information against the witness.

D. EXAMPLES OF SAFE HARBORS

Speaking with others about the case/ testimony (before and during trial). This area can give you some issues to cross examine upon, which are built on the premise that the witness is biased against your client.

Q. Did you meet with [opposing counsel, opposing party, expert] *in preparation for this trial?*

Q. *When?*

Q. *Where?*

Q. *Did anyone but anyone else coffee/dinner/drinks?*

Q. *How long did it last?*

Q. *Who was there?*

Q. *Where are they today?*

Q. *Substance?*

Q. *Recorded?*

Q. *Actions taken after conversation?*

Remember, some of the questions may yield information that is deserving of a Cross Exposition such as how much money was spent on a witness (say, for an expensive dinner for "trial preparation")—implying that the witness has been financially incented to testify for the other side.

Desire to be involved in case (subpoena vs. volunteer). I *love* a volunteer witness—that person who is there to make damned sure that he or she gets to try to throw your client under the bus. That reeks of bias, and is a great safe harbor.

Preparation for testimony. Showing that a witness has gone overboard shows bias. Showing that a witness has not prepared goes to credibility.

Q. *You knew this trial was set?*

Q. *You knew this date was coming?*

Q. *You had plenty of time to prepare?*

Q. You had the opportunity to read your report/deposition?

Q. You understand how important this trial is to my client?

Q. You understand how important this trial is to [opposing party]?

Q. You understand the jury needs accurate information in order to render a proper verdict?

Q. Yet you did nothing to prepare to testify?

Understanding of the oath. When a witness is all over the place, and making stuff up on you, go to the oath. Certainly you can use other methods of impeachment (prior inconsistent statements, negative impeachment, etc.), but use the oath. Jurors, as lay people, generally respect the judicial system and the concept of taking an oath to tell the truth. Using the oath is always a safe area, as no witness is going to make light of the oath.

Opportunities to give missing information/ testimony. Akin to negative impeachment (what is missing), would be cross examination on the failure to follow up and make sure the truth—the *whole* truth—comes out in the judicial process. Inquiring about a witness' continued ability to access the courts, the attorneys, or even at upon an innate internal desire that justice be done, is a safe harbor area from which witnesses cannot wiggle out.

Q. You have known about this case since the day the incident happened?

Q. Yet you have never told anyone before today that [what was said on direct]?

Q. You know how to get ahold of Mr. Lawyer?

Q. You know how to contact the court?

Q. You know how to contact the clerk?

Q. You have access to the internet?

Q. You have heard of Google?

Q. You know the number to 911, don't you?

Q. So there is no reason that you could not have made that fact known before today.

The "number to 911" question may be a little argumentative and flippant, but it makes the point.

Opportunities to fabricate. Witnesses changing their statements, stories, or testimony is usually linked to some other triggering factor. Exploring when a witness made a different statement is effective and safe, as it can be linked up later to the witness' lack of credibility.

Cutting out speculation. Establishing that the witness has no direct knowledge can be a great assent in your story. By cutting out any ability to speculate, or for the jury to assign some degree of direct knowledge to a witness, you can neutralize the witness.

Q. Officer Witness, you weren't there when all this occurred?

A. I was not.

Q. You didn't see any part of what happened?

A. I did not.

Q. You don't have direct knowledge of what the defendant did?

A. Nope.

Q. You don't have direct knowledge of what the defendant said?

A. Negative.

Q. You also don't know what the accuser did or said?

A. That is true, I do not.

Bias and prejudice. A great safe harbor is bias prejudice. The opportunities are too vast to list here, but simple questions like *"you do not like my client, do you?"* and the like are always safe, *if in fact the witness has the biases or prejudices.* Some witnesses, such as records custodians and law enforcement officers, are simply doing their jobs and don't have an ax to grind, so to speak.

7.3 TARGET DOCUMENTS

Target documents are those documents (and other items of tangible evidence) that you may use when cross examining the witness. The key word is *may*, because you never know what is going to happen. And if nothing else has been stressed in this book, flexibility and the ability to adapt is the name of the game.

Target documents can be anything, from an actual exhibit that has already been entered, to an item of evidence for which you are laying the evidentiary foundation for admission later. It can certainly be something you will need to impeach a witness. It can be something—almost *anything*—that can refresh a witness' recollection.

Here's the "don't forget": *never, ever, ever get up to cross examine a witness without having your target documents ready and right at hand.*

A.   ELECTRONIC FORMAT

I am a big fan of electronic (paperless) practice. If for no other reason, it is because I can access it whenever I want to, and work on my litigation cases at any time. There are times I am alone and think of a point; I can use my smart phone to access my files, review reports or depositions, and use my note taking app to jot down my thoughts. Nothing is lost, and I can capture my work product at any place and at any time.

However, not all courtrooms are up to speed with the paperless format. I make the distinction between court and courtroom, because there are many clerks' offices that are paperless, and the courtrooms down the hall have no presentation technology.

If you have the ability to use technology in the courtroom, take advantage. Jurors are no longer afraid of it; in fact, I believe that they expect it. I did an opening statement in a murder case in 1998 using PowerPoint to connect the mass of defendants (it was a gang fight with dozens of participants)—no one had ever seen anything like that before then. Now, jurors get tired and bored when you play with paper exhibits. Come into the 21st century already!

Whatever you use, and there are many options out there, be sure to have everything in place and *practice* using it.

Also, be sure to either check out the courtroom in advance, or take every possible cord and cable that you might need to make your presentation. My firm has actually taken a big-screen TV to the courtroom in order to conduct a cross examination. In other cases, we have been able to just "plug and play." It is critical that you take the time to know what you will need before you start—if not, you will be embarrassed. I was a part of the largest Medicare fraud case ever tried in the late 1990s—there were over 1800 boxes of documents! We expected that the presentation would be all electronic, with the government using scanned documents on the overhead. It didn't work—after waiting for hours on the first day of testimony for the government's tech guy to try to make it work, the judge ordered that the prosecutors use paper and the overhead projector. It was not pretty.

Do not assume that your technology will work with the court's technology, and be prepared.

B.   GOOD OLD PAPER

Paper is not bad. Countless trials were tried using paper exhibits for over a century—maybe longer—before courtroom technology began to take hold.

The persuasive power of paper. Paper still has a huge degree of acceptance and importance in the courtroom. Legend or lore has instilled in people a blend of reverence and fear of a "legal document." Papyrus, scrolls, sheepskin, parchment . . . all have played a huge part in documenting the journey of humanity. The most important documents in history were written on one of these forms. The Declaration of Independence, the Bill of Rights, the Magna Carta are some.

For jurors, important paper documents in their lives are marriage certificates, birth certificates, social security cards, diplomas, certificates . . . even a paycheck. The importance of a paper document is still alive and well.

But for courtroom practicality, paper can breathe life into the trial. When cross examining on a breach of contract, what more important than the contract itself? The inked page holds so much more power than a cold electronic version. Think of the impact to the jury when you hand the actual contract to the defendant, and make him or her answer questions while holding the very document he or she signed and then violated. The last time he or she held it, someone else was counting on him or her living up to what he or she was signing—that is not lost on the jury.

The same impact comes from anything a witness has written or signed—contracts, letters, memos, checks, receipts . . . the list goes on and on.

Evidentiary value of paper. Sometimes the paper itself is the star of the show. Think of the prosecution of Martha Stewart for lying to investigators—it was the ink on the paper that proved the lie. A stock sale memo figured prominently in the investigation of her for insider trading. The memo was written in blue ink, but *two different types* of blue ink. The single notation that was purported to establish a preexisting agreement to sell at a certain price point—"@60"—was written in a "scientifically distinguishable" ink from the rest of the memo. In that case, the paper itself would be critical to cross on—this is not an actual transcript, but we can only imagine it would have gone something like this:

Q. *You held this in your hand?*

Q. *You saw the writing?*

Q. *That writing in blue ink?*

Q. *You got another blue ink pen?*

Q. *You wrote "@60"?*

Q. *And you know that the FBI lab at Quantico has determined that ink is different than all the other ink on the page?*

A PDF ("portable document format") just wouldn't have the same impact.

Think about the ease of presentation as opposed to the impact you want the paper to have during your cross.

C. DISCOVERY DISCLOSURE AND FILING WITH THE COURT BEFORE TRIAL

Be sure to comply with all discovery rules consistent with the state, Federal, local rules and any pretrial orders. You do not want to be prohibited from using good material on cross simply because you did not disclose it to the other side.

Also check your jurisdiction's rules regarding filing requirements. Some courts require that deposition transcripts be filed before they can be used as impeachment material.

7.4 ETHICAL CONSIDERATIONS DURING CROSS EXAMINATION

Above all else, be ethical. No matter the skill—good or bad—of the advocate . . . no matter the experience level . . . no matter the issues or cause of action . . . the trial lawyer must act ethically.

Ethical issues arise in two ways: the physical behavior of the advocate, and the substance of the questions.

A.   THE ADVOCATE'S BEHAVIOR

Years of experience in the courtroom has taught this author that there are certain things that jurors just do not like. There are advocate behaviors that can alienate a juror and critically cripple your ability to persuade and win. Consider this non-exclusive list of behaviors one must exhibit in court and during cross examination:

- **Keeping the attitude in check.** This general reminder goes out as a reminder that trial lawyers—type-A alpha dogs—tend to be competitive and emotional. Monitor your internal level. Don't let the highs get too high, or the lows too low. Keep a "poker face".

- **Watch where you are and your physical movements.** Stay away from the jury. Don't get too close to opposing counsel, unless it's an agreed encounter (whispering about an item of evidence, etc.). Ask to approach the witness with any documents or items of evidence you may need them to see up close. Ask before moving a lectern, an easel, or anything else. Ask before you move to better see during an opposing witness' testimony about a diagram or exhibit. In other words, a "Your Honor, may I . . ." will prevent an admonition from the court. It's simply more professional.

- **Confidence without cockiness.** It's wonderful to win—it's the objective of undertaking the representation of a client. And while a win can take various incarnations based of the goals of a client, advocates are there to achieve that goal. You will encounter small victories in the multitude of battles that make up the war of a trial. Be humble, and be professional. Don't gloat. You are not the star of the show, and jurors don't know and don't care about your trial win-loss record. They get that you just smoked a witness on cross examination. You will make a more lasting impression by simply letting your work speak for itself. Get the victory, and move one.

- **Zeal without fanaticism.** In every courthouse, there is "that attorney"—the one that makes every case the trial of the century. "That attorney" is the one that objects to every question, angrily demands a sidebar for the simplest of issues, yells, rolls the eyes, and generally acts like a jerk. Don't be "that attorney."

- **Perseverance without showing disappointment or disagreement.** We all know about "The Little Train That Could"—a story we tell children to illustrate the attitude of perseverance in the face of adversity. You will have cases where the facts are kicking you in the teeth, opposing counsel is kicking you in the teeth, and the judge is kicking you in the teeth. Maintain your dignity and your professionalism. Watch facial expressions and body language; maintain the highest deference with your responses to the court and counsel. Keep your head in the game. Jurors see what is happening, and will note your can-do attitude—which can lend credence to your story and case theories.

- **Don't joke around.** Know the difference between a "moment of levity" and being unprofessional for making improper jokes. The moments of levity are natural and organic, and will arise on their own time and when everyone needs (consciously or subconsciously) a mental break in the action. Some things are just funny. Don't create or manufacture those moments. They make you look immature and unprofessional.

- **Be detailed without bogging down.** Know your audience, and tailor your cross (or

opening, direct, or closing) to what is needed
to do the job. This author has been noted
(more accurately, *criticized*) by opponents for
long cross examinations. Duly noted—but I
am not up there for my health or to pound on
collateral or irrelevant matters. If the cross
takes ten minutes, fine. If it takes an hour,
well, it will be done in a manner that will only
seem like ten minutes.

- **Be prepared.** Most jurors will do their civic
  duty without too much grief, but they really
  do not want to be there. They may find it
  interesting, or simply see jury service as
  something as important as military service
  . . . but they still have jobs, family matters,
  and general life obligations. If you are not
  prepared, they see it as a waste of time. Your
  floundering around will not go unnoticed. It
  will be met with resentment, and that will
  lead to dislike and consequently a rejection of
  your story. Be like a Boy Scout: *be prepared*.

- **Outbursts.** There is really no need to advise
  advocates to control themselves. However, if
  in doubt, think about Model Rule 3.5(d)
  ("Impartiality and Decorum of the Tribunal):
  *a lawyer shall not . . . engage in conduct
  intended to disrupt a tribunal.*

A word of caution—jurors are your peers. They are
your neighbors. They shop at the same stores you do,
and their children go to the same schools as the ones
your children attend.

In their mind, they are your equal. Your law degree means nothing in a courtroom. They see who you are. They quickly sense and attitude of "attorney entitlement." Jurors can get the impression—even wrongly—that you think you are better and smarter than the witness. Be very careful to not portray that to them.

The jurors on your care see themselves as your peers . . . your *equal*. Be sure to treat them that way be everything you do in a courtroom.

B.   THE SUBSTANCE OF THE QUESTIONS AND TESTIMONY

Ethics regarding the substance of the questions is of utmost importance. Without ethical advocates asking ethical questions and making ethical arguments, our system of justice will not work. While "truth" is always seen from different perspectives, there are limitations on *stretching* the truth.

If common sense and an internal since of ethics and morals are not enough, consider the American Bar Association Model Rules of Professional Conduct[1]:

---

[1]   ©2017 by the American Bar Association. Reprinted with permission. All rights reserved. This information or any portion thereof may not be copied or disseminated in any form or by any means or stored in an electronic database or retrieval system without the express written consent of the American Bar Association. Copies of the ABA Model Rules of Professional Conduct are available at shopaba.org.

Rule 3.1   Meritorious Claims And Contentions

A lawyer shall not bring or defend a proceeding, or assert or controvert an issue therein, unless there is a basis in law and fact for doing so that is not frivolous, which includes a good faith argument for an extension, modification or reversal of existing law. A lawyer for the defendant in a criminal proceeding, or the respondent in a proceeding that could result in incarceration, may nevertheless so defend the proceeding as to require that every element of the case be established.

* * *

Rule 3.4   Fairness To Opposing Party And Counsel

A lawyer shall not:

. . .

(b)   falsify evidence, counsel or assist a witness to testify falsely, or offer an inducement to a witness that is prohibited by law;

. . .

(e)   in trial, allude to any matter that the lawyer does not reasonably believe is relevant or that will not be supported by admissible evidence, assert personal knowledge of facts in issue except when testifying as a witness, or state a personal opinion as to the justness of a cause, the credibility of a witness, the culpability of a civil litigant or the guilt or innocence of an accused; or

(f) request a person other than a client to refrain from voluntarily giving relevant information to another party unless:

(1) the person is a relative or an employee or other agent of a client; and

(2) the lawyer reasonably believes that the person's interests will not be adversely affected by refraining from giving such information.

Cheap shots. You can't take cheap shots at a witness. You simply cannot ask questions that, whether by your question itself (actual or implied) or the answer, that is simply to put a bug in the mind of the jury that the witness is a bad person, or has done something illegal, when there is no actual basis for that accusation.

Rule 3.1 applies for purposes of cross examination because of the language "assert or controvert an issue therein." The themes and topics, and questions you use to get to your target facts, are all mini "issues". Thus, you may not undertake a line of questioning unless you have *a basis in law and fact for doing so that is not frivolous*. Further, Rule 3.4(e) clearly prohibits cross examining on an matter that is irrelevant and not supported by *admissible* facts.

Impeachment on irrelevant or collateral issues is not in good faith. Launching into questions about areas that have been excluded by pretrial order is not in good faith. It is the height of unethical behavior to ask a question simply to get inadmissible information into the mind of the jurors. Example:

> Q. *Mr. Witness, you are the accuser in this case,*
> *are you not?*
>
> A. *I am.*
>
> Q. *And your claim is that Mr. Defendant stole*
> *your dog?*
>
> A. *It is.*
>
> Q. *It is true that you're from North Korea, isn't*
> *it?*
>
> OBJ. *Objection, Your Honor, improper.*
>
> J. *Sustained. How is that of any relevance*
> *whatsoever, counsel??*

Clearly, that question was designed solely to impugn the character of the accuser (assuming that being from any particular county is in fact some sort of character flaw). Whatever the country of origin of Mr. Witness, he can still be the victim of a theft. Unless a question has a basis in fact AND in the law (under some statute or the Rules of Evidence), then it is just a cheap shot. Cheap shots are a violation of Rule 3.1 and the rule of your state bar.

Falsities—witnesses and counsel lying. The model rules prohibit allowing a witness to lie on the stand:

Rule 3.3   Candor Toward The Tribunal

(a)   A lawyer shall not knowingly:

(1)   make a false statement of fact or law to a tribunal or fail to correct a false statement of material fact or law previously made to the tribunal by the lawyer;

(2) fail to disclose to the tribunal legal authority in the controlling jurisdiction known to the lawyer to be directly adverse to the position of the client and not disclosed by opposing counsel; or

(3) offer evidence that the lawyer knows to be false. If a lawyer, the lawyer's client, or a witness called by the lawyer, has offered material evidence and the lawyer comes to know of its falsity, the lawyer shall take reasonable remedial measures, including, if necessary, disclosure to the tribunal. A lawyer may refuse to offer evidence, other than the testimony of a defendant in a criminal matter, that the lawyer reasonably believes is false.

(b) A lawyer who represents a client in an adjudicative proceeding and who knows that a person intends to engage, is engaging or has engaged in criminal or fraudulent conduct related to the proceeding shall take reasonable remedial measures, including, if necessary, disclosure to the tribunal.

(c) The duties stated in paragraphs (a) and (b) continue to the conclusion of the proceeding, and apply even if compliance requires disclosure of information otherwise protected by Rule 1.6.

(d) In an ex parte proceeding, a lawyer shall inform the tribunal of all material facts known to the lawyer that will enable the tribunal to make an informed decision, whether or not the facts are adverse.

There are many circumstances where you will be able to cross examine a favorable witness.

Unfortunately, that witness' favorability may be found in his or her willingness to lie for your client. You must think very carefully about undertaking a cross in such situation, as the flow of facts is from *you*.

Suppose you know that your client was in fact the person that committed the crime, and the government had eyewitnesses that placed him at the scene. Your defense witness wants to testify that she was with the defendant across town at the time. You know—or at least strongly suspect—she is lying about the alibi. Rule 3.3(a)(3) specifically prohibits you from (1) knowingly and (2) offering, evidence you know to be false. When in doubt, seek advice from an ethics attorney, and always err on the side of *not* violating the rule. "Knowingly", in the opinion of this author, includes "known or should have known"— check your local jurisdiction and you will likely find your Bar association and supreme court agree with me. "Offering" includes asking cross examination questions that elicit or otherwise perpetuate the lie.

Again, when in doubt, take the out in Rule 3.3(a)(3) and refuse to offer the evidence. If your client persists in that course of action, consult with an ethics attorney and consider withdrawing from further representation.

Another trick you see from time to time is for the cross examiner to pretend to look at a damning document, studying it while asking questions that are seemingly coming from the contents of that document. In reality, the document is a copy of a subpoena or docket sheet or something else totally unrelated. To give the false impression that the document has some really bad information about the witness is entirely improper.

In summary, avoid tricks and chicanery. Winners never cheat, and cheaters never win. And your reputation and bar license is far too valuable to engage in unethical behavior in court.

7.5 OLDIE BUT GOODIE RULES OF CROSS EXAMINATION

To be sure, cross examination has been around since there has been recorded thought. References to cross examination are found in the Bible:

Hear now my reasoning.

Listen to the pleadings of my lips.

Will you speak unrighteously for God, and talk deceitfully for him?

Will you show partiality to him?

Will you contend for God?

Is it good that he should search you out?

Or as one deceives a man, will you deceive him?

Job 13:6–9 (World English Bible, https://ebible.org/web/JOB13.htm)

He who pleads his cause first seems right; until another comes and questions him.

Proverbs 18:17 (World English Bible, https://ebible.org/web/PRO18.htm)

And, of course, there is the story of Daniel, whose cross examination of the local elders proved their lies and saved the life of Susanna. See Chapter 1.

In modern times, there are many works on cross examination (see Chapter 10). One of the very first well-known treatises on cross examination was *The Art of Cross Examination* by Francis Wellman. First published in 1903, it was reprinted for decades. Like many of the treatises out there, Wellman made a list of "golden rules" that are still practical today.

WELLMAN—1903	BODIFORD—2018
I. BE CONFIDENT, BE VIGILANT	
Except in indifferent matters, never take your eye from that of the witness; this is a channel of communication from mind to mind, the loss of which nothing can compensate. "Truth, falsehood, hatred, anger, scorn, despair, And all the passions—all the soul—is there."	• Look the witness in the eye, and make him or her look you in the eye. Show no fear, and that you are all business. Show you will get your answer and the truth. • While you are staring in without fear, watch the witness closely, for ticks and tells.
II. LISTEN FOR SEMANTIC GAMES	
Be not regardless, either, of the *voice* of the witness; next to the eye	• Listen not only to what the witness

this is perhaps the best interpreter of his mind. The very design to screen conscience from crime—the mental reservation of the witness—is often manifested in the tone or accent or emphasis of the voice. For instance, it becoming important to know that the witness was at the corner of Sixth and Chestnut streets at a certain time, the question is asked, Were you at the corner of Sixth and Chestnut streets at six o'clock? A frank witness would answer, perhaps I was near there. But a witness who had been there, desirous to conceal the fact, and to defeat your object, speaking to the letter rather than the spirit of the inquiry, answers, No; although he may have been within a stone's throw of the place, or at the very place, within ten

says, but *how* he or she says it.

- Do you hear hesitation?
- Do you hear frustration?
- Do you hear honesty?
- The maker gave you *two* ears for a reason—use them both.
- Listen to the words that are being said—is the witness splitting hairs?
- If you ask, were you at the corner of Sixth and Chestnut Streets at six o'clock, knowing good and well that the witness *was* there, and the witness answers "no"—is he or she playing a game of semantics? Was he or she not *directly* on the corner, but rather a few yards away? Was it 5:59,

minutes of the time. The common answer of such a witness would be, I was not at the *corner at six o'clock*.

Emphasis upon both words plainly implies a mental evasion or equivocation, and gives rise with a skilful examiner to the question, At what hour were you at the corner, or at what place were you at six o'clock? And in nine instances out of ten it will appear, that the witness was at the place about the time, or at the time about the place. There is no scope for further illustrations; but be watchful, I say, of the voice, and the principle may be easily applied.

instead of dead-on 6PM?

- If you catch the witness playing those games, use it against him or her.

III. DON'T BE A JERK

Be mild with the mild; shrewd with the crafty; confiding with the honest; merciful to the young, the frail, or the fearful; rough to the

- Be mindful of your tone.
- Don't get cute, don't be a jerk. Dignity and professionalism at all times.

ruffian, and a thunderbolt to the liar. But in all this, never be unmindful of your own dignity. Bring to bear all the powers of your mind, not that *you* may shine, but that *virtue* may triumph, and your *cause* may prosper.

Remember that before you can control someone else, you have to be able to control yourself.

IV. DON'T GO WHERE YOU DON'T KNOW

In a *criminal*, especially in a *capital* case, so long as your cause stands well, ask but few questions; and be certain never to ask *any* the answer to which, if against you, may destroy your client, unless you know the witness *perfectly* well, and know that his answer will be favorable *equally* well; or unless you be prepared with testimony to destroy him, if he play traitor to the truth and your expectations.

- Don't go fishing— have a purpose.
- Don't ask a question for which you do not already know the answer. It could blow up in your face.
- Use techniques for improvising cross examinations, and safe harbor questions.
- Otherwise, don't mess around too much with a witness you don't know anything about.

V. LOCK THE WITNESS DOWN	
An equivocal question is almost as much to be avoided and condemned as an equivocal answer; and it always *leads* to, or *excuses*, an equivocal answer. Singleness of purpose, clearly expressed, is the best trait in the examination of witnesses, whether they be honest or the reverse. Falsehood is not detected by cunning, but by the light of truth, or if by cunning, it is the cunning of the witness, and not of the counsel.	• Ask a limited, leading question, that deals with one fact, calls for either a yes or a no, and does not need further explanation. • Get a yes, or get a no. Either one. But get don't let the witness waffle or equivocate. • If he or she waffles, hold his or her feet to the fire and get your yes, or your no.
VI. CONTROL THE WITNESS AND YOURSELF	
If the witness determine to be witty or refractory with you, you had better settle that account with him at *first*, or its items will increase with the examination. Let him have an opportunity of satisfying himself either that he has mistaken	• Control your witness. Once you relinquish control, you can't tell your story. The witness is going to tell his or hers. . .*not yours.* You will not regain control once it is lost . . .

| *your* power, or his *own*. But in any result, be careful that you do not lose your temper; anger is always either the precursor or evidence of assured defeat in every intellectual conflict. | • . . . and you will look dumb in the process.
• Be strong, be confident, but do not lose your cool. |

VII. STAY ONE STEP AHEAD OF THE WITNESS

| Like a skilful chess-player, in every move, fix your mind upon the combinations and relations of the game— partial and temporary success may otherwise end in total and remediless defeat. | • Think in 3D.
• Use control techniques.
• Use Cross Expositions to stop errant witnesses. |

VIII. EVERYONE HAS A PLAN, 'TIL THEY GET PUNCHED IN THE FACE

| Never undervalue your adversary, but stand steadily upon your guard; a random blow may be just as fatal as though it were directed by the most consummate skill; the negligence of one often cures, and sometimes renders | • Listen.
• Think in 3D.
• Know your facts.
• Have a plan, have safe harbors.
• Don't give up, regroup and keep going. |

effective, the blunders of another.	
IX. ALWAYS BE PROFESSIONAL AND THINK THING THROUGH	
Be respectful to the court and to the jury; kind to your colleague; civil to your antagonist; but never sacrifice the slightest principle of duty to an overweening deference toward *either*. In "The Advocate, his Training, Practice, Rights, and Duties," written by Cox, and published in England about a half century ago, there is an excellent chapter on cross-examination, to which the writer is indebted for many suggestions. Cox closes his chapter with this final admonition to the students, to whom his book is evidently addressed:— "In concluding these remarks on cross-examination, the rarest, the most useful, and the	• Be the bigger person. Stay in control of your witness AND yourself. • Always be the consummate professional. • Sometimes less is more. • If you are not helping, you are hurting. • Everything you ask, ask it for a reason. • Fight hard, but know when to stop. • "More cross examinations are suicidal than homicidal." —*Emory Buckner* • Being careful, prepared, and professional is far more important— and effective—than

most difficult to be acquired of the accomplishments of the advocate, we would again urge upon your attention the importance of calm discretion. In addressing a jury you may sometimes talk without having anything to say, and no harm will come of it. But in cross-examination every question that does not advance your cause injures it. If you have not a definite object to attain, dismiss the witness without a word. There are no harmless questions here; the most apparently unimportant may bring destruction or victory. If the summit of the orator's art has been rightly defined to consist in knowing when to sit down, that of an advocate may be described as knowing when to keep his seat. Very little experience in our courts will teach you

being brash and flamboyant.

this lesson, for every day will show to your observant eye instances of self-destruction brought about by imprudent cross-examination. Fear not that your discreet reserve may be mistaken for carelessness or want of self-reliance. The true motive will soon be seen and approved. Your critics are lawyers, who know well the value of discretion in an advocate; and how indiscretion in cross-examination cannot be compensated by any amount of ability in other duties. The attorneys are sure to discover the prudence that governs your tongue. Even if the wisdom of your abstinence be not apparent at the moment, it will be recognized in the result. Your fame may be of slower growth than that of the talker,

but it will be larger and more enduring."	

7.6 TAKEAWAYS

- Practice litanies for refreshing, impeaching, and handling evidence.

- Always be beyond reproach with your ethics and professionalism.

7.7 EXERCISE

Exercise 1:

Memorize the common evidentiary objections, foundations, refreshing and impeaching. Practice with your cross sparring partner.

CHAPTER 8
CROSS EXAMINATION EXAMPLES

8.1 THE AUTHOR IN ACTION

After great personal debate about doing this, I am including some of my own cross examinations for your consideration.

I think it is important to obtain transcripts and, where available, audio or video of your courtroom advocacy, and to critically review it. First, it helps you grow as an advocate. The bad can be made better, and the good can be made great. What you may sense and react to in real time takes on a greater meaning when you have time to sit and think about it.

Second, having a record of what you do in court makes your parents happy to see what you're doing with that law degree!

As to the first point, the inclusion of some of my own work here is to demonstrate the system that I use and have attempted to set out in this book. My cross examinations are effective, but no particular one is "perfect". So, I will settle for effective. I hope that some of what I have practiced and delivered in court will assist you in finding your own voice as an advocate. While I think my way of doing it works, always work to find out what works best for *you*. You can only do that by watching, listening, reading, and practicing!

There is almost no way to include an *entire* trial as an example in book, so most authors use isolated transcripts. A good example of my cross examination techniques is found in a jury trial I litigated on the charge of driving under the influence ("DUI"). This example works because it was a one fact witness case (there were two witnesses related to the breath testing machine, but the arresting officer supplied most of the facts). Therefore, the entire trial is mostly encased in the testimony of one person.

A.   THE CASE

My client was arrested for a run of the mill DUI. A seemingly run of the mill DUI—she had one of the best videos I have ever seen, but blew *twice the legal limit* in Florida (which is .08, pursuant to Florida Statute section 316.193). Certainly there was some really great things to work with, but also a really bad fact that had to be overcome—the high breath.

This was the police report:

Video was available, and showed both the traffic stop as well as and the interactions with my client. She looked very, very good on the video—which was completely contrary to what was in the report.

B.   THE CROSS SHEETS

My cross sheets. I set my case up as follows:

Theory: Because the video showed my client driving without any issues, and performing the roadside tests almost flawlessly, the case theory was "believe your eyes, not what you are told." Boiled down to a word, it was a case of *believability*— everyone has seen someone who had too much to drink. People form their own opinions based on prior life experience.

Themes: Rush to judgment, not impaired, believe your eyes and not this cop

Topics: No bad driving, no indicators of impaired driving, cop predisposed to arrest, other innocent reasons for her appearance, excellent performance of physical tests.

The cross sheets looked like this (these are the actual sheets; these are an earlier and slightly different version of what is in Chapter 3.5):

JOSEPH C. BODIFORD, P.A.   CROSS-EXAMINATION SHEET

STATE v. ▮▮▮▮▮
CASE NO. ▮▮▮▮▮
WITNESS: OFC ▮▮▮▮▮
TOPIC: NORMAL FACULTIES: SEE, HEAR, WALK, TALK, DRIVE

THEME FOR CLOSING:
BELEIVE YOUR EYES:
NF's ARE OK !

Phase I, Veh in Motion   (V - 4)

- Weaving (across lane lines); straddling; Swerving; Turning w/ wide radius; Drifting; Almost striking obj/veh;
- Stopping problems; varying speed (Accel/decel); too slow; speeding
- Going wrong way on 1-way; wrong lane; Slow to respond to traffic sigs/ofc sigs; stopping for no reason; no headlights @ night; improper/unsafe turn; driving on other than roadway; inapprop. resp. to ofc; unusual behavior

"Appearing impaired"

- STOP: trouble w/ controls; trouble exiting; fumbling w/ docs; not understanding; slurred speech; leaning on veh; repeating q's; wrong answers; odor of alc
- ⊕ INNOCENT REASONS ~~FOR HER~~ DRIVING
- → "DRIVING" IS A NORMAL FACULTY

- ONLY 1 NHTSA "CUE"
  (Stop bar viol is NOT NHTSA)

- OTHERWISE, OPERATION IS FLAWLESS

- YOU CHANGED LANES IN INTERSECTION

1:30-1:45; business

- drifting to ⓛ, almost striking median [NOT IN REPORT] [NOT ON VIDEO]
- drifting "several" times [NOT IN REPORT]
- pulled ⓡ ? "EASY, SAFE" } YOUNG FEMALE
  — siren to get thrugh traffic

- ~~Eyes~~
  - Eyes
  - [watching me] [dog/sig intox] [NOT IN REPORT]

PAGE 1 of 4

JOSEPH C. BODIFORD, P.A.   CROSS-EXAMINATION SHEET

STATE v. ▮▮▮▮
CASE NO.
WITNESS: OFC ▮▮▮▮
TOPIC: NORMAL FAC's

THEME FOR CLOSING:
N/Fs ARE PERFECT

PHASE II: PERSONAL CONTACT

+ KNOW LT's EVERYDAY APPEARANCE?
  (So, no baseline?)

- YES: smoke, contacts, time & day, crying
- COOPERATIVE [Told you "BAD EVENING" - crying, alone ... ??
- FUMBLING - normal, everyone
- ALC. CONTAINERS.
- SLURRED SPEECH? ADVISE?

"QUESTIONING TECHNIQUES" -
  - Divided attention - purposely confuses
  - No unusual reactions
  - Followed instructions
  - got out, veh in gear, closed door,
    d/n lean, etc

⊗ INNOCENT EXPLANATION FOR
    APPEARANCE

DISTINCT
ODOR

1:20

TRYING TO TELL YOU WHAT
WAS WRONG - YOU JUST
WANTED TO DO FSTs?
(D/N care why having a bad
night)

PAGE 2 of 4

JOSEPH C. BODIFORD, P.A.   CROSS-EXAMINATION SHEET

STATE v. ▮▮▮▮▮
CASE NO.
WITNESS: OFC. ▮▮▮
TOPIC: FSES GREAT

THEME FOR CLOSING:

PHASE III: "PRE-ARREST" SCREENING

GOING TO ARREST ?!?

② COMPLEX INSTRUCTIONS IN SHORT TIME

WAT - GO THRU RPT FACTORS
         V
         VIDEO   (VIII-11)

NHTSA: "REQUIRES A DESIGNATED
         STRAIGHT LINE"

(if imaginary: what size? color? length?
         Where? she knew that?)

→ "IMAGINE"
-- "or as straight as you can"

SLOPE DOWN

OLS - PERFECT!

④ INNOCENT REASONS FOR PERFORMANCE:
     Fatigue
     Stress
     Nerves
     Pains in feet
     Lights in eyes

20 MIN -

"STANDARDIZED" ≠ VALIDATED

seconds mentally & physically @ same time
1 demo   DISTURB WALKED

8 "CLUES" - 4

Finger out - to tell
Jurors there's something
They can't see

4 "CLUES" - SWAYING
       "dropped foot"
         [NOT IN VIDEO]

[DEMONSTRATE..? → He gave
               ½ demo]

You're doing paperwork!

PAGE <u>3</u> of <u>4</u>

I have noted in the transcript below where the sheets change as I change themes and topics. You should be able to discern as you read the transcript where I was on the sheets. Remember, *I do not use a list of questions*. I think in 3D as I go, using the sheets as a guideline for my questions. My questions are born of telling the story from the skeleton of the sheets.

C.   THE CROSS

Here is the transcript of the cross exam. In regular font is the actual cross. In italic font is my commentary now, several years later. I am looking at what I could have done better, what I could have left out, and (of course) the GOOD STUFF.

The name of and references to my client has been omitted at my discretion, as she is a nice young lady who does not need to be memorialized as a criminal trial defendant.

BY MR. BODIFORD:
CROSS EXAMINATION

Q.   Good morning.

A.   Good morning, sir.

Below, I start with Cross Sheet 1, and set it up by using the witness to give some background of his training and techniques.

Cross Sheet 1 of 4:

NORMAL FACULTIES: SEE, HEAR, WALK, TALK, DRIVE

Q.   All right. Let's go through these—this investigation and all this. Now, you start with—there's three phases to a DUI investigation per NHTSA, right?

A.   Yes, sir.

Q.   And then—and NHTSA is N-H-T-S-A, right?

A.   Correct.

Q.   National   Highway   Traffic   Safety
Administration.

A.   Yes, sir.

Q.   And they're the ones that have somehow
standardized this process that you go through when
you're doing a DUI investigation.

A.   Correct.

Q.   And standardization means all of you
supposedly do it the same way—

A.   Yes.

Q.   —or supposed to do it the same way, right?

A.   Yes, sir.

Q.   There's a difference between standardization
and validation, correct?

A.   Yes, sir.

   *Now I proceed into the facts of the case, starting
with Cross Sheet 1 of 4.*

Q.   Okay. The first phase is vehicle in motion,
correct?

A.   Yes, sir.

Q.   Okay. And then your Phase I observations,
there's any number of things that you can look for
according to NHTSA, right?

A.   Yes, sir.

Q.   And you're familiar with those, right?

A.   Yes, sir.

Q. So things you could look for according to NHTSA are weaving, both within the lane, and across the lane lines, correct?

A. Yes, sir.

Q. Straddling the lanes as you drive down the street?

A. Yes, sir.

Q. Swerving?

A. Yes.

Q. Turning with a wide radius?

A. Uh-hum. Yes.

Q. Drifting?

A. Yes.

Q. And drifting is when they're kind of just going one direction, and they correct it, right? And they drift over, and they come back, correct?

A. Yes, sir.

Q. Okay. And almost striking a vehicle or object, that's a sign that you could look for as far as Phase I, correct?

A. Yes, sir.

Q. Other things that NHTSA puts out are stopping problems; do you agree?

A. Yes, sir.

Q. Varying speeds, meaning somebody'll go fast for a while, and then they'll go really slow for a while, that's a—that's a cue, right?

A. Correct.

Q. Or rapid acceleration, burning out at a stop sign, or slamming on brakes, deceleration, those could be clues, correct?

A. Yes, sir.

Q. People that just get over there and go too slow, they're going like 25 in a 55, that could be a clue of impairment, right?

A. Correct.

Q. And to the contrary, speeding could be a clue.

A. Correct.

Q. Could be a clue. Okay. How about going the wrong way down a one-way street? NHTSA says that's a clue, correct?

A. Yes, sir.

Q. And there's others, driving in the wrong lane; do you agree?

A. Yes, sir.

Q. Being slow to respond to traffic signals or an officer's direction, that's a clue, right?

A. Yes, sir.

Q. You know, when an officer's directing traffic, and the person just goes right by them, you know? Is that right?

A. Yes, sir.

Q. People that stop for no reason, that—that could be a clue of impairment per NHTSA, correct?

A. Yes.

Q. That would fall in the category of those folks that you see that are sleeping through a cycling green light, you know, they're just there for apparently no reason, that's a clue that somebody could be under the influence, right?

A.   Yes, it is.

Q.   Clearly. Somebody driving with no headlights at night, right, that's a clue?

A.   Yes, sir.

Q.   NHTSA also says that making an improper or unsafe turn is a clue of impairment, right?

A.   Yes, sir.

Q.   And also driving on somewhere other than the roadway, you know, like driving on the sidewalk, so to speak. That could be a clue of impairment, correct?

A.   Yes, sir.

Q.   Inappropriate response to an officer's signals, or other unusual behavior, those are all clues, correct?

A.   They can be, yes, sir.

Q.   They can be. And those are ones that are—that NHTSA has come out and said, officers, look for these things, right?

A.   Yes, sir.

Q.   Okay. Now, do you have your NHTSA manual with you today by chance?

A.   No, I don't.

Q.   You didn't bring it? Okay. NHTSA also says that looking at the actual stop itself once you've activated the lights to conduct the stop, that there's continued clues that you can continue to see, right? Such as trouble with the controls on their car, you know, they put the left blinker on; and then the right blinker; and then the left, that could be a clue, correct?

A.   Yes, sir.

Q.   Trouble exiting the car. You know, when people get out and they fall over, that's a clue, right?

A.   Yes, sir.

Q.   Now, fumbling with documents, you've told us about that, and certainly you think that's a clue, correct, that's a NHTSA clue?

A.   Yes, sir.

Q.   Not understanding what you as the officer are telling them, right?

A.   Correct.

Q.   So these are all things that you can look for as far as drivers and to determine whether they are impaired.

A.   Yes, sir.

Q.   Now, in this situation, you're telling us that you saw on her vehicle in motion, Phase I detection, before any contact with her, you've essentially seen her drifting to the left almost striking a median; is that what you said?

A.   Yes, sir.

Q.   Okay. Now you remember reporting this case; did you not?

A.   I did.

Happily, I just asked over 40 questions in a row with only a "yes" or "no" response—which is unusual. The questions, tone, and pace were designed and delivered in a manner to assure those responses from the witness.

Q. Do you have your report with you today?

Open-ended question—bad, but no harm done. If he said yes, he could not wiggle out of giving me the answer I wanted. If he said no, he would be revealed as a cop that showed up for court unprepared.

A. I have a couple of the pages, just my narrative—

Q. Okay.

A. —that I brought with me, yes, sir.

Q. Right. And in that narrative you mention drifting, but nowhere in your report do you say anything about almost striking a median, did you?

Negative impeachment—highlighting what should be there by showing it is not.

A. Just that she crossed over the line.

Q. Right. Now, that report was made that night, correct?

A. Yes, sir.

Q. And it was made based on your observations while they were still fresh in your mind, right?

A. Yes, sir.

Q. And the reason that you make the reports is so that you can have a fresh memory when you come in five, six months later at a trial, right?

A. Yes, sir.

Q. Okay. And it's important that you make those reports accurate? Yes?

A.   Yes

Q.   And it's important that they be all-inclusive—

A.   Yes

Q.   —correct? Good, bad, and the ugly?

A.   Correct.

By going through the timing of writing the report, and why it was important to write it, I was able to highlight its importance, and credit its contents.

Q.   Right. So almost striking a median is a fairly significant driving indicator, isn't it?

A.   Yes, sir.

Q.   And that's—but that's—conspicuously you've left that out of your written narrative at two different places in your report, you would agree?

"Conspicuously" is probably objectionable as argumentative. Bad.

A.   The actual wording of that, yes, sir, but—

Q.   Right.

A.   —I did put that she crossed over the line—

Q.   Right.

A.   —which there is a line right next to the median.

Saying "right" as he was explaining was not planned, probably done to convey "yes, we get that, but . . ." but it's not good to talk over the witness.

Bad for making a record, and may come across as condescending.

Q. But striking the median—striking a median, the first time we've heard of that is today in front of these jurors.

An admission that a fact was made up at trial—not an everyday occurrence, and certainly a great catch. Note, I used "in front of these jurors" to imply he was lying to them, not to me. It was designed to include them and personalize their investment in the trial.

A. Yeah. That she almost struck the median, yes, sir.

Q. Okay. And that's also not on the video.

A. Correct, yeah.

**NOTE: In the notes section on the right of Cross Sheet 1 of 4, you see my notes from direct examination about his "drifting" comments.

Add to the fact that it's not in the report, and he's just now making it up, the jury is reminded that the video is the true measure of whether he's telling the truth or not.

Q. Today you said that she drifted several times, right?

A. Several times to the left, yes, sir.

Q. Okay. And again, looking at your report, you say that she drifted from her lane of travel, then violated a stop bar. You say in your report she drifted once, correct? Are you—you've read your report in preparation for today, right?

Terrible question—compound—more than one fact. Bad!

A.   Yes, sir, I did.

Q.   Okay. And so you make it seem in your report is that there's one incident of drifting.

A.   Well, prior to the other one—there was the one that's—that I put in the report, but then the one that was not captured on video, which—she went towards me—

Q.   So you're only—

A.   —and put that on—

Q.   —putting on—in the report what's on the video?

A.   I—I don't know. Could I—if—if I could look at my report again.

Q.   Sure.

At this point, I knew that I had him on the ropes. What's better, I knew that he knew it, too. He was about to make up another fact, and I was going to let him and punish him for it.

However, we were talking over each other—I should have waited for him to finish.

MR. BODIFORD: Judge, may I approach?

Deference to the court.

THE COURT: Yes, you may.

THE WITNESS: Just to verify exactly what I said.

MR. BODIFORD: Mine—yeah, mine is the—your narrative's going to be on these two pages, and I've got some notes which I don't mind you—

THE WITNESS: Okay.

MR. BODIFORD:—seeing or anything like that.

I don't mind him seeing my notes and highlights. I have nothing to hide—does he?

THE WITNESS: All right, sir.

MR. BODIFORD: So that's—let's go (unintelligible) to your recollection is refreshed, and we shall proceed.

Not the cleanest refreshment—bad. Predicate was not clear.

THE WITNESS: (Witness reviewed documents). I stated that she was observed drifting from her lane of travel crossing the painted lane marker. Yeah, that's what I stated (unintelligible)—

MR. BODIFORD: Okay.

THE WITNESS:—drifting, that she drifted from her lane of travel, crossing the painted lane marker.

BY MR. BODIFORD (CONTINUING):

Q. All right. So in your report, you make it sound as if that's one incident (unintelligible), correct?

Now that his recollection is refreshed . . . I would have given him the facts for him to agree to, but he just repeated what he'd read in his report, so there was no need.

A. Yes, sir. But it was actually several.

Q. So now that we're in trial, now you're telling us there's more than just one.

A. There was at least two, yes, sir.

Q. Okay. And none of them are depicted on this video.

A. I believe they are.

I knew what was on the video from my pretrial preparation, and the jury had just seen it on direct. I knew it was not there, and it was going to be interesting to see him try to point it out.

Q. Can you—can you point out where she's drifting over a—on—over a lane marker—

A. Yes, sir.

Q. —in this video?

A. Drifting over to the left. I—I don't know if her tires actually crossed the lane marker, but she drifted over to the left several times.

He receded from the crossing the lane marker because it was not on the video, and he realized it.

He was now trying to claim going back and forth (essentially weaving) in the lane had resulted in her tires going over the line and consequently that she had left the lane of travel. I knew how to clear that up.

Q. And—and so we're clear, when you're driving a car in the state of Florida, you're allowed to use the entire lane, right?

A. Yes, sir.

Q. If you want to drive on this side of the lane, as long as you stay in that lane, that's cool, right? Yes?

A. Sure.

Q. And if you want to drive over on—move over to the left or right, and drive on that side of the line, as long as you don't go over, it's cool, right?

A. Yes, sir.

"Cool" is probably too colloquial, but he did agree to what I needed—that using the entire lane to travel, and not staying in a perfectly straight line, is not a traffic infraction. And he went with it. Time for the kill shot . . .

Q.   All right. And that's what's depicted on this video, correct?

A.   Yes, sir.

Q.   There's no—there's no swerving, there's no—let me ask it to you this way: Do you agree that all—all the other NHTSA indicators that we've talked about here this morning, other than this drifting issue, none of those are on the video.

Terrible question. Started bad, ended bad.

A.   She violated the stop bar, sir.

Even the bad question gave me something to work with: he went a different direction in an effort to get out of the mire he'd created. I wouldn't let him.

Q.   But that's not a NHTSA indicator now, is it?

We went through this at the beginning, and the jury heard all the things that are *indicators. Now he's trying to add something in—I had to highlight that.*

A.   It's a traffic infraction, it is a—

Q.   Do you—

A.   —NHTSA indicator.

Q.   In all the things that NHTSA has said, is failing to stop at a stop bar, or failing to obey a traffic light, or a stop signal, is it an indicator?

A.   Failing to stop at a stop bar is a traffic violation.

Q.   Okay. So a traffic violation would be an indicator of impairment, right?

A.   Yes, sir.

He was trying to gain some ground back by saying that stopping over the big white stop bar at the intersection is an infraction, and essentially any and all infractions are indicators of alcohol impairment. That opened a huge door for me . . . again, I knew the video incredibly well from watching it over and over in pretrial preparation . . . and I knew HE had committed a traffic violation! Time to use it against him.

Q.   Okay. Is failing to—or is changing lane at an intersection, is that a traffic violation? If you change lanes while you're in an intersection under a light, that's—

A.   I believe it's within 50 feet, yes, sir.

Q.   Okay. So you—you can't—so we're clear, if you're going under the light and you're in the four-way, you can't be changing lanes, right? That's a—

A.   You're not—

Q.   —traffic violation.

A.   —supposed to, yes, sir.

Q.   Okay. You do that on this video, don't you?

A.   I don't know if I was within 50 feet.

Q.   Okay. But you weren't impaired that night.

A.   No, sir.

Q. Okay. So by you committing a—a violation as you go through the intersection, that's not an indicator in any way of you being impaired, correct?

Point made—the video clearly shows him committing an infraction, and certainly he had not been drinking, so his traffic infraction was not an indicator of his *impairment. But he sensed it coming.*

A. I'm not sure where exactly you're talking about. I'm—I'm sorry.

Q. When—when you—when—

MR. BODIFORD: Let's see if I can make this thing work.

I was trying to talk and work the video at the same time, and couldn't. Thank goodness it was not followed by my usual colorful words used when technology fails me. . .

A. Okay.

(Whereupon, the video recording was published to the jury).

Q. Technology sometimes fails us, doesn't it, Officer?

A. I'm just not sure exactly at what—what intersection you're referring to, sir.

Q. Well, how many intersections did you go through with her? Do you recall?

Seemed to me he was trying to make it look as if I were trying to confuse him. Back it up, go forward again, and make it clear it's not me who's being duplicitous, it's him.

A.   Well, there was the one at Westshore, and then—I'm not sure if there was one prior—

Q.   All right.

A.   —to that.

Q.   I can't tell where on the video we are, but you are traveling, would you agree, looks like through— is that Lois? And you're in the—

A.   Yeah—

Q.   —middle lane.

A.   —that—that's—

Q.   There you go.

A.   —approximately Lois.

I am still talking over him, which is a bad habit. Bad Joe!

Q.   You just changed lanes in the intersection; did you not?

A.   Yeah, that's—that's right after I observed the vehicle, so I wanted to get—get up to the vehicle. Yes, sir.

There's the admission—he violated the law but was not drunk, so traffic infractions are not per se indicators of impairment.

Q.   Again, so we're clear—I'm not saying you need to write yourself a ticket—the point of the—the exercise we're going through is, you committed a traffic infraction.

A.   Yeah. I had a reason—

Q.   Okay.

A.   —as the law enforcement officer, I had a—

Q. Okay.

A. —reason for making that adjustment.

He was trying to justify what he did and avoid my point—

I was in control, and I did not let him wiggle out of it . . .

Q. But the point is is that just committing a minor infraction does not always mean somebody is under the influence of alcohol.

A. That's correct.

Finally—he admits it. But not after I had to hold his feet to the fire.

Time to move on . . .

Q. All right. And, in fact, many of these other things that we talk about as far as using the lane or—or, you know, going from one side of the—those can be the results of innocent behavior, right?

A. Can be, yes, sir.

Q. Yeah. In fact, October 1st, we just passed a law in Florida that now makes what illegal?

Not a leading question, but a permissive open-ended question to see if he knew the current status of the law. If he did, we move on. If not, his credibility is further called into question as not knowing his job.

A. Texting while driving.

Q. Right. Exactly. Everybody likes to drive with their knees, and text with their thumbs. It's a distraction, correct?

A. Yes, sir.

Q.   And distractions—looking at the CD player can distract you from the roadway, right?

A.   Yes, sir.

Q.   Looking at the GPS can distract you from the roadway, right?

A.   Correct.

Q.   A child in the backseat can distract you from the roadway.

A.   Yes, sir.

Q.   Looking for someplace to go can distract you from the roadway, right?

A.   Yes, sir.

Q.   And none of those have anything to do with being under the influence, right?

A.   No, sir.

Q.   So there are innocent explanations for driving patterns.

A.   Correct.

Another set of "yes" answers to helpful facts—there are non-alcohol-related reasons for some bad driving patterns.

Q.   Okay. So all in all here, we essentially have two—two clues in the vehicle in motion phase of the investigation, would you agree—

A.   Yes, sir.

Q.   —the drifting and the stop bar.

A.   Yes, sir.

Q.   Both of which can be, you agree, sometimes innocent behavior.

A. Yes, sir.

Q. All right. And yet you felt that was enough to go ahead and pull her over.

A. Yes, with a traffic violation and what I observed—

Q. Now—

A. —prior to that, yes, sir.

Q. —you—You're—you're—you're not a regular run-of-the-mill Tampa Police Department officer, you are a special DUI investigator, right?

A. Yes, sir.

The idea was to contrast the otherwise innocent driving to the shark in the water, looking for a kill . . .

Q. And your job, as you told us earlier, is to drive around Tampa and look for impaired drivers, right?

A. Yes, sir.

Q. And to arrest them. Right?

A. Correct.

Another nice run of "yes" and "no" questions and responses to helpful fact questions—re-exerting control once again.

Q. So if you smell alcohol on somebody's breath and they're behind the wheel, chances are, they're going to jail, right?

A. Not necessarily.

Q. That's why you're there, that's why you're on the street.

A. Not just based on the odor of—of alcohol, no, sir.

He—and no cop I've ever crossed in a DUI trial will admit this, but phrasing it as a "chances are" question—a possibility—I get the fact out to the jury that any alcohol on one's breath can potentially get them arrested. That creates concern in the mind of the jury—"if I have a glass of wine at dinner, and get stopped on the way home, am I going to jail?"

Q. Okay. Would you agree that other than this—this—this issue of the drift and this issue of the stop bar, otherwise her—her operation of the vehicle is—is fine? There's nothing else that would lead you to any—

A. Yes, sir.

Q. Okay.

A. Yeah, the stop bar was the reason for my stopping her.

**NOTE: in the notes section on the right of Cross Sheet 1 of 4, you see my notes from direct about an "easy, safe" place to pull over—and my noted that the driver was a "young female." Not part of my planned cross, but something I picked up on direct and incorporated.

Q. Now, you—you mentioned that it concerned you that she had not pulled off to the left, that she had passed two, as you say, safe places to turn off to the left.

A. Yes, sir.

Q. Those are dark streets down there though going—that you pass, aren't they?

A. She could have stopped right in the turning lane.

Q.   Well, yeah. But, you know, she—you now know she's a young female, correct?

And—yes? You've got to say out loud for the record.

A.   After the fact, yeah.

Q.   Hmm?

A.   I didn't know who was driving the vehicle at the time.

I know that he probably did not know the driver was a young female when he was following her, but he certainly did later. And that knowledge is something he ignored when he testified on direct that not immediately pulling over was a sign of impairment.

Q.   I understand that. But you also base your arrest of her—by the time you arrest her and you know who she is; you base that on the totality of the circumstances, right?

"I understand that" is improper. Bad.

A.   Correct.

Q.   So—so we're clear, you're not saying that her not taking those two lefts that she could have, you're not saying that's indicative—indicators of impairment, is it? Because that's what I thought you said on direct.

Bad question. Should have been "[d]idn't you tell this jury on direct that . . ."

A.   It—it's involved in the whole situation, yes, sir.

Q.   Okay. So let's talk about it then. So if you're going to—if you're going to count off on her, or put into your totality of the circumstances this issue that she didn't turn down a dark street, once you know who she is, and once you see that she's a—a young female alone in a car, and you see that she's decided then to go to a well lit mall parking lot, doesn't that actually indicate good judgment?

Question is too long. Bad.

A. I don't believe it was good judgment for her to cross over two lanes of traffic with other vehicles present—

Q. Well, you had to—

A. —no, sir, I don't.

Q. —you mentioned your siren. Your siren was about that white car that was to your right that wouldn't get out of your way, correct?

A. Yes, sir.

Q. So—so let's talk about that white car for a second. She's trying to get over, the white car won't move for a full Tampa—marked Tampa police car with lights and siren on. That—that's what happened essentially, right? You're blowing your siren at this knucklehead next to you.

A. Yeah, well, she—she cut across, and then by the time I started to move over, the other vehicle was in the other lane, I couldn't get over.

Q. That other vehicle was not yielding to her or you, correct?

A. That's correct. But she—she shouldn't have cut over across the lanes.

He is trying to wiggle back to my client, while I am trying to demonstrate that the other driver of the

white car was exhibiting more "signs of impairment"
than my client. I exerted control by forcing him to
stay on that issue.

Q.   That notwithstanding though—

A.   Yes.

Q.   —this other vehicle—

A.   —bike lane, yeah.

Q.   —was also exhibiting clues of possibly being
impaired by not responding to an emergency
situation; do you agree? It's not her fault that the
siren came on; do you agree with that?

A.   For the siren, no, sir.

Q.   All right. Now, we go to phase—the next phase
of the three phases, and this next phase is known
as personal contact. Right?

A.   Yes.

MR. BODIFORD: Hold on.

   **Now we move on to Cross Sheet 2 of 4: "Normal*
Fac's [faculties]"

Q.   And the personal conduct—I'm sorry, personal
contact phase of the investigation is—is strange
because you don't have a baseline to start with with
these people. Do you understand what I mean by a
"baseline"?

A.   If you could explain just what you're—

Q.   You've never met ▮▮▮▮ (phonetics)—

A.   —referring to.

Q.   —▮▮▮▮ before that night in your entire life,
had you?

A.   Correct.

Q. Okay. So not having any knowledge of her, you don't know what she's like under regular circumstances, do you?

A. That's correct.

Q. Okay. You have to take her as you find her.

A. Yes.

Q. Now, with you—you said that when you first got up to her, you noticed several—several things that added into these clues or cues of—of impairment, what you call the totality of the circumstances? One of which was that her eyes were red, right?

A. Yes, sir.

Q. 1:30 in the morning, certainly an innocent explanation for having red eyes is that somebody's just been up for a long time, and they're tired, correct?

A. Correct. It could be.

Q. And somebody that may have been in a place where somebody was smoking, smoke can cause eyes to turn red; do you agree?

A. Yes, sir.

Q. She told you she was wearing contact lenses, didn't she?

A. Yes, sir.

Q. And certainly contact lenses can make somebody's eyes red, right?

A. Possible, yes, sir.

Q. Is there anything else about Ms. ▮▮▮▮ that night that you observed that would have led you to believe why her eyes were red—or understand why her eyes were red, other than alcohol?

So far, this part of this topic went well. He has given me lots of yeses to my favorable fact questions. He knows that the video shows my client crying and upset at the time of the very first contact, and her explanation of why. He knows I am going to make him out to be a bad guy for arresting her after she fought with her boyfriend.

**NOTE: this was on the note section of Cross Sheet 2 of 4, from my notes of his direct testimony.

A.   She said she had a rough night. I don't know if it was pertaining to a boyfriend or some situation. But—

Q.   And she was—

A.   —she did state that. At one point she started crying, yes.

Q.   She was crying. She was crying when you got up to her. And crying will make your eyes red, won't it?

A little bit of "counsel testifying" but it was on the video. Bad Joe!

A.   It can, yes, sir,

Q.   It can. And that's—crying is not an indicator of being under the influence of alcohol, is it?

A.   She wasn't crying when I first walked up to her.

Q.   Well, it's interesting you talk about that. First of all, she was fully cooperative with you, you agree with that.

A.   Oh, yes.

Q.   Okay. Now, as far as this having a bad evening, she—she stops and tells you initially, I'm having a bad night. And there's a long pause in the video, and you begin to talk to her again, and she says, I'm having a bad evening. She starts to try to tell you, she—she pauses—do you remember that, she pauses, and you're listening, right?

A.   Okay.

I don't blame him for simply answering "okay" as it was a convoluted question. Should have broken it into multiple questions. Bad!

Q.   You've got to—do you remember that on the video?

A.   Yes.

Q.   Okay. You've got a young female who's alone in a car at 1:30 in the morning who's crying. That you knew at that point in time, correct?

A.   Yes, sir.

Q.   And when she pauses saying she's had a bad evening, you didn't say why; you said, let's get out and do field sobriety exercises, didn't you?

A.   Yes, sir.

Q.   You didn't care why she was having a bad night, did you?

A.   I was there to do my job, sir.

Q.   So the answer is, your job—your job—does your—well, let me ask you this: Does your job not entail caring about a young female driver who is obviously crying in a car?

Terrible start, but otherwise good question. Trying to make him look like the shark in the water, looking for a meal, and doesn't care who he eats.

A.   I believe I demonstrated care and concern for her throughout the whole investigation.

Q.   But you didn't want to know why she was crying or why she was upset.

A.   Because she—

Q.   The day—

A.   —she'd stated that she just had a bad night, and I believe she stated that—

Q.   Okay.

A.   —something to do with a—a boyfriend or something like that and (unintelligible).

Q.   And so then we, out the door, and let's go do field sobriety test, right? Because your job is not to care, your job is to arrest her for DUI. That's your job—

A.   My job is not to get into peoples' personal life, sir.

Q.   Oh, okay. Wouldn't somebody having had a fight with a significant other and being under some emotional distress have some bearing on whether they could actually properly do the physical sobriety exercises when you got to them? If she was mentally distraught?

A.   It's possible.

Q.   Sure. And wouldn't it be something that when we talk about the physical sobriety and the divided attention, her emotional state, wouldn't that go under her ability maybe to hear and process the—the commands that you were going to give her regarding these field sobrieties?

A.   Possible.

Q.   Sure. But you didn't bother to try to find out what was wrong with her. I want to know why.

A.   No, sir.

Q.   I—I—I think this jury would like an explanation as to why when this poor girl's crying in the car, and you have an opportunity to figure out why, the first thing you do is, hey, let's go do the—

UNIDENTIFIED SPEAKER: (Unintelligible).

(Whereupon, a side bar conference was held that is unintelligible).

I do not recall what the sidebar was about, but likely an objection to my line of questioning. Admittedly I was arguing with him more than I was using leading, one-fact questions to tell my story. Bad, bad Joe! Apparently it was not a sustained objection, as I continue on the topic.

BY MR. BODIFORD (CONTINUING):

Q.   All right. So finally, if you will, please explain why that when given the opportunity to find out what had been going on with her that evening, you chose instead to do the physical sobriety exercises.

Took a chance here, asking for an open-ended narrative. I am comfortable using this, but do not recommend to everyone. I knew he'd just spit out all his "totality of the circumstances" points and I would address them one by one. I was ready for it Cross Sheet 2 of 4.

A. Well, based on my observations up to that point; and the distinct odor of an alcoholic beverage coming from her breath; the fact that she was fumbling around with her paperwork, at that point I was ready to conduct a DUI investigation, ask her to step out of the vehicle. If I would start diving into a conversation as far as what's going on with her that evening, I would have gotten off track as far as my investigation. And as a police officer, every time I stop somebody for whatever reason, everybody always has a story or a personal situation that they're going through. And if I took the time to listen to everybody's situation every time I made a traffic stop, I'd never get my job done.

He were go . . .

Q. Distinct odor of an alcoholic beverage. So from this distinct odor, can you tell us, was it strong, was it moderate, was it weak, or was it just distinct?

A. Enough to smell it coming off of her breath, yes, sir.

Q. Okay. And just smelling something on somebody's breath does not give you an indication of how much they have had to drink, right?

A. Correct.

Q. Or what it was they had to drink, right?

A. Only that it was an alcoholic beverage, yes, sir.

Q. But you can't distinguish beer, wine, liquor, any of that. Just that it's there.

A. Correct.

Q.   Okay. Or when, you can't tell from that odor when they had it, right?

A.   Correct.

Q.   And this—this issue of fumbling, now, are you telling us that she's in there just—you know, there's papers flying everywhere; or was it that you're telling us that she was looking for these things?

A.   She was looking for the items and passed over them several times when they were right in front of her.

Q.   You have in your report noted that she had fumbling fingers, right?

A.   Yes, sir.

Q.   Nowhere in there do you say, and she passed over the documents that I had asked of her—

A.   No.

Q.   —did you?

A.   That's—that's inclusive in the fumbling of— the fumbling of fingers.

Q.   Okay. So the first time you've articulated that she passed over documents is here before this jury today, right?

A.   That's my explanation as far as fumbling fingers, yes, sir.

Having gone through what he said he observed, I move to what could be an indicator of impairment that he did not *observe.*

**NOTE: this was NOT on my Cross Sheet, but something spontaneous that I felt was important in telling my client's story.

Q. Okay. You didn't—one of the things that NHTSA tells you in this second phase personal conduct—contact section is to look for things like whether somebody has slurred speech. She didn't have slurred speech, did she?

A. No, sir.

Q. Okay. And that's generally a big one when somebody's under the influence of alcohol, that's kind of the first thing to go is the speech, right?

A. Sometimes it's present, yes, sir.

Q. Yeah. And not only slurred speech, be people can become abusive or combative; or to the contrary, happy drunks, and then there's laughing, giggling at everything, right?

A. Sometimes, yes, sir.

Q. That didn't happen with her, did it?

A. No, sir.

Q. She was coherent; do you agree?

A. Yes, sir.

Q. She gave you appropriate answers to the questions that you asked, right?

A. Correct.

Q. And one of the other things that—two other things that NHTSA talks about that you can look for as far as influence is open containers. You know, somebody's got a road soda there with them. There was no open containers in this vehicle, correct?

A. That's correct.

Q. And the other thing they—another thing they talk about is cover-ups. You walk up, and all of a sudden, somebody's got a mouthful of mints and a cigarette and a cigar, and a Binaca blast. No cover-ups here, right?

A.   Correct.

Q.   But she never covered up anything from you, she agreed to take your breath test at the end of this, too, didn't she?

A.   Yes, sir.

Back   to   the   Cross   Sheet,   "Questioning Techniques"...

Q.   Uh-hum. All right. Now, your questioning techniques. NHTSA talks about how to do these questioning techniques to, if you will, simulate this driving divided attention skills thing, right? You're trained how to do that.

A.   Yes, sir.

Directly from the Cross Sheet . . .

Q.   So when you're up—up at the car, and you're asking for this, and you're talking about that, that whole interaction is designed to divide the driver's attention, isn't it?

A.   When you ask for, like, several different documents, yes, sir.

Q.   Right. So you're coming out of the gate trying to trip somebody up.

A.   I wouldn't say I'm trying to trip them up, I'm just trying to introduce a question that would cause them to have to use divided attention.

Q.   Uh-hum. And she—at your Phase 2 personal contact with her at the car, she did those things correctly, didn't she?

A.   Yeah. She—I asked her for the documents, and like I said, she had difficulty locating them, but eventually did.

Directly from the Cross Sheet . . .

Q.   Uh-hum. And no unusual reactions other than her crying, right?

A.   Correct.

Directly from the Cross Sheet . . .

Q.   She followed your instructions while at the car; did she not?

A.   Yes, sir.

Directly from the Cross Sheet . . .

Q.   And when she got out of the car, NHTSA says if somebody gets out and they're leaning and, you know, not being able to balance, that's a clue. She didn't exhibit those clues, did she?

A.   Correct.

Q.   She was able to get out, close the door, and go directly to where you wanted her to stand, right?

A.   Yes, sir, she did.

Q.   And she stood there like a statute; did she not?

A.   She stood there, yes, sir.

Free-styling off the Cross Sheet, I incorporate the video that the jury has just seen.

Q.   What—when you—when she first goes and stands behind the car while you're moving hers, are you telling us that there's something wrong with the way she's standing there that gave you any clues at—at that point in time—

A.   No, sir.

Q.   —she was under the influence?

A.   Not at—no, she stood fine.

Q.   Okay. Now—and again, back to these—this totality of the circumstances, you're adding these clues into your overall investigation as you're going, right?

A.   That's correct.

Q.   Okay. So—but by the same token, all of these things that we've just talked about when we first get to the car are all also very indicative of innocent behavior, too. Right? Like a distinct odor of alcohol on her breath, of—of—of alcohol on the breath, it's not illegal to drink and drive, right?

A.   Correct.

Q.   It's illegal to drink too much and drive.

A.   That's correct.

This was addressed in jury selection, so now I have the arresting officer admitting what the jury knows to be the law. They can now hold him to that standard.

Q.   So that odor in and of itself is consistent with innocent behavior; is it not?

A.   It can be, yes, sir.

Q.   Right. And—and the fumbling and trying to get the documents, you've probably stopped thousands of people in your time, and that's something you see all the time, isn't it?

A.   Sometimes it happens, yes, sir.

Q.   Even with people who are stone cold sober.

A.   Sometimes.

   **NOTE: now I move on to Cross Sheet 3 of 4, "FSE's [field sobriety exercises] *Great"; you will note there are more notes from direct on my sheet than with the other sheets. You will see below how I incorporated them into my cross.*

Q.   Right. Okay. Now, the next phase, Phase 3, what is Phase 3 called? It's called pre-arrest screening.

A.   Yeah. Pre—yes, pre-arrest.

Q.   NHSTA calls it pre-arrest screening. You're familiar with that, right?

A.   Yes, sir.

Q.   And you're trained on that, right?

A.   Yes, sir.

Q.   And pre-arrest screening begs the question that this is going to lead to an arrest, doesn't it?

A.   Possible.

Q.   Well, they don't call it pre-let-them-go screening, do they?

   The jury thought this was funny, which signaled to me that they were with me and understanding the story I was telling about this cop being prone to arrests.

A.   Well, if someone does the exercises and fails to demonstrate clues of impairment, then they would not be placed under arrest.

Q.   And—and so we're clear on how this works, your—your pre-arrest screening captured on the video so that once you—you've arrested them, you've got a record to show the jury. Very simple how—why this video is taken, correct?

A.   Yes, sir, that's—that's a part of the reason, yes, sir.

Q.   All right. Now—and we've talked a little bit about this before, but you described for Ms. Muller (phonetics) the fact that the—these instructions are designed to be both mentally—give a mental and a physical thing at the same time to simulate this divided attention. In other words, you want to distract them while you're giving these instructions, correct?

A.   That's correct.

Q.   Yeah. But distraction isn't the same as impairment. You can be a distracted driver and not be impaired, right?

A.   Could—could be, yes, sir.

The following came from my notes on the Cross Sheet from the direct examination, regarding there being "complex instructions in short time".

Q.   Okay. So the idea behind these are to give these things—but these are—you know, give these divided attention instructions. But don't you agree, there are a lot of instructions in a very short period of time. Right? Stand like this, I'm going to tell you to do this, put your hands down, you walk here, you turn this way, you walk back, you got it? Go. That's how it works in a short period of time. Right?

A.   I understand what you're saying, yes.

Q.   So it is—you—do you agree—

A.   I don't think it's a lot—

Q.   —that the idea—

A.   —of instruction. But—

Q.   Hmm?

A.   I don't think it's a lot of instructions. But—

Q.   But the—

A.   It's enough to cause divided attention.

Q.   Okay. Right. There you go. And—and—and so you—you demonstrate that here, now, you've done these exercises countless times—

A.   Yes, sir.

Q.   —agreed? Okay. The walk and turn. Now, the factors—well, stop here real quick. These things are pass/fail, right? You either pass them, you go home; you fail and you go to jail. That's how it works, right?

A.   It's not a pass/fail, it's whether they demonstrate any of the clues of impairment.

Q.   Okay. So you don't look at it and say, boy, they really failed that exam. You're just trying to build whatever clues you can find to make an arrest.

A.   I look for clues of impairment, yes, sir.

Q.   All right. Now, the walk and turn. You said that NHTSA gives us eight actual clues to look for. And those are the ones that you're looking for, no more, no less—

A.   Correct.

Q.   —right? Uh-hum. And on this one, she, in your estimation, exhibited four, or—

A.   Right.

Q.   —50 percent of the—of the—of the ones that are out there.

A.   That's correct.

Q.   All right.

MR. BODIFORD: Judge, if I could have a moment to try to turn this thing back on.

THE COURT: Yes, sir.

(Whereupon, the video recording was published to the jury).

MR. BODIFORD: Aye yai yie (phonetics). No, wait a minute. I might have actually figured out a way to fast forward it.

Don't talk to yourself while you're on the record. Bad Joe!

BY MR. BODIFORD (CONTINUING):

Q.   All right. Let's stop here real quick. One of the things that NHTSA tells you in their manual is if somebody's wearing high heels, they can take them off, correct?

A.   That's correct.

Q.   She did that, right?

A.   Yes, sir.

Q.   She stood on those, what, 3- or 4-inch high heels, bent down, unbuckled them, took them off, and never even teetered, did she?

A.   I—I think she did a little.

Q. Well, you've done the—you've done these—

A. Right.

Q. —field sobriety tests a billion times. You ever stood in high heels and tried to bend down and take them—

A. Never wore—

Q. —off?

A. —high heels in my life.

Q. Okay. So we know that you're not trying to take them off either. That's a pretty impressive feat that she just does there, isn't it?

A. Yeah, I would have to say yes. I don't know how anybody walks in them.

That was the kill shot in the trial—and he knew it. There was no way he could overcome by his testimony the images on the video. My client in no way appeared to be under the influence of alcohol or drugs.

Q. Well, I'm not talking about walking on them, I'm talking about taking them off. That's even more impressive the way she does it. Look. She's not wavering; her heels and toes don't come off the ground, do they? And she's basically almost standing on top of her head. Let me ask you this, Officer: Would you agree that that exercise she just performed there is harder than any of the ones you gave her?

A. I don't know about that. I don't know how often she wears high heels, and—

Q. Well—

A.   —I mean, I—

Q.   —knowing what you know about alcohol influence though, and—and being a TPD officer, you would expect somebody that's really under the influence of alcohol to have bit the dust when they pulled that, wouldn't you?

A.   It's possible.

Q.   Really? It's possible—then you would expect that if somebody's under alcohol, they couldn't do that.

A.   I've seen people under the influence do—

Q.   Which—

A.   —much better than that.

Q.   You've got to give it to her, at that stage in the game, okay, she did that pretty well, right?

A.   I—I've already admitted that.

Q.   Okay. So why didn't you stop, just let her go home, say, this woman's not under the influence of alcohol?

I probably could have stopped before this, but the question I just asked is important to the story—the story that she was not under the influence, and should not have been arrested.

A.   That is our field sobriety exercises, sir.

Q.   I was going to ask you if there was any men that wrote—or any females that wrote the physical sobriety exercises, but you probably don't know that. So—

(Whereupon, the video recording was published to the jury).

Q. All right. Let's go through this walk and turn here real—by the way, she picks them up, walks appropriately, sets them down appropriately, comes back, no problems, right? Still no problems, correct?

A. Correct.

Q. Okay.

(Whereupon, the video recording was published to the jury).

Q. Okay. The first thing you said was imagine a straight line between her—where you're at and the car.

A. Correct.

Q. Now, NHTSA says—NHTSA says that in order to do the walk and turn, it requires a, quote, designated straight line, right?

A. If possible. If it's available.

Q. You're in a mall parking lot, aren't you?

A. Uh-hum.

Q. There's about 5,000 straight white lines within 20 feet of you, aren't there?

A. It was a very lit area, and I decided to do it just right there because I don't like taking people away from the scene.

Q. Parking lots are right over here, on the other side of this (unintelligible), right?

A. Uh-hum.

Q. Yes?

A. Correct.

Q.   I mean, this is, what, Westshore Mall, is that what it's called?

A.   Yes, sir.

Q.   Okay. And—and—so you had the opportunity to put her on a white line, you just chose not to is what it is.

A.   I chose to do the exercises right there, yes, sir.

Q.   Okay. So you're telling her, imagine this line. This imaginary line, how long was this imaginary line?

A.   I just told her to imagine it from where she was standing, towards my vehicle.

Q.   Well, did you tell her how wide to imagine it?

A.   No. I just—

Q.   Are you talking about a—

A.   —I just told here I just wanted her to walk as straight as possible.

Q.   Okay. Well, were you—or were you wanting her to imagine a pin-stripe, or say, like maybe a football, or likely be a stop bar? Did you tell her?

A.   No, I didn't specify, sir.

Q.   Okay. And you didn't tell her what color this imaginary line was or how long this imaginary line was, or anything, did you?

A.   No, sir.

Q.   Okay. And that's not what NHTSA standardizes, is it?

A.   NHTSA said to use a line if it's available—

Q.   Okay.

A. —in—the best location.

Q. All right. So—by the way, while we're standing here, so that we're all clear, she's not leaning like this to her left, is she?

A. Could be the camera—

Q. It—

A. —is slightly—

Q. —would you agree—

A. —angled.

Q. —with me that—

A. Yes, sir.

Q. —this light and this oak tree—

A. Yeah. Sometimes the camera gets—

Q. Okay. So we're—just so we're clear that she's not—

A. Correct.

Q. —you know, doing a Michael Jackson here. All right. Fine. Now, one of the things you said was that she made—she failed to maintain her balance during the instruction that she, quote—

(Whereupon, the video recording was published to the jury).

Q. —what you said this morning, she steps off the line. Now you tell us when she steps off the line.

A. When she fails to maintain, you mean?

Q. Okay. Now, she's in position.

A. Yes, sir. Watch her. Just watch her feet. While I'm demonstrating.

Q. Uh-hum. Is that it?

A.   There's one more after that.

Q.   Now, it—

A.   Right there.

Q.   —part of the—Okay.

A.   Right there.

Q.   So when you're walking in front of her, then she—she—

A.   Moves her—

Q.   —moves her—

A.   —foot to the side.

Q.   —she moves her right foot—Okay. At this point in time, she's been standing one foot and the other for almost 30 seconds, correct?

A.   I didn't time it. I don't know, sir.

Q.   But that's part of the test. That's part of what the test is, is just saying, okay, sit here and listen to me, you put them in this position—

A.   Correct.

Q.   —because you know that it—at some point in time, the likelihood of them falling out of that position is going to be very real. Right?

A.   Just following what I'm trained to do, sir.

Q.   Okay. So then we go through—does not touch heel to toe.

(Whereupon, the video recording was published to the jury).

Q.   Now, your explanation of that was that you're giving a signal on a video to—

A.   Correct.

Q. —to what, to them, to the jurors?

A. Just indicated on my video that when she missed this heel-to-toe.

Q. Okay. So what would—what would be the downside of shooting this from the side so we could actually see whether they're touching the heel to toe?

A. Sometimes I do. It all depends on where my vehicle is and where I line up the camera.

Q. Okay. Well, you could have—you know, you had any number of options, but you told her very specifically, you took her to that spot, and you told her, walk towards the camera.

A. Correct.

Q. And you know that that's not going to show whether she's heel-to-toe. You've done this 1,000 times. You—

A. Well, if—

Q. —know whether or not it shows—

A. —if it clearly doesn't show, that's why I always point my finger out.

Q. So basically you're—you're trying to tell the jurors something they can't see.

A. I—I'm not sure what you're implying, sir.

Q. Well—

A. Are you saying I'm lying or—

Q. No. I'm saying that—that the way this video was set up, we cannot see whether she's heel-to-toe, so you're on the—you have the good vantage point, and you're signaling when she misses to us.

A.   That's why I'm—

Q.   If that signal—

A.   —signaling.

Q.   Hmm?

A.   That's why I'm signaling.

Q.   Okay. So the signal is so you can tell them what they might not be able to see with their own eyes.

A.   I guess so, yes, sir.

Q.   Okay.

(Whereupon, the video recording was published to the jury).

Q.   Now, again, when she gets to the end, she turns around, and you've told her to do pivots; instead, she turns around, she doesn't fall, she gets back in line, she keeps going. And you—you said that's an incorrect turn, correct?

A.   That's correct.

Q.   And that's just based on the fact that NHTSA wants it to be clean, turn, turn, turn, turn, get back in the light, keep going.

A.   That's correct.

Q.   Okay. So if somebody spun around like Michael Jackson, didn't fall, and looked great doing it, they would still get counted off for that.

A.   That's correct. Not following instructions.

Q.   Not—not following instructions. So it's not necessarily the turn that's the problem, it's that she's not following instructions that you're counting her off.

A.   It's—it's both.

Q. Okay. Now, obviously, there could be innocent reasons for how she did those couple of things, you know, like failing to maintain her balance, fatigue factors into somebody's performance on physical sobriety exercises; does it not?

A. It could.

Q. Stress? Stress of a situation could factor in, correct?

A. It can, yes.

Q. Nerves, you know.

A. Uh-hum.

Q. People get nervous when they talk to officers.

A. Sure. Uh-hum.

Q. Somebody walking in bare feet on pavement could also affect how they're able to perform this particular walk and turn, correct?

A. Possible, yeah.

Q. Yeah. And also if somebody's—if lights were shining up in their eyes, that can impact how they do certain physical sobriety exercises, right?

A. It can.

Q. Okay. Now, the next one was the one leg stand, which has, according to the National Highway Traffic Safety Administration, four indicators of impairment. I—I ask you this in the same vein as I asked you about her taking off her shoes. She stands on one leg perfectly still for 30 seconds. What's—why is that not a complete pass?

A.   She had a noticeable sway, sir; and right at the end, she dropped her foot, even though I didn't mark it in the report, but she did drop her foot.

Q.   So—so this—so this—this exercise, this test of standing on one foot, of being able to accomplish that, while looking down, which the looking down messes up the equilibrium, doesn't it? Designed to do that, isn't it?

A.   That's part of it, yes, sir.

Q.   Right. And following—and doing all that, keeping the hands down by the side, you do all that, and you still get docked if you moved a little bit to side-to-side.

A.   It was a noticeable sway, yes, sir.

Q.   And it would be noticeable on this video?

A.   As much as possible of the—the camera aligned, yes, sir.

Q.   Other than the sway though, wouldn't you agree, that's one of the best one leg stands you've ever seen?

A.   I wouldn't say that.

Q.   And again, there are innocent reasons for why she may have done what she did: Fatigue, stress, nerves, all of those things could factor in, right?

A.   That's possible, yes.

Q.   Okay. And by the way, you're counting—you're having her count to see whether or not she's— you're looking at your watch while she's counting to see if, again, mentally she's able to keep—and she kept pretty dang close, didn't she, doing her, one, Mississippi; two, Mississippi.

A.   Yes, sir.

Q.   I mean, she maybe got off a second or two, right?

A.   Yes. She did—

Q.   And that—you agree—

A.   Very well counting, yes, sir.

Q.   She did well counting, correct?

A.   Yes, sir.

Q.   Okay. All right. So you go out to the—you go out to the—oh, before you leave there—so you arrest her, she doesn't flip out on you, correct?

A.   Correct.

Q.   She understands and is still cooperative with you, correct?

A.   Yes, sir.

Q.   And, in fact, she has presence of mind enough to tell you about the flat shoes in the car. You were nice enough to say, hey, do you want to—what do you want to do with your shoes; and she remembered that there were those shoes in her car, and you got them for her, right?

A.   Correct.

Q.   So it's a combination of you, you know, being nice to her; but also her having the presence of mind to be able to respond and to remember that that was there. And that's certainly not an indicator of somebody who is under the influence, right?

A.   I—I don't know, sir. But it—

Q.   What, the ability to—

A.   —that is (unintelligible).

Here, I get into the final Cross Sheet, Cross Sheet 4 of 4, regarding the normal faculties.

Q.   —well, do you—do you understand what—you know what the normal faculties are, correct?

A.   It all depends on someone's level of impairment.

Q.   Right. But what are the normal faculties, if you'll explain to the jury. What—what do we define the normal faculties as for DUI work?

MADAM STATE ATTORNEY: Objection.

THE COURT: Approach.

(Whereupon, a side bar conference was held that is unintelligible).

BY MR. BODIFORD (CONTINUING):

Q.   So, Officer, what are the normal faculties that we are looking to see if they are impaired, what are they?

A.   A normal faculty would be someone who's able to listen, comprehend, and perform normal functions would be normal faculties, if I understand what you're asking—

Q.   Uh-hum. Yeah.

A.   —and saying.

Q.   No—I mean, you—but I mean, you're vested with enforcing the DUI laws, correct?

A.   Correct.

Q.   And—and so the definition of normal faculties, do you not have a succinct legal definition for what normal faculties are?

A.   I'm just not sure what you're asking for. I mean, I—I would—

Q.   Please define—

A.   —give you my personal opinion what normal faculties are. I mean, normal faculties are basically a person who's able to perform the normal day-to-day activities and—and—is that what—is that what you're asking?

Q.   Well, no. Because—I'm actually asking you if you know what the legal definition is because you're the one that says that she broke that law. So for you to be able to know what law she broke—to be able to say whether she broke a law by driving with normal faculties impaired, it would seem that you would know what the normal faculties are. So please tell the jury what the legal definition of normal faculties is.

A.   I base—if I can elaborate a little bit—

Q.   Sure.

A.   —I based my conclusion on making a DUI arrest based on whether or not they demonstrate clues of impairment. I don't particularly look for normal faculties because I've seen, and then certain—in all the DUI arrests and investigations I've done, there are some people who can look perfectly normal and act perfectly normal, but they are impaired.

Q.   How about the ability to see, is that a normal faculty?

A.   Sure.

Q.   Hear?

A.   Correct.

Q.   Walk?

A.   Yes, sir.

Q.   Talk?

A.   Correct.

Q.   Judge distances?

A.   Yes, sir.

Q.   Respond to emergencies?

A.   Sure.

Q.   Drive an automobile?

A.   Sure.

Q.   And as you've said, do all the daily mental and physical tasks that we have in our normal lives, those are normal faculties, right?

A.   Yes, sir.

Q.   Okay. And—but you put those aside, and all you do is just plug the person—or run the person through the NHTSA standards and see whether or not they're yes or no.

A.   Yeah, I would have to agree with that. I mean, we—we look for the abnormal faculties, the—you know, for a person doing out of the norm is what stands out as far as possible clues of impairment.

Q.   So what do you give greater weight to, what you know to be normal faculties, like you've described somebody's ability to do daily functions; or the NHTSA standards? What do you give greater weight to when formulating probable cause to arrest her?

A.   I would have to lean towards the NHTSA standards and look for the clues of impairment that people demonstrate, because that's—that's what we're looking for.

Q.   So in other—

A.   (Unintelligible)—

Q.   —words, you just disregard your own common sense.

A.   I wouldn't say that, no, sir.

MR. BODIFORD: Judge, I have nothing further.

THE COURT: Okay. Any redirect?

MADAM STATE ATTORNEY: Yes, Your Honor.

(Whereupon, the Cross Examination was concluded by Mr. Bodiford, and Redirect Examination was conducted by the State.)

MADAM STATE ATTORNEY: Nothing further.

THE COURT: All right. May the witness be excused?

Mr. Bodiford, do you have any other questions?

MR. BODIFORD: Well, just one if you'll allow—

THE COURT: Of course we will. It's something that is—

MR. BODIFORD: Yes.

THE COURT: In response to something just asked by the State?

BY MR. BODIFORD:

RECROSS EXAMINATION

Q. Well, you—you said that you demonstrate these things for folks on the walk and turn, and you only gave half a demonstration though, didn't you?

A. I didn't take the full nine steps if that's what you're asking.

Q. Okay. All right.

MR. BODIFORD: Nothing further.

THE WITNESS: Yeah.

THE COURT: Okay. May the witness be excused? Do you want him to remain in the area?

MADAM STATE ATTORNEY: He may be excused, Your Honor.

THE COURT: All right. Thank you.

(The witness was excused from the courtroom.)

(Whereupon, the excerpt of the Recorded Jury Trial in the above-referenced proceeding was concluded.)

The jury returned a not guilty verdict, notwithstanding the fact that her breath test results were over .16.

8.2 A REALLY, REALLY BAD CROSS

This is from a real case. The basic facts of the case are that the defendant, his girlfriend, and an acquaintance (his co-defendant) went to an apartment, ostensibly to buy marijuana. Instead of buying marijuana, once inside the defendant went in a back room, everyone heard a gunshot, and the defendant ran out and both left. One of the residents of the apartment was shot in the head with a shotgun and was dead.

The shooter wore a mask, and the whole defense revolved around identification. This witness, one of the apartment residents, was the only witness from the apartment who provided any identification of the defendant. She testified on direct that she recognized the defendant's eyes, and had picked him from a photopak lineup.

The actual names of the attorneys, defendant, and witnesses have been changed or omitted in this example for obvious reasons.

CROSS EXAMINATION BY MR. ███████ :

Q.   Good morning. Ma'am, I'm so sorry about what you went through.

Defers to the witness, making her the star.

THE COURT: Mr. ███████ , will you please use the podium?

MR. ██████ : Of course.

Reprimanded by the judge, losing control.

Q.   (By Mr. ███████) I'm sorry about what you went through.

A.   Thank you.

Repeats the deference, reinforcing that she is a victim (who cares—victims can lie and make mistakes).

Q.   I listened to you testify and I believe we met sometime ago and I took some notes and I would like to talk to you about some of the notes I have.

Attorney is not the witness, so his notes are immaterial and irrelevant.

A.   Yes, sir.

Q.   It is your testimony, is it not, that a light was in your face while this was happening, is that fair?

"Is that fair" is not asking her to agree to a fact, but asking her to agree to his interpretation, which is immaterial and irrelevant. "Is that fair" and "it is your testimony" could be left out, and there would be a perfectly good one-fact, leading question.

A.   It was shining in, yes.

Q.   And it's your testimony that you didn't know Mr. ▇▇▇▇ prior to this, correct?

Same problem.

A.   Yes.

Q.   And it's your testimony that at the time you didn't know who it was, but later everything added up and that's why you feel it was David, is that fair?

Again, same problems.

A.   For ▇▇▇▇?

Q.   Yes.

A.   Seeing his mugshot and seeing his eyes is what I can picture him. I can point him out from anybody as soon as I seen his mugshot it was him.

Control of the witness is lost. She is now giving the facts.

Q.   When you said things added up, is that what you are referring to, or referring to other telephone calls and what other people said?

This is a deposition question—the attorney does not know the answer and is confused. Instead of using facts that he knows to control the witness, he resorts to an open-ended question and permits the witness to fill in the blanks.

A.   I thought he was referring to [the co-defendant] because I didn't—I saw [the co-defendant] but I wasn't as close to [the co-defendant] as I was to Mr. ▮▮▮▮▮▮.

Q.   Did you tell us that you knew [the co-defendant] from before this?

Leaving off "[d]id you tell us that . . ." leaves a perfectly good cross question.

A.   Yes.

Q.   You certainly acknowledge that at all points more confident as to [the co-defendant's] involvement than anybody else's that is fair right?

Objectionable as counsel testifying, and certainly improper to ask a witness to agree with the attorney's interpretation of the evidence.

A.   Uh-huh.

Q.   Yes?

A.   Yes.

Good to get an actual "yes" or "no" rather than a guttural sound, to make a clean record.

Q.   Now, today you told us that after you heard the "boom" which would have been the shotgun firing.

Today did you tell us at that point the gentleman you believe is Mr. ███████ went back to the room where it happened, is that your testimony today?

Why reinforce her direct testimony—the most damning testimony against his client?

A.   Yes.

Q.   And forgive me for picking or quibbling, but would you acknowledge that when you first gave a statement what you said was you heard the "boom"?

THE   PROSECUTOR: Objection.   Improper impeachment.

THE COURT: Sustained.

Properly   sustained—terrible   attempt   at   an impeachment.

(By Mr. ███████) Have you been consistent with your statements throughout?

An attempt at a "safe harbor" question, but not a good one.

A.   Yes.

MR. ███████: We might call her later.

THE COURT: Redirect.

    * * *

MR. ███████:   Judge,   may   I   ask   one   further question?

THE COURT: Approach the bench.

(At the bench:

THE COURT: I don't do redirect [sic—the judge means "recross"] unless there is good reason. I don't think he went outside the scope. What do you want to ask?

MR. ███████: He asked her about what she saw when the face was covered and she acknowledged it was covered and she said the eyes and he basically went over again and my question would be to specifically get her to specifically how much of the eyes were exposed.

THE COURT: I'll allow it, but try to ask all your questions on cross next time.

(Bench conference concluded)

RECROSS EXAMINATION

BY MR. ███████:

Q. How much of the eyes were exposed?

A. It was a ski mask so this part of his eyes around here you could see.

MR. ███████: That's all I have, Judge.

THE COURT: Okay. May she be excused or does she need to remain?

THE PROSECUTOR: She may be excused.

THE COURT: Mr. ███████?

MR. ███████: She may be excused.

The witness was never recalled in the remainder of the trial.

Let me be clear, this was not my cross examination. This attorney was an experienced attorney at the time of the trial—the failure to make even some attempt to discredit the eyewitness identification is inexplicable. Non-leading questions and compound questions relinquished control to the witness. Regurgitating the direct examination is never effective. Needless to say, the defendant was convicted and is currently (as of 2018) fighting a life sentence.

8.3 CROSS OF A LAW ENFORCEMENT OFFICER IN A CRIMINAL CASE

The following is another of the author's cross examinations. Very similar to that above, but with some unique differences. Specifically, this trooper's credibility was seriously in question because he arrested two people in the same car for the same drugs, and failed to preserve the video of the stop and car search. That was an issue, as two people were charged with possessing the same drugs.

This cross examination is rather long—probably over forty-five minutes. However, it is succinct and does not repeat or drone—or at least I did not get the sense from the judge or jury that it did.

(Whereupon, the following is an excerpt of the Video Recorded Jury Trial in the above-referenced proceeding beginning with the Cross Examination of Trooper Mark Baker.)

MS. GRIFFITH: No further questions.

JUDGE SHELFER: Mr. Bodiford.

MR. BODIFORD: Thank you, Your Honor.

BY MR. BODIFORD:
CROSS EXAMINATION

Q. How you doing, Trooper Baker?

A. How you doing?

Q.   Well, thank you. Trooper, do you think you would recognize photos of the car if I showed them to you?

A.   Oh, very much so.

MR. BODIFORD: Your Honor—Your Honor, may I approach?

JUDGE SHELFER: Yes, sir.

(Defendant's Exhibits 1–7 marked for identification.)

BY MR. BODIFORD (CONTINUING):

Q.   I'm going to show you what has been previously marked for identification as defense Exhibits 1 through 7. Just ask you to take a look at them; let me know when you're done.

A.   Were these the ones that were in the evidence custodian, taken by—

Q.   I—I can't testify, Trooper Baker, all I can do is show you photos.

A.   This seems to be the inside. I—there's no pictures of—really of the outside of the vehicle for me to properly identify it. But it seems to be the sort, yes.

Q.   Okay. Now, you—you just mentioned the other photos. Did you take photos of the inside of the car?

A.   Not that I'm aware of. I cannot recall—I don't recall taking photos, or otherwise it would have been put in as evidence.

Q.   Uh-hum.

MR. BODIFORD: May I approach, Your Honor?

JUDGE SHELFER: Yes.

THE WITNESS: If you're inquiring that what I was talking—

MR. BODIFORD: I—I didn't—

THE WITNESS:—about putting—

MR. BODIFORD:—I'm sorry, I didn't—I—I didn't ask a question, so let me just move on. So—

THE WITNESS: Go ahead.

MR. BODIFORD: Thank you.

BY MR. BODIFORD (CONTINUING):

Q.   All right. Now, since you've been on the Florida Highway Patrol, do you have your book there of all your certificates?

A.   Yes.

MR. BODIFORD: Judge, may I approach?

JUDGE SHELFER: Yes.

BY MR. BODIFORD (CONTINUING):

Q.   Do you mind if I take a look at those?

A.   Yeah. Sure. It goes from here, all the way back.

Q.   Sure. Okay. Mind if I take it over there while I'm talking?

A.   Yeah. Go ahead.

Q.   Thank you. So since you've been on in 2009, you have received a great deal of training—

A.   Yes.

Q.   —right? In looking at your book here, we have—the first thing I come to is Commission on Criminal Justice Standards and Training. That's speed measurement.

A.   Yes.

Q. Advanced training. Okay. That doesn't have anything to do with detecting drugs, right?

A. No. You're going to have to go all the way back to—

Q. Okay. So Radar Speed Measuring Certificate, that has nothing to do with detection of drugs.

A. You're going to be doing this a long time. That's—I've got multiple certificates.

Q. So the answer is no, that has nothing to do with the detection of drugs?

A. No

Q. Okay. And something from Williams Communications. So we have a wireless technology company that has certified you for use of a speedometer, right?

A. Very much so.

Q. And that has nothing to do with detection of drugs, right?

A. It can—I guess you could be. It goes into our traffic stops and every day, how we get involved with it. So my—and my enforcement with the violators usually comes from a probable cause stop. So, yes, I guess it could be interdicted into that, yes.

Q. But you don't patrol anywhere other than on streets, so everything you do involves another car, right?

A. Not necessarily, no. I—I do houses as well. I've done warrants, whatever I need to do.

Q. So warrants don't have anything to do with speedometers.

A.   Not in that case, no.

Q.   All right. Laser speed measuring, same thing, that's not on drug recognition, right?

A.   Uh-hum.

Q.   Breath test operator, that has nothing to do with drug recognition, right?

A.   No.

Q.   It doesn't have anything to do with how to properly search and preserve evidence—

A.   No

Q.   —right?

MS. GRIFFITH: I'll just object at this point, the relevance going through each and every certificate I think is (unintelligible).

JUDGE SHELFER: Okay. Go ahead.

MR. BODIFORD: Thank you.

BY MR. BODIFORD (CONTINUING):

Q.   You have the basic recruit certificate, 775 hours. Now, that's the important one, right?

A.   There we go.

Q.   That's the one that says, I'm a—a—a trained and certified law enforcement officer in the state of Florida.

A.   Yes.

Q.   And in that 775 hours, you receive training on how to collect evidence, right?

A.   Well, the way it is, that is actually done through FHP.

Q.   Right.

A.   So ev—every different division you go to or department you go to has different ways they intake evidence and how they go through. So that certificate itself is actually going through the commissions of getting your law enforcement certificate.

So then you have a—what—we have a—what they call a breakout, and then we learn all the FHP policies and different things that go along with that.

Q.   And—by the way, is it at the FHP Academy that you learn how to testify?

A.   Yes.

Q.   Because you receive training on how to testify, don't you?

A.   Very small, but, yes.

Q.   Yeah. But you have been trained on how to sit in front of these folks and how to turn and how to address them, right?

A.   Well, I've—I've done this multiple times, so—

Q.   But you receive training on it, right?

A.   I—I bring it more towards my experience, I learn more in my experience than I would from the Academy.

Q.   So—but the answer is, yes, you've been trained on it, right?

A.   I have some small training.

Q.   And before you ever took the stand in a trial, somebody told you how to talk to these folks, didn't they?

A.   Not necessarily, no.

Q.   They weren't—so what did they do, just say, wear your uniform, and show up for trial?

A.   Show up for trial, give—give your testimony, be truthful with what you say, give—give everything as you talk about the—if you're talking about—And I'll expand on what he's saying. So when you go—

Q.   Well, no, I have to ask you a direct question.

A.   Okay.

Q.   Okay?

A.   Well, you're addressing it, so I was going to address that issue.

Q.   And you did—

A.   So—

Q.   —and I appreciate that.

A.   Go ahead.

Q.   Thank you. But part of it is—is—is that you were taught as to turn and to address them, right?

A.   I was taught that through childhood. So—

Q.   Uh-hum. We've got breath test operator again; nothing with drug recognition, right?

A.   Uh-hum.

Q.   CJIS Full Access Certification. That's teaching how to use a computer, isn't it? CJIS is the Crime—

A.   C-J-I-S—

Q.   Yeah.

A.   —System. So it's the N—NCIC, FCIC, different things like that.

Q. And—and because you have this CJIS certificate, this proves to all of us that you actually know how to access the Clerk of Court database and look up cases, right? That's what C-J-I-S is, isn't it?

A. Yes. And we can go through it, yes.

Q. And you know how to do that, don't you?

A. Yeah. I've gone through them. Do I use it on a daily basis, no.

Q. When you arrested Mr. Hernandez in this case—

A. —no, I did not use CJIS.

Q. You never looked, did you?

A. Nope.

Q. You never looked to see if this case was still pending.

A. No. For what?

Q. After you arrested him, you never checked to see if his case was still pending or anything—

A. I had no idea until the attorney called me the other day.

Q. Alcohol testing; again, nothing about drug recognition, right?

A. Yeah, and the same as before.

Q. Uh-hum. Speed measuring, not—that has nothing to do with drug recognition or interdiction, right?

A. Uh-hum.

Q. This just says PR-24, Basic Course Recertification. A PR-24 is a—

A.   Baton.

Q.   —baton—

A.   Yeah.

Q.   —right?

A.   Uh-hum.

Q.   Basic patrol rifle course. That's shooting, not drug detection, right?

A.   Yes. That—that would be an actual patrol rifle.

Q.   All right. You've gone through this FEMA—

A.   Uh-hum.

Q.   —field course operations in Anniston, Alabama. That's the emergency preparedness, right—

A.   That's—

Q.   —disaster relief.

A.   That's riot controls, yes. I'm—I'm the instructor for that, yes.

Q.   Right.

A.   Yeah.

Q.   But not for drug recognition and interdiction, right?

A.   You're getting there, don't worry.

Q.   I'm sorry?

A.   We're getting to that point.

Q.   Okay. So just to run through them: IA and attention and distraction—

A.   Uh-hum.

Q.   —another FEMA certificate, another FEMA certificate, low visibility occurrence risk index—

A.   Yep.

Q.   —field training officer school.

A.   There you go.

Q.   What, you learned drug interdiction in field training officer school?

A.   I have to—I have to teach other people about it.

Q.   Okay. How many hours did you—were—

A.   I did 32—

Q.   —trained in—in that? On a 32-hour clock of—the entire (unintelligible) field officer school—

A.   Uh-hum.

Q.   —how much did you spend on teaching others drug interdiction, 4 hours, 2 hours?

A.   Just depends—well, that goes on to a case of it's a person-by-person basis, how quickly do they catch on to it.

Q.   So your—your training—

A.   Uh-hum.

Q.   —you're trained on how to train others was a total of 32 hours.

A.   Yes.

Q.   That is on the (unintelligible) everything.

A.   Yeah, 32 hours. So it's like a week long, I've got to be there every day.

MR. BODIFORD: (Unintelligible).

BY MR. BODIFORD (CONTINUING):

Q.   So we've got active shooter, basic homicide—

A.   Uh-hum. TIM's (phonetics) training.

Q. Traffic incident management, right?

A. Uh-hum.

Q. Another instructor technique course.

A. Uh-hum.

Q. What do you mean "uh-hum"?

A. Yes.

Q. Does that mean—does that mean that taught you how to do drug interdiction?

A. No. I'm—I'm just going—I'm saying, yes, I have that. Go ahead.

Q. Firearms instructor.

A. Yes.

Q. Impaired driving enforcement.

A. There you go.

Q. What do you mean, "there you go"?

A. ARIDE? That—they teach us all kinds of drugs in that course; including DUI, how to detect DUIs and drugs; what kind of drug is to do what. We go through matrixes and different things that go from deceptive anesthetics to—to cannabis to cocaine, stimulants, depressants. And we're det—we're trained to detect on the use of that, and to identify what drugs, if we find them, try to find—to identify them. There's one.

Q. All in two days.

A. Hmm?

Q. All in two days.

A. Is it 24 hours?

Q. Sixteen.

A.   Sixteen hours? The ARIDE course? I forget—

Q.   All—

A.   —I think it was a three-day.

Q.   All of that—

A.   Uh-hum.

Q.   —in just three days.

A.   Uh-hum.

Q.   Okay. Then the Commercible book, learn vehicle interdiction.

A.   Uh-hum. That would be another drug care class.

Q.   That was 8 hours.

A.   Yes, that's a full day where they—deal with it, using it.

Q.   Precision immobilization techniques—

A.   That would be—

Q.   —that's to learn the PIT maneuver, isn't it?

A.   Very much so.

Q.   And a PIT maneuver is put it in the trees, right?

A.   PIT—mobilization technique. So that's—it's— God forbid, if someone's fleeing or eluding, or something along those cases, we're able to—I mean, I don't see the reference into it—but we're going to go—that's how we stop the vehicles from going.

Q.   Right.

A.   Yeah.

Q.   Exactly. And a (unintelligible). So—

A.   Uh-hum.

Q.   —although you are a—an exceptionally well-trained trooper—

A.   Uh-hum.

Q.   —very little of your training has to do with collection of evidence.

A.   To—to an extent, most of it is—comes from the road itself.

Q.   Right. And a lot of it comes through your standard operating procedures, correct?

A.   I believe—yes. To an extent, yes.

Q.   And you are, in fact, familiar with your standard operating procedures; are you not?

A.   Yes. Do I know it verbatim, off the top of my head, no.

Q.   No. And prior to the trial starting this morning, I offered you a copy of them, and you accepted them, didn't you?

A.   Uh-hum.

Q.   And you have them with you up there, don't

A.   No. I actually—they're out in the hallway right now.

Q.   You left them in the hallway?

A.   Yes.

Q.   Okay. Well, would anything refresh your recollection as to these procedures?

A.   You can go ahead and I—I'll address them as I come—

Q.   All right.

A.   —to them.

Q.   That's fine. Well, the—you are trained though, and part of the training is to learn what's required of you as far as collection of evidence, right?

A.   Yes.

Q.   Uh-hum. And how to package it, right?

A.   Yes.

Q.   How to preserve it?

A.   Yes.

Q.   How to store it properly?

A.   I can go in-depth in that if you'd like me to.

Q.   Well, the question is: You were trained on how to store the evidence.

A.   Very much so.

Q.   And you were also trained on how to make sure it's available for a trial, right?

A.   Yes.

Q.   And you know from your standard operating procedures that you are, in fact, required to have them for trial, right?

A.   Yes. We do everything we can to try to get everything to trial.

Q.   Now, is—as far as the physical evidence, the standard operating procedure of the Highway Patrol requires all employees to properly collect, document, process, and control all evidence and property items that come into their possession, correct?

A.   Very much so.

Q.   And the objective of this SOP is to protect the rights of the individuals involved, right?

A.   Yes.

Q.   Okay. Now, there you deal with actual audios and and videos, there's a whole separate set of operating procedures that you have to work under, correct?

A.   Yes.

Q.   And—and they mandate—first and foremost, you're familiar with 17.22.04, that the purpose of using an MVR—MVR is what?

A.   You're getting into a bunch of that—acronyms now. So go ahead.

Q.   Would anything refresh your recollection as to what MVR is?

A.   If you'll let me take a look at it.

Q.   I'm going to—

MR. BODIFORD: Judge, may I approach?

JUDGE SHELFER: Uh-hum.

BY MR. BODIFORD (CONTINUING):

Q.   Okay. Just ask you to read that top line, let me know when you're done, read it to yourself. Let me know if that refreshes your recollection.

A.   Okay. Do you want me to say it out loud for you?

Q.   Yeah. Do you know what MVR is?

A.   Yes.

Q.   What is it?

A.   It's Mobile Video/Audio Recording.

Q.   Also known as the in-car camera, correct?

A.   Yes.

Q.   And you are aware that the purpose of having the in-car is for accurate documentation of events, actions, conditions, and statements made during arrests, traffic stops, and other incidents to enhance members' reports, collection of evidence, and testimony in court, correct?

A.   Very much so.

Q.   Well, you—are aware of that, right?

A.   I am.

Q.   And you were aware of it on October the 8th of last year, right?

A.   I am.

Q.   Okay. And you were aware that operating procedure 17.22.05, Subsection B, Subsection (c) says that the MVR equipment shall be used in every traffic stop, right?

A.   Yes.

Q.   And you did that in this case.

A.   As it's equipped, yes.

Q.   And your car was equipped.

A.   It was.

Q.   And you turned it on.

A.   Uh-hum.

Q.   And you recorded everything.

A.   Uh-hum.

Q.   And pursuant to that same SOP, Subsection 3, it says, the MVR will record the actions of suspects during interviews when undergoing field sobriety tests, or when placed in custody if the recording would prove useful in later judicial proceedings.

A.   Um-hum.

Q.   You were aware of that SOP on that date, correct?

A.   I—I am.

Q.   And you knew that you had made a felony stop that day, right?

A.   Very much so.

Q.   Any you knew that you had made two felony arrests that day, right?

A.   Yeah.

Q.   Now, you know from being on the Florida Highway Patrol for five years, that felony arrests don't stop with you just taking people to jail, correct?

A.   Correct.

Q.   They then go to court.

A.   Most times; not always, but yes.

Q.   Well, sometimes they do, but most times they go to court, right? Yes?

A.   That's a case-by-case basis. So go—go ahead.

Q.   So the point of it is is that you know that after the arrest is made, the case is going into the court system.

A.   It—it starts its courts trial.

Q.   And it could end up one day—

A.   Uh-hum.

Q.   —in an environment like we're in today, couldn't it?

A.   Very much so.

Q. And—and you knew that on October 8th, right?

A. Yes.

Q. And you know that the standard operating procedure also says that that MVR is to record the circumstances at crime and accident scenes, or other events such as the confiscation and documentation of evidence or contraband.

A. Uh-hum.

Q. The idea is that when you find something, your video shows essentially where you're at in the car—

A. Uh-hum.

Q. —and also allows you with your Lavalier mic on to give a narrative play-by-play of what's going on, right?

A. Yes.

Q. And the video also is for the purpose of you, when you're near a suspect, to capture what the person is actually saying on that Lavalier mic, which then can be recorded and used in front of a jury. You knew that, right?

A. Yes.

Q. Now, part of the rule requires—and this is a standard operating procedure—requires that evidentiary digital recordings be uploaded as soon as reasonable. And you did that, right?

A. Very much so.

Q. Now, the MVR recordings then have a—a dropdown menu that you can choose a particular purpose for the stop, right? Like a DUI or a felony arrest—

A.   That's—

Q.   —or a misdemeanor arrest, right?

A.   That's done at the end of the recording of the individual video.

Q.   So you do it while you're in the car.

A.   Yes.

Q.   Right. Okay. So in this particular case—well, more broadly, you are aware that the MVR recording shall be retained in accordance with the needs of judicial prosecution, correct?

A.   Yes, I have—that's not me, but yes. I upload it; after it gets uploaded, I—I have nothing else to do with it.

Q.   Okay. Once it's uploaded, you have nothing else to do with it.

A.   Uh-hum.

Q.   Okay. Now, it says that—and this is a standard operating procedure that you—

A.   Uh-hum.

Q.   —should be aware of, and you are aware of—

A.   Uh-hum.

Q.   —that these recordings containing information that they be of value—

A.   Um-hum.

Q.   —for case prosecution or in any criminal civil adversarial proceeding—that means trial, right?

A.   Um-hum.

Q.   —shall be safeguarded as other forms of evidence and placed in the evidence property room. Were you aware of that SOP?

A.   Yeah. It immediately uploaded into there.

Q.   Into the room?

A.   Yeah. That's where her office is, the evidence custodian, it's in the room itself.

Q.   So—so what you're telling this jury is that once it uploads, it goes wherever, and you never see it again.

A.   So bas—basically when I go into upload, so I— I pull into the station. So it's on a wireless system. So we pull in and we log in to our server. So I click the button to log in to the server, it tells me what videos are downloading, what it's not downloading. Just like you would be downloading a video off-line, it's the same concept.

So we download the video, and it uploads into a server. So as it goes from the server into it—it clears my bank. So I have 32 hours of open data that I can put onto the system.

So as it goes from the server onto—or from my server that's in the car, goes on to a server itself, I— I don't have access to it at that point in time, it is now inside the server itself.

Q.   But you're the case officer, right? Meaning you—

A.   Yes.

Q.   —you made the arrest.

A.   I did, yes.

Q.   And ultimately, you're going to be the one responsible for sitting in front of seven people, right?

A.   Very much so.

Q.   And you're aware that—now, just so we're clear, you are aware that depending on what tag or what purpose for stop—

A.   Uh-hum.

Q.   —you choose at the end of the recording—

A.   Uh-hum.

Q.   —that that will impact how long the—the video stays on the server, right?

A.   Yeah.

Q.   Okay. And you know, for instance, a felony arrest, it'll stay there for 365 days, correct?

A.   Yes.

Q.   But a regular traffic stop, it only stays for 30 days, right?

A.   I think they bumped it to 90 now, yes.

Q.   Okay. But in this case, you should have picked felony arrest, right?

A.   Yeah. Very much so.

Q.   And you didn't.

A.   Yes.

Q.   And the video is gone.

A.   Yes. I can articulate though if you like.

Q.   No. I'm going to ask you the questions.

A.   Okay.

Q. The question I'm going to ask you is that when—you're familiar with CJIS and you know how to check cases on-line, correct?

A. Yes.

Q. Now, you have the ability to say, all right, this guy's arraignment that's coming up, this first court date, let me make sure this video is still available for the prosecutor. You have the ability to do that, don't you?

A. Yes.

Q. You never even thought to do that before this second, have you?

A. No. I—I don't—I don't usually check the cases based on, because most of—I'll explain on that. So whenever we—

Q. Well—

A. —get cases—

Q. —let me—but I have to ask you the questions, and then you tell me—

A. Go ahead.

Q. —the answer. You are required—you are aware that the member, meaning you, may request a MVR recording be retained for more than 30 days. You're aware of that SOP, aren't you?

A. Uh-hum.

Q. And—and in these SOPs, there's actually a big boxed area boxed out—you're—you're aware of this particular provision, aren't you, that says: Prior to erasing any audio/videotapes, the member must ensure that all court proceedings are completed. And you didn't do that, did you?

A.   No. Because based on what I recollected, I had chosen felony. So after—like I said before, I—from my recollection, I put in a felony because I put case numbers and everything associated with it. So when it goes into the system—like I said, I—it's a computer system, so I don't have—know how it purges, whatever it does. When I upload to the system, it goes in as a felony stop. I enjoy having the video here to be able to see everything that you can have. In this case, whatever the situation was, if you get it uploaded however the data gets collected through my—my car, believe me, it goes up and down—I call it about a—probably on a biweekly basis, that the system working or not working out of—whatever the situation is. So it could have been due to the fact that it didn't go in. And I don't think there's anyone here that can testify that I didn't upload it as a felony, and it's only to the fact that we don't know what happened to the system once it got in. So if it got purged, again, like I said, I have no—I have no recollection. Believe me, I would have been more than happy to have the video. But unfortunately Mr. Hernandez was in Sergeant Smith's vehicle, so he wouldn't have been caught on my in-car video camera on the inside anyways, but he would have been outside.

Q.   Oh. So there's yet another video that we don't have. So—

A.   No. He—

Q.   —there's one in Sergeant Smith's vehicle.

A.   —he didn't have one.

Q.   Ah.

A.   Ah.

Q.   So you ever sent an email to the wrong file and waiting for a response that you never got? You ever sent an e-mail to the wrong person waiting to hear back from them?

A.   Uh-hum.

Q.   Realize later you sent it to the wrong spot and had to resend the e-mail?

A.   Sure.

Q.   Now, turning your attention to the report that you wrote in this case—and you've testified to us earlier about finding marijuana in the back—

A.   Uh-hum.

Q.   —and finding a roach and finding cocaine in a black Coach bag, correct; do you remember that?

A.   Correct.

Q.   Now, when you write your—your reports, it's very important to write exactly what happened, correct?

A.   Yes.

Q.   And you're trained that the idea is so that, number one, you have it while it's fresh in your mind and you can put it to paper, right?

A.   Very much so.

Q.   And the other idea behind writing an accurate report, so if you're ever sitting in front of a jury, you can tell them exactly what happened, correct?

A.   Yes.

Q.   And in this case, your report is full of words like "they" said—

A.   Uh-hum.

Q.   —correct?

A.   That could be multiple people, yes.

Q.   And "we" said—

A.   Yes.

Q.   —correct? None of which is attributed to one or other person, right?

A.   No, it would be—they—they both either said it or agreed to it after the one said it, with a nod or a—

Q.   Well, which was it?

A.   —or a gesture.

Q.   So—so let me ask a question. Do you understand the difference between broad and narrow?

A.   Very much so.

Q.   And understand the difference between accurate and vague?

A.   Uh-hum.

Q.   And singular versus plural?

A.   Yes.

Q.   And specific versus general? You understand the difference between all those, right?

A.   Very much so.

Q.   And—and using the broader of all those terms creates confusion, doesn't it?

A.   Are you saying that—if there's something in the report you'd like me to verify, then you can go ahead and ask.

Q.   Well, what you just told this jury before I asked that line of questioning was that—

A.   Uh-hum.

Q.   —it was X, or it was Y. In other words, they both said it, or one of them said it, and the other one nodded along. So which is it, Trooper Baker?

A.   It's going to be a case-by-case said. If you'd like to ask me, I can tell you.

Q.   So Trooper Mark Baker, are you telling this jury that you wrote this report in a broad manner so that you can come in front of them and sort it out later?

A.   No. Not—not whatsoever. That'd be like me asking you this: So we come up—

Q.   Well, let me ask you the questions—

A.   Sure. Go ahead.

Q.   —and not give examples. You agree that the video would be specific, wouldn't it?

A.   I'm sorry?

Q.   The video would be specific, wouldn't it?

A.   Yes.

Q.   And the video would be narrow, right?

A.   To an extent, yes.

Q.   What do you mean "to an extent"? The video is exactly what happens—

A.   Yes.

Q.   —right?

A.   But it only captures a fixed point. It's not something that follows around with me.

Q.   The Lavalier mic that is on you follows you around, doesn't it?

A.   To an extent. It only goes so far. So it only—

Q.   (Unintelligible) have a range?

A.   Yes, it has a range.

Q.   Did you check the video before you uploaded it to see whether it accurately recorded everything?

A.   I—I watched parts of the video of me catching the—or finding the drugs and stuff like that, after I found the drugs and the test kits for them—

Q.   Was your—

A.   —and the—

Q.   —microphone working?

A.   From what I recollect, yes.

Q.   And the video, if we had it, would actually be accurate as to who said what, wouldn't it?

A.   Very much so.

Q.   Now, it was, in fact, not ever Mr. Hernandez's statement that there was marijuana in the trunk of the car, right? He never said, there's marijuana in the trunk of the car. Right?

A.   My recollection, they both stated that—they were aware of the drugs inside the vehicle.

Q.   And Mr. Hernandez over here never said, there is cocaine anywhere in the vehicle, did he?

A. They both stated that they were aware of the drugs inside the vehicle.

Q. Now, you—a second ago you said to the best of your recollection. You'd have to watch the video to be 100 percent sure—

A. No, I just refer to my report, which is sitting in front of me at the mic.

Q. And you would agree that the video is much more accurate than your report.

A. Not necessarily, no. Because the video only captures again a fixed point. So what I see—I'm—I would love to have one that I could go stick on me and you'd see what I'd see. But as we go in—into the car, it—I—I disappear from the video. That's all you see or hear, me rustling around. That's really all you hear when you get inside the vehicle because I'm moving around so much.

Q. But you're also trained to do like a John Madden color commentary as you're finding stuff so that you can remind yourself of things later, right?

A. No. We're never—we're never trained to do that. But I—I tend to do that, yes. If it were—

Q. And that would exist in this case, would be whatever you're saying as you're finding things and where you're finding them.

A. Usually when I find things, I bring—

Q. Yeah.

A. —it immediately out of the vehicle as soon as I find it, and then I walk it to the front of my car, and I place it on the front of the car (unintelligible)—

Q.   Now, what's—

A.   —evidence you saw.

Q.   Thank you. Let's talk—again, back to a little bit about your investigation. Now, and throughout the course of your five years, not only with your training, but with your experience, you have studied investigation techniques, right?

A.   Different ones, yes.

Q.   Had hundreds and hundreds of cases, right?

A.   Very much so.

Q.   You know what tools are available to you to investigate cases, right?

A.   Yes.

Q.   And you know what methods are available to you to investigate cases, right?

And you know that items such as the ones we have here, not only are they evidence, they contain evidence, don't they?

A.   Yes.

MR. BODIFORD: Madam Clerk. Thank you.

BY MR. BODIFORD (CONTINUING):

Q.   By the way, on State's Exhibit Number 2, when you write the suspect's name, the only name you wrote was Giovanni Martinez (phonetics), right?

A.   Uh-hum.

Q.   Okay. Now, on these particular items, they are evidence. By the way, you said earlier, you weren't sure if the roach is in here?

A.   Hmm.

Q.   It is—can't you look and figure out if there—

A.   I could probably try to dig through, but I'm not—not allowed to open it, see? There's quite a bit of marijuana in there unfortunately.

Q.   You know that these things could contain fingerprints, right, both this State's 2 and State's 1. There could be fingerprints on there, right?

A.   To an extent, yes.

Q.   Yeah. Now—

A.   Could be, yeah.

Q.   —do you recall when we took your deposition back at the end of June—

A.   Uh-hum.

Q.   —I asked you about fingerprints.

A.   Uh-hum.

Q.   Do you remember that? And you remember you said, it can be done before trial?

A.   It could be.

Q.   Did you?

A.   No. In this case, no. Because as you can see on the cocaine one, it's covered in powder, different powders and stuff like that, so it's going to be hard to get a fingerprint off of that.

But the marijuana kit itself usually you give to the State's Attorney and we'll—we'll find out what the situation is on the—and it wasn't—again, it wasn't a possession, it's a constructive possession case. So—which means you—you're familiar with it, or you know the drugs are inside there. Neither one of them—if one of them would have said, hey, that's mine, I wouldn't have even charged the other one.

Q. Well, we'll—

A. That's the case that—

Q. —let's come back to—we'll talk—let's talk about constructive possession in just a second. But fingerprints can be on bags, right?

A. Could—yes.

Q. Basically on—

A. Depending on the surface, it depends on what it (unintelligible).

Q. Sure. And you—and you know what it is, it's the sweats and the oils on your fingers that when it contacts something that has other maybe cleaning products or dirt, the—the sweat and the oil transfers from your hand to whatever surface it—it transfers to, right?

A. Yes.

Q. Okay. And it could be on cell phones, right?

A. Uh-hum.

Q. Yes?

A. Yes.

Q. It could be on containers, just about anything, right?

A. Yes. Depending on the surface, yes.

Q. And you—you—so you know how fingerprints work, and you know that you could have lifted them, right?

A. I don't have any kits to lift them, no. But we—

Q.   But you know how to get it lifted, right?

A.   You'd have to send them away.

Q.   You—

A.   (Unintelligible)—

Q.   —and you know how to do that.

A.   Again, we—you talk with—I already addressed this issue. We talk—I talked with the State's Attorney, if we found out it was a valid thing that needed to be done, then we would get it done.

Q.   So what you're telling this jury is that you and the prosecutor said, we've got a constructive possession case where we don't actually know who may have touched it; and we made a conscious, joint effort between the two of us not to test for fingerprints on any of it.

A.   So when—

Q.   Is that a yes or a no? And I'll let you explain.

A.   Rephrase the question again. Go ahead.

Q.   You and the prosecutor got together—

A.   Uh-hum.

Q.   —and you made a joint decision between the two of you, whether it was Ms. Griffith, or somebody else in the office, that on a constructive possession case where we don't actually know who this belongs to, and we could perhaps solve it by fingerprinting it, we made the decision not to do it. Are you saying that's—that you did that with a prosecutor in this case?

A.   Not—it doesn't go into that extent, but yes. Usually the—at a point it's addressed if it comes up to it. And if we do come and talk about it, it'd be like, hey, we've got to get these fingerprints done. It's not—if—if it's a thing and say, hey, do you think the fingerprints could help with this, then we address the fingerprint issue.

Q. Then most cases—

A. Most of the time—

Q. I'm sorry. Finish.

A. Go ahead.

Q. This case has been out there for over a year, and you've never had any of this fingerprinted.

A. No.

Q. Now, you also know how DNA works, right?

A. Yes.

Q. And you've collected DNA evidence before, right?

A. Yes.

Q. Now, I'm not going to embarrass you or I by asking either one of us to say what DNA stands for, but we know that it is just about any biological transfer from sweat, all the way up to pieces of skin or hair—

A. Uh-hum.

Q. —that can be tested—

A. Uh-hum.

Q. —and—and conceivably linked back to a suspect, right?

A. Yes.

Q. In a nutshell.

A.   Yes.

Q.   And there's a whole database out there of people, when they get a felony conviction, they get their DNA, and we're building a database—

A.   Yes.

Q.   —across the country, right?

A.   Very much so.

Q.   And you know that DNA can be taken from clothes, right?

A.   Uh-hum.

Q.   Yes?

A.   Yes.

Q.   And luggage, right?

A.   You can't—again, depending on what it is.

Q.   And in this case, there's been no effort to do any DNA analysis to see who this belongs to.

A.   No.

Q.   When you—when you first approached the car, Trooper Baker—

A.   Uh-hum.

Q.   —you had said that Mr. Hernandez, who was nervous, right?

A.   Yes.

Q.   That's common for a traffic stop. People get nervous being pulled over by the police all the time, right?

A.   That's again a case-by-case basis.

Q.   Okay. At some point in time after the stop, Giovanni Martinez (phonetics) is the driver that was on his cell phone; do you remember that?

A.   I know at different points of the time, yes, he was.

Q.   Okay. And that was prior to you taking him into custody, him being arrested, he was being allowed, so to speak, to use his cell phone?

A.   I believe so, yes.

Q.   Okay. And you ultim—so you identified one cell phone as his; Mr. Hernandez had a cell phone, correct?

A.   I don't recall.

Q.   Okay. Do you remember there being a cell phone in the backseat of the car?

A.   I don't recall.

Q.   Hmm. Do you—you remember this black Coach bag—

A.   I do.

Q.   —correct? That was not his bag, was it?

A.   They—both subjects stated that it wasn't their bag.

Q.   Okay. So as you sit here today, you have zero proof whatsoever that the black Coach bag wherein State's 1 cocaine was found—

A.   Uh-hum.

Q.   —belonged to—was in any possession of this man here, correct?

A.   In actual physical possession? It was in the trunk itself.

Q.   So the answer is no, it was not in his possession.

A.   Not in physical possession, no.

Q.   And it's not under his control, was it?

A.   No, it was in the trunk—in the front seat.

Q.   And there was nothing to establish he had any ownership of it, right?

A.   No.

Q.   Did you inventory the contents of the black bag or photograph the black Coach bag where the cocaine was found for us here today?

A.   No. I don't have a camera unfortunately. I would love to have one.

Q.   What type of phone do you use?

A.   Oh, I'm not—use my personal phone?

Q.   Yeah.

A.   No, I'm not using my personal phone. We're— if—we're told not to use our personal phone.

Q.   Really?

A.   Yeah.

Q.   You—you do realize that there is a—

A.   Uh-hum.

Q.   —a—a   provision   standard   operating procedures—

A.   Uh-hum.

Q.   —17.22.06 called Use of Personally Owned Audio/Video Devices—

A.   It—

Q.   —are you familiar with that? And it essentially says that any member requesting to use personally owned audio/video recording devices must adhere to the FHP mobile video/audio recording equipment specs, (unintelligible) requirements, and guidelines.

A.   Uh-hum. Which, again, it has to be approved by the department itself. And—which my—I guess my phone is not. So—

Q.   But to save—

A.   Go ahead.

Q.   —to tell this jury you're not allowed to use your phone is not accurate, is it?

A.   Because my phone doesn't meet the specs or requirements.

Q.   So we don't have any photos; we don't have the backpack; and we don't have an inventory of the backpack, other than the cocaine, right?

A.   The—that was the only evidence found in it, yes.

Q.   Okay.

A.   There was no IDs or anything associated with it, or otherwise I would have addressed that issue.

Q.   Okay. And it—at some point in time, do you recall taking a cell phone that belonged to an unknown person and—and threatening the two guys there that you were going to use that phone to call the owner of it and try to see who—see if you could get that person to come—

A.   No, I—

Q.   —back and admit that they were the owner—

A.   No. I asked—

Q.   —of the cocaine?

A.   —I asked them, they said it was a friend of theirs.

Q.   The phone.

A.   No, no, no, no. The bag. There was a phone—

Q.   There was—

A.   I don't even remember there being a phone at all.

Q.   You don't remember dropping a third phone into the bag?

A.   Not that I recall.

Q.   Where—so at this—if this vehicle is used in a drug situation and all the contents of it are being impounded—

A.   Uh-hum.

Q.   —what happened to the black backpack that had the cocaine?

A.   Since it—it belongs to whoever it is, that's not necessarily being used for the crime itself. The compartments—or the Tupperware itself was someone that was hiding it. We take it out of its compartment. Just like the Tupperware container itself, I'm not going to take all the carpet around the carpet—the container because it held it. I'm not going to take the—the top off of the—the car just because it contained what was in there.

Q.   You say the top off the car?

A.   Yeah. You see where—you see what I'm getting at?

Q.   Yeah.

MR. BODIFORD: Judge, may I use the overhead with defense 1 through 7 that he's previously—

JUDGE SHELFER: Yes.

MR. BODIFORD:—see if he recognizes it? Any objection?

JUDGE SHELFER: Do you want the lights down? You want the lights down?

MR. BODIFORD: It would be up to the jury, Judge, whatever is their—

JUDGE SHELFER: Turn them down so they can see better.

BY MR. BODIFORD (CONTINUING):

Q.   All right. Trooper Davis (sic), you recognize this as being the front driver's seat of the car that you stopped that day?

A.   Again, I—I—I can't—can't see it now.

Q.   Would it (unintelligible) lights back on (unintelligible)?

A.   Again, I—I can't see. We don't have a tag number or vehicle. I—I—it looks like a convertible.

Q.   But you can't say for sure that was the same car?

A.   I cannot.

Q.   Okay. Does the computer (unintelligible) a Sebring convertible?

A.   It looks like convertible-ish.

Q.   Okay. What about—

A.   And different (unintelligible)—

Q.   —this particular backseat?

A.   It looks—

Q.   Now, do—do you recognize this as the—

A.   It seems to have been the same style of vehicle that we were out with, yes.

Q.   Okay. Now, you had mentioned finding the— State's Exhibit 2, the large—

A.   Uh-hum.

Q.   —stained container of marijuana back behind a seat.

A.   Uh-hum.

Q.   Now, would that be behind where my laser pointer is, and down from there?

A.   Yeah. If it's the same make and model, there's—a level plane so the back of your car usually has where the speakers are in the back, that's where that area is that's behind that seat.

Q.   Would that be something akin to what is depicted in—for the record, this would be defense Exhibit Number 6. Kind of where the hat is, would that be down in the well behind the seat, just so—

A.   Yeah. I'm—I'm trying to picture whether it was that, but—

Q.   Well, let me back one up for you.

A.   Yeah. If you can be a little bit broader, I—I focus—that—that looks a little bit better, yeah.

Q.   So this is kind of part of the backseat. You're—oh, airing (phonetics) out a part of the car when you searched it?

A.   No.

Q.   Never saw that? Okay.

A.   No.

Q.   But essentially, if we look on this, going down behind the seat, there's a well, right?

A.   It's not even a really well. You can see it straight from the back window.

Q.   You could look in through the back window.

A.   Yeah. As you walk up to it on the—on the back window, you—you—you'd be able to see right into that back area. It's the best—almost like—like that.

Q.   Well—so regarding the hat that I showed you earlier—

A.   Um-hum.

Q.   —the hat would essentially down in that dip area; is that fair to say?

A.   Yes. If that's the same area.

Q.   Okay. And your testimony is that if you're looking from the backseat towards that area—

A.   Uh-hum.

Q.   —you couldn't see something if you were—from the vantage point towards the car, right? If you're standing behind it looking down in, you could see what's in here; do you agree?

A.   Yeah. It just depends on where your positioning and the vehicle is.

Q.   Okay. Now, what else is in that compartment besides the marijuana?

A.   That was the only (unintelligible).

Q.   You don't have an inventory of whether there were shirts or pants or hats or anything else in that little compartment. Your testimony is just the marijuana.

A.   No. I believe there was an inventory done on the vehicle itself.

Q.   Okay. So you would have been the one to do the inventory?

A.   Me or Sergeant—Sergeant Smith.

Q.   And it would have been part of your report?

A.   It should have been a packet, yes, it's turned in with the packet.

Q.   Okay. So where is—do you have it with you here today?

A.   That—I believe she has my packet.

Q.   You don't—you don't have the—you didn't bring your police report with you?

A.   I—I have my police report.

Q.   Okay.

A.   It's right here.

Q.   But you didn't bring anything else other than just your narrative.

A.   Other than my narrative directly to everything, no.

Q.   So as we stand here, as you sit there and testify, you can't tell us what was in there other than just you're saying just the marijuana. (Unintelligible).

A.   Yeah. I—I'd have to—I'd have to look at the vehicle inventory report and see what was in it.

Q.   All right. Now, Mr. Hernandez, let's talk about his appearance and demeanor, if we can, just real quick. He—when you—when you met with him, he was nervous, but he did not appear to be under the influence, correct?

A.   No, not—he—he's not a driver. It's a—it's under—under the influence—

Q.   What does—

A.   —(unintelligible).

Q.   —that have to do with anything? Either he was under the influence or he wasn't.

A.   Well, it has a big issue because you were talking with DUI? Are you talking about just under the influence? He's not my driver, so I'm—I don't know what you're trying to ask. I—

Q.   So you didn't—you didn't even look to see whether the guy looked like he had been smoking marijuana or something like that?

A.   You just talking about having some marijuana?

Q.   So—okay. So other than his statement that there was some somewhere, he didn't appear to be having—he didn't appear to have used marijuana.

A.   No, he wasn't doped out if that's what you're asking.

Q.   He didn't have red eyes.

A. I think he had conjunctiva, if I remember correctly.

Q. Uh-hum. So that's a medical condition.

A. To an extent, yes.

Q. Yeah. Now, you're—

A. But he—

Q. You're not a drug recognition expert, right?

A. I—I am not.

Q. Right? And a drug recognition expert is somebody that actually trains to be able to look at somebody; observe certain symptoms, signs of physical displays, and within a relative degree of certainty, say that person is on X particular drug. That's what a DRA (sic) is, right?

A. And that's why we go to the ARIDE class, that's the step before it. So whenever we go to ARIDE, we're able to—you get—it's basically a basic course of the DRE class. So you're able to identify certain issues that pop up. And once you go to that, you get an application to go to the DRE school, and they accept you, which mine's in April.

Q. So you've applied but you haven't been.

A. No.

Q. So the answer is, no, I'm not a DRE.

A. I was ARIDE, but that's not DRE.

Q. So all right. ARIDE means nothing; DRE is where—what you need.

A. Well, to be a complete expert, yes.

Q. He was alert, correct, Mr. Hernandez?

A. From what I recall, yes.

Q.   He was coherent, right?

A.   He was nervous other than that.

Q.   Do you understand the difference between nervous and coherent?

A.   Yeah.

Q.   Do you understand what coherent means?

A.   Yeah.

Q.   Coherent means your ability—able to talk and listen and give responses correctly—you know, appropriate answers, right?

A.   Yes.

Q.   And he was those things, correct?

A.   Yes.

Q.   And he—

A.   The nervous—

Q.   —was serious.

A.   —the nervousness behavior also calls him with coherency, so he's not able to answer because he's stuttering or whatever the consideration is.

Q.   And he was serious, right?

A.   Yes.

Q.   He wasn't laughing?

A.   No, he didn't laugh.

Q.   He wasn't smiling.

A.   No.

Q.   He wasn't moving around a lot.

A.   I didn't have eyes on him the whole time, I couldn't tell you that.

Q.   Okay. Other than you noting that he's nervous, as you approached the vehicle, you did not see there being any what we call furtive movements, right?

A.   Like someone—like someone trying to hide something?

Q.   Correct.

A.   No.

Q.   And you didn't see anything being passed between Mr. Hernandez and the driver, did you?

A.   No. Usually when you get pulled over, that—you stop what you're doing anyway.

Q.   So the answer is no, I did not see them—

A.   No.

Q.   —passing anything between them.

A.   No.

Q.   Okay. And Mr. Hernandez was quiet, correct?

A.   For—for the most part, yes, he was.

Q.   The main talker was Mr. Martinez, right?

A.   Yes.

Q.   Okay. Now, when we get into—and I'll start summing—summing up here and getting towards the end. I'm sure everybody's very happy about that.

A.   Go ahead.

Q.   When we talk about possession, Trooper Baker, we—there's two types: There's actual and constructive, right?

A.   Very much so.

Q.   Now, my laser pointer, you would agree, is in my actual possession, right?

A.   Uh-hum.

Q.   Your badge is in your actual possession, right?

A.   Yes.

Q.   Your hat, however, is in your constructive possession—

A.   Constructive possession, yes.

Q.   —is that right; do you agree?

A.   Yes.

Q.   And the hat is—is in a spot where you yourself can control it, right?

A.   This one is, yes.

Q.   Well, that's the one I'm talking about.

A.   Yes. Yes.

Q.   Well, do you have another hat (unintelligible)—

A.   I have lots of hats.

Q.   Well, which one did you think I was talking about?

A.   Go ahead.

Q.   You thought I was talking about that one?

A.   Oh, yeah.

Q.   Okay.

A.   We're good.

Q.   That hat is in your—you have the ability to control it right now, you could pick it up and put it on your head if you wanted to.

A.   Uh-hum.

Q.   Right?

A.   Yes.

Q.   I come over and try to pick it up and put it on my head, you're probably going to stop me, correct?

A.   Probably, yeah.

Q.   Right. It's called what we—we—we talk about having dominion and control; do you understand those words?

A.   Yes.

Q.   Okay. And in this particular place, we don't have any actual possession by either of these persons, correct?

A.   No—

Q.   Nothing in their hands?

A.   Nothing.

Q.   Nothing in Lazaro Hernandez's person, meaning in his pockets or, you know, in a shirt pocket, nothing like that. Right?

A.   Other than the remnants on the floorboard itself, but I guess that could be considered possession itself.

Q.   Do you understand the difference between a floorboard and somebody's pocket?

A.   Yes. If you're talking about having it in all of his person?

Q.   The question is: Was it in his pockets?

A.   No.

Q.   Was it in his shirt pocket?

A.   No.

Q.   Was it in his back pocket?

A.   Nope.

Q.   BY the way, this stuff you're saying was on the floor, did you scrape it up and did you—and bring it in so these folks could see what you're talking about?

A.   It's—it could take a long time to do all that. But, no, because I already have the—

Q.   Well, don't—

A.   —marijuana itself.

Q.   It would take a long time to do that. Don't you think it's important when you accuse somebody of possessing an illegal substance—

A.   Well, you—

Q.   —that you have the proof of it?

A.   Agreed. But his issues, you also have cat hair that's involved with it and everything like that. So if I were to—if that's the car that—if you saw how dirty it was. So it's going to be kind of hard to get all that information up there, and it kind of looked like a big ball of dirt.

Q.   So these folks have to rely on your describing and determine what's important and what's not.

A.   To—what I deem as evidence.

Q.   Okay. Now, there is no controlled substance that was in a container in his hand, was there?

A.   No.

Q.   And there was no controlled substance that was in a container on his person, meaning, for instance, in—for example, my mints in my bag in my hand.

A.   No.

Q.   So there wasn't any containers like that. And there was no containers that he actually was in control of, right?

A.   No.

Q.   There was no containers that were close enough to be within his ready reach.

A.   No, no containers, no.

Q.   Okay. So, in fact, he was not in actual possession of anything at all.

A.   In actual possession, no.

Q.   Okay. Now, constructive is the other issue, right?

A.   Yes.

Q.   And you know from being a trooper that you have to pr—you have to—to consider when you're arresting somebody—

A.   Uh-hum.

Q.   —as to whether they're aware of the presence of the substance.

A.   Yes.

Q.   All right. Now, your report, your testimony, you say they both said they knew it was there.

A.   Uh-hum.

Q.   —both the marijuana—

A.   Hmm.

Q.   —and the cocaine, right?

A.   Yes.

Q.   But you can't tell these jurors when they—when Mr. Hernandez learned that the cocaine was there, can you?

A.   No.

Q.   You didn't ask him that.

A.   When I—

Q.   Yeah.

A.   —knew he was there?

Q.   Well, if you know it was there, when did you find it out, Mr. Hernandez? I mean, you're conducting the interview, you didn't ask that question?

A.   I said—I asked how long—or where the black bag came from.

Q.   And they said, it's somebody else's.

A.   Yes.

Q.   Okay. Did you say, and when did that somebody else tell you he had cocaine in his black bag, Mr. Hernandez? You didn't do that, did you?

A.   I individually questioned them, yes.

Q.   But the answer is, no, I did not ask him when he found out that there was cocaine in the bag. That's the answer, isn't it?

A.   He stated that he knew that the cocaine was in the black bag.

Q.   And that's the extent of what you know—

A.   Yes.

Q.   —is that this—this statement somewhere that he said, I know who's cocaine—or we—

A.   Prior to the stop is what it got to, yes.

Q.   Okay. But that's all you can tell us.

A.   No, that's all—

Q.   So all you can tell these jurors, that's all I know—

A.   That's all I—

MS. GRIFFITH: (Unintelligible) calls for possible (unintelligible).

Thank you.

JUDGE SHELFER: Go ahead.

BY MR. BODIFORD (CONTINUING):

Q.   All you can tell these jurors is that at some point in time, somebody said, either Martinez or Hernandez, there's cocaine in the thing, and either somebody said, yes, or somebody nodded their head along with that. Or something like that. That's the extent of what we have, correct?

A.   Yes. I questioned them, and they stated they were aware of the drugs located inside the vehicle prior to me making the stop.

Q.   All right. Now, in addition—so that's only one thing that you as arresting officer have to be able to—to have and to prove before making arrest. There's actually two other things, right?

A.   Uh-hum.

Q.   For constructive possession, the substance you find has to be in a place over which the person has control.

A.   Uh-hum.

Q.   Right? But you just got done telling the jurors for actual possession that the marijuana roach was not in a place over which he had control of it.

A.   It's in the—I believe the roach was in the center console area. So it wasn't—

Q.   Did you put that in your report?

A.   I believe so.

Q.   The roach was actually on the floorboard—

A.   I have to find it myself. One moment.

THE WITNESS: May I have just a moment, Your Honor?

JUDGE SHELFER: Uh-hum. I'm going to need to give the jury a break. Is this a good time to do that?

MR. BODIFORD: That'd be fine, Judge.

JUDGE SHELFER: Let's do that. I know everybody needs a—a break. So let me remind you not to talk among yourselves about what has transpired. And we'll come—there should be some coffee in there for you. And we'll come back and then try to get you out of here at 12:00 o'clock for lunch. Okay?

UNIDENTIFIED SPEAKER: Just leave your notes there.

(The jury was excused from the courtroom.)

THE WITNESS: I find it. It says driver's side floorboard.

JUDGE SHELFER: Okay. We will—anything before we go to recess?

MS. GRIFFITH: No, Your Honor.

JUDGE SHELFER: We'll be in recess.

MR. BODIFORD: Just that—admonish the witness the rule of sequestration is invoked, and not to discuss the case with anyone.

JUDGE SHELFER: You understand that? Okay. (Recess.)

(Discussion off the record.)

(The jury returned to the courtroom.)

JUDGE SHELFER: All right. Everyone be seated. The record can show that the jury has returned to the courtroom, and that Mr. Hernandez is at counsel table with Mr. Bodiford.

And you were still inquiring, Mr. Bodiford.

MR. BODIFORD: Thank you.

BY MR. BODIFORD (CONTINUING):

Q. Trooper Baker, before we left, you had—we were talking about where the little—

A. Roach.

Q. —roach was found. And you had initially said you believed it was in the center console. Is that what you told the jury initially?

A. Yes.

Q. And, in fact, you checked your report, and that roach was found on the driver's floorboard, correct?

A. Yes.

Q. Which would have been at the feet of Mr. Martinez, right?

A. Yes.

Q. So, of course, Mr. Hernandez has no ability to control that roach while it's at the feet of Mr. Hernandez (sic).

A.   Not necessarily. I mean, you have access—you saw the pictures of where it was. I mean—that'd be like me reaching over the judge's desk, not that I would ever do that.

Q.   Yes—well, that's the point. That's the point. What independent proof do you have, Trooper? Tell this jury—

A.   We don't—we don't—

Q.   —that (unintelligible). Hmm?

A.   We don't have any proof—one way or another, not that he did or he didn't.

Q.   Let's move it on back to the marijuana that's behind the seat in the well.

A.   Uh-hum.

Q.   You have no proof that he was able to have any control over what was behind that seat, do you?

A.   Rephrase your question. Because I—had no control over it, like—as in how?

Q.   Well, let's back it up one step. It wasn't his car, right?

A.   No.

Q.   It belonged to Giovanni Martinez's (phonetics) mom, correct?

A.   Yes.

Q.   And—so you—you have no proof whatsoever that Lazaro Hernandez had placed that stuff back there, right?

A.   That's the—that's the thing is we don't know where—it doesn't grow there, so it's got to come there somehow.

Q.   Right.

A.   So someone—someone placed it there.

Q.   But it's not what you know, it's what you can prove, isn't it?

A.   Exactly.

Q.   And so you have no proof that this man sitting behind me put it there, right?

A.   And I have no proof that he didn't.

Q.   And you have no proof that—so—you have no proof whatsoever that he had the ability to go back there and say, hey, I'm taking this, I'm going to do whatever with it, do you?

A.   Say that—say that again?

Q.   Didn't know that he—that—the issue is—what we're getting at is that when you arrest for constructive joint possession, you have to be prepared to prove that the substance was in a place over which the person has control.

A.   Has control. So inside the vehicle, you're in a vehicle, that—that—as you could see, it's open all the way to the back. I can get anywhere in that vehicle that I want to. He has control over the vehicle, he can if he gets out, hey, give me the keys, he can unlock the trunk. I mean, that's like he—someone riding with someone, I have—I can do whatever I want to in that vehicle.

Q.   You're speculating—

A.   —whenever.

Q.   —now, right?

A.   No. No. That's a fact.

> Q.   Well, like if I—well, you leave here and I go get your FHP car—
>
> A.   Uh-hum.
>
> Q.   —and I start climbing all over it like a three year old—
>
> A.   I'm going to kick your ass.
>
> Q.   Because I don't have the ability to control what's in there, do I?
>
> A.   Again—
>
> Q.   Right.
>
> A.   —if you had—let's put it this way then: You bring something in my vehicle and you put it in the backseat. Grab it whenever you want.
>
> MR. BODIFORD: May I have just a moment, Judge?
>
> JUDGE SHELFER: Uh-hum.
>
> MR. BODIFORD: Thank you, Trooper, I have no further questions.

I do not subscribe to the theory that "less is more" or "keep it short". I have a story to tell, not just a short list of questions to ask. If it takes a while, then it takes a while. I keep animated, move around, and gesture to the witness and jury to keep them involved. If they signal they have had enough, I will wrap it up. In this case, they were very attentive and did not give me any indication that they were anything other than understanding and believing my story—*my client did not know the dope was there, and this sketchy investigation can't prove otherwise. You can't be guilty of possessing something you didn't know was there, much less have any control over!*

On a final note, the judge granted a judgment of acquittal (like a directed verdict in civil cases) after the State rested, so the jury didn't even get to deliberate!

8.4 CROSS OF AN EXPERT IN A CIVIL CASE

This is a cross examination that is found on an attorney's website. I thought it very well done, and offer it to you as an example of a well-prepared and concise cross examination. While the style is different than mine, the content and delivery clearly get across the story that—

Take a look at Chapter 4.7 (Expert witness cross). You will see this attorney use many of the techniques I list therein.

I have redacted the names of the parties for obvious reasons.

CROSS EXAMINATION OF DR. ███████:

Q. Good afternoon. Doctor, my name is ███████. You and I have never met, have we?

A. That's correct, sir.

Q. Let me introduce you to T. D., the man you've never met also. I know you've already testified that you've never examined him. But you've never even laid eyes on him until you walked in the courtroom, correct?

A. Yes, sir.

Q. You didn't lay eyes on him when you were contacted by Mr. Opposing Counsel's firm to write a report, did you—had you seen him by then?

A. That's correct, sir, I have not.

Q. Okay. You didn't lay eyes on him when you actually wrote the report?

A. No, sir.

Q. And you were provided just some records on his medical condition, correct?

A. I was provided with a fairly copious amount off records.

Q. But no films?

A. No, sir.

Q. You've never seen one MRI film on this man?

A. I've seen the report, sir.

Q. Excuse me. My question was, have you ever seen an MRI film on this man?

A. No, sir.

Q. How many films has Dr. W. seen?

A. I believe he saw the X-rays.

Q. And the MRIs?

A. Yes, sir.

Q. As far as any other doctors who have actually treated T.D., you haven't been provided all of the information that they have because they've had access to radiological films themselves, and Dr. W. has actually been inside this man's back, would you agree?

A. I would agree, sir.

Q. I've heard a phrase used by counsel for the trucking company many times already in this trial. Now to be fair or let's be fair—as a matter of fact, I think I heard it during your direct examination, didn't I?

A. You did, sir.

Q. Okay. To be fair, would you tell the jury how many times your opinion has been limited or stricken by a court of law in a case like this? To be fair, tell them, please.

A. To the best of my knowledge, sir, it has not been.

Q. Well, you were an expert in the KJM v. MNA Inc. company case that happens to be—have been filed and is pending right next door, in the Court next door, the ██th District Court of ██████ County, ████████, correct?

A. I don't know, sir.

Q. You're not familiar with an order signed by the judge literally in the next room?

A. No, sir. I have not been provided with that.

Q. That eliminates your testimony? Who's the lawyer who hired you in that case?

A. I don't know, sir. I don't recall. If you would like to hand me that, I would look at it.

Q. You've never seen anything provided to you by the lawyer who hired you in that case right next door telling you about any part of your testimony being stricken?

A. No, sir.

Q.   Okay. You ever heard of D.—Judge ███ next door?

A.   I may have, sir.

Q.   But you are familiar with that case?

A.   I recall the name.

Q.   Okay. And you're still an expert in that case?

A.   I don't know, sir.

Q.   You've been deposed in that case?

A.   I don't know, sir. I have no memory.

Q.   How many other cases has your testimony been or limited by a judge?

A.   As I said, sir, I have not ever been provided information that my testimony has been stricken.

Q.   Are you saying you don't know how many times?

A.   I am saying that, sir.

Q.   I just heard you say that a discogram should to determine whether surgery was necessary on Mr. D.; is that right?

A.   That's correct, sir.

Q.   Do you remember your patient by the name of D.R.?

A.   I do.

Q.   Does that ring a bell?

A.   I do.

Q.   Your own medical records on her indicated that if there are no changes since March last year, we will recommend a lumbar discogram to see whether the pain is coming from the L-4, 5 level if indeed the discogram is concordant at that level.

And she and I will talk about anterior lumbar inter body fusion.

A. What was the date of that report, sir?

Q. First of all, did you write that?

A. I did. I believe I can recognize my report.

THE COURT: Why don't you hand it to him if that's his. Let him identify it.

THE WITNESS: Thank you, sir.

THE COURT: Um-hum.

MR. ██████: May I approach?

THE COURT: Yes, you may. Go ahead.

THE WITNESS: May I see the report?

Q. (BY MR. ██████) Looks like the date is ██████ the 9th, 2003.

A. Um-hum.

Q. I'm referring to the last page of your—the last two.

A. May I see the report?

THE COURT: Give him the whole report.

THE WITNESS: Thank you. Her accident was in 2002, and she had none of the disqualifying factors that the defendant does.

Q. (BY MR. ██████) I don't think I asked you anything about that, Doctor.

A. I'm sorry.

Q. Did you recommend a discogram and if was concordant with lumbar pain at L-4 5, then the two of you would talk about doing surgery on her?

A. Back then I did, yes, sir.

Q. How many other patients have you done discograms on?

A. In—as I said to defendant's counsel, sir, I have done it in the past. I no longer do it.

Q. You understand that other doctors and different types of specialists continue to use discograms as a valid medical tool, don't you?

A. It's not valid, sir, but they do use it. It's been disqualified by many societies at this point.

Q. You're not a neurosurgeon, are you?

A. I'm an orthopedic spine surgeon, sir.

Q. Does that mean you're not a neurosurgeon?

A. That's correct, sir.

Q. You're certainly not board certified in neurosurgery, are you?

A. No, sir.

Q. You never attempted to become board certified in neurosurgery, did you?

A. No, sir.

Q. As a matter of fact as far as your patient, Ms. R., was concerned, not only did you recommend a discogram and indicated that if it was concordant with the pain, that is consistent with the pain, that you would go ahead and recommend surgery to her. Not only did you do that, but this was in a collision where the amount of the damage to her car was, in your terms, minor approximately $2,000, correct?

A. Correct, sir.

Q.   Less than the damage to his car, to T.D.'s car, wasn't it?

A.   Yes, sir.

THE COURT: Okay. Will you attorneys approach real quick?

Ladies and gentlemen, why don't y'all stand up and make noise.

(Discussion off the record)

THE COURT All right. Here we go. Go ahead, Mr. ███████. I'm sorry.

Q.   (BY MR. ███████) And as a matter of fact in that patient, surgery was done on Ms. R., wasn't it?

A.   It was. I've made mistakes. That was one of them.

Q.   Then it's possible that you have made a mistake coming in to this courtroom at a $1,000 an hour for the defendants to testify that the treating doctor should not have even used a discogram, should not have done the surgery on a patient who you've never seen, talked to, or not even seen any films on; isn't that correct, Dr. B.?

A.   Well, at this point, sir, I know much more about the medical literature than I did in 2002. And I would not do it again. So I would say that the vast way to the medical evidence and my knowledge of Mr. D's condition would say that I have not made an error.

Q.   Is that a yes to my question?

A.   I would say I have not made an error in this case.

Q.   Do you know how much knowledge, medical knowledge, experience, and training as a neurosurgeon that Dr. W. has?

A.   He has about the same professional training as I do, sir.

Q.   Do you know how much experience he has?

A.   I believe that he is board certified about the same time I am, sir.

Q.   Do you know how much experience in doing back surgeries he has?

A.   About the same as I do, sir.

Q.   Now you don't know that, do you?

A.   I looked up when he graduated from medical school, sir.

Q.   That's not going to tell you how much experience he has during—doing back surgery, does it?

A.   Not an exact number, sir.

Q.   And you are a person who really doesn't even like to do back surgery, aren't you?

A.   No, sir. I do surgery when it's indicated, and I think the patient is going to get better.

Q.   Have you ever said that you—you think you're very, very, very careful and that's why you don't operate on a lot of people, you ever said that?

A.   I said I was very careful.

Q.   Have you ever said you don't operate on a lot of people?

A.   I don't operate on as many people as others do.

Q.   You've stated before that you don't operate on a lot of people, don't you?

A.   I'm not sure what a lot of people is, sir.

Q.   Well, what did you mean when you said that you don't operate on a lot of people?

A.   There are a lot of people who come to me asking for surgery, and I choose not to operate on them because I don't think that they're going to get better because I don't think that they're going to get better because of issues in litigation, depression, or secondary gain.

Q.   Now, as a doctor, don't you have an ethical professional obligation to turn another doctor in if you think that that other doctor has committed malpractice on a patient? Don't you have such an obligation?

A.   Yes, sir.

Q.   Have you contacted the ▮▮▮▮ State Board of Medical Examiners about Dr. W.?

A.   There is a difference between disagreeing whether something is necessary and committing malpractice, sir.

Q.   Have you contacted the ▮▮▮▮ State Board of Medical Examiners on Dr. W.?

A.   I have not, sir.

Q.   Have you contracted the ▮▮▮▮ State Board of Medical Examiners on any physician who as treated T.D. in this case?

A.   I have not.

Q.   As a matter of fact, not only did you sat that you didn't think discograms are worthwhile and that Mr. W. shouldn't have done that, shouldn't have used it in any consideration for surgery, you even go farther and say epidural injections and facet injections are not useful in individuals with this type of back pain after a car wreck?

A.   For long-term relief, they're not, sir.

Q.   You yourself have ordered injections on your own patients who have been involved in car wrecks, haven't you?

A.   I have, sir.

Q.   So on one hand in your report for the trucking company, you put in here that epidural injections and facet injections are not very useful, but at the same time you go ahead and prescribe them for your own patients?

A.   When I have informed the patient that they're for short-term gain only and that the patient understands that, yes, sir.

Q.   You don't know anything about that, though, regarding the facet injections that T.D. received, do you?

A.   I don't know what, sir?

Q.   You don't anything about what the gain was to be accomplished short-term, long-term, you don't know either way, do you?

A.   I'm sorry I only know what was in the records, sir.

Q.   That's right. You have a very limited knowledge of this case, don't you?

A.   I have the knowledge of the medical records, sir.

Q.   And that's all?

A.   Correct, sir.

Q.   But that didn't it keep you from writing this report indicating that epidural injections and facet injections are not useful in the report that you did for the trucking company, did it?

A.   There are several references in the medical literature that were appended to that opinion, sir.

Q.   Medical literature, let's talk about that for just a second, because you do provide a couple of references in the report that you did?

A.   I did, sir.

Q.   As a matter of fact, I believe that you even wrote MRI is a very poor indicator of the source of lower back pain?

A.   I did.

Q.   That's what you wrote, right?

A.   Um-hum, yes, sir.

Q.   And, Dr. B., I went and looked at those articles that you cited. And that's some of them.

A.   Those are the two that I believe that I cited that said that lower MRI is a very poor indication of the source of lower back pain.

Q.   And what the article really says is that MRI alone may be a poor source without clinical correlation, examining the patient, and finding out what the patient's symptoms are to see if they connect with the findings on the MRI, as opposed to just looking at an MRI in a vacuum without any context relating to the symptoms and examination of the patient. That's what the article says, isn't it?

A.   Um-hum, It says in that last sentence, therapeutic or prophylactic interventions should not be based solely on magnetic resonance abnormalities in the absence of clinical indicators.

Q.   And clinical correlation is essential to the importance of abnormalities on MR images, right?

A.   That were not present in this case, yes, sir.

Q.   You've never seen the films?

A.   I've seen the report, sir.

Q.   But you've never seen the films, have you?

A.   I agreed to that, sir.

Q.   And you didn't put the full statement in your report, you only put part that MRI is a poor indicator. You didn't put anything about the clinical correlation that should be used with an MRI, did you?

A.   I actually quoted that sentence from a textbook that directly quoted these two articles.

Q.   I'm talking about the articles that you cited. You left out part of the critical information from some of the articles that you cited, didn't you?

A.   These articles were written one in 2001, one in 1996. And I'm telling you what they've come to mean at this point.

Q.   Wasn't my question, Doctor. You left out part of the critical information from some of the medical articles that you cited when you wrote the report from the trucking company, didn't you?

A.   In my report, I drew a conclusion and cited the reference, yes, sir.

Q.   Now, you know that a motor vehicle collision can cause a spinal injury, don't you?

A.   Yes, sir.

Q.   And just like Ms. R., for example, in the collision that she had that had even less property damage than Mr. D's car, she ended up with not only a spinal injury but a spinal surgery, didn't she?

A.   She did.

Q.   But when a defendant hires you—and I think you said that you do, what, 75, 80 percent of your work for defendants like the trucking company in this case; correct?

A.   Yes, sir.

Q.   When a defendant comes and hires you, you really want to look at the situation to see if you can avoid connecting the trauma with the injury, don't you?

A.   No, sir. What you want to do is prepare a fair evaluation of what happens. And about 50 percent of the time, you are able to make that connection. And obviously a report or testimony is not required in those cases.

Q.   What trucking company were you working for when you wrote your report on J.P.?

A.   I was not working for any trucking company, sir. I was hired by the defense attorney.

Q.   Okay. What defense attorney representing a trucking company were you working for when you wrote your report on Mr. J.P.?

A.   May I see the report, sir? Mr. J, W.J.

Q.   In ███████ ?

A.   I believe so.

Q.   That was a case where in 2005, Mr. P. was injured after 18-wheeler struck—truck struck a building and Mr. P. was caught underneath the collapse of the building that the truck ran into, correct?

A.   Yes, sir.

Q.   What was the weight of the material that fell on him?

A.   We never established that anything fell on him. He was caught in an air pocket underneath the desk, sir.

Q.   So you don't know how much weight fell on him?

A.   I don't, sir.

Q.   Initial primary complaints centered in his low back?

A.   Yes, sir.

Q.   What type of material fell on him? Were these concrete blocks, were they stucco walls, what type of material—even though you don't know how much they weighed—how much—what type of material was it that fell on him?

MR. OPPOSING COUNSEL: Judge, I'll object at this point as relevance in this case. I don't think, thank goodness, anything fell on Mr. D.

MR. ███████ : The point to establish that even with a history and knowledge of a building collapsing on an individual after a truck ran in to the building, primary complaints of low back and pain ultimately as we can probably—

THE COURT: I'll give you some leeway, limited leeway. We'll get through this.

Q.   (BY MR. █████) Just a few more questions. What type of material was it that fell on him?

A.   I don't remember. I believe that it was the metal side of the building.

Q.   You go to great lengths to criticize his operating surgeons too, don't you?

A.   Yes, I do. I just—if you're going to keep asking me, I'd like to refresh my memory. Thank you, sir.

Q.   What type of doctors were you accusing in this case of doing in appropriate things?

A.   I was not—

MR. OPPOSING COUNSEL: Your Honor, excuse me. I object. This doctor never said that Dr. W. did anything inappropriate. And if we're going to keep down this line—

THE COURT: I sustain it. Rephrase the question, Mr. █████.

Q.   {BY MR. █████} What were you accusing these doctors of doing that you were saying they should not have done?

A.   In that case—sir, first of all, I accused no one. I said that the scientific evidence states that the— one of his doctors was trying to say that the disk bulge was directly related to the accident, which as we know is not true. He also did a procedure that scientifically has been shown not to make any difference, if not a negative difference. In other words, it's hurt more people than it's helped before he then went on to do the fusion, which also did not help that person.

Q. Did you report these doctors that you felt so strongly about to the ▮▮▮▮ State Board of Medical Examiners?

A. There's a difference between best levels of care which we achieve and something well down here which is below the standard of care which is called medical malpractice. So no, sir, I did not report that.

Q. You just—

A. However, as a portion of our society, we have been working as best as we can to stop some of these things from happening.

Q. You just got through saying that the procedure utilized by these doctors were produced even negative effects to patients. And yet knowing in your own mind that these doctors were performing a surgery that produced negative effects on patients, you didn't turn them into the state authorities?

A. When you say "negative effects," sir, you mean—what I mean by that is that their medical condition did not improve and sometimes declined after it.

Q. What type of doctors were you critical of in this case?

A. Dr. X. is an orthopedic surgeon.

Q. And Dr. M.?

A.   Dr. M. is a neurosurgeon. And, of course, you didn't ever examine a patient in this case either, did you?

A.   No, sir.

Q.   And as a matter of fact, you didn't even look at any films in this case, did you?

A.   I don't know, sir.

Q.   And if none are listed on here, if no films are listed, would that mean you didn't see any films?

A.   No films were listed at the time of that report. I believe that I did see films later, sir.

Q.   Now, I want to finish up. We're short on time. But you've got cases pending all over North ▮▮▮▮ as a records reviewer, don't you?

A.   I do.

Q.   And as a matter of fact, not only did you have testimony stricken by the judge next door concerning opinions from you, but you've got at least one other case presently pending right now in the court next door, the ▮▮th District Court—

THE COURT: That's me.

MR. ▮▮▮▮:—concerning—

THE COURT: That's me.

THE WITNESS: That's you.

MR. ▮▮▮▮: I'm sorry.

Q.   (BY MR. ▮▮▮▮) It's right here. We don't even have to go next door. You've got another case pending right in this court. The D. case, does that sound familiar?

A.   With just the name, no, sir.

Q.   D. and A. D. v. J.R.?

A.   I'm sorry. I've had to see them.

Q.   You know when that case is set for trial?

A.   No, sir.

Q.   You got a case—and you were just a records reviewer in that, weren't you?

A.   May have been, yes, sir.

Q.   In a case of—okay. In some of the studies that you cited, the people that were studied, some of them had no back complaints, didn't they?

A.   That's why they were studied, sir.

Q.   That's not like Mr. D., is it?

A.   What those studies do is what they show the unreliability of a study in a normal person.

Q.   That's not like Mr. D, is it?

A.   It prevents us from drawing a conclusion about the cause and effect on Mr. D, no, sir.

Q.   You're still charging a $1,000 an hour?

A.   Actually, it's a set fee forth is afternoon, sir.

Q.   So they are getting a break, the defendants are getting a break then?

A.   Depends on how long you talk, sir.

Q.   Well, you've been over here since 12:30. It's five o'clock. So they are getting a break, aren't they?

A.   That depends on your definition. I agreed to a set fee, sir.

Q.   Haven't you stated that it's important to look at MRI films?

A.   When possible, yes, sir.

Q.   Doctor, you can't come in here and actually state that you're in an equal position to give medical opinions on T.D. compared to someone who has actually treated, examined, and actually operated on Mr. D, actually been inside his spine. You are not in an equal position to that physician, are you?

A.   In some ways, I'm in a better position because I've been able to review the whole record. I also don't have to defend my own work, sir.

Q.   You are not in an equal position to somebody like Dr. W., are you?

A.   I have not treated him, no, sir.

Q.   Is that a yes to my question?

A.   I'm sorry. I was agreeing with you. I'm sorry.

Q.   Okay. So if I gathered up medical records on everyone in this courtroom, regardless of how long anybody in this courtroom has been seeing a particular doctor, maybe a specialist, you'd be willing to come into court for a $1,000 an hour and testify to your medical opinions based only on records and feel that your opinions were just as valid as a doctor who knows the patient so well?

A.   Only if it were the truth, sir.

Q.   You'd be willing to do that?

A.   If it were the truth, yes, sir.

Q.   And it doesn't matter how much more information the treating doctor might have on anybody in this courtroom, it doesn't matter, you'd be willing and able to come in to court just based on some records and be willing to dispute, if you wanted to, whatever the treating doctor might say about a patient that they have known, examined, treated, and maybe even operated on; isn't that true?

A. Yes, sir.

Q. Thank you. I appreciate you letting me visit with you.

MR. ███████: I'll pass the witness.

THE COURT: Is there any redirect?

MR. OPPOSING COUNSEL: Three questions.

THE COURT: Okay.

MR. OPPOSING COUNSEL: You can count them.

REDIRECT EXAMINATION

BY MR. OPPOSING COUNSEL:

Q. Are you aware of any limit at this judge has put on your testimony in this case before this jury this afternoon?

A. No, sir.

Q. Question No. 2, do you feel as though Dr. W. committed malpractice?

A. No, sir.

Q. Question No. 3, after Mr. ███████ gets done grilling you, tell this jury what opinions you want to change.

A. None, sir.

MR. OPPOSING COUNSEL: Pass the witness.

THE COURT: Mr. ███████, do you have any follow-up cross?

> MR. ███████: I think he's answered all my
> questions. Thank you.
> (End of Excerpt of Proceedings)

This was a fantastic cross examination of an expert witness.

8.5 CROSS OF A LYING WITNESS

Another one of my cross examinations. This cross examination was of the alleged victim of a violent domestic battery charge. She made a statement to the police officer who arrived on scene the night of the incident. She then went to the prosecutor's office a few days later and wrote—while under oath—a complete recantation. At trial, she went back to her original statement.

The case theory was not really that the battery did not happen, as much as it was that the witness was so unbelievable and uncredible that no one knows what to believe. The cross was organized like this:

> MS. SCOTT: I don't have any other questions.
> JUDGE FITZPATRICK. Mr. Bodiford.
> MR. BODIFORD: Thank you, Judge. Your Honor, may I reposition this podium?
> JUDGE FITZPATRICK: Sure.
> MR. BODIFORD: Thank you.

BY MR. BODIFORD: CROSS EXAMINATION

Q.   Ms. Jakes, do you need to throw away any of your tissues there that you've been using, or you can—

JUDGE FITZPATRICK: I have a trash can.

BY MR. BODIFORD (CONTINUED):

Q.   —throw them away behind you. If you need to stop and use one of those, go ahead, all right?

A.   All right.

Q.   Okay. You get nose bleeds every once in a while, too, don't you?

A.   No.

Q.   You don't suffer from nose bleeds?

A.   No.

Q.   Okay. Now, let's talk about—first about the—the trailer that you were living in. You saw the photograph—

A.   Yes.

Q.   —right?

A.   Yes, sir.

Q.   That's—where that oven door is is exactly where Tate (phonetics), your stepdad, left it, isn't it?

A.   No, it was standing up more so.

Q.   It was on top of the stove?

A.   It was standing up on the stove.

Q.   What does "standing up" mean? Describe standing up for this—the members of this jury.

A.   It wasn't laying flat, it was standing up.

Q. On top of the stove.

A. It was on the stove. It was standing up like this bottle.

Q. So you're saying it was up where the burners are?

A. It was—the—this the stove, this the—the part that it was standing up on.

Q. So like it's shown in the photo is how he left it; am I right?

A. No.

Q. So—

A. This the stove, this the oven piece is standing up on the stove.

Q. Okay. So it—so when it got hit, did it fall down?

A. Yeah.

Q. So—

A. It fell down.

Q. —so if it was standing up, it went like that.

A. Yeah.

Q. Okay. So who put it back up for the picture?

A. Say it had to—somebody had to pick it up.

Q. So it wasn't you though you're saying?

A. Ung-ugh.

Q. You didn't go in and clean up the scene before somebody got there?

A. Ung-ugh, I wasn't—I wasn't cleaning up the scene.

Q.   But you told Ms. Griffith (sic) just a second ago that the door wasn't knocked off of the stove because of Mr. Rollins, right?

A.   Yeah, he didn't knock it off the stove.

Q.   Okay. Your statement was regarding this night is that we started fighting.

A.   Uh-hum.

Q.   Do you recall telling her that?

A.   Yeah.

Q.   So you admit to fighting?

A.   No, we started fighting.

Q.   Okay. So the answer is yes, I admit to fighting. You can tell us.

A.   Yes. We went to fighting.

Q.   Now, what you told the police that night is that you were punched in the face.

A.   Yeah, I was punched in the face.

Q.   Now, were you punched like that [indicating by punching into my own hand]?

A.   Just like that.

Q.   Just that hard, or harder?

A.   He punched harder.

Q.   Okay. Right in your nose?

A.   Uh-hum.

Q.   How many times, once?

A.   I think. I—I wasn't worried about it at the time, I was worried about getting away.

Q.   Was it at least once? Yes?

A.   No.

Q.   He didn't punch you in the face once?

A.   Ung-ugh.

Q.   So where did he punch you then? Tell these folks so they understand your story.

A.   I don't remember how many times he punched me in my face, but I remember he punching me in my face.

Q.   Okay. So the answer is, he punched you at least once, right? Yes?

A.   No.

JUDGE FITZPATRICK: Okay. Listen to the question. He's saying punched you at least once.

THE WITNESS: He punched me more than once.

JUDGE FITZPATRICK: Okay.

MR. BODIFORD: Fine. That's what—

JUDGE FITZPATRICK: At least one time then.

BY MR. BODIFORD (CONTINUING):

Q.   Okay. Would you say he punched you twice?

A.   Yes.

Q.   And was the second one also that hard?

A.   Yes.

Q.   Okay. Did he punch you a third time?

A.   No, sir.

Q.   Just twice.

A.   He could have been twice.

Q.   Find something funny today, Ms.—

A.   No.

Q.   —Jakes? No?

A.   No, sir. No.

Q.   Now, he—you also told the police that night he bashed your head into the floor.

A.   Yeah.

Q.   On the—on the—on the floor of the—of the mobile home, right?

A.   Yes, sir.

Q.   Like this hard [indicating by slamming my palm into the courtroom floor]?

A.   Yeah. Yeah, hard.

Q.   Or harder?

A.   He was over me. He was harder.

Q.   So what's he doing to you, he's—

A.   It was hard.

Q.   —grabbing you by your hair, just smashing your head into the—

A.   My hair was over—my hair was on the floor.

Q.   Your hair was on the floor? Was—like your weave or just straightened your hair or what?

A.   It was my hair.

Q.   It was your hair. Just little strands of your hair, right?

A.   No. It was my hair.

Q.   Strands. You—

MS. SCOTT: Asked and—

Q.   Let me ask you—ms—answered.

BY MR. BODIFORD (CONTINUED):

Q. —this. Are you—are you telling this jury that that picture that we just saw up there a minute ago, is that—there was a whole—

A. (Unintelligible)—

Q. —flock of your hair ripped out?

A. That's what the picture says.

Q. Do you know if—whether the officer—well, we already said that. Where was your hair on the floor? Where in this room was your hair?

A. By the door.

Q. Okay. So the officer would have seen this obvious bald of your hair that was ripped out.

A. The officer pointed it out to me.

Q. Uh-hum. Did you bleed where the hair was ripped out?

A. No.

Q. So back to the head bash. He's over you bashing your head in the floor. How many times, once?

A. He was standing over me bashing my head on the floor.

Q. How many times, more than once?

A. Yeah.

Q. Twice?

A. It was once, for a long time.

Q. Long time. A minute?

A. Ung-ugh.

Q. What does that mean, yes or no?

A.   No, sir.

Q.   Was it more than a minute?

A.   Yes, sir.

Q.   So for 2 minutes?

A.   About—about 3 minutes.

Q.   About 30 minutes.

A.   About 3 minutes.

Q.   Three minutes. Okay. So did he—are we saying it's bash, wait; or is he just bashing your head like this (indicating)? Is it more like the second one, is that what you're saying?

A.   He wasn't just bashing my head in the floor, he was actually punching me as he had my head on the floor.

Q.   Okay. Are you face up?

A.   No, I was face down.

Q.   Okay. So your nose, your chin, your cheeks, they're making contact with the floor as he's bashing it. Is that what you're telling these folks?

A.   That's how I got a rug burn in my face.

Q.   Oh, and the rug burn in the face, is that reflected in these photos?

A.   (Unintelligible).

Q.   Okay. Were you—

MR. BODIFORD: (Unintelligible).

MS. SCOTT: (Unintelligible) the pictures that are—

MR. BODIFORD: Judge, may I approach?

JUDGE FITZPATRICK: Yes.

BY MR. BODIFORD (CONTINUING):

Q. Showing you what's been previously entered into evidence as State's 2-A, 2-B, and 2-C. If you would, kindly show those jurors rug burn.

THE WITNESS: (Unintelligible).

JUDGE FITZPATRICK: Can you point it out in the pictures?

THE WITNESS: (Indicating).

JUDGE FITZPATRICK: Well, you need to point it out to them.

THE WITNESS: Oh.

JUDGE FITZPATRICK: Hold it up there and show it to them.

THE WITNESS: Burned both of my cheeks.

BY MR. BODIFORD (CONTINUING):

Q. That's rug burn.

A. Yeah.

Q. Okay. You never told the officer that night anything about rug burn, did you? Why are you looking at Mr. Rollins?

A. He didn't (unintelligible)—he's not—I ain't going to get nobody in trouble.

Q. I'm sorry. What did you just say?

A. Nothing, sir.

Q. No, you just said, I don't want to get nobody in trouble.

A. Yes, sir.

Q. Okay. So are you changing your statement again here in court as to what Mr. Rollins did to you?

A. When I changed my statement in the State Attorney's, I was forced to—

Q. No, no, ma'am. Listen to my question.

JUDGE FITZPATRICK: Hold on. You asked her a question, she's just finding (phonetics) the question.

THE WITNESS: Sir?

BY MR. BODIFORD (CONTINUING):

Q. Are you changing your statement here today after you've taken a fourth oath?

A. No.

Q. Okay. Now, choking you around your neck.

A. Yep.

Q. So he's behind you, what, he's got you in like a head lock like a wrestler?

A. Yeah. He tries—he choked me like he was going to put me to sleep.

Q. Okay. How long did that last, a minute?

A. I was trying to get myself out of it, I don't remember.

Q. You scratch him?

A. Yeah. Did you scratch him to try to protect yourself?

A. I don't know what I did.

Q. Did you hit back?

A. Yeah.

Q. Did you bite?

A.   Ung-ugh.

Q.   Did you kick?

A.   I was kicking trying to get loose.

Q.   And—and you told the officer that—that night that you got hit in the head with a bat, right?

A.   I told her it was something like a bat.

Q.   In the head.

A.   No, on my back.

Q.   On your back. And that's as you were leaving, as you were running out the door? Okay. Is that a yes?

A.   Yes, sir.

Q.   Okay. Did you try not to make that noise while we're—

A.   Yes, sir.

Q.   —in court. Okay. Now you ultimately go to the hospital by ambulance.

A.   Uh-hum.

Q.   Okay. You had no injuries, did you?

A.   Ung-ugh.

JUDGE FITZPATRICK: Okay. You have to use words, okay?

THE WITNESS: No, sir.

JUDGE FITZPATRICK: Thank you.

BY MR. BODIFORD (CONTINUING):

Q.   So not only was the baby okay, that you told Ms. Scott, but you were okay, correct.

A.   Yeah.

Q.   And this—this—this is what happens when you cry, isn't it, your nose bleeds, doesn't it?

A.   No.

Q.   So you run over to your neighbor's house. Curtis is gone at that point, correct, he leaves.

A.   He was still at my house while I ran to the neighbor's house.

Q.   And as soon as you left, he left, correct?

A.   Yeah.

Q.   Okay. He was no longer a threat to you at that point, right?

A.   Curtis wasn't trying to hurt me that—he was aggravated with me, and he wanted sex. He was on—he was on some—he was—he was—he was, I don't know, on alcohol. He was hurting me, he wasn't trying to hurt me, he was just aggressive. Curt got a bad temper.

Q.   Did—wait. Did you say he was on alcohol?

A.   He was on something, alcohol, drugs, I don't know.

Q.   Did you tell the officer that night that—

A.   Uh-hum.

Q.   —you thought he was on drugs?

A.   Yes, sir.

Q.   Did you smell alcohol on his breath that night?

A.   No, sir.

Q.   So you know he wasn't drinking alcohol.

A.   Well, he was doing something, sir.

Q. Okay. But the question is—back to my question. The question is: Once you left, he left. He left your—he left—

A. He left because he know I was going to call the police.

Q. You told him, I'm going to go call the police, right?

A. Yes, sir.

Q. And you were mad.

A. Yes, sir.

Q. And you knew that if you called, because he's on probation, you could get him locked up. Right?

A. When me and Curt was in the house, I did told him to leave from (unintelligible). He told me he wasn't going nowhere.

Q. The answer is: You knew though that you held the key to the jail cell; isn't that right?

MS. SCOTT: I'd object to that question.

JUDGE FITZPATRICK: I'll allow it, go ahead.

THE WITNESS: Yes, sir.

BY MR. BODIFORD (CONTINUING):

Q. All right. So all you had to do was make the call, Curtis is in jail.

A. I wasn't trying to put Curtis in jail, I was trying to make sure I myself was okay.

Q. So again, back to where we go is that once you left, Curt, what, did he leave to go cool off?

A. No. He left to call his mom.

Q.   Okay. But he was no longer a threat to you once you went to the neighbor's house, right?

A.   No.

Q.   He didn't follow you.

A.   No.

Q.   He didn't chase after you.

A.   Ung-ugh. He—

Q.   He didn't yell at you?

A.   He snatched me back in the house.

Q.   Well, that was before you went.

A.   He didn't want me to go out of there.

Q.   Okay. And that's when the big clump of hair came out, right?

A.   No.

Q.   Hmm. All right. So back to the neighbor's house. Once you're there, he doesn't bother you any more, right?

A.   Ung-ugh.

Q.   Okay. Now, let's—let's turn our attention to after he gets arrested. You told Ms. Scott, you still cared about him for a period of time, correct.

A.   Yes, sir.

Q.   And you had lots of calls with him, right?

A.   Yes, sir.

Q.   And—and you've listened to them?

A.   Uh-hum. Yes, sir.

Q.   Okay. And nowhere on—well, first of all, he asks you to admit to your lies, doesn't he?

A.   Did Curt ask me to admit to my lies?

Q. Yeah. He said, I want you to go down there and tell them you lied. That's what he said on there.

A. No, sir.

Q. You didn't hear that on there?

A. No, sir.

Q. And you—but you listened to that.

A. Yes, sir.

Q. Uh-hum. So Curt never said, go lie to them.

A. Well, he told me to lie for him.

Q. Oh, he did.

A. But he didn't tell me to admit the lie.

Q. You never once on any of those tapes, or ever in any of your calls told Curtis, I'm not lying, did you?

A. I told him I wasn't lying for him.

Q. You never once said to him, Curt—Curtis, you need help; you need counseling. You never told him anything like that, did you?

A. No.

Q. You never confronted him in any of these jail calls with why would you do something like that to me, did you?

A. No, sir.

Q. You never exercised the option to just simply not accept his calls when he called you collect. You took his calls, didn't you?

A. Yes, sir.

Q. And during those calls, you never—when he would tell you, I want you to go down there, tell those people you lied; you never said, I don't know what you're talking about, and hung up on him, did you?

A.   No, sir.

Q.   You did what he asked, didn't you?

A.   Yes, sir.

Q.   Because it was the right thing to do, wasn't it?

A.   Yes, sir.

Q.   Now, in addition to talking to him on the phone, you also visited Curt at the jail, didn't you?

A.   Yes, sir.

Q.   Now, but you did it in a special way, right?

A.   Yes, sir.

Q.   Now, so the jury knows, when you're going to go visit somebody, you've got to put their name down and you have to tell them your name, right?

A.   Yes, sir.

Q.   First you say, my name is Janie Jakes (phonetics), right?

A.   Yes, sir.

Q.   And the jail says, who would you like to see, right?

A.   Yes, sir.

Q.   And then you say the inmate's name, right?

A.   Yes, sir.

Q.   But in this situation, when you would go to see him, you didn't use the name Curtis Rollins, did you?

A.   No, sir.

Q.   Because you knew the State Attorney's Office would be looking at that list to see whether you were visiting, right, didn't you?

A.   No, sir.

Q.   So you would use the names like Derrick Baker (phonetics); does that ring a bell?

A.   Never even been—

Q.   Who is Derrick Baker (phonetics)?

A.   The same person that was in a park with Curtis.

Q.   The guy in the park with Curtis. So when you told the jail you wanted to see Curtis—Derrick Baker (phonetics), that was a lie, wasn't it?

A.   Yes, sir.

Q.   You, in fact, went and saw Curtis instead, correct?

A.   Yes, sir.

Q.   And in addition to Derrick Baker (phonetics), you also gave the name Tony Dixon (phonetics), right?

A.   Yes, sir.

Q.   And when you told the jail that you're going to see Tony Dixon (phonetics), that was a lie; was it not?

A.   Yes, sir.

Q.   You also used the name Michael Scott, another person in the pod with Mr. Rollins, didn't you?

A.   Yes, sir.

Q.   And you told the jail that you were going to see Michael Scott, that was a lie.

A.   Yes, sir.

Q.   You also wrote letters to him, didn't you?

A.   Yes, sir.

Q.   And you would sign those letters with the name Money Rollins, right?

A.   That's when he wrote me, Money Rollins.

Q.   But you—you still have the name Money, don't you?

A.   Yes, sir.

Q.   That's your—that's the name you gave yourself, isn't it?

A.   That's my nickname.

Q.   Are you rich?

A.   (Unintelligible).

Q.   Oh.

A.   That—

Q.   And certainly your last name is not Rollins, is it?

A.   No, sir.

Q.   So if you gave the name Money Rollins, that would be a lie, wouldn't it?

A.   I really (unintelligible). The letters said Money Rollins.

Q.   Turn your attention to Trina's house. Trina Price is Curtis's mother, right?

A.   Yes, sir.

Q.   Now September the 14th, prior to the incident we're here for today, y'all were living at her house, weren't you?

A.   Yes, sir.

Q.   That wasn't—that—that situation wasn't about a bag, it was about sex, wasn't it?

A.   No, sir.

Q.   You wanted to have sex with Curtis, and you're trying to grab Curtis to get up from watching TV and he wouldn't do it, right?

A.   No, sir.

Q.   It's okay, you can tell them.

A.   No, sir.

Q.   In fact, at one point in time, you went over and—and grabbed him by his private parts and tried to pull him up off the couch, right?

A.   No, sir.

Q.   And he—and he slapped you away, and you got mad, didn't you?

A.   No, sir.

Q.   And you chased him into a room. You did kick a door open to get to him, didn't you?

A.   That's after fighting, I try to get my son.

Q.   After the fight and you tried to get your son?

A.   My son was in the room with Curtis.

Q.   Hmm. And you kicked the door open, and you stabbed him with the scissors, didn't you?

A.   We went back to fighting.

Q.   Uh-hum. And you were mad that night, too, weren't you?

A.   Yes, sir.

Q. But that night Curtis Rollins when the police hit him said he didn't want to press charges on you, right?

A. Yes, sir.

Q. But they didn't (unintelligible) you, did they?

A. No, sir.

Q. Now, as you sit here today, Ms. Jakes, you are on probation with this court, aren't you?

A. Yes.

Q. And the charge that you pled to, you know that charge, don't you?

A. Agg (unintelligible) with a deadly weapon.

Q. Aggravated battery—

A. —with a deadly—

Q. —with a—

A. —weapon.

Q. —deadly weapon; is that right?

A. Yes, sir.

Q. And you went to court November the 21st of last year, and you took an oath, didn't you, in front of the judge?

A. Yes, sir.

Q. You swore to tell the truth, didn't you?

A. Yes, sir.

Q. And you entered a plea to that charge.

A. Yes, sir.

Q. Now, the deal that you got, you didn't go to— spend any time in jail, did you? Other than when you got arrested, you didn't spend any time in jail, did you?

A.   No, sir.

Q.   Nope. You got probation.

A.   Yes, sir.

Q.   Probation means that you're on supervision by an officer that works for the County, correct?

A.   Yes, sir.

Q.   And everything that you do, they watch, right?

A.   Yes, sir.

Q.   Okay. You have to report in to them, don't you?

A.   Yes, sir.

Q.   Okay. And that's going to go on for three years.

A.   Yes, sir.

Q.   Now, they also assigned you to do 480 hours of community service, right?

A.   Yes, sir.

Q.   And you haven't done any of those hours yet, have you?

A.   Yes, sir.

Q.   The—the bigger issue is they asked you is (sic) to do an anger management class, right?

A.   Yes, sir.

Q.   And did you do your anger management class yet?

A.   No. I'm doing my community (unintelligible).

Q.   I'm sorry, say again?

A.   I've been doing my community (unintelligible) hours.

Q. So you're doing community service hours, as opposed to doing anger management.

A. Yes.

Q. And those things were assigned to you because of the things that you did to get yourself on probation, right?

A. Yes, sir.

Q. Your temper?

A. I was protecting my kids.

Q. You're protecting your kids when you confronted a lady about stealing—

MS. SCOTT: I'd object to—

BY MR. BODIFORD (CONTINUING):

Q. —your DVD player?

MS. SCOTT:—him (unintelligible), Judge.

THE WITNESS: She stole it—

JUDGE FITZPATRICK: Hold on.

THE WITNESS:—(unintelligible) my house.

JUDGE FITZPATRICK: Hold on. Hold on. I'm going to allow it because she made a statement about the—what the nature of the crime was. So go ahead.

BY MR. BODIFORD (CONTINUING):

Q. Well, let's talk about that. You're—you were protecting your kids when this happened. You actually thought a lady had taken a DVD player from you, didn't you?

A. No, sir.

Q. And you—and you went up to that lady, Narobi Warren (phonetics). You know Narobi Warren (phonetics), right?

A. Yes, sir.

Q. She lived in the Cathedral Drive trailer park with you, uh-hum? Right?

A. Yes, sir.

Q. You went out and you confronted her about that DVD player.

A. No.

Q. And when she didn't tell you what you wanted to hear, you began hitting her in the head with a brick, didn't you?

A. No, sir.

Q. Right in front of, not only Narobi (phonetics), who's getting hit, you know Yolanda Kilpatrick (phonetics)?

A. No, sir.

Q. Well, the officer came, you told the officer, yeah, she pointed her finger at me, and we went to fighting. That's true, isn't it?

A. No, sir.

Q. None of that's true? So—so let me make sure—none of that's true that when you went to court and raised your hand and you took the oath and pled guilty, was that a lie, too?

A. No. I told her what happened.

Q. This lady actually was beat in the head so bad that the ambulance had to come get her, wasn't it?

A. Yes, sir.

Q.   So you did beat her in the head?

A.   Yes, sir.

Q.   Now that you're on probation, there's a special condition of your probation. You're familiar with the conditions of your probation, aren't you? Your probation officer's been over them with you, correct?

A.   Yes, sir.

Q.   Uh-hum. And are you familiar—it's not a special condition, it's a standard condition. Are you familiar with standard condition Number 5?

A.   No.

Q.   No? Are you familiar with: You will live without violating any law? Are you familiar with that?

A.   Uh-hum.

Q.   Probation officer told you, you can't commit any law violations, can you?

A.   No, sir.

Q.   And also it goes on to say, you've read this: A conviction in a court of law is not necessary for such a violation of law to constitute a violation of your probation. Means you don't actually have to get charged with another crime for you to commit a law violation, does it; isn't that right?

A.   No, sir.

Q.   Uh-hum. And—and lying under oath, you understand that to be perjury, don't you? You know what perjury is?

A.   Yes, sir.

Q. Okay. And if you commit perjury, then you could violate your probation, right?

A. Yes, sir.

Q. If you violate your probation, they take you back to jail, right?

A. Yes, sir.

Q. And then you're looking at going to prison for 15 years, all right?

A. No, sir.

Q. No?

A. Twenty years.

Q. Hmm. Doesn't a charge of aggravated battery with a deadly weapon carry a maximum sentence of up to 15 years?

A. Yes, sir.

Q. Right. And you were told when you pled that any violation, you could be sentenced to the maximum, right?

A. Yes, sir.

Q. So the maximum was 15 years, right?

A. Yes, sir.

Q. So if you violate your probation, you could get 15 years?

A. Yes, sir.

Q. All right. So if you got arrested on this, you don't like being in jail, do you?

A. No.

Q. You have to be away from your family, right?

A. Yes, sir.

Q.   You'd have to be away from your children, right?

A.   Yes, sir.

Q.   People tell you what to do.

A.   Yes, sir.

Q.   They tell you what to wear.

A.   Yes, sir.

Q.   They tell you what to eat.

A.   Yes, sir.

Q.   They tell you when to eat it.

A.   Yes, sir.

Q.   They tell you when you're going to go to sleep.

A.   Yes, sir.

Q.   And they don't even give you a light switch, they turn the lights out for you, don't they?

A.   Yes, sir.

Q.   And you don't like that, do you?

A.   No, sir.

Q.   Don't like being told what to do, do you?

A.   Ung-ugh. No, sir.

Q.   And certainly you don't want to violate your probation and risk being locked up again, do you?

A.   No, sir.

Q.   And you're willing to do what it takes to avoid that, aren't you?

A.   Yes, sir.

Q.   Now, when you were out there on January the 20th, you made a written statement; do you recall that?

JUDGE FITZPATRICK: Can you answer the question?

THE WITNESS: Oh, I'm sorry.

BY MR. BODIFORD (CONTINUING):

Q. Were you looking at something important?

A. No. I didn't think you were talking to me.

Q. Back on January the 20th, you made a written statement, right?

A. Yes, sir.

Q. And we're talking January 20th of actually 2014. Three years ago.

A. Yes, sir.

Q. So have you had a chance to review the written statement before you got on the stand today?

A. No—no, sir.

MR. BODIFORD: Judge, may I approach?

JUDGE FITZPATRICK: I think it was 2015, you said 2014.

MR. BODIFORD: Judge, for the record, at the bottom, the officer, because it was January, was still writing '14.

JUDGE FITZPATRICK: Okay.

MR. BODIFORD: So that's what I was looking at. So—

JUDGE FITZPATRICK: All right.

MR. BODIFORD: May I approach, Your Honor?

JUDGE FITZPATRICK: Show it to Ms. Scott first. Go ahead.

(Defendant's Exhibit 2 marked for identification.)

BY MR. BODIFORD (CONTINUING):

Q.   Ma'am, I'm going to show you what's been premarked as Defendant's Exhibit 2 for identification purposes. Going to ask you to take a look at it, read it to yourself, take your time, and let me know—

A.   Yes, I read this.

Q.   You read it prior to today?

A.   Yes, sir.

Q.   Okay. And that's your signature at the bottom there?

A.   Yes, sir.

Q.   Do you recognize the handwriting?

A.   Uh-hum. Yes, sir.

Q.   Is it the same—same document that you wrote out the night that this incident allegedly occurred?

A.   Yes, sir.

Q.   Okay. Does this appear to be a true and correct copy—

A.   Yes, sir.

Q.   —of your actual—

A.   That's true.

Q.   —written statement?

A.   Yes, sir.

Q.   No, I'm saying, a copy. Is the copy an exact copy of what you wrote?

A.   Yes, sir.

MR. BODIFORD: Judge, I'd move in defense Exhibit Number 2.

MS. SCOTT: Under what basis? I'd object to hearsay.

JUDGE FITZPATRICK: He just asked her questions about it, which he said the police officer, he cross examined her. I don't think the document itself can come in.

BY MR. BODIFORD (CONTINUING):

Q. When you were provided this piece of paper, the officer just handed you the paper, didn't he?

Now, he wrote in some things like your name and the address. He wrote those for you, right?

A. Yes, sir.

Q. Okay. And he told you to read it, didn't he, this whole part up here? He told you to read that, didn't he?

A. Yes, sir.

Q. Did you read it?

A. Yes, sir.

Q. Do you—did you understand it?

A. Uh-hum. Yes, sir.

Q. Okay. And it says: I do solemnly swear or affirm that the information given by me in this case is the truth, the whole truth, and nothing but the truth. Do you recall reading that?

A. Yes, sir.

Q. And did you understand it that night?

A. Yes, sir.

Q. It also says: I understand that making a material false statement under oath is a crime, a misdemeanor of the first degree, and punishable as provided under Florida Statute 837.012. Do you remember that?

A.   Yes, sir.

Q.   And you read it that night, you understood it, didn't you?

A.   Yes, sir.

Q.   And then it says: I am willing to make this statement, I understand, I know what I'm doing; no promises or threats have been made to me; and no pressure or coercion of any kind has been used against me. Raise your hand—

A.   Yes, sir.

Q.   —do you swear to tell the truth—

A.   Yes.

Q.   —and your answer was yes, right?

A.   Yes, sir.

Q.   And that's when you wrote this. And I turn your attention to when you went to the State Attorney's Office on January—on February the 9th, you gave another statement, didn't you?

A.   Yes, sir.

Q.   Okay. And have you had a chance to look at it before you took the stand today?

A.   Yes, sir.

Q.   All right. And in that one—now, you're—what you told the jury is Trina picked you up from your mom's house, right?

A.   Trina picked me up from my mom's house.

Q.   You got in the car—

A. Rode off.

Q. —voluntarily with Trina, right?

A. Yeah.

Q. What did you say, both of them?

A. I said rode off with her.

Q. Rode off with her. Right. I mean, she didn't have to drag you kicking and screaming in the car, did she?

A. No, sir.

Q. Okay. You were willing to come down here and make this statement.

A. Yes, sir.

Q. And she was just the mode of transportation that was provided, correct?

A. Yes, sir.

Q. Your mother certainly wasn't going to bring you down here to do it, was she?

A. I kept a secret from my mom.

Q. Your mom doesn't like her.

A. I don't like her, not now.

Q. You didn't have any other way to get here, and Trina volunteered to take you, right?

A. Trina called my phone and told me she gonna take me.

Q. Hmm. And did you tell her, no, you're not?

A. No. Because I was still in love with her.

Q. So you got in the car, and you came down to the State Attorney's Office, this building we're in here, correct?

A.   Yes, sir.

Q.   And you went to the Fourth Floor?

A.   Yes, sir.

Q.   And you told them why you were there, didn't you?

A.   Yes, sir.

Q.   And you met with some people from the State Attorney's Office, right, your attorney or a victim's witness person, or somebody like that, didn't you?

A.   Yes, sir.

Q.   Okay. Now, Trina wasn't in there for that, she stayed out in the lobby.

A.   Yes, sir.

Q.   So when you were back there, you didn't tell these people, look, Curtis's mom just made me come down here—

A.   No, sir.

Q.   —she thinks I'm dropping charges—

A.   No, sir.

Q.   —but I really don't want to. You didn't do that, did you?

A.   No, sir.

Q.   They—they talked to you about the case, didn't they? They said, what happened, and you told them, I lied. Didn't you?

A.   Told them I lied.

Q.   Uh-hum. And they gave you a piece of paper and asked you to write out a sworn statement, and you said you would, right?

A.   Yes, sir.

Q.   And the statement that you made that day—

MR. BODIFORD: Actually, Judge, may I approach the witness?

JUDGE FITZPATRICK: Sure.

(Defendant's Exhibit 1 marked for identification.)

BY MR. BODIFORD (CONTINUING):

Q.   Let me show you what's been marked as defense Exhibit Number 1 for identification. Do you recognize that?

A.   Yes, sir.

Q.   And what is it?

A.   A lie.

Q.   Is that the statement that you made up at the State Attorney's Office?

A.   Yes, sir.

Q.   Okay. Is your signature at the bottom?

A.   Yes, sir.

Q.   Do you recognize the handwriting?

A.   Yes, sir.

Q.   Okay. And does this—does this appear to be a true and correct copy of the actual original that you filled out yourself?

A.   Yes, sir.

MR. BODIFORD: Judge, let me move defense Exhibit Number 1 into evidence.

JUDGE FITZPATRICK: Any objection?

MS. SCOTT: (Unintelligible) objection to hearsay.

JUDGE FITZPATRICK: It is still hearsay, but you can ask her questions about it.

BY MR. BODIFORD (CONTINUING):

Q.   The statement that you signed, right above your name, it says: Under penalties of perjury, I declare I have read the foregoing document, and that the facts stated in it are true.

A.   I was—

Q.   Did you—did you see that before you signed

A.   No, sir.

Q.   Oh, you just didn't read that part?

A.   I just went to writing.

Q.   Okay. And so the lady, Ms. Helene Potluck (phonetics), who came in as the notary public, who said that she—that the document was sworn to and subscribed to her, she made you raise your hand, didn't she.

A.   Yes, sir.

Q.   And she said: Do you swear to tell the truth?

A.   Yes, sir.

Q.   And you understood that, didn't you? And your testimony is that you lied anyway?

A.   Trying to help her.

Q.   So an oath to tell the truth means absolutely nothing to you, does it, Ms. Jakes.

A.   It means a lot to me.

Q.   You just say whatever it is that's convenient for Janie (phonetics); isn't that true?

A.   No, sir.

Q.   So when you went to the—the chief prosecutor of this Circuit, went to their office, and you said, I want to drop charges on Curtis Rollins because I told the police a lie about Curtis hitting me, that wasn't true?

A.   No, sir.

Q.   And when you said, I called the police—the reason I called the police is to get his VOP in. Are you saying that you went to the State Attorney's Office and bold-faced lied to them, right in their face?

A.   Yes, sir.

Q.   And when you made the statement: Yes, he hold me so I would not hit him, but he never hit me back—

A.   That was a lie.

Q.   —that's something—you just looked at these people's face and lied to them.

A.   Yes, sir. Well, I got the CD that—him telling me on the phone about his saying that we talked about.

Q.   You've got the CDs?

A.   No, I don't have the CDs. I listened to the CDs, the same thing—

Q.   The ones that Ms. Scott—right. Uh-hum.

A.   Yes, sir.

Q.   And—but, no, he's telling you, you need to go down there and tell those people you lied.

A.   Yes, sir.

Q. Right. And you did just that, didn't you? Because an oath means nothing to you, does it, Ms. Jakes.

A. Because I was trying to help Curt.

Q. Now, you talked about pressure, and you said that his family was pressuring you—

A. Yes, sir.

Q. —to make this second statement. That was—is that what you told this jury?

A. Yes, sir.

Q. Okay. But the pressure wasn't coming from him, coming from his family.

A. Yes, sir.

Q. All he asked you to do was say, go tell those people that you lied for me. That's all he ever said, isn't it?

A. Uh-hum.

Q. That's all he ever demanded of you.

A. Yes, sir.

Q. Uh-hum. And you know that perjury is a crime, right?

A. Yes, sir.

Q. And you know that making a false report to a law enforcement officer is a crime, don't you?

A. Yes, sir.

Q. So you're backed into a corner in front of this jury, aren't you?

A. Yes, sir.

Q.   Uh-hum. You created the pressure here, didn't you?

A.   No, sir.

Q.   The pressure is being felt today because if you don't do the right thing, you could violate your probation.

A.   Yes, sir.

Q.   So you've got a—you've got to try to make everybody happy so that Janie (phonetics) doesn't get in trouble, right?

A.   Yes, sir.

MR. BODIFORD: May I have a moment, Your Honor?

JUDGE FITZPATRICK: Sure.

MR. BODIFORD: Thank you, Judge, nothing further.

(Whereupon, the excerpt of the Video Recorded Jury Trial in the above-referenced proceeding was concluded.)

8.6 TAKEAWAYS

- The heat of a cross examination brings many unexpected things. Stay cool and go to your fundamentals.

- Always stay in control.

- Everyone has a different style, but the fundamentals are all about the same. *Lead* and *limit*.

8.7 EXERCISES

Exercise 1:

The best exercise for learning any advocacy skill is to *go watch a real trial*. No matter your level of experience, you can always benefit from watching a trial.

So, go watch a trial!

Note what the advocates say, how the move about, and what questioning they undertake. See if you can figure out the back story—if you get a chance, discuss the case with the bailiff, or even one of the attorneys. Do not approach the jurors!

Exercise 2:

Taking a lead from your humble author, watch or read a transcript of you conducting a cross examination. Some jurisdictions have the ability to video the proceedings, and all you have to do is order a copy from the electronic reporter in the same manner as you would a paper transcript from a traditional court reporter.

Look at your cross, and start with red-lining all the non-leading questions. Then look at questions containing more than one fact. Look for "and" or "um" words that you used and did not even realize it. Check to see if you are saying "okay" or "thank you" every time the witness responds. Look at objections, and how you responded. Were you prepared, and was is succinct? If you were caught off guard, why? What did you miss?

Ask someone else to look at or read your cross. Ask that person if he or she can tell you what your client's story was, or if your cross totally confuses him or her. Be sure to ask your critique to be honest, and promise him or her that you will not take it personally (and don't!).

If you have the time, start from scratch and redesign the cross. What would you have done differently?

Exercise 3:

Using one of the examples above, create "reverse engineer" the cross and create Cross Sheets. Can you figure out the themes, topics, and target facts? What would you have done differently?

" I HAVE NO FURTHER QUESTIONS OF THIS WITNESS."

CHAPTER 9

CROSS EXAMINATION TOOL BOX

9.1 CASE LAW FOR ALL OCCASIONS

Having case law ready is being able to either (1) change a judge's mind and getting a favorable ruling, or (2) making a record for appeal.

This idea is not original, as good trial preparation includes anticipating legal issues and having precedent ready. My favorite version of the case law file was a friend who drug an old banker's box from trial to trial, containing cases he gathered over the years and in different trials. It was a rag-tag looking set up, but he had case law for all occasions.

Each part of the trial has potentially troubling legal issues. Cross has its own specific set of problems: the judge limiting the cross, preserving the record by properly arguing objections, mistrials, and opposing counsel continually objecting to try to stop your magnificent cross examination presentation.

A.   JUDGE LIMITING CROSS

Cross examination is a fundamental, Constitutional right. The Confrontation Clause of the United States Constitution is the source of that right. That is coupled with the century of case law that stresses the critical importance of cross examination to the truth-finding process. Thus, judges can only limit cross examination in few circumstances.

Federal Rule of Evidence 611 gives the judge fairly broad power to control the courtroom:

Rule 611. Mode and Order of Examining Witnesses and Presenting Evidence

(a) Control by the Court; Purposes. The court should exercise reasonable control over the mode and order of examining witnesses and presenting evidence so as to:

(1) make those procedures effective for determining the truth;

(2) avoid wasting time; and

(3) protect witnesses from harassment or undue embarrassment.

(b) Scope of Cross-Examination. Cross-examination should not go beyond the subject matter of the direct examination and matters affecting the witness's credibility. The court may allow inquiry into additional matters as if on direct examination.

An excellent discussion of limitations on cross examination is found in *Douglas v. Owens*, 50 F.3d 1226 (1995):

We review a district court's ruling concerning the allowable scope of cross-examination for abuse of discretion. *United States v. Werme*, 939 F.2d 108, 117 (3d Cir.1991) (citing *United States v. Reed*, 724 F.2d 677, 679 (8th Cir.1984)), cert. denied, 502 U.S. 1092, 112 S.Ct. 1165, 117 L.Ed.2d 412 (1992).

We begin our analysis by noting that a party is guaranteed "only 'an opportunity for effective cross-examination, not cross-examination that is effective in whatever way, and to whatever extent, the defense might wish.'" *Kentucky v. Stincer*, 482 U.S. 730, 739, 107 S.Ct. 2658, 2664, 96 L.Ed.2d 631 (1987) (quoting *Delaware v. Fensterer*, 474 U.S. 15, 20, 106 S.Ct. 292, 294, 88 L.Ed.2d 15 (1985)) (emphasis in original). We also recognize that the district court is required to strike a balance between the opportunity to cross-examine and the need to prevent repetitive or abusive cross-examination. *United States v. Casoni*, 950 F.2d 893, 919 (3d Cir.1991). Thus, the district court may properly exercise its discretion in this area by imposing reasonable limits on the scope of cross-examination, weighing such factors as undue prejudice, relevancy, and delay due to repetition. As stated recently by the Court of Appeals for the Eleventh Circuit, "[t]rial judges retain wide latitude to impose reasonable limits on cross-examination based on concerns about, among other things, confusion of the issues or interrogation that is repetitive or only marginally relevant." *United States v. Baptista-Rodriguez*, 17 F.3d 1354, 1370–71 (11th Cir.1994).

To properly evaluate a witness, a jury must have sufficient information to make a discriminating appraisal of a witness's motives and bias. See *United States v. Abel*, 469 U.S. 45, 52, 105 S.Ct. 465, 469, 83 L.Ed.2d 450 (1984). It is an abuse of discretion for a district judge to cut off cross-examination if the opportunity to present this information is not afforded. *See Harbor Ins. Co. v. Schnabel Foundation Co.*, 946 F.2d 930, 935 (D.C.Cir.1991) (district court abused its discretion in cutting off cross-examination because it was not collateral, irrelevant, or prejudicial and had a direct bearing on the weight to be given the witness' testimony by the jury), cert. denied, 504 U.S. 931, 112 S.Ct. 1996, 118 L.Ed.2d 592 (1992).

It is my opinion, and I would think the opinion of most judges, that if you are not being repetitive, continually plowing relevant new ground, and not being argumentative, you can proceed through your cross examination without limitation. If you use the Five Fundamentals and stick to telling a story, and not just digging or badgering, you should be fine.

However, you may find that you have a judge that wants to exert too much control over the flow of evidence, for whatever reason. You may unfortunately run into judges that want to exert control simply to speed up the trial. Some may want to dominate you just to show "who's the boss", as sad as that may be. Having the law at your fingertips can even the playing field with those judges, right the ship and let you finish your cross, or set the issues up for reversal on appeal. The following issues are where you might find a judge being too aggressive and unduly limiting your cross examination.

- Foundations
- Offer of proof

- Outside the presence of the jury

- Time limits

- Subject matter issues

- Impeachment issues

Be sure to argue the relevance of your questions, and how prejudicial and unfair it would be for you not to be able to explore areas of questioning with the witness. If necessary, make a proffer of the questions (and anticipated answers) as soon as you are outside the presence of the jury.

B.   ARGUING COMMON OBJECTIONS

Space does not permit a case law compilation for all the objections and evidentiary issues discussed in Chapter 5. Of course, pretrial motions are the best way to resolve those issues before trial starts. Otherwise, I highly recommend going to court with a courtroom evidentiary manual—there are many, and you probably have a favorite from law school. The *Summary Trial Guide* available from eLEX Publishers (www.eLEXPublishers.com) is an excellent tool to have handy; it contains the rules of evidence as well as an evidentiary objection guide.

Of course, you can reconstruct your own version of the Objection Guide in Chapter 5.

"Advocacy muscle memory" should be exercised and practiced, so common objections are on the tip of your tongue at all times. For example:

RELEVANCE:

Your Honor, this testimony is irrelevant as it does not make any material fact more or less probable.

OR

Your Honor, the probative value of this testimony is outweighed by its prejudicial effect.

HEARSAY:

Your Honor, the testimony is an out of court statement that is being offered for the truth of the matter asserted.

IMPROPER IMPEACHMENT:

Your Honor, this is an improper impeachment—the methods for impeaching a witness are specific, and not following those methods is prejudicial to this witness and my client.

If you cannot memorize the basics, write them down and have them handy at trial, or have your objections sheet on the table in front of you.

C.   MISTRIAL STANDARDS

No one wants a mistrial, except perhaps for the obviously guilty criminal defendant. But advocates who have worked incredibly hard to bring a case to trial want it to conclude. There is only so much financial, physical, and emotional capital litigants have, and trying cases more than one time can quickly drain those important resources.

There are times, however, when there is no alternative other than to ask the court to declare a mistrial. In the context of a cross examination, this could be when a rogue witness decides to blurt out overwhelmingly prejudicial information about the defendant that was ordered excluded from the trial. It can also be in a situation where the opposing side fails to disclose information that prohibits an effective cross examination.

The standard for a mistrial is "manifest necessity." *Arizona v. Washington*, 434 U.S. 497, 98 S.Ct. 824, 54 L.Ed.2d 717 (1978); *Renico v. Lett*, 559 U.S. 766, 130 S.Ct. 1855, 176 L.Ed.2d 678 (2010). Of course, asking for and getting a mistrial in a criminal case brings up the issue of whether the case is barred from further prosecution by double jeopardy. While that is a discussion worthy of its own law review article, suffice it to know that something really bad has to happen in order to constitute "manifest necessity" for a mistrial. The denial of a mistrial will be reviewed for abuse of discretion. *Id.*

D.   OTHER COMMON ISSUES

Have all target documents with you at the podium.

Be sure to have all your exhibits, demonstratives, pens, etc. ready.

To the extent possible, show what you have to opposing counsel before the trial, or at least before the cross examination, begins. You do not want to have to stop and argue why you should not be allowed to use something or the other. My philosophy is to tell my opponent how I am going to beat them, then beat them how I told them I would.

1. Sequestering Witnesses

A very important thing to remember is that you do not want witnesses to prepare for your cross examination. There is a way to prevent that: *the sequestration of witnesses.*

Rule 615. Excluding Witnesses

At a party's request, the court must order witnesses excluded so that they cannot hear other witnesses' testimony. Or the court may do so on its own. But this rule does not authorize excluding:

(a) a party who is a natural person;

(b) an officer or employee of a party that is not a natural person, after being designated as the party's representative by its attorney;

(c) a person whose presence a party shows to be essential to presenting the party's claim or defense; or

(d) a person authorized by statute to be present.

By asking that the court "invoke the rule", you can keep almost all witnesses out of the courtroom.

2. Surprise Witnesses

Fundamental fairness dictates that all sides have a fair chance at the trial. Most courts will have strict pretrial discovery rules. Be sure to have the rules and any pretrial orders ready when arguing violations and prejudice.

9.2 SUSTENANCE

It is not the pinnacle of legal scholarship, but it bears mentioning. When you are in trial, you are on an island in a world isolated from everything else. You have to be able to exist and survive. Much like the shows on TV where the host is dropped in a remote location and has to survive, you have to be able to survive in trial.

You have to maintain your strength during a trial. Your trial toolbox should have good food, bottled water, any medicine you need during the day, and perhaps some loose change for a vending machine if the situation gets dire.

There are other disasters that can happen in trial. New shoes can lead to blisters. A broken pen can stain fingers (I once got stains on my fingers from a leaky marker, and inadvertently rubbed ink all over my face without realizing it; I later found out the judge and bailiff found it quite entertaining). Beyond food, consider having the following in your trial toolbox:

- a sewing kit and/or some extra safety pins
- a glasses repair kit and lens cleaner
- plastic bandages
- some sort of headache relief
- a detergent/stain remover pen

- handiwipes
- extra charging cables, connectors, and miscellaneous technology

Being prepared for anything is comforting. If something happens, you deal with it. Juries respect your preparation for the unknown, and professionalism in mottling through. Once you have their respect, they will listen to your story.

9.3 CROSS TOOLS

With regard to your target documents, today's courtroom offers many options for the presentation of your cross examination. Anyone who has attempted any project around the house knows that having the right tool for the job is critical.

For cross examination, the physical, in-court tools available can really make the job not only easier, but more effective.

Highlighting certain words and phrases, having a witness mark on or highlight a point of impeachment on a blowup of a document or photo, or making a witness use a laser pointer to point out a target fact can work wonders.

In this chapter, we will discuss and explore some choices of tools for the cross examiner, including that which available electronically and going "old school" with paper and dry erase.

A.   PRESENTATION BY VIDEO

First and foremost, you will be limited by whatever technology is available in the courtroom, and your imagination.

If the courtroom has overhead presentation technology, great. You can use just about anything you can plug in to the system. My firm uses Apple TV—we plug that in the overhead, grab the Wi-Fi (if the courtroom does not have one, we bring our own "hotspot"), and run a laptop, tablet, or smartphone to present . . . *anything*. It is a small setup, very portable, and has other uses in the firm. And the costs is *de minimus*, as the Apple TV is very affordable, and most folks already have a tablet or smart phone.

Other alternatives are limited only by the system you are hooking into—so have plenty of cable choices. Also try to know what system the courtroom has available, so you can know what presentation software to use. Some popular ones are:

- ChromeCast

- Evernote

- PowerPoint

- KeyNote

- TrialDirector

B.   EASEL AND DRY ERASE

The surefire way to avoid technology problems is to avoid using technology. A trust easel and a dry erase board are tried and true. They are also inexpensive.

Whether you use electronic or "old school", have a pointer or a laser pointer.

C. BLOWUPS

Blowing up exhibits is an excellent advocacy tool. Everyone can see them, you can more easily question the witness about the exhibit, and it looks prepared and professional.

Every city has a printer that can put the exhibit on a Styrofoam backing. This is costly, however. If you are on a budget, have the exhibit blown up as a blueprint enlargement, which is substantially cheaper but on thin paper. Then go to one of the big-box stores and purchase a plastic poster frame. They are usually 24 inches by 36 inches, and have thin plexiglass see-through covers. You can use your dry erase markers on those frames, over and over. Very economical, and they look great.

D. DEMONSTRATIVES

If you make exhibits for demonstrative purposes, be sure they will be usable. I have seen firms spend thousands of dollars on mock ups, models, and the like, all to not be able to use them at trial. Remember, the exhibit has to be relevant, which includes it being somewhat to scale and representative of the thing it depicts. It is an excellent idea to bring the issue up before the trial, with a proposal of the thing so the other side and the judge can discuss it with you. Better an early reveal than a destroyed cross at trial.

9.4 TAKEAWAYS

- Be prepared with case law on issues you think may come up at trial.

- Be sure to ask that the "rule of sequestration" or "the rule" be invoked, and that the other side's witness leave the courtroom.

- Prepare your presentation tools in advance of trial.

- Be sure to take everything you need—technology, food, etc.

9.5 EXERCISES

Exercise 1:

From an advocacy book, find a sample case file that contains exhibits. Have a friend or co-worker (for more impact, someone who doesn't mind giving you a hard time) learn the witness role that uses the exhibits. Practice a cross examination where one or more of your target facts use the exhibits.

Contact the trial team at your local law school. Invariably they will have leftover exhibits from competitions past. They can give you a copy of the case file as well as let you borrow the blown up exhibit. Practice using it with a "mock" witness.

Exercise 2:

Explore the many cross tools that are out there, such as Trial Director (one of the author's personal favorites), PowerPoint, OnCue, Sanction, ExhibitView, and others. Any that are free, download them and try them out. Use them on both your laptop or desktop as well as your mobile device. Use the exhibits from Exercise 1, above, and try the cross using technology.

Exercise 3:

Contact the IT department at your local clerk's office, and ask to come in and have a courtroom technology discussion. Most IT professionals are happy to share what is available. If time permits, ask to practice your cross from Exercise 1, above, in an actual courtroom.

Exercise 4:

If you are in law school, check out the school's courtroom technology. Run your practice exercise in the courtroom, both with a paper exhibit and with the e-exhibit. Have friends sit in the jury box, and discuss with them the effectiveness of both and what they prefer.

STEVE RUSHING

"I have no more questions of this witness."

CHAPTER 10

RECOMMENDED CROSS EXAMINATION RESOURCES

10.1 A LAWYER NEVER STOPS LEARNING

My mother, Jane, told me when I was going off to law school, "a lawyer never stops learning." I didn't realize how right she was. Think about the use of expert witnesses—the trial lawyer has to become an expert in his or her own right, to be able to understand and present the complicated subject matter to the jury. Think about a cause of action you've never litigated, or a statute you have never used. Trial lawyers really, truly, never stop learning.

Advocacy is a "never stops learning" discipline. If you don't stop learning, you will never improve. As you go along in your career, the actual courtroom experiences can be few; you have to find ways to stay fresh and current.

Keep a trial journal. List your trials and hearings, what the issues where, who your judge and opponent were, and what was the outcome. Critique yourself—be honest. Look for your good as well as your "needs improvements". Keep that journal over your career.

Watch trials. Go to the courthouse and sit through a trial. Find out who the great trial lawyers are, and go see them live. Time watching trials is the greatest teaching tool—you get to see great advocates, and some bad ones. Learn from both.

Finding trials is as simple as calling member of the bar, or judicial assistants, or the clerk of court. I like to go see high-profile trials—they are as easy as looking at the front page of the newspaper.

Don't forget that your local law school, and many undergraduate schools, have mock trial teams. You will see some of the finest advocacy ever from law student advocates.

Read. You are here because you are reading about cross examination (this author thanks you!). There are some fantastic treatises on cross examination, as well as advocacy in general. Don't limit yourself to books, though—get trial transcripts and analyze cross examinations. You will learn amazing things from the records of actual trials.

Use online resources. There are many, many great resources on the internet. YouTube has entire channels dedicated to advocacy teachings. Law school professors have blogs, podcasts, and webpages with great advocacy skill content. Never be afraid to send an email to a professor or another attorney, to ask for help or advice. You'll be surprised how willing trial lawyers are to help each other.

Remember, this is a *skill*. You must exercise the advocacy muscles. That is why we call it the *practice* of law—we are always having to practice in order to get it right!

10.2 RECOMMENDED RESOURCES

A. BOOKS

I recommend these books to you because they are in my own collection. I have read and relied on them over the years. Note, I am recommending the edition I own, but there may be newer editions available. Sadly, some are out of print—but Amazon and eBay are great sources for all sorts of great *used* advocacy books (hint, hint).

- Roberto Aron, Kevin Thomas Duffy, Jonathan L. Rosner, *Cross-Examination of Witnesses: The Litigator's Puzzle* (1989)

- Jules H. Baer & Simon Balicer, *Cross-Examination and Summation* (2nd ed. 1948)

- F. Lee Bailey & Henry B. Rothblatt, *Cross-Examination in Criminal Trials* (1978)

- American Bar Association, *The Irving Younger Collection: Wisdom & Wit from the Master of Trial Advocacy* (2010)

- Terrence F. MacCarthy, *MacCarthy on Cross-Examination* (2007)

- Peter Megargee Brown, *The Art of Questioning: Thirty Maxims of Cross-Examination* (1987)

- Leonard E. Davies, *Anatomy of Cross-Examination: A History of the Techniques of an Ancient Art* (2d ed. 2003)

- J.W. Ehrlich, *The Lost Art of Cross-Examination* (or Perjury Anyone?) (1970)

- John Nicholas Iannuzzi, *Handbook of Cross-Examination: The Mosaic Art* (2nd ed. 1999)

- Larry S. Pozner & Roger J. Dodd, *Cross-Examination: Science and Techniques* (2nd ed. 2004)

- Louis E. Schwartz, *Proof, Persuasion, and Cross-Examination: A Winning New Approach in the Courtroom* (1973)

- Francis L. Wellman, *The Art of Cross-Examination* (1903)

Perhaps one day this book will be worthy of addition to this list!

Some books that I do not own, but have checked out of law libraries and reviewed, and recommend are:

- James Kenway Archibald & Paul Mark Sandler, *Model Witness Examinations* (4th ed. 2016)

- F. Lee Bailey & Kenneth J. Fishman, *Excellence in Cross-Examination* (2013)

B.   VIDEOS AND WEBSITES

Seven Steps to Cross Examination

(https://www.youtube.com/watch?v=-Kha__fMWI g&t=6s)

Professor Charles H. Rose III discusses the tactics of cross examination and how to structure your questions most effectively and persuasively. *NOTE: pretty much anything Professor Rose does is worth every second of your time to watch and take notes.

Mastering Cross Examination—In the Courtroom

(https://www.youtube.com/watch?v=yyn-ykG7 GF8_)

Another video from Professor Rose, presenting a goal-oriented approach to cross examination.

Irving Younger's 10 Commandments of Cross Examination

(https://youtu.be/dBP2if0l-a8)

An excerpted clip from UC Hastings College of the Law in San Francisco of the late great Irving Younger delivering some key points of his much referenced 10 Commandments of Cross Examination in the 1970s. A true classic in the history of American legal education, Younger's Ten Commandments of Cross Examination are often cited, debated and over analyzed, but certainly not without their merits in at least familiarizing yourself with them.

OJ TRIAL; F Lee Bailey VS Mark Fuhrman

(https://www.youtube.com/watch?v=U_A4xDj6 DO)

An excerpt from the most-watched criminal trial ever. Many people, including me, believe that the cross examination by the legendary F. Lee Bailey was the reason the jury acquitted Mr. Simpson. This cross is a model of control and storytelling on cross examination.

The Art of Cross Examination

(https://www.youtube.com/watch?v=6z9pBpM-fI4)

Experienced trial lawyer John Rosen talks about the ultimate goals of cross examination and how to have the most substantial impact on the courtroom.

10 Tips for Effective Cross Examination

(https://www.youtube.com/watch?v=-FmPzpMU tmc)

Associate Justice David Lillehaug of the Minnesota Supreme Court outlines best tips for taking your cross examination to the next level.

Two Quick & Easy Cross Examination Tips

(https://www.youtube.com/watch?v=hQ0wiVM8ZT k)

Great, short video from my friend and colleague, and great advocacy teacher, Elliot Wilcox.

10.3 AMERICAN BAR ASSOCIATION MODEL RULES OF PROFESSIONAL CONDUCT[1]

Rule 1.1 Competence

A lawyer shall provide competent representation to a client. Competent representation requires the legal knowledge, skill, thoroughness and preparation reasonably necessary for the representation.

Rule 1.3 Diligence

A lawyer shall act with reasonable diligence and promptness in representing a client.

Rule 3.1 Meritorious Claims and Contentions

A lawyer shall not bring or defend a proceeding, or assert or controvert an issue therein, unless there is a basis in law and fact for doing so that is not frivolous, which includes a good faith argument for an extension, modification or reversal of existing law. A lawyer for the defendant in a criminal proceeding, or the respondent in a proceeding that could result in incarceration, may nevertheless so defend the proceeding as to require that every element of the case be established.

Rule 3.2 Expediting Litigation

A lawyer shall make reasonable efforts to expedite litigation consistent with the interests of the client.

Rule 3.3 Candor toward the Tribunal

(a) A lawyer shall not knowingly:

(1) make a false statement of fact or law to a tribunal or fail to correct a false statement of material fact or law previously made to the tribunal by the lawyer;

(2) fail to disclose to the tribunal legal authority in the controlling jurisdiction known to the lawyer to be directly adverse to the position of the client and not disclosed by opposing counsel; or

(3)   offer evidence that the lawyer knows to be false. If a lawyer, the lawyer's client, or a witness called by the lawyer, has offered material evidence and the lawyer comes to know of its falsity, the lawyer shall take reasonable remedial measures, including, if necessary, disclosure to the tribunal. A lawyer may refuse to offer evidence, other than the testimony of a defendant in a criminal matter, that the lawyer reasonably believes is false.

(b)   A lawyer who represents a client in an adjudicative proceeding and who knows that a person intends to engage, is engaging or has engaged in criminal or fraudulent conduct related to the proceeding shall take reasonable remedial measures, including, if necessary, disclosure to the tribunal.

(c)   The duties stated in paragraphs (a) and (b) continue to the conclusion of the proceeding, and apply even if compliance requires disclosure of information otherwise protected by Rule 1.6.

(d)   In an ex parte proceeding, a lawyer shall inform the tribunal of all material facts known to the lawyer that will enable the tribunal to make an informed decision, whether or not the facts are adverse.

Rule 3.4   Fairness to Opposing Party and Counsel

A lawyer shall not:

(a)   unlawfully obstruct another party's access to evidence or unlawfully alter, destroy or conceal a document or other material having potential evidentiary value. A lawyer shall not counsel or assist another person to do any such act;

(b)   falsify evidence, counsel or assist a witness to testify falsely, or offer an inducement to a witness that is prohibited by law;

(c)   knowingly disobey an obligation under the rules of a tribunal except for an open refusal based on an assertion that no valid obligation exists;

(d)   in pretrial procedure, make a frivolous discovery request or fail to make reasonably diligent effort to comply with a legally proper discovery request by an opposing party;

(e)   in trial, allude to any matter that the lawyer does not reasonably believe is relevant or that will not be supported by admissible evidence, assert personal knowledge of facts in issue except when testifying as a witness, or state a personal opinion as to the justness of a cause, the credibility of a witness, the culpability of a civil litigant or the guilt or innocence of an accused; or

(f)   request a person other than a client to refrain from voluntarily giving relevant information to another party unless:

(1)   the person is a relative or an employee or other agent of a client; and

(2)   the lawyer reasonably believes that the person's interests will not be adversely affected by refraining from giving such information.

Rule 3.5   Impartiality and Decorum of the Tribunal

A lawyer shall not:

(a)   seek to influence a judge, juror, prospective juror or other official by means prohibited by law;

(b)   communicate ex parte with such a person during the proceeding unless authorized to do so by law or court order;

(c)   communicate with a juror or prospective juror after discharge of the jury if:

(1)   the communication is prohibited by law or court order;

(2)   the juror has made known to the lawyer a desire not to communicate; or

(3)   the   communication   involves misrepresentation,   coercion,   duress   or harassment; or

(d)   engage in conduct intended to disrupt a tribunal.

Rule 3.6   Trial Publicity

(a)   A lawyer who is participating or has participated in the investigation or litigation of a matter shall not make an extrajudicial statement that the lawyer knows or reasonably should know will   be   disseminated   by   means   of   public communication   and   will   have   a   substantial likelihood   of   materially   prejudicing   an adjudicative proceeding in the matter.

(b) Notwithstanding paragraph (a), a lawyer may state:

(1) the claim, offense or defense involved and, except when prohibited by law, the identity of the persons involved;

(2) information contained in a public record;

(3) that an investigation of a matter is in progress;

(4) the scheduling or result of any step in litigation;

(5) a request for assistance in obtaining evidence and information necessary thereto;

(6) a warning of danger concerning the behavior of a person involved, when there is reason to believe that there exists the likelihood of substantial harm to an individual or to the public interest; and

(7) in a criminal case, in addition to subparagraphs (1) through (6):

(i) the identity, residence, occupation and family status of the accused;

(ii) if the accused has not been apprehended, information necessary to aid in apprehension of that person;

(iii) the fact, time and place of arrest; and

(iv) the identity of investigating and arresting officers or agencies and the length of the investigation.

(c)   Notwithstanding paragraph (a), a lawyer may make a statement that a reasonable lawyer would believe is required to protect a client from the substantial undue prejudicial effect of recent publicity not initiated by the lawyer or the lawyer's client. A statement made pursuant to this paragraph shall be limited to such information as is necessary to mitigate the recent adverse publicity.

(d)   No lawyer associated in a firm or government agency with a lawyer subject to paragraph (a) shall make a statement prohibited by paragraph (a).

Rule 3.7   Lawyer as Witness

(a)   A lawyer shall not act as advocate at a trial in which the lawyer is likely to be a necessary witness unless:

(1)   the testimony relates to an uncontested issue;

(2)   the testimony relates to the nature and value of legal services rendered in the case; or

(3)   disqualification of the lawyer would work substantial hardship on the client.

(b)   A lawyer may act as advocate in a trial in which another lawyer in the lawyer's firm is likely to be called as a witness unless precluded from doing so by Rule 1.7 or Rule 1.9.

Rule 3.8   Special Responsibilities of a Prosecutor

The prosecutor in a criminal case shall:

(a)   refrain from prosecuting a charge that the prosecutor knows is not supported by probable cause;

(b)   make reasonable efforts to assure that the accused has been advised of the right to, and the procedure for obtaining, counsel and has been given reasonable opportunity to obtain counsel;

(c)   not seek to obtain from an unrepresented accused a waiver of important pretrial rights, such as the right to a preliminary hearing;

(d)   make timely disclosure to the defense of all evidence or information known to the prosecutor that tends to negate the guilt of the accused or mitigates the offense, and, in connection with sentencing, disclose to the defense and to the tribunal all unprivileged mitigating information known to the prosecutor, except when the prosecutor is relieved of this responsibility by a protective order of the tribunal;

(e)   not subpoena a lawyer in a grand jury or other criminal proceeding to present evidence about a past or present client unless the prosecutor reasonably believes:

(1)   the information sought is not protected from disclosure by any applicable privilege;

(2)   the evidence sought is essential to the successful completion of an ongoing investigation or prosecution; and

(3)   there is no other feasible alternative to obtain the information;

(f)   except for statements that are necessary to inform the public of the nature and extent of the prosecutor's action and that serve a legitimate law enforcement purpose, refrain from making extrajudicial comments that have a substantial likelihood of heightening public condemnation of the accused and exercise reasonable care to prevent investigators, law enforcement personnel, employees or other persons assisting or associated with the prosecutor in a criminal case from making an extrajudicial statement that the prosecutor would be prohibited from making under Rule 3.6 or this Rule.

(g)   When a prosecutor knows of new, credible and material evidence creating a reasonable likelihood that a convicted defendant did not commit an offense of which the defendant was convicted, the prosecutor shall:

(1)   promptly disclose that evidence to an appropriate court or authority, and

(2)   if the conviction was obtained in the prosecutor's jurisdiction,

(i)   promptly disclose that evidence to the defendant unless a court authorizes delay, and

(ii)   undertake further investigation, or make reasonable efforts to cause an investigation, to determine whether the defendant was convicted of an offense that the defendant did not commit.

(h)   When a prosecutor knows of clear and convincing evidence establishing that a defendant in the prosecutor's jurisdiction was convicted of an offense that the defendant did not commit, the prosecutor shall seek to remedy the conviction.

Rule 3.9   Advocate in Nonadjudicative Proceedings

A lawyer representing a client before a legislative body or administrative agency in a nonadjudicative proceeding shall disclose that the appearance is in a representative capacity and shall conform to the provisions of Rules 3.3(a) through (c), 3.4(a) through (c), and 3.5.

Rule 8.4   Misconduct

It is professional misconduct for a lawyer to:

(a)   violate or attempt to violate the Rules of Professional Conduct, knowingly assist or induce another to do so, or do so through the acts of another;

(b)   commit a criminal act that reflects adversely on the lawyer's honesty, trustworthiness or fitness as a lawyer in other respects;

(c)   engage in conduct involving dishonesty, fraud, deceit or misrepresentation;

(d)   engage in conduct that is prejudicial to the administration of justice;

(e)   state or imply an ability to influence improperly a government agency or official or to achieve results by means that violate the Rules of Professional Conduct or other law;

(f)   knowingly assist a judge or judicial officer in conduct that is a violation of applicable rules of judicial conduct or other law; or

(g)   engage in conduct that the lawyer knows or reasonably should know is harassment or discrimination on the basis of race, sex, religion, national origin, ethnicity, disability, age, sexual orientation, gender identity, marital status or socioeconomic status in conduct related to the practice of law. This paragraph does not limit the ability of a lawyer to accept, decline or withdraw from a representation in accordance with Rule 1.16. This paragraph does not preclude legitimate advice or advocacy consistent with these Rules.

INDEX

References are to Pages

EXHIBIT USE IN CROSS

EXPERT WITNESSES

FACIAL EXPRESSIONS

FACTUAL ISSUES

IMPROVISING CROSS EXAMINATIONS

PRESERVATION OF ERROR

PRIOR CONVICTIONS

PRIOR INCONSISTENT STATEMENTS

PROFESSIONAL PRACTICE

PROFFERS